# ROOTS & ROUTES

# Roots & Routes

## Memoirs and Musings of a Dublin Nomad

Brendan Cardiff

The Liffey Press

Published by
The Liffey Press
Ashbrook House, 10 Main Street
Raheny, Dublin 5, Ireland
www.theliffeypress.com

A catalogue record of this book is
available from the British Library.

ISBN 978-1-905785-75-9

Printed in the United Kingdom by MPG Biddles.

# CONTENTS

# Acknowledgements

My good friends Liam and Lucy Kelleher are to be thanked, some might suggest held accountable, for accidentally initiating this little narrative. I had attended a dinner party in their home one winter's evening on retirement from the Commission. As a consolation prize, and an attempt to prove that retirement was the ideal occasion to start a new life, I was about to set off for distant parts. I fell into conversation with a charming young lady who thought that shipping out of Ushuaia in early January, bearing due south across the Southern Ocean to the Land of the Midnight Sun, was an original alternative to armchair and remote control, if not slithering terminally under the duvet. I did not know that she was the presenter of a Radio Eireann programme, a Sunday morning favourite of mine during occasional visits to my home city. She later asked if I would agree to be interviewed on the programme, *Snapshots*. For some months I demurred fearing that the utterly charming but forensically probing Carrie Crowley might disinter gruesome memories of an African terror state of the 1970s during her customary unrehearsed interview. I relented when encouraged by niece Eithne O'Dwyer to confront past demons. I prepared a short, annotated CV, out of which these pages escalated. Producer Mary Duffy managed to whittle our lengthy conversation down to programme length. Some listeners suggested I put my recollections down on paper; I was encouraged by the accomplished author Elizabeth Healy, sister-in-law of Denis McGowan, then editor of the EU's internal newspaper *Commission en Direct*. Jonathan Williams, another alumnus of the IPA, provided further encouragement.

I am indebted for memories and details of Dublin of earlier days to Fred and Beth Reid, Tom and Bernadette Reid, Joy and Miriam Reid, Bernadette Sheridan, Rita Neary, Patrick Brennan, Nuala Malone, Lily Butler, Jim and Siobhan Leech, Jerome and Maire O'Carroll, Mat and Ruth O'Donoghue, Ken and Claire Douglas, Stella Walsh, Norman and Diana Hudson Taylor, Joe and Joan Swan, Sinead Dolan, Larry McArdle and Sheila Geaney. Noelle Grothier and Eilish Murphy of the Department of Defence, Bernadette Marks of Fingal Genealogy, Jeremy Black of Fingal Local Studies Library, Andreas O'Brien of Dublin City Archives, Nuala Canny of the Board of Works, Tim Carey of Dun Laoghaire-Rathdown County Council and Dermot Mulligan of Carlow County Museum all provided valuable information, helping to redeem from relative obscurity historical facts about northwest Dublin. Dennis and Patricia Marks elucidated the historical importance of the formula which Hamilton scratched on Broombridge.

Details of family history were clarified and recalled by Jim, Catriona and Edward Cardiff, Finbarr, Simone and Daniel Hannigan, Desmond Madden, Joan and Cecil Fallon, Maura Hatfield, Greg and Gail McCann, Karel Kiely, Frank Cardiff, Barbara Parker nee Cardiff, Kevin Cardiff, Dick Bates, Moira Cardiff, Hillary Murphy, Hugh Fitzgerald Ryan, Sally T. Griffiths and Rachel Bewley-Bateman.

Fading memories of enchanting Roman days and lyrical nights at the opera were refreshed by Maureen Lemass, Pat Cosgrove, Elizabeth McKenna and Valerie Lombard.

Fond memories of UCD days are revived during the convivial dinners regularly attended with fellow alumni of Group IX A, Economics, Politics and Statistics, Liam Kelleher, Michael Casey, Denis Fahey and Tom Haughey, as we reflect on the human condition at our favourite Indian bistro retreat in Monkstown. Susan Copeland of OECD kindly furnished me with a copy of Professor Paddy Lynch's 1965 report *Investment in Education*.

Valuable comments were made by Mark Callanan and Fran Lawlor at the IPA, Martin Burbridge of the IDA and Brendan Don-nelly of Enterprise Ireland. Carolyn Gormley of the IPA helped find some nice old photos of Tom Barrington and Patrick Lynch. Joan Flanagan and Theodor Moga of the Commission Information Office, and Heidi Standecker of External Relations, provided many historic Community photographs.

My good friends Cathal Cavanagh and Roger O'Keeffe commented on and provided critical insights into the Commission, and the economic and education services in particular. Maurice Guyader made some very convincing criticisms of the addendum on development. I am indebted to innumerable other ex-colleagues, especially Mary Preston, for evoking fond memories of imagination and ferment during early pioneering days at the Commission. My efforts to build transatlantic bridges were assisted by many enthusiastic contributors, too many to list in their entirety: on the Commission side Tom O'Dwyer has retired to his Tipperary idyll with his lovely lady Margaret, while former assistant and invaluable financial controller Susanne Pelz has happily returned to the unit in charge of external relations to rekindle team work with Margaret (Maggie) Nicholson of Fulbright Belgium, and Frank Frankfort of the FIPSE office in the Department of Education, Washington DC. Secretary of Education Richard Riley, know as the 'Great Statesman of US Education', has retired, though not before receiving an honorary PhD from UCD. William (Bill) Glade, too, has retired from the State Department to academia, as have Charles (Buddy) Karelis and Charles (Chip) Storey from FIPSE. Sadly, Winnie Warnat, the irrepressible and charismatic Director for Vocational Education at USED has left us all. David Michael Wilson of USIA Brussels, who helped overcome innumerable obstacles in the early days of our proposed cooperation, has retreated to the Maryland countryside. In Canada, Alain Dudoit, Peter Egglington and Brian Long have all taken their leave of the Foreign Affairs Department, as have Martha Nixon and Michelle Bonin-Stewart of Human Resources. Frank Deeg and Helen Donoghue, of the Commission Delegations in Ottawa and Washington have also moved on to other activities.

Paul and Sandi Ballinger, wonderful Canadian neighbours, were an invaluable source of encouragement, inspiration and practical

help as I struggled to make the transition from the delights of dip-
ping pen into ink to the disembodied formalism of Word 2003,
then to navigate the entanglements of Word 2007, as well as helping post samples of old Kodachromes to Picasa. Sandra and Giulio
Maggioni helped clean up many dusty and fading slides and prints.
Solange Pissort-Protin attempted to bring a degree of tidiness to an
anarchic den.

All-important editing and publishing contributions were provided by David Givens of The Liffey Press, an enlightened publisher
who risked accepting a novice manuscript encompassing a cascading miscellany of reminiscences along a protracted odyssey, judi-
ciously selecting and pruning them into a more concise and coherent narrative. I was fortunately saved from enduring embarrassment by the professionalism of the discerning and accomplished
editor Elizabeth MacAulay who undertook the honing of drafts rife
with serial infelicities. Her eloquent redrafting proved especially
valuable as my spelling is sufficiently erratic to drive my PC's spell-
check to digital distraction, my punctuation random and, while favourably disposed to syntax, I was, as ever, daydreaming when Mr
(Spud) Murphy, my English teacher at "Brunner", expounded that
still elusive concept.

The cover design is by the exceptionally creative Sinead
McKenna of Sin E Design. Research for appropriate maps was assisted by Cliodhna Ni Anluain, Conor McNamara, Colette O'Daly,
Siobhan Leech, Diana and Norman Hudson Taylor, though limitations of space prevented fully exploiting the fruit of their efforts. All
photographs in the colour sections of the book were taken by the
author.

Finally, responsibility for all sins of omission and commission is
mine alone. I have not attempted to provide a formal, objective record of events, merely the personal retrospective of a mellowing
expat. Any unintended misrepresentations are accidental and due
to interpretation from the personal angle, and an impairing memory. To the host of others who influenced my thinking and stirred
recollections of a bygone era I extend my sincere thanks.

*For Ma, Pa, Maureen, Jim, Catriona, Edward, Finbarr,*
*Simone, Daniel, Sarah, Elliot and Ophelia.*

'All the world's a stage ... and one man in his time plays many parts'
– William Shakespeare, *As You Like It*

# PROLOGUE

THESE PAGES RESULT FROM AN INTERVIEW on Radio Telefís Éireann shortly after my retirement in 2005. Ms Carrie Crowley quizzed me about the hometown of my youth, schooldays, incidents of guiding travellers around Rome, adventures while meandering through foreign parts in earlier times, and recollections of working in Dublin and on the Continent. Some survivors of the travels suggested that I should set my recollections down on paper. For one seeking a new rhythm to life, spasmodic scribbling became therapeutic – males apparently find it more difficult to adjust to retirement than our lady colleagues. Despite the redoubtable Dr Johnson's contention that 'no man but a blockhead would ever write, except for money', this blockhead found it fun and enormously fulfilling to relive memories I had little time to reflect on during the relentless flurry of working life. Not having kept diaries during my days, and some somnambulistic nights, on the open road, I had to resort to the misty crystals of old Kodachromes to unlock memories of bygone landscapes. Hopefully, this little text will succeed in evoking memories of Dublin of yore, former travel companions and destinations, former colleagues at the IPA, IDA and the Commission, and fading snapshots of other lost worlds. To paraphrase playwright Micheál MacLiammóir, I'm only writing to my friends.

I had the good fortune to savour the beguiling charms of historic Rome, to be captivated by that city of intoxicating artistry for four enviable summers in the early 1960s, before it was blighted by a tsunami of tourists. The Eternal City of *dolce vita* days buzzed in the euphoria of post-war recovery. There are many fabulous cities in the world but in terms of history, art, architecture and ambience, none comes even close to equalling that centre of aesthetic delight – not even the City of Light. I recall, too, a winter wonderland of snow-enveloped villages in the Tirol in the early 1960s, the exhilaration of waltzing down an apron of pristine snow, the wind whistling in one's ears, the gelid air causing eyes to moisten. Nowadays it seems rare to see snow in villages below 1,500 metres after January. Ablation of glaciers, which are said to store two thirds of the earth's hydrologically-cycled fresh water, releasing it slowly over the spring and summer to water thirsty farmlands, continues apace. The summertime melt-water endings of glaciers in the Tirol have retreated by hundreds of metres, while others have simply disappeared altogether.

The halls and corridors of Earlsfort Terrace were physically restricting, even for the student numbers in 1960s' UCD, but the place had a character, an *esprit de lieux,* all of its own; it buzzed like the interior of a beehive between classes as scholars and teachers poured from tributary corridors and stairways to join a humming, rambunctious confluence in the main hall. Nearly all faculties shared the one building, embodying the traditional concept of a *universitas* of learning. We may not have fully appreciated it at the time, but we were well served by many distinguished mentors, men and women of outstanding intellect and dedication. A number of them, in economics, politics and history especially, played a major role in revitalising a country still psychologically fatigued in the long aftermath of WWII. They helped shape the outlook of a new generation of citizens, piloting the transition to a more open, liberal society, and eventual integration into a wider European partnership.

Later, I had the good fortune to work for a number of organisations in Ireland and Brussels headed by charismatic and inspiring leaders – men of integrity fired by the desire to promote better governance, nationally and regionally, end the curse of involuntary emigration and promote quality employment. Dedicated and inspirational public servants such as TK Whitaker, TJ Barrington, P Lynch, MJ Killeen, whose focus was not on their own egos but on the long-term betterment of the community, helped to lift a country, still feeling sorry for itself, out of the stultifying 1950s into a springtime of hope on publication of the groundbreaking blueprint *Economic Development*. Four decades before Obama they invoked confidence in the 'yes we can' society. In Japan such individuals are apparently designated 'living national treasures'.

In 1973 Ireland was actively to join in that noble endeavour, the peaceful construction of the new European Community, just as a millennium earlier Irish teachers had shown their affinity for Europe when they spread across the Continent helping Charlemagne restore the heritage of western culture lost during the Dark Ages. But my return to the Continent was conducted in far more favourable circumstances than my relatives of less than a century earlier: they had been sent as fodder to the depravity and carnage of the Western Front, fighting other European teenagers they had never before encountered. We bypassed Flanders' blood-sodden fields to work peacefully and harmoniously with our new-found neighbours in historic Brussels. Again, I was fortunate to work, in the pioneering day of the Commission, within a multicultural team open to ideas and melded to draft a new and peaceful chapter in European history. I reflected at my first staff meeting that, had we been born 60, yea, 30 years earlier, half of us would have been aiming guns at the other half. Noting a number of lady colleagues in our unit I recalled that it was at the insistence of the Community that Irishwomen no longer had to resign their jobs the day they tied the knot.

The founding fathers of this new Europe were at once visionaries and pragmatists. They realised that the best means to banish further slaughter was to intertwine the Continent industrially, raising living standards by removing restrictions on commerce with neighbours. The idea was to interlock commercial structures so incontrovertibly as to make it economic suicide to go to war with partners. Yet, their main motivation was moral. As former Commissioner Peter Sutherland has pointed out: 'The founding fathers of the EU were explicitly philosophical in their approach. The philosopher who influenced the EU's chief architect Robert Schuman ... was Jacques Maritain, with his concept of forgiveness, and his idea of personalism, of the dignity of man not being linked to race. Forgiveness – after the bloodiest war in history – was the key to it.... It proceeded as an attack on nationalism, which has led to the wars."[1]

Of course, the Community was set up by visionary leaders during a period which demanded heroic statesmanship. They could thus propose bold, long-term strategies in the turmoil of post-WWII Europe; in later and less demanding times the electorate has tended to select more accommodating and popular governments. Maybe that cantankerous old scribe Plato had a point when he argued in favour of political leadership by philosopher-rulers – they might take a longer term view of policy.

The idealism and altruism of the Community of nine was not restricted to raising living standards throughout outlying regions but in helping less fortunate neighbours in other parts of the world, coyly referred to as less developed countries, or LDCs. Many of these were former colonies of France and Britain and such cooperation was also seen as a means of making amends. But the range of conditions and challenges faced by the LDCs was far greater than first realised – either by the architects of the Lomé Agreement or by its operatives in the field. Idealism and harsh reality were to confront each other on the frontline, especially in Uganda, where I was posted.

Unfortunately, my efforts to promote development in that magnificent land were dashed by unrelenting repression and social meltdown, the country's infrastructure crumbling and institutions usurped by a psychopathic despot. What had been a scenic paradise, hailed by Churchill as the original Garden of Eden, was turning into a tropical necropolis, a paradise lost, the populace in constant risk of being 'disappeared' by the rival secret police services. A psychosis of fear pervaded the land: the law was but the dictator's latest whim. One indication of the difficulty of helping progress was the clamping down on any critical thinking by 'intellectuals', i.e. schoolteachers, who were arrested en mass. Ultimately, it was impossible to provide the envisioned infrastructural aid, a

---

[1] *Financial Times*, 3–4 January 2009

key ingredient of long-term development, instead only short-term humanitarian assistance was possible.

Yet, amid the callous cruelty and cynicism, the humanity of some courageous spirits stood out. Exemplary ladies, including Irish medical missionary sisters, provided a moral compass amid an enveloping despondency. They were an inspiration to those who risked losing faith in the innate goodness and compassion of humanity, and confirmation of the resilience of the human spirit. They were assisted by other plucky characters, including some volunteer medics who toiled heroically in the bush, especially in the daunting fastness of remote Karamoja.

Though my efforts at anything other than humanitarian help were largely frustrated they did, paradoxically, provide a valuable insight into the chasm between theory and practice where development is concerned. I realised that the accepted building blocks of growth, skilled labour, equipment, irrigated land, physical infrastructure, were less a priority than addressing the obstacles to development – strongmen leaders and withering public administrations, lack of honest, effective civic institutions, democracy, rule of law, failure equitably to share the fruits of progress, as people's aspirations suffocated. The Marshall Fund had shown that success in regenerating an economy depends on there being a basic social infrastructure in the first place – and, as Ireland showed later, in replacing an apathetic community spirit with hope-filled vision and enthusiasm. Later when I wandered within less developed countries in Africa, Asia and Latin America, many of outstanding natural beauty, I also reflected on the stark contrast of bountiful nature and the degradation of poverty, the frustration of knowing that, with some elementary concern by the ruling elites, and an elementary knowledge of tropical hygiene and agriculture, heart-breaking toil and debilitating diseases could be eliminated at little or no cost. (These reflections are enlarged on in the addendum on development.) I have since thought that the best we can do for the LDCs is to avoid judging our success at assistance purely on the basis of monetary aid handed out, but to offer the means, the instruments and core institutions, whereby the partner nations can learn to develop themselves. (One recalls the maxim often attributed to Confucius: 'give a man a fish and he will eat for a day; teach a man to fish and he will eat for a lifetime'.) Having lived among Africans one develops a great admiration for their courage in the face of adversity, especially the self-sacrifice and determination of the womenfolk to look to the welfare of their extended families. In view of the moral vacuum which has opened in Ireland's hedonistic bubble economy and amid wrenching stories of clerical malfeasance it is both reassuring to note the continued tradition of self-sacrifice by such inspiring role models as the supremely compassionate and caring Margaret Hassan of Care, who paid the ultimate price, and, more recently, Goal volunteers Sharon Cummins, and her Ugandan colleague Hilda Kawaki. It is entirely fitting that the two Darfur heroines should have been awarded the Monsignor Hugh O'Flaherty International Humanitarian Award named as it is in honour of another outstanding but oft overlooked hero of WWII who helped escaped Allied POWs find safety, and saved the lives of so many resistance workers and Jews from the Rome Gestapo after 1943.

Given the scale of meltdown in the developed economies and the likelihood of less aid being offered as austerity beckons, it would be wise for new policies, including a systemic review of long-term aid, to crystallise around institutional and aspirational assistance, encouraging latent entrepreneurship and initiative. But such a transformation is most likely to be successful within open societies, and the reluctance of many African countries to encourage reform in their most egregious neighbours in a mistaken sense of solidarity, is not encouraging.

The European Community is generally perceived by outsiders, especially those requesting membership, as a union of peace and prosperity. In the 1970s and 1980s the pioneering Commission was suffused with a great sense of aspiration and energy, even passion. It was not bogged down by cumbersome procedures. The objective was to turn political ideas into concrete action. A few landmark decisions of the European Court, and resolute leadership by the Council of Ministers, helped breach long-standing logjams and revive unity of purpose. We did not notice it over time but success was, paradoxically, sowing some seeds of apathy. With successive enlargements the earlier sense of common purpose was being replaced by a desire for *a la carte* engagement, leading to a risk of centrifugal unravelling.

Community membership has been more conducive to mitigating ancient tensions between Ireland and our neighbouring island than is generally acknowledged. It surely would be an egregious historic mistake were we both to be relegated to a semi-detached periphery as a result of our own short-sightedness. It is most unfortunate that our nearest neighbour seems to have become disillusioned with the Community, allowing emotion to prevail over pragmatism, never mind vision. Many of us old-timers at the Commission recall with respect the great contribution many outstanding British officials (Chris Patten instantly springs to mind) made to Community development in the pioneering days after 1973. The British were then enthusiastic members, strictly upholding the rules, and later dedicated supporters of efforts to complete the internal market. But their leadership of the day baulked when Jacques Delors proposed that the potential gains of this risky initiative be shared with all segments of society, not just the business classes. This led to a realignment of British politics regarding Europe. The shackles of nostalgia still linger in the suburbs and shires of the Sceptr'd Isle. These sentiments are probably understandable since many Britons can still remember the old glory days when Britain ruled a quarter of the Earth's surface and had emerged victorious in two world wars. There was a natural reluctance, even an element of wounded pride, to join a club founded by the defeated of former conflicts, including former enemies. Meanwhile, the Continental members were rapidly turning past catastrophe into future success. In 1957 British PM Eden vetoed Community negotiation, so the country which was commendably to the fore in setting up the European Court of Human Rights, fluffed its chance to become a leader of the newer organisation. The Continental six went ahead and drafted the rules of the game, far less to the later advantage of the UK than had she accepted the proffered torch. As Timothy Garton Ash remarked recently, '... Britain has reverted to type, preferring to play second fiddle to Washington rather than take its place in the front row of the European orchestra'.[2]

Britain needs her Continental partners just as they need Britain, the country which heroically saved Western Europe, including the Emerald Isle, from tyranny in the darkest days of 1940, and prevented all Germany and probably the Benelux, France, Greece and Italy from falling to the transcendental awfulness of Soviet hegemony in 1945. Another British commentator, the eminent historian Max Hastings, observed, '[m]any British people are so preoccupied with the relatively minor inconveniences imposed by the EU upon this country that they ignore its triumph in bringing peace and stability to many societies that had not known these things in living memory'.[2]

One aspect of membership of the Community which has arguably failed to receive as much attention as it deserves is the potential for constructive dialogue and conflict resolution offered by constant meetings of politicians and officials, thus allowing states in bilateral dispute the ideal opportunity to discuss and treat with each other on the sidelines of plenary sessions. Irish and British ministers, politicians, civil servants and civil society made frequent use of such propinquity to cultivate friendly relations during the trying days of the 'Troubles' in the North of Ireland. In the absence of such contacts and friendships the situation could well have been aggravated instead of attenuated. The contribution made by the intensive cooperation with the Central and Eastern European countries and Russia after the fall of the Berlin Wall, smoothing their reintegration into a new trans-European neighbourhood, is also little remarked on. Yet it represented one of the most peaceful break-ups of empire in all history – especially compared to the disintegration of the Turkish Empire in the Balkans and the Middle East. The magnanimous approach of the then Soviet Russian leadership, especially Mikhail Gorbachev, contributed greatly to the process. He disposed of a couple of million troops and a vast arse-

---

[2] *The Guardian*, 26 March 2009
[2] *The Guardian*, 18 August 2008

nal of weapons. Had he not agreed that each of the old Warsaw Pact countries was free to make its own choice the result could have been as blood-soaked as many other dismantlings of empires.

I recall my pleasant surprise when once visiting my scintillating home town, maybe in the early 1990s. The new Taoiseach, Albert Reynolds, of whom I knew little apart from his liking for country and western music, was quizzed by a TV reporter about some distant injustice inflicted on the long-suffering Irish by our unruly cross-channel neighbours. Expecting a damp-eyed evocation of the outrage and a reflexive expression of historic injury, I was delighted when he told the reporter to cop on and start looking to the future rather than harping on about the past – he said he had to live for his children and grandchildren, and everyone else's too. Well, good for you Mr Reynolds, I thought. It was thanks to people like him, Garret FitzGerald, John Major, Bertie Ahern, Tony Blair (maybe even a late mellowed Mrs Thatcher) and that inimitable icon of Irish-British and European reconciliation, John Hume, that we are finally approaching a peaceful resolution of our historic antipathy.

Meanwhile, with the passage of time, a younger generation of Europeans recalls less of past traumas and enmities. They forget the original *raison d'etre* of the Community. Many consider peace, stability, democracy and prosperity as part of the natural order and consider institutional arrangements for enlargement rather arcane. Thus, it is possible that the very success of the European movement may lead to bland acceptance that peaceful cooperation with neighbours is the natural fallback condition of relationships.

Educational cooperation programs such as Erasmus and Leonardo have been exceptionally successful in creating a sense of cross-border community among the young – rapport across former minefields. Over two million young people have now spent part of their study period in neighbouring countries, creating a community of teaching and learning, sharing ideas, becoming integrated into the culture of the host country, and building future business and personal networks. I was honoured to have been in a position to help open further portals to friendly academic and vocational cooperation with the wider international community.

The 2000 Lisbon Strategy was a clarion call for the Community to invest in science and education if we are to maintain former standards of living in a more open trading world. It emphasised the provision of skills and know-how essential for quality, environmentally-friendly jobs, an economy based on intelligence rather than muscle. It contained echoes of the OECD-Irish Government report of 1965, *Investment in Education*, commissioned by Dr Patrick Hillery who was later to become Ireland's first European Commissioner. The Irish had earlier shown that, with substantial investment in human resources and sustained efforts to encourage advanced technological investment, both domestic and overseas, a previously calcified society could awaken, fire its latent wit and energy, and raise standards to those of its advanced partners. This admirable strategy was eagerly pursued by the more innovative and creative Nordic nations, while its earlier protagonist grew complacent and opted for more facile, speculative, alternatives. The Irish were to provide another lesson – how easy it is to sacrifice hard-won success when a country is seduced by excessive exuberance, the delusion that soaring property values, dubious financial instruments and profligate credit creation can replace productive investment and diligence.

The tale ends, to be followed, on a slightly more unconventional note, with an addendum on the nature of development. Having occasionally had to address problems and suggest solutions to obdurate backwardness at national and regional level, as well as competitiveness at the other end of the technology spectrum, and having travelled extensively within some of the most deprived countries in the world, I have often tried to find a deeper reason than mere lack of financial investment for failure to achieve take-off. So I have succumbed to the temptation to muse on the deeper underlying causes. Should this evince any well-intentioned reader to deeper reflection and insight, and a greater concern for those the French writer Franz Fanon called the wretched of the earth, then the small effort involved will have been worthwhile.

# 1

# ROOTS

*O*
*Tell me all about*
*Anna Livia! I want to hear all*
*about Anna Livia. Well, you know about Anna Livia?*
*Yes, of course, we all know Anna Livia. Tell me all.*
*Tell me now.*

– James Joyce, *Finnegans Wake*

I WAS NOT AT ALL CONSULTED ABOUT THE event, neither timing nor venue: but in 1941 my good parents had the foresight to ensure I was born into an oasis of tranquillity. In contrast to the convulsing events of the most momentous year of the twentieth century my suburban idyll was a sleepy backwater. Unlike some scribes I have no vivid personal recollection of my early years: premonitions, obviously, of a very late developer. My first real recollection was of the breakfast table one morning, my mother reading a note my father had left on departure for work: 'Agnes, the war is over'.

The scene of my arrival into this wonderful world was in the townland of Castleknock, parish of Chapelizod. The former village was celebrated by the poet Wordsworth, while the latter is the setting for Joyce's *Finnegans Wake*, though I was unaware of this work for many years as many of Mr Joyce's verbal pyrotechnics were anathema in Irish homes in an era stifled with dogmatism. In keeping with the prevailing orthodoxy I was conveyed within days to the parish church of Chapelizod and baptised forthwith, lest premature ill-health and subsequent demise condemn my eternal soul to Limbo, a destination only recently declared theologically extinct.

The tranquillity of my early days was uneventful: I was too young to be aware of the background canvas of wartime shortages, blackouts, the stertorous droning of Luftwaffe bombers as they arrived to bomb Dublin's North Strand, never mind such conflagrations as Stalingrad, Kursk, Midway or Normandy. One bomb did land somewhat near our house, over the wall of the Phoenix Park, by the cricket clubhouse, between Áras an Uachtaráin and the US Ambassador's residence. My father, who was on police duty nearby at the time, heard a piece of shrapnel whistling past and retrieved it from a tree trunk in the light of the following day. It was about seven inches long, weighed over a pound and the thought of connecting with such a jagged, cruel missile as it whizzed through the air was a convincing reminder of the awfulness of modern warfare. This was our family's closest encounter with Round II of Europe's twentieth century civil war – involvement with the earlier 1914-18 bloodletting had been much closer to home.

I have been informed that my first words were 'all gone', followed later by 'ice cream'. This importuning was accompanied by an opening of mouth to a position photographers would call full aperture, a tiny finger was pointed deep down towards the consumption chamber to prove that no remains of previously inserted sweets, lollipops, chocolates or ice cream were left, that further replenishment was required. Spluttering or resolute closing of jaws was employed against insertion of normal nutrition, which was only achieved using a method close to force feeding. Apparently these limited early rhetorical flowerings were considered by their author adequate for requirements and not further supplemented for almost another year, causing my parents to fret that their offspring was beyond redemption, a mere machine for consumption of sugary foodstuffs, and would possibly remain sufficiently inarticulate as to jeopardise future employability, never mind the chances of being accepted by a nice girl.

I was conscious of the presence of my older brother James, or Jim as we called him, in the manner that a junior sibling becomes aware of superior entities, especially when he is oft condemned to be the recipient of clothes outgrown by the older sibling. He was expected to act as a role model to be looked up to; not so my younger sister Maureen who was a mere porcelain face in a bundle of swaddling clothes, and a wee bit spoiled as the only young lady. So, as piggy in the middle, I was left largely to my own devices, partially responsible for rearing myself, as can happen with middle children.

Kid sister's backstage role was rudely abandoned one morning when Jim and I were having breakfast; the blond moppet, beatific smile on porcelain face, all of a year and a couple of months, had managed to escape from her cot and, on her very first unaided stroll, wobbled into the breakfast room unannounced, grabbed the poker from the fireside companion set and proceeded to belay the grating like a demented hard rock drummer, eyes sparkling with wistful glee, mouth fixed in an impish grin which slowly enveloped a cherubic countenance. Jim and I were fascinated at this evidence of early iconoclastic impulse and fell around laughing, while her horrified Mum dashed in from the kitchen in a rush of Yatesian foreboding that 'mere anarchy is loosed upon the world'.

I shared one common trait with my younger sister: we both hated cabbage and, ever more so, its coprolitic cousin, spinach. We were forced to consume these revolting vegetables, being exhorted to by a certain lady doctor who broadcast a weekly medical slot on Radio Éireann extolling the virtues of cabbage, full of iron and vitamins essential for growth. I offered to suck iron nails as an alternative. We were reminded that Africa was full of starving children who would give anything to partake of the cabbage on our plates. Maureen and I instantly offered to sacrifice all those vitamins, help our parents package our culinary nemesis and post it off immediately to the malnourished. Somehow this offer was never acted on. We eventually resorted to sabotage. Father, a dedicated gardener of vegetables as well as flowers, had planted a few rows of cabbages in the back garden and these were, to our horror, growing rapidly, far too rapidly for our comfort. We partially cut through the stalks using his cut-throat razor, presuming any failure of the crop would be put down to adverse weather conditions or some bug. Unfortunately that night a wind blew all the plants over, and our indiscretion was compounded when the razor was found to be particularly blunt next morning. It did not require Sherlock Holmes to detect that the loss was not an act of nature. As the ringleader I had my bottom spanked and we were both deprived of pocket money for a month.

From then on we surreptitiously resorted to an ecological form of sabotage, gathering any snails and caterpillars we could find and inserting them into the hearts of the cabbage plants. Unfortunately, the snails seem to have shared our dislike and slid off in the direction of the more appetising strawberries a few rows away. I have always harboured the thought that if one's taste buds reject a foodstuff then it surely must be noxious for that particular person's metabolism. Years later a young Amerindian lady, who taught the Brazilian army jungle survival methods, confirmed my hunch: her rule was that if a fruit or leaf tasted OK it might be edible; if it tasted foul it probably was poisonous and should be spat out at once.

One year my father dug out some early potatoes he had planted and my mother called on the critical skills of our good neighbour Mrs Sheridan, an avid gardener herself and a most discerning judge of flowers and vegetables. She pronounced the sample not so much potatoes as mere *póiríns*. I looked up the word in Dinneen's Irish dictionary some time later to find that it means a pebble or a marble.

## Hinterland

The northwest corner of Dublin was the epicentre of my youth. Our bungalow home, with front flower-garden and rear vegetable, was located beside the Phoenix Park, that wonderful lung for Dubliners, who proudly declare it as the largest enclosed urban park in Europe, if not in the whole wide world. Its sylvan setting was our childhood playground and I looked upon it as the nearest thing to the great parks we read of in *National Geographic* magazine. This belief was reinforced by the herd of fallow deer which grazed there. Between our house on Nephin Road and the River Liffey, Joyce's *Anna Livia Plurabelle*, was the area known as Oxmantown, or Ostmans' town, the ancient redoubt of the Vikings. To the east lay Cabragh, nowadays Cabra, once the farm of the infamous 'hanging judge' Lord Norbury (more of him later). This was in its turn bordered by the Royal Canal upon whose Broombridge William Rowan Hamilton graffitied the formula for quaternions. Beside that were the abandoned, ivy-covered ruins of old Cardiff Castle, and the Dunsink Observatory. No doubt a sophisticated visitor from Pall Mall, Manhattan or Beverly Hills would have considered it an insignificant corner of an inconsequential land but to me, for years, it was a childhood fantasy-land; by my own doorstep I had the plains of Africa, with deer running wild across the boundless expanses of the Fifteen Acres. Nor was there a lack of the great carnivores or the 'Big 5', even if they were firmly locked up in the Zoological Gardens which formed part of the Park since 1831. Particularly when the wind was blowing from the south, as it usually did, we could hear the occasional roar of a moody lion.[1] There was primary forest, secondary forest, stands of thorn trees, history, culture, even the dark, foreboding horrors of old Cabragh farmhouse stalked by the shades of the hangman.

The cultural topography of our neighbourhood was almost entirely Catholic and conformist. It was an accepted fact that the Good Lord, despite the minor technical detail of his being born a Jew in Bethlehem, was at heart an Irish Catholic. We had a small number of Church of Ireland (Protestant) neighbours, all fine, righteous members of the community, generally more affluent than the rest of us as they were mostly families of business executives. Relations between both faiths were generally excellent but with one main exception – this was before the acceptance of ecumenical religious services. I recall with deep regret and embarrassment one occasion when an elderly Protestant neighbour passed away and we followed the coffin to his church, but could not go inside to the service. That good *mensch*, John XXIII, and his *aggiornamento*, had

---

[1] Dublin Zoo, after 1927 and the arrival of the 'talking' movies, was home to MGM's Leo the Lion; his mane was deemed more magnificent and roar more spine-shiveringly impressive than the original Californian trouper.

yet to arrive with his message of mutual tolerance and understanding. There were few Jews in our neighbourhood but some of our very best friends were of Dublin and Jewish descent – I realised early on that there is no better combination of original humour and banter than that of Dubliners and Jews. Since they were direct descendants of Aaron Figatner, mentioned in the Sirens' Episode of James Joyce's *Ulysses*, it is no wonder.

Though our family was far from privileged I have no recollection of any shortages of the necessities of life, certainly not of foodstuffs, though luxuries were few and far between; we had no car and, initially, no phone. Central heating was unknown in private houses; we had fireplaces in each room, but those in the bedrooms were only lit if one were confined to quarters due to illness. So most mornings in winter we arose to windowpanes frosted over with extraordinary floral designs. We always had a radio, even one with the latest 'magic-eye' tuning technology. TV was not available until some time in the early 1950s when the serene and elegant young Princess Elizabeth decided to get married or crowned or both, and a goodly number of ideologically schizophrenic republicans trooped out to make their first such investment – and invite other neighbours around to observe, enthralled by the sheer extravagance of the historic event. (As if to encourage the surreptitious inquisitiveness of their republican neighbours, the British authorities kindly erected a powerful transmission mast in the Mourne Mountains, north of the border, just before the event.) It was mainly watched by the wives as coronation day was a working and school-going day. But the general populace seemed to agree that the Princess was a fine and exceptionally well-mannered, if highly privileged young lady.

Though not short of clothes, we did not have the endless selection available to children today. I recall having a few jackets and short pants, including short pants suits, usually bought in Clery's of O'Connell Street (incidentally claimed as one of the world's earliest supermarkets). I always had my own, not-handed-down 'Sunday suit' which was worn on that day or when visitors were expected.

I recall talk of the possible visit from one ominous visitor, the 'glimmerman', an inspector from the gas company, whose task it was to check that housewives were using gas during restricted hours, or turning the taps to the maximum position. He was authorised to make an unannounced visit to your kitchen, check the temperature of the griddles and cut off supply to the offenders. I was probably too young to have encountered such a person. But his presence was still invoked whenever we turned the taps to maximum. My only other recollection of wartime or post-war restrictions was on the occasion, in the early 1950s, when we visited Northern Ireland, but could not buy most articles temptingly displayed in shop windows, such as sweets, because we did not have the appropriate British ration cards. Down south we practised a more elementary form of rationing – that of money.

Toys were strictly offered and gratefully received at Christmas and, to a limited degree, at birthdays. But toys were toys, and the provision of new clothes or shoes was considered cheating if offered at those times. Clothes were a basic requirement parents had to provide, ordained in some Geneva Convention or an obscure clause of the Constitution, so were not categorised as real presents. I recall one Christmas morning receiving a beautiful new leather school bag. Pleased as I was with it I did not count it as a Christmas gift. Excitement was so high on Christmas Eve we stayed awake longer than usual anticipating the bounty which awaited us at the end of our beds on Christmas morning. Somehow the presents materialised without Santa ever waking us.

We did not anticipate fancy foreign holidays and, consequently, did not miss them. In the late 1940s our Aunt Rebecca ventured to take an aircraft to Jersey or London for her annual holidays and we subsequently greeted her returning DC 3 Dakota at Collinstown Airport as if we had our own lunar astronaut in the family. Our holidays comprised mainly day excursions and picnics to the bracing seaside resorts near Dublin, Dollymount, Malahide, Killiney, Bray, or weekends at a resort a little further away. We dipped in the Irish Sea, retreated shivering, hides purple, to extol the water's be-

nign temperature. Nowadays just recalling the 'summer' temperature of the Irish Sea brings on goose pimples.

My one and only feeling of social deprivation occurred not with
our lack of a family car but with the realisation that the Meccano
set I had been given one Christmas was only the basic no. 1, while
my elder brother was deemed worthy of a no. 3. OK, elder brothers
always get better and more advanced presents, but there was still a
feeling of discrimination. Fortunately, a key attribute of Meccano,
in addition to being one's own fantasy factory, was the inter-
operability of its parts, and an upgrading system whereby adding a
1A supplement to no. 1 converted it into a number 2, and so on.
With additions, my set soon reached if not exceeded the no. 2
model, while my brother's slipped *pari passu* in the ratings. Still,
my sense of deprivation was not alleviated each time I opened the
box. The cover shamelessly depicted a couple of affluent and obviously spoiled English kids assembling a reproduction of London
Bridge which would have required two boxes of the stratospheric
model no. 10 to assemble. Had our family ever drawn a promising
filly in the Irish Hospitals Sweepstakes I had no doubt what represented the zenith of my dreams.

I recall being taken for a trip by the 'Da', at the suggestion of
'Senior Management', on one of the last electric trams, before they
were replaced by motorised buses and, indeed, on one of the last
steam trains. As an indication of just how dynamic and innovative
our neighbourhood was, the two rival suppliers of bread, Johnston,
Mooney & O'Brien, and Boland's Bakeries, and twin milk suppliers
Merville Dairies, and Hughes Brothers, switched over from horse-
drawn to motor-driven vans. The supply of milk was initially ladled
out from a large churn using pint measures with a little *tilley* added
to make sure people weren't short-changed. The milk suppliers later
changed to bottles of pasteurised milk, which no longer needed to be
collected in person, but could be left on the doorstep. The bottles
were protected by cardboard stoppers but the local birds learned to
peck through these and drink down as far as their beaks would allow.
Later metal foil tops were substituted but the wily aviators learned to
penetrate these as well. Milk was delivered early, the delivery men

began loading up at the dairy at 3.00 a.m. so that the school kids could enjoy the still warm brew before leaving home.

## Transannalivia – Northside Story

Northwest Dublin is not generally regarded by discerning social arbiters as the most fashionable quarter of a city divided by the languid Liffey.[2] In fact, many southsiders believe it was condemned by natural geography to obscurity, still drying out after the retreat of the last glacial maximum, the ethnologically-distinct aboriginals only recently emerging from their hibernacula. For us it was not just an exceptionally tranquil if sleepy corner of the world but one with a captivating local history. If pushed by more socially-obsessed southsiders we could always counter that we shared our *quartier* with the President who lives in *Áras an Uachtaráin*, the old Vice Regal lodge, situated in the Phoenix Park alongside the American Ambassador and the Papal Nuncio. We could always remind them that the youthful Winston Churchill spent his early days playing nearby in the First Secretary's lodge – presuming Churchill Minor ever played.[3]

## The Phoenix Park – Dublin's 'Lung'

Dublin, considered the Second City of the Empire from 1660 to 1860, is blessed with many tranquil oases, beautiful parks, gardens and green areas: Herbert Park, St Anne's, the Botanical Gardens, Iveagh Gardens and, of course, *la crème de la crème*, the Phoenix Park. With the rapid expansion of the city this is now a vital and

---

[2] Hence the old joke, 'what divides primitive from civilised man? The Liffey...'

[3] Apparently this was not the first Dublin connection with the Churchill family. The original John Churchill, Duke of Marlborough, had supported Charles I and reputedly lost his property while his mentor lost his head. He was restored to position under Charles II when appointed to some advantageous sinecure in Dublin Castle. He lived on Bridge Street, unfortunately for the purposes of this tale, on the south side of the river, though close enough to the main road which led to the north side. Later, Edmund Burke, father of conservatism despite being a Norman Catholic rather than a member of the Protestant ascendancy, had the better sense to reside on the north side, on Arran Quay.

much-appreciated 'lung' of 700 hectares within the modern city boundaries. It is as large as all of London's parks put together. On last observation it is still lit by gas lamps – tended apparently by the son of the original lamplighter of my youth, a genial gent who knew all the neighbours and lived on Blackhorse Lane.[4] The Park was our childhood playground, a hundred yards from our suburban house.

Since I could only dream of visiting the various parks depicted in *National Geographic*, I fantasised that different corners of our local facility were fair alternatives to the Serengeti, Yosemite, and the Masai Mara (especially where thorn trees grew). Other trees may not have been as large as I imagined the Californian redwoods to be but there were some pretty impressive imitations.[5] The ponds in the Phoenix Park's Furry Glen might not compete with Lakes Naivasha or Rudolf, but they seemed equally stocked with birdlife, even if the representative species was more duck and the odd blow-in Malahide seagull, than shoe-billed stork or flamingo. Quarry Lake is quaintly covered with white water-lilies in summer.

The Phoenix Park originated on the demesne of the Barony of Castleknock and included land which belonged to the monastery of the Knights Templar, established at Kilmainham in the 1170s, just after the Norman invasion. When these were suppressed in 1312 the lands passed to the Knights Hospitaller of St John of Jerusalem. During the Reformation the monastery was confiscated by Henry VIII, following which its grounds became a Royal Deer Park and hunting ground, most of the does presumably enjoying greater life expectancy than His Majesty's queen-consorts. Later, it became the location of the Viceroy's lodge. Later still the monastery ruins at

---

[4] During the War of Independence many Dublin lamplighters, excluded from curfew restrictions, acted as the eyes and ears of the Volunteers.

[5] There is a large redwood in the nearby Botanical Gardens in Glasnevin, though it is at least a thousand years shy of its homeland competition. The Gardens included a giant *Victoria Regia* water lily from the Amazon, floating on a heated pool in a stove-heated aquarium specially designed for the exotic import. Seedlings and specimens were introduced as far back as 1849, but only grew successfully in 1854, flowering in 1855: with its steamy humidity and unprecedented temperature, a visit to the Victoria glasshouse was the next best thing to a trip to the Amazon itself.

Kilmainham were rebuilt as a Royal Hospital for old soldiers, based on the design for *Les Invalides* in Paris. In 1680 a wall was constructed around the present Park, excluding the Royal Hospital, which lies across the river on the southside. This space was opened to the great unwashed of Dublin by the good Viceroy, Lord Chesterfield, in 1745. The four-kilometre-long Main Avenue is named after this foresighted philanthropist.

During the eighteenth century the Viceroy would invite VIP guests over from England for a spot of hunting royal deer and fowl, a concession to the senior aristocracy when HM was not in residence. I recently spoke to a Dublin neighbour, local historian Patrick Brennan, who confirmed what my brother-in-law Finbarr told me that 200 years ago some of the most magnificent residences in Dublin were located around Montpelier Hill, near the main gate to the Park. Among those who maintained such homes were the Duke of Cambridge and other figures of London high society.[6]

In the eighteenth and nineteenth centuries many elegant buildings and monuments were added to the Park, including an upgraded Viceregal Lodge, the Chief and First Secretarys' Lodges, and the Under Secretary's Lodge. After Independence the Viceregal Lodge was to become the residence (in Irish the *Áras*) of the President (*Uachtarán*) of the new Irish Free State. The First Secretary's Lodge, where Churchill played as a child, has become the Civil Defence College and the Under Secretary's, hitherto Ashtown Castle, became the Papal Nuncio's residence. More recently, when his ecclesiastical eminence was chased out by dry rot, a most instructional new Park Information Centre was established there. I recall Pa showing me the 'prairie', facing the Hole-in-the-Wall pub, where a herd of cattle had been incinerated and buried during an outbreak of foot-and-mouth disease in the late 1930s. The adjacent watering hole is said to date back to medieval times, but apparently got its name from the gap in the wall through which pints were

---

[6] Apparently the said Duke married a Dublin actress, so the marriage was considered morganatic, his heir was not recognised and the title died out.

passed to slake the thirst of provincial cannon fodder mustered in the fields opposite in 1914 before being shipped through Kingstown to the Western Front. Today it has been extended and contains numerous salons, a charming restaurant and a wine shop offering a discerning selection of mouth-watering *Bordelaise*. During the war years and until the late 1940s vegetable allotments for city dwellers who wished to supplement their diets were located between Ashtown Castle and the Park Racecourse. The latter facility was the scene of some excitement during the war. Almost all open fields were staked so that foreign aircraft or gliders intent on invasion could not land with impunity. One exception was the final straight of the racecourse. On 8 December 1942 a pilot landed his craft, extricated himself and was desperately trying to light matches in a vain attempt to set it on fire, fearing it might fall into the wrong hands, when Mrs Peard, the formidable lady superintendent of the racecourse (Clerk of the Course) and a Lieutenant with the Local Security Force, came complete with shotgun to what she presumed to be a nefarious Nazi bomber, and threatened to blow his head off if he did not desist. The pilot was identified as an American on a training course from Derry who had got lost. My brother Jim was playing in the front garden when the plane flew over our roof just before landing: an event which was to prove his very earliest childhood recollection. The plane was disassembled, transported to Baldonnel, the Irish Air Corps base, repaired and later that month handed over to a Wing Commander Riddle who took off for some unrecorded destination.

One of the tallest obelisks in Europe was erected within the Park to the memory of Dublin-born Arthur Wellesley, Duke of Wellington, after his victory at Waterloo. As with Nelson's Pillar in Sackville Street, later O'Connell Street, members of the British armed forces 'volunteered' a day's pay to finance the construction. Around the base there are bas-relief tableaux depicting the Duke's victories in India and at Waterloo. These were cast from cannon captured from the French, which presumably saved money as well as cocking a snoot at the defeated enemy. The statues of the various belligerents and conquerors provided handy grips for us in our first attempts at rock climbing, but the sheer sides of the granite superstructure above defied all our attempts to imitate Hillary and Tensing.

Another prominent Phoenix Park column was sited in the middle of Chesterfield Avenue, with an eponymous sculptured fowl atop. To the less culturally sophisticated citizenry this was usually identified as the 'Eagle Monument'. Yet the ordinary citizens were not alone with their misnomer; the highly-educated Lord Chesterfield presumed that the origin of the popular name 'Phoenix' had classical resonances, whereas it derived from the Gaelic *fionn uisce,* or clear water, due to the presence of an old chalybeate (mineral) spring. According to Dillon Cosgrave in *North Dublin City and Environs* (Nonesuch Publishing, Dublin) the spring was located at what is now the northern extremity of the Zoo.[7]

I faintly recall another statue to a famous British general, a magnificent equestrian statue of Limerick-born Viscount Hugh Gough, the Napoleonic and (Indian) Sikh Wars' veteran, at the crossroads between Chesterfield Avenue and Serpentine Road as it leads to the Wellington monument. His representation was not appreciated by the more fundamentalist patriots and was blown up on a number of occasions. I recall hearing the final 1957 blast; the Office of Public Works (OPW) then tired of restoring the much beset jockey to his innocent mount and retired them both, apparently to a storage yard in the Royal Hospital filled with Victorian statuary, comparable to the post-Soviet statuary graveyards to be visited in the outposts of the old Soviet Empire.

It is quite probable that the republican zealots who blew up the statue were not fully versed in their Irish history and mistook him for his great nephew, Sir Hubert Gough, ringleader of the Curragh Mutiny and later of Somme fame – or infamy. Apparently both generations shared the same mental shortcomings: tactically obtuse generals they believed in the supreme efficacy of the frontal assault, regardless of the loss of men, and were ignorant of intelligent mili-

---

[7] Our local post office, located on the nearby Navan Road, was called The Brook, after a stream which flowed close by, past Martin's forge on Nephin Road towards the Park and it was probably that which fed the original spring.

tary tactics.[8] However, the story has an interesting ending: the remains of the statue were acquired in 1984 by the owner of Chilling-
ham Castle, in Northumberland, where they were fully restored and
re-erected in 1990. In the context of recent Anglo-Irish amity there
is now talk of his repatriation, to reoccupy the pedestal still in the
charge of the OPW.

As a historical fact, the oldest monuments in the Park are two
*cromlechs*, ancient burial monuments 1,000 years older than the
pyramids. One is to be seen at Knockmary, near St Mary's Hospital,
the other in the Zoo Gardens. The Park also contains the largest
Viking cemetery outside Scandinavia.

The Royal Hospital at Kilmainham was something of a ruin during our childhood. We avoided it not so much because of our sensitivity to its decrepit architecture as to its situation, lying that little
bit outside our radar screen on the south shore of the Liffey. In the
1970s the Office of Public Works decided to refurbish the old building, situated as it is on a magnificent site, thus creating a fine new
Irish Museum of Modern Art (IMMA). The work progressed from
1980-84, costing £20 million. In 1985 the IMMA won the *Europa
Nostra* award as a distinguished contribution to the preservation of
Europe's architectural heritage.

Some of the other residences and monuments were not spared
our youthful visits. My best pal Fred and I often popped over the
retaining ditch[9] around the *Áras*, once or twice seeing President
Sean T O'Kelly strolling along the pathways engrossed in a book.
He spotted us intruders peering from within the bushes a few times
but the kindly old gentleman never summoned the hounds. We
visited the Nuncio's residence on occasion, as well as that of the
Ordnance Survey, but they lacked the glamour of the *Áras* with its
magnificent stands of trees and ponds – a large chunk of which was

---

[8] The later Gough was protected by Haig from the ridicule of other British Army
officers of WWI, until his disastrous performance at the battle of Ypres.

[9] A prominent feature of the landscaping of the Park is that of the sunken-fences
(called 'ha-has') around the perimeter of the major demesnes, as described by Dr
John A McCullen in his erudite and lavishly illustrated history of the Park published by the Stationery Office, Dublin, 2009.

recently donated by President McAleese as an extension to the Zoo-logical Gardens. For some reason, and not necessarily because of security, the US Ambassador's residence held no attraction for us. Much further outside the Park walls was Luttrellstown Castle. It too lay outside the normal locus of our playground, but it featured briefly following the shooting of the film *Ivanhoe* in its grounds, word having reached us that the Hollywood crew were not particu-larly assiduous at recovering the many thousands of arrows shot off during the production. For weeks afterwards we played Knights of the Round Table: we had the professional arrows but, unfortu-nately, not the equivalent standard bows.

## Oxmantown

Between our house on Nephin Road and the River Liffey, *Anna Livia Plurabelle*, was the area known as Oxmantown, the ancient redoubt of the Vikings which predated the Battle of Clontarf: it was probably considered by these unruly gents as the then equivalent of a modern retirement resort on the Costa Brava. Apparently in 1098 timber from Oxmantown Wood was used to build the roof and ceil-ing of Westminster Hall in London.

A road threaded its way close to our house which in ancient times linked the Hill of Tara with a Wicklow port on the south of the Liffey, across the ford of the hurdles, *Áth Cliath*, which gave Dublin its old Irish name. Dublin Bay tended to silt up and was not used as a deep water port until after the Bull Wall was built on the advice of Captain Bligh (recently decommissioned from command of the *HMS Bounty*) in 1800; the tidal scouring which resulted cleared a channel in the Liffey's mouth and had the serendipitous effect of creating the bird sanctuary of Bull Island from the mud and sand which would previously have been carried out to sea. The second oldest church, St Michan's, on the eponymous Church Street, was the oldest construct on the north side of the river, built in 1095, after Dublin Castle and Christ Church Cathedral. In the antiseptic air of the crypt of St Michan's (it is claimed) lies the body of an old Crusader in a perfect state of preservation. Two other monasteries were located north of the Liffey, but these did not survive the attentions of the friends of King Henry VIII during the dissolution of the monasteries. One was an old Dominican monastery located where the Four Courts now stand; the other was the great St Mary's Abbey of which only the old crypt remains, off Mary Street. Apparently after the dissolution the stones of the venerable monastery were used for other buildings being erected, just as the Colosseum in Rome was used as a quarry during the Renaissance.[10]

## Cabragh

The road which passed near our house was the old Cabra Road whose original starting point was near Stonybatter (the stony *bóthar* or road) and Manor Street; it then continued out towards Ashbourne and Rathoath. During the eighteenth century a portion was renamed Prussia Street in honour of Frederick the Great who had notched up some victories again the French, much appreciated by the authorities at that time. It continued along what is now called Ratoath Road, past Little Cabragh House at the corner of Blind Lane. Little Cabragh House and Farm was once the country estate of the odious and notorious 'Hanging Judge', parvenu John Toler, Lord Norbury, as mentioned earlier. The Cabra Road then continued to pass over the Tolka River at Cardiff Castle Bridge. Good friends of our family, the children of Frederick and Marie Reid, once lived in the old Cabragh House which was eventually torn down in the late Forties when the Cabra housing estate was built. Among those who lived on the lands of Cabragh was the family of Jim Lacey the author of an engrossing local history *A Candle in the Window: A History of the Barony of Castleknock* (Marino Books, Dublin, 1999). Jim Lacey describes the history of the Barony, originally comprising 12,000 acres when granted by King Henry II to Baron Hugh de Lacy. He also pointed out to me that the Kerdiffs (later Cardiffs) had owned part of the lands of Greater Cabragh, which later became the location of Cabra Convent. I first learned

---

[10] I have often thought that in destroying the old monasteries, churches and their internal artworks, Henry's men committed as great an act of cultural vandalism as the Spanish conquistadores in Central and South America.

from this engaging work that Wordsworth had lauded Castleknock
and the nearby Tolka River when visiting his friend, the aforementioned mathematician, Sir William Hamilton.

## Hanging Judge Norbury

John Toler was at once a revolting and interesting character; it was
he who conducted the notorious trial of Robert Emmet 'the Darling
of Ireland'. Starting off from a humble Cromwellian planter background in Co. Tipperary he climbed the greasy pole of social advance on the basis of a consummate facility for deception, corruption and a fawning obsequiousness, to become a senior judge in the
late eighteenth century. His career as a callous opportunist continued as an MP at the Parliament on College Green, and was further
bolstered to membership of the Lords when divers blandishments,
threats, chicanery and bribery were resorted to in order to ensure
passage of the Act of Union. He was notoriously partial to a bottle
of port. So infamous was his addiction to donning the black cap for
the least crime, the story was told that his ghost could be seen, on
wintry nights of course, crossing the fields between Cabra and the
Navan Road in the guise of a black dog. Back in the days when a
host of crimes merited the rope, including the stealing of a few of
apples by a starving child, Toler seemed to derive a salacious pleasure in condemning his prisoners. One session of his court on Green
Street was reputed to have been interrupted by the braying of an
ass outside: on inquiring what was the noise he was informed, 'Just
an echo of the court, your Lordship'. He obviously was what Dubliners would consider a glib but utterly unscrupulous 'chancer'. He
had a reputation for issuing obsequious invitations to the more
prominent members of Dublin society to visit his country estate;
one naïve couple, presumably a few notches lower on the scale of
polite society than he sought to cultivate, landed at the door with
horses, carriage and a mountain of luggage – a sinister indication of
the length of their stay. Old Norbury spotted them, quickly dashed
out the front door and exclaimed, 'Now my dear friends, this is so
kind of you, I'll really take no excuse, you must positively oblige me
by staying for dinner.'

The government of the day obviously knew who to select as senior judge for the trial of Robert Emmet following the failure of his rebellion. Just as other vengeful regimes would later depend on the biased adjudications of Friesler and Vyshinski, so the administration of the day knew they could count on Norbury. He and his two judicial sidekicks had no difficulty in finding Emmet guilty of treason against the Crown and championing Republican France during a one-day trial in Green Street Courthouse. Emmet's speech from the dock, during which he thoroughly cheeked old Norbury, even reminding him he might drown in the blood of his victims, has gone down as one of the greatest speeches ever delivered, and is reputed to have been learned by heart by the great Abraham Lincoln, he of the iconic Gettysburg Address.[11] Emmet obviously realising he had no hope of mercy and, deciding he may as well be hung for a sheep as a lamb, went on the attack, despite the desperate efforts of Norbury to silence him:

> What have I to say why sentence of death should not be pronounced on me, according to law? I have nothing to say which will alter your predetermination, nor that it would become me to say with any view to the mitigation of that sentence which you are here to pronounce, and by which I must abide ... I have no hope that I can anchor my character in the breast of a court constituted and trammelled as this is. I only wish ... that your lordships may suffer it to float down on your memories untainted by the foul breath of prejudice, until it finds some more hospitable harbour to shelter from the rude storm by which it is at present buffeted ... My Lords, you seem inpatient for the sacrifice. The blood for which you thirst is not congealed by the artificial terrors which surround your victim – it circulates warmly and unruffled through the channels which God created for noble purposes, but which you are now bent to destroy, for pur-

---

[11] Similarities in styles are remarkable: 'Fourscore and seven years ago our fathers brought forth upon this continent a new nation, conceived in liberty, dedicated to the proposition that all men are born equal ... The brave men, living and dead who struggled here, have consecrated it far above our powers to add or detract ... we here highly resolve that the dead shall not have died in vain, that this nation, under God, shall have a new birth of freedom; and that government of the people, by the people, and for the people, shall not perish from the earth.'

poses so grievous that they cry to heaven ... I am going to my cold and silent grave: my lamp of life is nearly extinguished; my race is run; the grave opens to receive me and I sink into its bosom. I have but one request to ask at my departure from this world: it is the charity of its silence. Let no man write my epitaph; for as no man who knows my motives dare now vindicate them. Let not prejudice or ignorance asperse them. Let them and me rest in obscurity and peace and my name remain uninscribed, until other times and other men can do justice to my character. When my country takes her place among the nations of the earth, then and only then, let my epitaph be written.

Emmet was sentenced to a traitor's death: hung, drawn and quartered outside St Catherine's Church on Thomas Street on 20 September 1803. Ireland's 'Great Liberator', Daniel O'Connell, despised the jumped-up Toler and was later to succeed in having him removed from the bench for egregious misconduct.

## Broombridge

Slightly further along the old Cabra Road from the ruins of Cabra Farm one comes to Broombridge over the Royal Canal and the Galway-bound railway. It was when crossing over this bridge one evening in 1843, on his way to a meeting of the Royal Irish Society, that the director of the local Dunsink Observatory, William Rowan Hamilton, had a flash of inspiration: lacking pen and paper he scratched the result of his thinking, $i^2 = j^2 = k^2 = i\,j\,k = -1.$, with a stone on the wall of the bridge. Previously he had believed that to represent 3D geometry with the algebra of complex numbers he would just have to devise a formula along the lines of $x$, $y$, $z$. But he suddenly realised that as well as the x, y, z vectors he would need a $w$ scalar, in other words a 4D or *quaternion* solution. This formula which, according to my American friend Dennis Marks, is hedged with qualifications, equals the interval between events in special relativity, and is the basis for quantum mechanics and relativity. Top 'quarks' to Dr Marks!

Depending on one's opinion Hamilton was a man you would either like to befriend or strangle; as a super precocious kid he became fluent in Greek, Latin and Hebrew at five, and a half dozen other exotic Eastern languages by thirteen, and then entered the field of mathematics. Though eminently successful at linguistics, maths and imbibing, he proved somewhat less successful at his preferred discipline of poetry and as a swain, possibly because he tried to woo his *inamorata* by showering her from a distance with copious compositions. A less cerebral competitor was faster off the mark, offering more tangible evidence of his amour, leaving poor Hamilton to seek refuge in the bottle. I have often wondered if the dearth of clear skies over his observatory compounded his addiction to a glass or ten. His acquaintance with glassware may have had the serendipitous result of his opening up the science of optics, the geometry of light and its refraction through lenses – providing a further interpretation of quaffing the light fantastic.

Apparently he mellowed with age and was the epitome of the absent-minded professor, sometimes falling asleep during important meetings of the Royal Society – not just the Dublin but the London branch – and presenting himself to the lectern at Trinity College when indicating signs, as well as the orbiting aromas, of copious lubrication. On his way through England to attend meetings of the London Society he would call on his friends William Wordsworth and Samuel Coleridge. He expressed a wish to shine as a poet. Wordsworth rather diplomatically advised his friend against 'allowing the poetic parts of his nature to seduce him from the path of science'. Like many of the old Anglo-Irish squirarchy, he must have been a real fun fellow to know, even if not a good marriage prospect.

Between Broombridge and Dunsink Observatory were the archaic ruins of the old Cardiff Castle which my father often pointed out to me. I wanted to believe it belonged to long-lost relatives who had decamped to a newer and even more elegant pile – if not awaiting the rediscovery of distant relatives (including one who would have appreciated a no 10 Meccano set). But there is no record that the original owners were related to our side of the family, at least not in recent times; in fact, the original building was more of an old 16th century manor house with an adjacent iron mill than a real castle, which had been owned by a Cardiff from Co. Meath. These Cardiffs were probably descended from Kerdiffs who owned large tracts in counties Meath and Kildare since Norman times but forfeited them when they supported the Catholic side (Gaelic and Norman-Irish) against the Protestants (both Royalists and Puritan) in the 1641 rebellion. When Cromwell had crushed all opposition by 1653 any landowner who could not prove he had been loyal to the Parliament had his land confiscated, some being promised compensation in Connacht, which gave rise to the saying 'to Hell or to Connacht'. Cromwell also packed off a number of the more recalcitrant to the West Indies as slaves, hence the number of Irish names on certain islands, such as Montserrat. The remains of Cardiff Castle were bulldozed in those less environmentally-conscious days of the Fifties to make way for the Finglas housing estate. All that now remains are some roads bearing the name, and the bridge.

## Family Provenance

As indicated, I was the middle child, genealogically-interposed between a respected older brother Jim and a golden-curled moppet, Maureen.

Our family of three children contrasted with the 12 siblings of my mother's family, she being the penultimate arrival, and my father the only surviving child of his. The Dublin maternal grandfather, John Geraghty, ran a small team of builders. What he built is lost in the recesses of time, though I recall my mother telling me he was responsible for roofing the Guinness residence of Farmleigh, which is now the official state guesthouse.

My father hailed from Co. Kildare farming stock, coming from near the Curragh Camp, one of the largest British army bases and airfields in the UK of the time. The Curragh is also historically noted for its racecourse, the limestone of the local geology being reputed to contribute to the excellent bone structure of the bloodstock. From what I heard furtively whispered the size of grandfather Cardiff's farm diminished *pari passu* with the increasing affluence of the local turf accountants.[12]

---

[12] Presumably his friends failed to advise him that the only sure way to become a millionaire betting on the nags is to start off as a multimillionaire.

I recall in my youth visiting elderly Kildare neighbours of his who lived beside Martinstown House, then occupied by an elderly, secretive German who, it later emerged, was none other than the notorious Waffen-SS Obersturmfuehrer Otto Skorzeny, Hitler's favourite commando. He was a ruthless, though courageous and resourceful commando, an unthinking Nazi fanatic who had rescued Mussolini in 1943, tried to capture Tito, was later in charge of German troops dressed as American military police who misdirected US units during the initial stages of the Battle of the Bulge, when it was rumoured he also wanted to capture General Eisenhower. He abducted the Hungarian dictator Horthy when he was about to cut a deal with the approaching Soviets and replaced him with a pro-Nazi alternative. Among his other unfortunate distinctions was to put down the Von Stauffenberg putsch against Hitler in 1944, taking the initiative to seize control of Berlin. He was probably a leading member of the *ODESSA* escape line for Nazi war criminals. He was tried after the war and was about to be sentenced for resorting to false flag actions during the Battle of the Bulge, when a British officer confirmed that the allies too had occasionally used opponents' uniforms.

Sometime during the so-called 'economic war' of the 1930s my father abandoned farming to join the *Garda Síochána*, the replacement service to the Royal Irish Constabulary, which had been set up subsequent to the establishment of the Irish Free State in 1922. Since he joined some years after the Gardaí were set up, and promotion was mostly on the basis of 'Buggin's turn', it was some years before he was offered promotion, though he had apparently already passed the requisite exams. We kids were in school when promotion was proposed, and this would have entailed moving to some God-forsaken town in the midlands or west of the country which did not have any secondary school (what comedian Jimmy O'Dea would have called Ballygobackwards). Following much discussion my parents decided their children's education was more important than his career and the offer was refused three times. In those days the Gardaí applied an early version of the 'three strikes and you're out' rule, so he remained a regular cop to the end of his days. But he never complained: as long as he could cultivate the garden, ride his bicycle through the Park and along the banks of the Liffey, hear the news on Radio Éireann and the BBC Home Service, listen to Tommy O'Brien presenting his fascinating selection of historical classical records, read teach-yourself books on science or astronomy and take a week's holiday annually away from home, all was well in his universe. I have met a considerable number of other third-level students and successful professionals whose fathers were also in the Gardaí and who also self-sacrificingly refused promotion rather than jeopardise their children's educational prospects.

It must have been as a result of his travelling around his rural Kildare home in the evenings, along unlit roadways, that he gained his practical knowledge of astronomy. When I buy a newspaper I start reading sequentially from the first page. One good friend looks first to the sports pages. Another opens the racing pages and dumps the rest. My father's tendency was to first scrutinise the obituary page to see if anyone of his acquaintance had crossed over the Jordan River. Then he would look to 'Today's Weather' and 'The Sky this Night' column and make a mental note of which planets were to be seen, the vagaries of Irish weather permitting. Though in the eighteenth and nineteenth centuries our green and misty island was a major centre of astronomy, I can only wonder how they succeeded in making empirical contributions to that branch of knowledge. Maybe it was frustration caused by the same meteorological vagaries and not unrequited love which drove the above-mentioned Professor Hamilton distracted as Director of the nearby Dunsink Observatory. Still, 1,000 years before the Egyptians built the pyramids the ancient inhabitants of our cloudy isle managed to build a large megalithic tumulus at Newgrange, incorporating a long corridor which perfectly aligns with the rays of the sun at dawn during the winter solstice.

Judging by his library of books, many of which could be categorised as the 'teach yourself' genre, and bought before the diffusion of radio, never mind Open University TV, and when access to higher education in Ireland was greatly restricted, there seemed to have been as much a demand for self-instruction as there is nowadays for life-style improvement and diet. Before being posted to

Dublin, and because he could speak some Irish, he was sent to Salthill in Galway. From there he had plenty of time to pursue further education through correspondence courses he engaged in with distance-learning institutes in England, as was popular at the time.

The 'Da', as we irreverently referred to him – behind his back – had two other accomplishments. He could forecast the weather with surprising accuracy, and taught himself how to repair clocks. The first facility was usually put to the test when my mother, distrusting Radio Éireann's usual mantra of 'sunshine and occasional showers' would, prior to leaving the house, have him step outside the door, peer at the sky, sniff the atmosphere and make his *pronunciamento* as to the need to equip herself with an umbrella. This talent can be traced back to an incident in his youth when there was a discussion among local farmers as to whether to harvest some crop immediately, or leave it to ripen for a few more days. The Da, sensing some ominous lowering of pressure, deduced that a long spell of fine weather was about to end and recommended immediate harvesting of crops. Some followed his advice, some did not. The subsequent thunderstorm established his reputation. During the Emergency (as WWII was referred to in Ireland), Radio Eireann did not broadcast weather forecasts as they were deemed to help the Kriegsmarine, so any meteorological oracle had a certain standing amongst their neighbours. His other aptitude was developed accidentally, again, as a young man. Some neighbour had an old grandfather clock which had seemingly given up the chronological ghost but was retained as an imposing piece of furniture. The Da had a look at it, somehow spotted there was a hair spring protruding near an empty hole, the original retaining wedge missing. He nipped out to the hedgerow, broke off a thorn, inserted it into the hole to retain the hair spring and tapped the pendulum. The grandfather clock immediately resumed operation. This intervention was considered concrete evidence of my father's burgeoning mechanical proficiency. But such a reputation had its own inherent drawbacks. The days of the throwaway society had not yet dawned in Ireland, it was even the days of a Radio Éireann programme 'making and mending', so any friend or acquaintance of a friend with a dicey timepiece was wont to turn up at the door and leave it for repair, something not appreciated by the senior custodian of his schedule.

Another indicator of a vanished era in the pre-electronic banking days was his habit of bringing home his pay-packet unopened. He recognised that my mother's pre-matrimonial business experience made her the better manager. He indicated his usual modest requirements and was duly funded, while she paid bills and budgeted for expenditures. There were never any arguments about money or spending. I recall later in life when electronic calculators became standard in supermarket checkouts she distrusted such innovations and, being a dab hand at mental arithmetic, would double-check the totals.

## Genealogy

The Cardiff name first appeared in Ireland during Strongbow's Norman invasion of 1169. According to Hilary Murphy in his book *Families of Co. Wexford* there is a reference to a John de Cardiffe living near Dungarvan in 1233. Cardiffs also came to live in Naas, Co. Kildare, which was a Welsh-Norman town, around 1200. A townland north of Naas is still called Kerdiffstown, after James Cardiff of Cardiffstown who lost his lands for his part in the Rebellion of 1641, as mentioned above. There was a concentration of Cardiffs recorded around Rathoath near the Dublin/Meath border, but they too all forfeited lands subsequent to 1641. It would be interesting to know if one of these was the original owner of Cardiff's Castle by the Tolka River or of the land which formed part of Greater Cabragh House. Although my father hailed from Co. Kildare he believed that the Cardiff name on his side had come from Wexford. On my paternal grandmother's side the family name was Traynor. In 1760 one of her Traynor grandfathers married a Quaker lady, Catherine Pim. One Traynor relative fought on the side of Wellesley in the Spanish Patriotic War (also called the Peninsular War). Apparently he thought so highly of the weather there, not to mention the *vino* and the *muchachas*, he stayed on and there are now a few hundred Treñors in the Valencia phone book.

My father used to enjoy tracing the family tree for us but we kids were not interested in great grandfathers or grandmothers or third cousins; unfortunately he never set down on paper the complex relationships involved. Some Cardiffs in Australia, notably Frank, Barbara and Michele, are active in tracing the genealogy of the name and greatly help to fill the lacunae.

It was said of the Normans in Ireland that they eventually became more Irish than the Irish themselves. Thus the father's ancestors became fully integrated. Though Catholic they seem to have maintained a great respect for the Quaker traditions: I can recall the Da telling me how kind the Quakers were during the Famine. When other churches required a change of allegiance in return for food the Quakers gave assistance to anyone who needed it, regardless of faith, no strings attached. My great-grandparents knew, or knew of, another Kildare Quaker family, the Shackletons. A son Ernest joined the British Navy and became one of the boldest explorers of the Antarctic. My father oft recalled the adventures of Ernest Shackleton's great 1914-16 expedition when his inspired leadership and tenacious willpower turned a series of mishaps, especially the trapping of his ship *Endurance* in the winter pack ice of the Weddell Sea, into one of the greatest feats of seamanship and survival in the history of exploration. By a curious coincidence I was to work later in the Commission with Louise-Marie du Plexis de Gerlache, the grand-niece of the great Belgian nineteenth century Antarctic explorer, Baron Adrien de Gerlache, who had sold his new Arctic exploration ship *Polaris* to Shackleton who renamed it *Endurance* after the family motto. This was the iconic spectre ship photographed in winter darkness, the rigging encrusted in a ghostly rime, beset, its hull slowly crushed by pressure ridges in the open ocean pack-ice of the exceptionally cruel Antarctic winter of 1915.

Both sides of the family were affected by World War I. In each case the young men immediately signed up for the (British) Army in 1914. At only eighteen years of age the Dublin branch duly trooped down to Great Brunswick Street to join up and, following some elementary training, were packed off to the trenches of Flanders. On my mother's side one uncle had the good foresight to join the Navy – wherein the most senior officers were separated from a dunking in the briny by the same inch-and-a-half of steel as protected the lower ranks; he returned home hale and hearty.

Following the 1916 Rebellion, or more precisely, the subsequent executions of the leaders of that ill-organised event, no further relatives joined the British Army, choosing instead the Irish Volunteers. Those who survived the trenches to come home also joined the Volunteers when the War of Independence intensified. A cousin of my father's, Thomas (Tom) Traynor, was captured during an ambush on the Black and Tans in Great Brunswick Street. Though interrogated at length he did not inform on his colleagues and was executed by hanging in Mountjoy on 26 April 1921 and buried in the prison yard with nine other comrades, including Kevin Barry, also executed during the War of Independence. A monument to his memory was erected in Tullow, Co. Carlow. The 'Forgotten Ten' were reburied, nine including Tom Traynor, in Glasnevin in October 2001.

When the rift occurred in 1921 between those who accepted the Treaty proposals and those opposed to them, the division seems to have been that the ex-British service personnel took the Treaty side, those who had gone directly into the Volunteers supported the Anti-Treaty side. This was real civil war, even more fratricidal than that of the US experience where the division was mainly on a geographical basis. In Ireland it was ideological, with brother fighting brother at times. On one occasion my maternal grandfather was horrified to hear that one of his sons, on the Treaty side, was being sent by his commandant to flush out some Anti-Treaty supporters holed up in the Black Church, one of whom was my uncle Joe, the youngest son.[13] During the Civil War two cousins of my father's who had taken de Valera's side were caught carrying arms and executed in the Curragh.

---

[13] Joe gave his parents a further reason to worry: one day their house was raided by the Tans who emptied drawers and stabbed mattresses for the presence of hidden arms. Luckily they did not check the pockets of an overcoat Joe had hung in the wardrobe or they might have been invited out to the wall of the back yard, buckets placed over their heads, for administration of summary justice.

As a result of these traumatic events politics was considered taboo at the dinner table in our house. (Religion and sex were also taboo: the former because there was no criticism of the patriarchal magisterium of the church in those more deferential days, hence no scope for debate; the latter, because there was no sex in Ireland in the period of pristine spirituality between the establishment of the Maynooth Seminary and of Radio Telefís Éireann, or more precisely, Gay Byrne's *Late Late Show*.) The Da had himself seen service with the Volunteers as a scout when a young boy but never discussed activities, except to excoriate the atrocities of the Tans, and the even less squeamish Auxiliaries, while the regular Tommies were considered decent enough guys. The Tommies may have been adversaries – if they shot at you it was because that was their job – but the Tans and Auxiliaries, who were reputed to be paid the princely sum of seven pounds per week, enjoyed killing and causing mayhem. They, and their boss Lloyd George (the Machiavellian Welshman had obviously thought he could crush Irish insurgency as that of the Indian mutineers of the 1850s had been defeated by the 'Army of Retribution'), were considered the real enemy.

## Exit, Pursued ...

The Da did recall, self-disparagingly, the occasion he was scouting on his schoolboy bike for the local battalion prior to a planned ambush of the Tans one evening. The ambush had been organised by another battalion in Athy and his group was detailed to obstruct the road to prevent the arrival of reinforcements from the main British base at the Curragh Camp. These heroes had obviously learned enough of Archimedes to save themselves the trouble of chopping down a large tree, so they tossed ropes over the top, allowing the law of the lever to work its charm. Their tactic proceeded perfectly except that the tree had a substantial root system embedded in the ditch and its fall tore open a gaping hole. In keeping with the principle that any battle plan never survives first contact, there just happened to be a large and irate bull in the field that was greatly perturbed by the commotion. The hubris of heroes prepared to take on the victors of WWI dissipated instantly when a pulsating near-ton of prime Kildare sirloin exited to chase the bold warriors down the road. It was one thing to open fire on the Tans, another on a neighbour's valuable bull. The Da thus gained an early insight into the unpredictability of asymmetrical warfare.

Although the family politics were moderately nationalist this was expressed, as with many other Irish people of the time, mainly as opposition to British government policy and not as antipathy to individual English people, many of whom lived in our midst anyhow, while a few relatives were content to live and earn their livelihood in England. The general perception was that your average Englishman and woman was a decent enough person who took a live-and-let-live attitude. But opposition was reinforced when the British Government introduced economic warfare against the Free State in the mid-1930s. This blockade, which was eventually lifted in 1938, had a devastating effect on the incomes of the farming community in particular. I have often wondered if this discordant episode, forgotten by most English people, did not irreparably sour the chances of Irish participation in WWII.

After the War many American and British tourists came to visit Dublin. The English may have been the less affluent and stayed in guesthouses rather than hotels but they were almost uniquely well behaved and were charming ambassadors for their country. We looked up to these paragons of exemplary manners as model tourists. Judging by the comportment of the latest generation of visitors from our neighbouring island, especially those who frequent the Temple Bar area for prenuptial bacchanalia, it is difficult to echo the admiration of Gregory the Great when he first encountered fair-haired Britons in the Roman slave-market, *Non sunt Angli sed Angeli.*

# 2

# Growing Pains: Schoolboy with Satchel

*Then the whining school-boy, with his satchel*
*And shining morning face, creeping like snail*
*Unwillingly to school.*

– William Shakespeare, *As You Like It*

*Knowledge is not the sole route by which the human*
*personality emerges from its chrysalis. There is also the*
*development that comes through the spectrum of such*
*activities as character formation, moral training, cultural*
*awareness, which result in the production of the mature person*
*adjusted to his spatial and temporal environment and*
*conscious of his limits and capabilities.*

– OECD Report, 1965, *Investment in Education*

MY EARLY EDUCATION TOOK PLACE at home. I was initially deposited at a nearby nursery school, run by an enterprising neighbour, wherein the main pedagogies consisted of playing with plasticine. Since this did not require any special vocational demands she delegated the instruction to the older pupils while she got on with her own housework. My delegated tutor was a charming neighbourhood girl, my senior by at least six months. When quizzed after class by my mother as to what pearls of wisdom I had picked up I naturally described the marvellous incunabula I had created under the tutelage of my charming mentor. Being something of a businesswoman mother decided I could fool around with plasticine at home without the payment of any fee and I was returned to the domestic hearth for another year. The world of art will never know if a budding young Irish Picasso was cut off from inspiration in the prime of his creativity.

For the next year while mother was washing and ironing I had to recite my nursery rhymes, being regularly subject to spot checks to spell the hardest words, and attain a thorough knowledge of multiplications tables up to twelve by twelve. I could eventually spell everything in an illustrated guide to animals from aardvark to yak and on to zebra. On safari at the nearby Dublin Zoo I was eager to spot the various animals whose names I could now spell and was most disappointed that there were no aardvarks or yaks on show.

## For Whom the Bell Tolls

Then, when six years old, I was packed off to the local St Dominic's College, Cabra, a junior school for boys run by the Dominican nuns, a subsidiary institution to the better-known girls' school, St Mary's College. These religious ladies were of a steely disposition and ran a tightly-disciplined ship. Since it was fee-paying they obviously felt they had to justify the modest fees by emphasising elocution. One of the primary objectives of instruction at St Dominic's was to ensure that their charges spoke with proper accents. To further emphasise the difference between the college and the local national school we were encouraged to play rugby rather than soccer or, heaven forbid, Gaelic football. And to further emphasise that being nuns was no deterrent to their commitment to muscular Christianity, virtuous minds in sturdy bodies, they encouraged the noble art of boxing. Despite being a scrawny kid with small hands and thin wrists I was somehow volunteered into trying my hand as a putative pugilist. I should have been much more wary when reassured that my partner, who hailed from one class above me, was experienced and would teach me a lesson in boxing and, so to speak, show me the ropes. I was inserted into the gloves like a gladiator preparing for action in the Colosseum, or Scott departing for the South Pole, whereupon my ephemeral supporters withdrew and I was left to face the opposition alone. My mentor confirmed that boxing was a gentleman's sport by shaking hands or, rather, gloves in the best Marquis of Queensbury tradition. I was delighted to have made friends with a guy who appeared to be cut out to be a natural sportsman. Unfortunately, appearances can be deceptive: my new found friend promptly whacked me one in the face and sent me and my pugilist career reeling. Over and out while the school bell, rung to open hostilities, was still reverberating, its diminuendo in synch with the mounting crescendo in my throbbing ears. I prematurely retired from the field of combat to this dissonant duet.

My rugby career lasted somewhat longer – about five minutes longer. I tried to tackle some retreating player along the lines I had observed among the experienced role models, but merely collected the heel of his boot in my mouth and promptly lost the last of my milk teeth. Once again I managed to retire from the field of Mars just managing to avoid tears.

## The School around the Corner

Two or so years later my parents decided that attendance at a nuns' school was probably not a best preparation for the rough and tumble of life and decided to send me to a much more robust institution – St Paul's Christian Brothers' School, North Brunswick Street – a prominent educational incubus for that corner of Dublin. The Brothers had a reputation for being dedicated, tough, if not entirely in tune with the meek and brotherly Christians of early church literature, but for providing a good education. My induction began immediately when my new classmates decided they did not care for the new arrival or, more precisely, his accent. I spent over a year of playground misery; my nose being constantly rubbed in the playground mud, before all inflections of the Dominican elocution were finally eradicated and I became accepted as a member of the tribe.

At Brunswick Street the teaching staff comprised an equal number of religious and lay teachers. Like all institutions there were the good and the bad, the popular and unpopular among the teachers.[1] Some teachers were naturally dedicated to teaching; others obviously did it as a job. I recall two in particular who taught English and who obviously had an infectious enjoyment of literature and poetry. One exceptionally capable and demanding teacher of maths unfortunately died during our third year. He was replaced by a teacher who had himself not done honours mathematics in his own finals. No doubt this poor individual spent many exhausting evenings preparing for us ungrateful wretches the following day, but I think we paid the price for his lack of competence. When teaching us calculus for the first time he suggested that we need not understand in detail what it really meant to take differentials, just to know how to use the technique. He compared the procedure to a workman using a pneumatic pump who does not know how it works, but who can manipulate the contrivance. For years afterwards this convinced me that I should not try to understand what was inside the black box of calculus. In fact, having somehow secured a temporary teaching job later, I realised that if taught logically the concept is quite straightforward and even simple. I often wonder how many children are put off maths because teachers are just not qualified to teach it.

In my mind the pleasant and tranquil years at school elide into each other, interspersed with school holidays and carefree days of youth. Being a day pupil my playmates were not necessarily from Brunswick Street, but neighbouring urchins. We moved house to the main Navan Road when I was about twelve years old. For me this had the great advantage that it backed onto the grounds of a sports club, with tennis courts, an athletics track and club house. It became my personal playground though I was too young to become a formal member. Unfortunately my favourite house did not last longer than two years. My father, being a keen gardener, disliked

---

[1] One primary school instructor was Paddy Crosby, who presented a popular programme on Radio Éireann, *The School around the Corner*.

the fact that our rear garden was too small, while the larger front flower garden, which he kept meticulously, was invaded frequently on a Wednesday morning when the Dublin Cattle Market took place. In the early 1960s few farmers had access to transportation and herded cattle on foot. Hundreds of the creatures were driven down the Navan Road to the markets on the North Circular Road. Some of these famished creatures showed their appreciation of his gardening by breaking through the gate, gobbling up his herbaceous border and trampling the manicured lawn. In those days cattle were then driven on the hoof from the markets down through the city to the docks. I recall in my youth cattle being driven down Bachelors' Walk, past O'Connell Bridge, to the north docks, to the inconvenience of the relatively few car drivers, not to mention the discomfort of pedestrians when the animals invaded the pathways and left their bucolic calling cards. Later I learned that, at the same time, on Sunday mornings shepherds still drove sheep down the now elegant Via del Corso in Rome.

### Sic Transit ...

My own halcyon days risked ending with the passing of the Leaving Certificate examination. As happened in Catholic schools in Ireland in the days before final exams a 'recruiting sergeant' from a religious order visited our school, encouraging us to consider a career as missionaries in Africa. We were invited to spend a weekend visiting the seminary which was located north of Dublin in Co. Cavan. One thing led to another and I ended up trying my luck as a potential future missionary, prepared to revitalise Africa. In those days in Ireland idealistic youth did not think, as in Britain, of joining the army: there was no gap year of voluntary service abroad, nor were there voluntary organisations such as Trócaire, Concern, Goal, or Gorta, under whose direction one could realise a youthful idealism. Various publications extolled the justifiably honourable exploits of Irish missionaries, male and female, mainly in Africa. Other countries sent their soldiers to conquer the world: the Irish sent their youth to assist the developing world with initiatives, not just doctrinal, but also inspired by humanitarian impulses, such as building hospitals, teaching tropical hygiene practices and modern methods of agriculture, and providing education and a sense of self-worth to the deprived in the towns and in the bush.

I spent a couple of happy years in the same rusticated seminary, though my memories are now hazy, especially regarding the 5.30 a.m. morning calls and somnolent attempts to indulge in Gregorian chant. We were kept in strict purdah, firmly isolated from the opposite sex, presumably in the hope that what one does not see one does not miss. Studies consisted of Plato[2] and Aristotle, with lashings of, or as Maritain more elegantly opined, a luminous flood of, the Angelic Doctor, St Thomas Aquinas. For Aquinas, Aristotle alone was 'The Philosopher'. Unfortunately, I did not stay long enough to find out if Jacques Maritain, the French neo-Thomist, was on the curriculum. He seems to have been a most interesting person, an anti-Vichy Christian democrat; he availed of his exile as philosophy professor in Canada to assist Jews escape from the Nazi-dominated Continent. His promotion of 'natural law' ethics meant he was called upon to help draft the UN Declaration of Human Rights and advise Schuman on the drafting of the Treaty of Rome.

My career in the church continued and included a few months at college in Rome, studying in the mornings at the university and afternoons in a charming house of studies on the Aventine Hill, beside the Baths of Caracalla, a short distance from the Circus Maximus. At weekends we were free to visit the innumerable ruins and monuments of classical, early Christian and Renaissance Rome. The ambiance was wonderful, relatively open-minded and intellectually enlightened, especially for one coming from an Irish Catholic background – after all John XXIII was recently installed up the road at HQ, and the progressive ecumenism of the Second Vatican Council was about to blow a welcome breath of fresh air into the fossilised structures of the Church. Among the studies was Roman archae-

---

[2] Years later, when I was exposed to the thinking of Karl Popper of 'Open Society' repute, I came to appreciate the excessive influence of Platonic philosophy on Catholic clergy, with his emphasis on rule by a knowledgeable caste in society, and belief that 'the wise shall lead and rule and the ignorant shall follow'. Confucius was of a similar mindset.

ology. I greatly enjoyed the field trips, especially to the ruins of the old Roman port city of Ostia Antica, and the many catacombs which surround the Citta Antica, especially those of Santa Priscilla where some newly discovered galleries were just being explored. Being archaeology students qualified us to enter sites off limits to ordinary visitors. These provided a wonderful insight into the beliefs, art and customs of the early Christians. Numerous insights into early Christian devotion and respect for the dead and martyred are provided by the many graffiti, in the elegant simplicity of the Latin and Greek calligraphy, painted and crafted on the walls by these early believers, almost 2,000 years ago.

One interesting feature of the early Christian catacombs is that among the iconography there is practically no depiction of the crucifixion – the paintings of the day are mostly of the Good Shepherd with a lamb on his shoulders (influenced by the classical figure of Orpheus similarly depicted carrying a lamb), or of a fish, the Greek spelling of which, ICHTHYS, corresponds to the initials for Jesus Christ, Son of God, Saviour. Occasionally, the symbol of an anchor is presented upside down representing the cross. Apparently it was hundreds of years later that the Byzantine church introduced the cross and the crucifix to the Western church, which I thought was a pity – the symbolism of a shepherd is more redolent of a kinder, caring faith. This belief was to be confirmed when I visited an old Spanish church in Ecuador and was numbed by a crucifix which my *Insight* guide described as showing the most anatomically excruciating wounds to be seen outside an operating theatre.

Our house of studies included a most eclectic gathering of students from all over the western world, apart from the countries on the other side of the Iron Curtain. Among the students and teachers were doctoral researchers and experts of long standing in many fields of study, including Biblical Studies. To qualify for the latter one had to be a bit of a linguistic genius and, preferably, have spent some time studying in Jerusalem. I recall being asked to help proofread the English language references in a draft *opus magnum* by one of these eminent sages. The basic text was in Latin and it not only included the Greek, without which a Biblical scholar wouldn't even begin to qualify, but Hebrew, Amharic, Syriac and Coptic. Apparently this elderly palaeographer could speak a dozen arcane languages and write and read many more. I just pitied the poor typesetters and compositors; setting *Finnegans Wake* must have been child's play in comparison.

I was overwhelmed by the vast history and archaeology of the most fascinating city in the world which, with Athens, constitutes the wellspring and patrimony of western knowledge and culture. The coming of early underground Christianity, with the initial emphasis on a forgiving, rather than retributive God, the philosophy of doing unto others as one would have done to oneself, of creating a compassionate society, injected a breath of fresh civilising air into the brutalising lifestyle of the old Romans. The Colosseum is a magnificent, iconic structure but it inevitably recalls the gruesome barbarism of gladiatorial games, the publicly-paraded torments and executions of the less fortunate, all played out as a spectator sport for Sunday afternoon family entertainment. During the early days of their faith the very sight of this arena of death must have stirred revulsion in Christians, just as the sight of a concentration camp would be for a Jew – in fact it would have had an almost similar effect on a Jew of the time since construction started by the Emperor Vespasian was completed under Titus in 80 AD, using Jewish slaves taken prisoner at the fall of Jerusalem.

To a great degree the coming of Christianity, and its forging in the crucible of persecution during the first two centuries in Rome, provided an initial introduction to the concept of human rights into the callous public ethos of the day. Unfortunately Constantine was to co-opt the Church into the political structure, instead of leaving religion and state separate or, better still, at a standoff. The temptation proved too great to resist and the Church grew to enjoy its temporal authority, the Christian Imperium, not realising that power inevitably corrupts. A millennium and half later the European Enlightenment evolved to adopt, in turn, a somewhat patronising superiority towards peoples of the non-Western world.

## Demobbed

Meanwhile, I wrested with a nagging concern I would not easily adapt to the Irish church milieu, with its culture of unquestioning deference, secrecy and misogyny, at the end of those halcyon days in the Eternal City: I realised I was a bit of a nonconformist, increasingly receptive to new ideas, starting to forge my own identity. It was a wonderful interlude of learning but not of creative thinking. There was also the distant but inevitable menace of commitment to lifelong celibacy and obedience.[3] I discussed it with colleagues who very helpfully advised me that, if I was not certain it was to be the life for me, better to jump ship there and then. Having decided to leave I organised a modest celebration with my admirably understanding colleagues. They kindly escorted me to the Stazione Termini, where I bade *arrivederci* to my early formative years, and boarded a train to cross my personal Rubicon.

I hoped that at some time in the distant future I might, again, *torna a Roma ... magari ....*

---

[3] Though abjuring possible partnership with a charming lady was heartbreaking, a *coup de foudre* was unlikely for a student constrained by nocturnal curfew, so a distant promise of celibacy was somewhat academic: without a real life *inamorata* it involved resignation to the pangs of unrequited love. Much more ominous was the looming declaration of obedience which presaged irretrievable suspension of critical thinking to an indeterminate roll call of superiors, any one of whom, with an inflated view of his own importance, I might find it difficult, if not impossible, to respect.

# 3

# UNCORRALLED:
# APPRENTICE NOMAD

*This wonderful graveyard [the Roman Forum] where the heart
of the ancient world lies buried ... can only become alive and
understandable if one is able, in imagination, to restore the
missing columns and re-gild the vanished roofs.*

– H. V. Morton, *A Traveller in Rome*

*Rome is an introvert and secretive place that hides
its treasures; even after living there for twenty years
it can spring surprises.*

– Georgina Masson, *The Companion Guide to Rome*

IT WAS JUNE 1962 IN DUBLIN, TOO EARLY to enrol at college, so some
form of gainful employment was called for. I first tried my luck
with Aer Lingus, then portrayed as the Green and Friendly Airline.
As debonair as an awkward, though spotlessly laundered youth
could manage, I entered their offices on O'Connell Street, Dublin.
A comely and impeccably groomed young sales lady, who looked
like she had just popped out of their most prestigious brochure,
summoned me. I announced that I was offering my services, and
was ready to take up a suitable appointment immediately. I was
graciously but firmly informed I would have to wait until they had

published an appropriate advertisement in the newspapers. I countered that I wished to start the following morning or, at the very latest, the following Monday. I received a further polite smile and the next customer in line was summoned. I retired, tail between legs, down but not yet out.

Next to be tested were the offices of Pan Am, TWA and BOAC. Finally, I was directed to a newly-established travel agency, which was said to be starting a series of summer package tours to Italy, with Rome as the operational hub. A helpful lady at the desk suggested I write in to the managing director, Joseph Herman Walsh, and apply for the post of representative in Rome which was vacant. I had a letter in the post that evening by 8.00 o'clock which, in those days, would guarantee delivery by early the following morning.[1] A day later I was called for interview.

JHW was a bluff, larger-than-life Belfast man, a supremely combative businessman who radiated energy and with a well-honed capacity for effective expression. He did not initially confirm if my application was successful. Yet I was called back for interview on numerous occasions, not so much to be interviewed as treated to a managerial onslaught which might have formed the basis for a course on business management. Mr Walsh was not given lightly to sacrificing vigour in expounding his business philosophy. As one of his very earliest employees the private tutorials he provided were unique – management consultants have charged a fortune for lesser insights. Presumably he was just mentally codifying his new business philosophy and needed an audience on which to practise his tutoring. Later when he proved highly successful as a businessman I was grateful he had forgotten the virtuoso performances, or he might have sent a substantial bill to my subsequent employers for initial vocational training. I was informed that knowing a bit of old Roman archaeology was far from sufficient to become a successful representative of the burgeoning JWT corporation which then to-

---

[1] Our local letterbox was located in the wall of the Phoenix Park and depicted Edward VII, his original red bas-relief profile having been over-painted a patriotic green.

talled almost 10. I would have to deal with a load of potentially du-
plicitous foreign hoteliers and local transportation companies, and
ensure they provided a level of service appropriate to our esteemed
clientele. As one who would have to purchase locally lots of services
on behalf of the company I too would have to absorb and emulate
the forceful, no-nonsense commercial culture of my new employer.
I slowly began to identify in my mind less with the poor Roman
Christians at the mercy of the lions and more akin to an impresario
of that spectacle. Or even, since I was being sent to Rome by a Belfast man who had a substantial clientele of forceful Northern Irish
Catholics, as a poor lion being thrown to the Christians.

Joe Walsh had come to Dublin a few years earlier to work for a
well-established British tour organiser which specialised in sending
Irish travellers of the period on their first trips abroad, mainly to
Lourdes and Rome. Since tour organisers took the big risks of char-
tering aircraft they also stood to be much more profitable than
travel agents who merely worked for a fixed commission on sales.
JHW soon linked up with two experienced post-war Continental
travellers and quondam civil servants who became co-directors, the
erudite Martin Ryan who radiated conviviality and avuncular authority, and the self-effacing Sam Lombard, a taciturn sage of sur-
passing financial acumen who applied himself as the ever-
dependable sphinx of the back-office. Both Sam and Martin had
explored Europe extensively in the post-war period when few Irish
males ventured further than Ballybunion for their annual holidays.[2]
Getting more involved with the travel business they both severed
their links with the civil service, this at a time when few ever resigned from such permanent and pensionable jobs.

Joe Walsh's philosophy was to stick to the basic bread-and-
butter business of organising package tours to Lourdes and Italy,
making sure he filled every last seat on his chartered aircraft. At

---

[2] I recall Martin telling me of his times in Germany in the late 1930s. He got into
the only taxi at a rank one evening, the driver informed him that he could not depart until another taxi had arrived, as the law decreed there always had to be a cab
at each stand. They waited for over a half an hour before relief arrived and they
could set out on their ten-minute trip.

this he proved exceptionally successful. Within a few short years the Spanish seaside market opened up heralding the start of the mass tourism market. Behind his tough businessman persona he could be a bit of a softie on occasion, particularly in relation to old acquaintances.

## Arrivederci Roma

I was designated representative in Rome; my main counterpart in the field was Breda Hickey who was in charge of affairs in the other main resort of Lourdes, in the southwest of France. A refined and gracious lady, she could maintain her serenity despite late arrival of aircraft, shortages of accommodation, coach breakdowns and disappearing guests. Though she had done the job for only one year she was already an institution among the newly-travelling Irish public. I briefly entered her territory when, en route to taking up my position in Rome, I had to help her with an exceptionally large group of travellers going to Lourdes one week. I was very apprehensive as to whether I would be up to the task as, not only was I entirely unacquainted with dealing with the sick and invalids, but I was rather reluctant to encounter the sentimentalist form of religion I feared was practised in Lourdes. I wondered how I might get along conversationally with a clientele all of whose pieties and certainties I might not necessarily share. It is not that I lacked respect for those with less questioning beliefs but did not wish to get involved in discussions which might hurt the feelings of those with sincerely-held, ingrained attitudes. Having travelled much *in partibus infidelium* where many exotic religions are practised, my now-mellowed and more tolerant philosophy is that my neighbour is free to practise what religion he or she wants and I will respect him or her, as long as they do not try to impose their beliefs on me. I welcome other opinions but tend to take a soft line when dealing with persons of advanced years for whom belief is the essence of their existence and who are unlikely to change.

Dealing with the visitors to Lourdes, especially the sick, was an eye opener. I was briefly taken in charge by some experienced *brancardiers* and soon learned that the last thing the sick and terminally-ill wanted when being wheeled around the town was sympathy or silky pieties. They were just delighted to escape from a hospital or sanatorium in Ireland, even if it were only for a few days and even if they knew it might be their last holiday abroad – or anywhere. They were usually in such high spirits that it was the most natural thing in the world to carry on a normal conversation. The whole adventure seemed to give a great psychological lift to them. I'm not surprised there are some extraordinary recoveries. Although some locals may cash in on the simple beliefs of the visitors, with their serried ranks of gaudy religious souvenir shops, at least the authorities keep the vendors out of the shrine areas around the Basilica. I left after a few days with great admiration for those who devote a week or so of their annual holidays acting as *brancardiers* in the restrained dignity of Lourdes.

I arrived in Rome to assume my new responsibilities as general factotum for the agency. This consisted in making arrangement for accommodating, guiding and providing pastoral care for guests who arrived each week by charter flight, spent a week in Rome and them departed to Sorrento and the Amalfi coast. Here they would in turn be greeted by my colleague Anna Napoli in the exquisite little Hotel Minerva, perched above the cliff just outside Sorrento, with a commanding view of the magnificent Bay of Naples and the distant silhouette of the rock-garden Isle of Capri, set like a jewel amid the shimmering, turquoise waters of the bay.[3] I was so overwhelmed by the sublimity of the vista some long dormant thespian voices bestirred and from the recesses of Intermediate Certificate poetry I recalled the lines of Shelly:

---

[3] Some years later as JWT expanded operations, Finnuala Kelleher was appointed as representative on the Adriatic coast. A young lady of enormous charisma and energy, hailing from a highly cultured Kanturk, Co. Cork, teaching family, and with an abiding love of Italian culture and history, an erudite guide to the glories of Ravenna and Venice, she soon gained a loyal following of clients who, in subsequent years, requested to be sent to the resort in which she was in charge. Later still, the gregarious Eugene McGee and the charismatic Elizabeth McKenna, 'La Liz', in love with Italian culture and history like Finnuala, built up a similarly loyal clientele.

Thou who didst waken from his summer dreams
The blue Mediterranean, where he lay,
Lulled by the coil of his crystalline streams,
Beside a pumice isle in Baiae's bay,
And saw in sleep old palaces and towers
Quivering within the wave's intenser day,
All overgrown with azure moss and flowers
So sweet, the sense faints picturing them!

## Largo al Factotum

Rome the eternal was the hub of our activities. My first contact
with the guests was when I met them on arrival off their charter
flight in the early hours of Monday morning at Fiumicino Airport,
tired zombies of pallid gaze. Many had never been out of Ireland
before. I would look after them for a week before packing them off
to Sorrento, Positano, Amalfi or Capri at the end of the week, while
I went out to the airport to pick up and process another group of
lost souls. Thus there were always two groups in Italy. At the end of
the second week the Sorrento crowd returned to Rome Airport to
be replaced by the arriving consignment of fresh palefaces on the
charter flight.

The key to successful tour operations is to fill both 'legs' of a
charter flight. It also helps if a good aircraft is available and at the
right price. In 1962 Aer Lingus used Vickers Viscount aircraft, with
their characteristic four Rolls Royce turbo-propellers, between
Dublin and Rome. This involved a necessary but time-consuming
refuelling stop in Zurich. Since it took a Viscount a good seven
hours to make each leg of the trip, Joe Walsh and Martin Ryan tried
to convince Aer Lingus somehow to provide a medium-sized jet.
But the only jets the airline then flew were their Boeing 707s (actually the 720 model), all allocated to the transatlantic route. So the
ever-enterprising Joe and Martin went over to London Heathrow
one Sunday afternoon and looked out for any jet they deemed to be
'gathering dust overnight'. They identified a few craft, especially a
Comet 4C of Middle East Airlines which arrived from Beirut in the
afternoon and, in the leisurely fashion of the times when aircraft

spent most of their time on the ground, did not take off again until late the following Monday morning. The 4C normally had 84 seats on board, except when some affluent sheikh arrived at Beirut with an entourage of *habibis* and demanded extra first class seats, and it could make the Dublin to Rome trip fully laden without the need to refuel en route. Since MEA had no licence to fly out of Dublin lengthy discussions were held with Aer Lingus until they agreed to charter the MEA jet themselves, so that anyone observing the elementary departure board of the time in Dublin airport would notice an odd-numbered Aer Lingus departure to Rome, and an even more surprising craft. Such was the bedrock belief in the reliability and safety record of Aer Lingus at the time that many Irish were just not prepared to fly with foreign carriers, except maybe British European Airways to London, but not some unknown Middle Eastern carrier. Some stared at the strange markings on the aircraft, declared their doubts and demanded a change of vehicle from one with a cedar tree on its tailfin to a big, reassuring, green shamrock. Informed that no refund would be forthcoming if they declined they eventually resigned themselves, threatened future legal action for unimaginable amounts of damages, sat down and took their chances. But the 4C was a good sturdy aircraft, since the problems of the preceding models had been thoroughly rectified – though not before the Boeing 707 had captured the market. We had no mishaps with the Comet or its crew, and no further complaints on the safe return of our punters. My major problem concerned the sheikhs, who had tourist class seats removed to be replaced by larger first class ones so that the craft often arrived with 79 instead of 84 seats and I had to seek volunteers to stay behind.

## Under Rome's Thrall: Non Basta una Vita

Our main basis during the first year was a *pensione* hotel, the Fabrello-White, on the busy Via Vittorio Colonna, a street located on the Trastevere side of the river Tiber which linked the Castel' San Angelo and the Vatican to the main historic centre of Rome on the other side of the river on which is located the Forum, Colosseum, Capitol, Piazza Navona and Central Station. The pensione was located on the third and fourth floor of an old palazzo and was managed by an elderly and highly-cultured Austrian Jewish gentleman, Stefan Popper, assisted by co-director Ms Eva Sintenis, a young German lady who had lost all her brothers on the Eastern front during the Second World War. She fled the martial remnants of Prussia to the relative pacifist ambience of post-war Italy. The palazzo was like many other buildings in the old centre of Rome, a palimpsest, or historic series of overlaid buildings, the most recent an eighteenth or nineteenth century palazzo, built onto a medieval construction, all of which had been added on top of solid travertine marble foundations dating from pre-Christian Rome. To demonstrate how much history lurked in the most surprising spots all over the city, Stefan pointed out a couple of bumps on the travertine jambs of the portico to our palazzo, about shoulder high. They initially looked like potatoes. Stefan explained to me that they were what was left, after two thousand years of being polished by myriads of passing shoulders, of the busts of ladies which advertised the building as a good-time emporium whose residents would extend a warm welcome to generous gents. Yet there they were, sandwiched between a jeweller's shop and an electric store, completely ignored by the unsuspecting and insouciant throng which trod this busy modern Roman street. Their location is not as surprising as the ruins of a genuine Roman bordello located in the second basement of a church on the Piazza Navona, and whose fraying artwork and raffish frescoes are in evident contrast to the pious themes and styles depicted upstairs. This confirms that there is a wealth of history every few yards within the old Eternal City. A lifetime is not sufficient, *non basta una vita*, to begin to learn the history of a city which may be beaten by Damascus for longevity but has experienced both upheavals and embellishments of successive republican and imperial styling, the flowering of early Christian architecture, then the medieval, renaissance, the exuberant Baroque and, finally, unification remodelling of the city.

Stefan was a mine of information and advice regarding a successful adaptation to my new hometown. One day I returned triumphant having purchased a new suit at a particularly keen price and showed off my prize to Stefan. 'Brendano,' he advised, 'I'm too poor a man to afford cheap goods.' Next time he took me to his own tailor who charged four times the price for ten times the quality – *su misura.*

Over the first few weeks I put together a program which consisted of a tour of the city on the visitors' first Monday morning, taking in the Colosseum, Arch of Constantine, the Roman Forum, Capitol Hill, Piazza Venezia, Trevi Fountain, the Pantheon, the Piazza Navona, Piazza di Spagna, Via Condotti, Castel' San Angelo, Pincio Hill, the Vatican and St Peter's and, finally, the Janiculum Hill.

The balmy Roman evenings were filled by visits to the Via Veneto and Trevi Fountain, Piazza Navona, Spanish Steps and the Barcaccia fountain (fed by the delicious Acqua Virgo, the sweetest water in Rome), open air opera at the Baths of Caracalla and the fairy-tale delights of the illuminated Villa d'Este fountain-gardens in the Latin Hills at Tivoli by night. Other day-time trips consisted of visits to the charismatic villages in the nearby Alban Hills and the catacombs alongside the Via Appia Antica outside the Aurelian Walls of the historic centre. Most important of all was organising attendance at the weekly Papal audience, usually hosted at the Papal retreat up at Castel Gandolfo in the Alban Hills, during the summer months.

The pace of life in Rome of the early 1960s was very different to the Rome of today. This was before the arrival of pervasive air-conditioning and jostling platoons of tourists who invade Italy all year round. Italy had just recovered from the cataclysm of war, just as Virgil described the country in the *Georgics* some two thousand years earlier, similarly recovering from a lengthy, devastating civil war. Before air conditioning was generally available an afternoon siesta was *de rigeur,* as was escape from the stifling, enervating heat of the city in August. Rome that month, especially after the Feast of the Assumption on the fifteenth, was like an apocalyptic city which had been contaminated by plutonium or some deadly virus, and abandoned. Not so many years before that the Pontine Marshes, flooded by the breaching of the aqueducts by invaders on the fall of the Western Empire, remained a source, not of *mal aria,* the deadly marsh air which was considered to cause the eponymous illness, but of legions of *zanzari*, or mosquitoes, the real vector for the spread of the infection. Fortunately Castel Gandolfo was above their peak flying altitude. Hence Romans liked to desert their city in hot weather, especially when the *sirocco* was blowing up from the Sahara and mosquitoes on the wing. Nowadays with the widespread diffusion of air conditioning, not to mention the draining of the marshes, and new patterns of tourism, places shunned in the 1960s are routinely engulfed even in the middle of August.

Mondays heralded the obligatory tour of the city which *capo gruppo* Brendano had confected to take in the main sites. As long as the microphone worked in the 50-seater touring coach he was in his element; if not, Mr Carlo Ricci of the Ricci Coach Company got an earful[4] and Brendan ended up with a much degraded throat. Though traffic jams were not unknown in the evenings, during the daytime travel around the old city even with a large coach was relatively easy. We complained if we had to park our bus over 100 metres from the Trevi fountain or the Pantheon. A tourist bus could cruise around the Piazza Navona in those days.

One perennial irritant to smooth organisation of city visits was caused by the disposition of normally reticent northern European ladies, demure Irish maidens included, to shed clothing and innate modesty when the temperature passed 25 degrees centigrade. Many believed that they were in the tropics and should dress accordingly. But the custom of the local matrons, and their strictly-chaperoned daughters of the day, was the opposite, to cover up when the sun was at its strongest and when visiting a church. The miniskirt fashions of Carnaby Street had not breached the bulwarks of the Alps and the only minis to be seen were worn by northern tourists, or those alluring Roman sylphs of dubious piety who vaunted their charms along the Via Veneto *di sera*. The only impediment to entry to St Peter's was the length of the ladies' dresses or lack of sleeves. Sleeveless dresses were a bogey; entry was refused by the censorial gendarmes at the main door unless a covering cardigan could be

---

[4] This was my only point of contention with the perennially unruffled and debonair director of that enterprise.

procured. I frequently ended up leaving the immodestly clad out-side, entering the hallowed sanctuary of the basilica with the meek of the earth, then grabbing any cardigans I could borrow with which I would exit the side door to restore the modesty of the awaiting black sheep, thus qualifying them to rejoin the rest of the group inside. Wearing a cardigan in St Peter's in summer posed no problem: such is the colossal size of the basilica walls that they act as a natural heat-sink, taking all summer to warm up and all winter to cool down – natural air-conditioning.

Shepherding the charges back to the bus in St Peter's Square was also a problem due to the proximity of souvenir sellers and shops on the nearby Via della Conciliazione. In the case of the dehydrated male Hibernians, revitalising bars beckoned, into which they flocked like a troop of thirsty hippopotami chancing upon a water hole. The ladies were mainly afraid that if they did not immediately snap up the souvenirs, cataracts of which tumbled out of myriad stores onto the pavements, supply would dry up, never to be replenished. Maybe it was a hangover from wartime economics, and that insights into supply-side economic theory had yet to be expounded, but ladies with spending money in their purses were loath to chance the effi-cacy of the invisible hand. Some stores were brazen enough to adver-tise in English 'Special Prices for Tourists'; one need never overesti-mate the intelligence of some travellers in distant lands.

## Caveat Venditor

Not all tourists are irredeemably naïve. I constantly advised my charges against buying anything from ambulant salesmen, espe-cially the type who offered glittering bracelets, rings and watches in guaranteed gold. One young lady from a provincial town, who probably had a discerning eye for a calf or yearling, decided she knew full well how to drive a hard bargain, even from a slick Italian entrepreneur. On the beach she was approached by a man, wading inland, trousers rolled up to the knee, as if he had just strolled over from France or Switzerland, flashing a case of enticing jewellery, who whispered 'smuggled watches, very special price'. Our astute young lady asked the price of a particularly attractive Omega, and offered but ten per cent of the quoted price – insisting not one lira more. The salesman eventually ceded to her steely determination. She subsequently approached me with her investment, an eminently satisfied look on her face. 'How much you think this cost?' she enquired. I put the timepiece to my ear and turned the winder – SKREEK, SKREEK, SKREEK. 'About three shillings, no, let me try it again, two shillings.' She was about to slap my face for casting aspersions on her commercial wisdom, but had second thoughts. I advised her to just listen to the winder and compare the noise level to any other watch, and maybe calibrate its timekeeping over the next few hours. She approached me a day later, an even more contented smile on her face. With the moral assistance of a couple of determined compatriots she had stalked the unsuspecting peddler and nabbed him. The three redoubtable maidens strong-armed the hapless huckster, threatened to throw him and his collection into the briny, before escorting him to the *questura* (police station), if he did not offer a full refund. One should not underestimate the audacity of some resolute colleens in foreign parts.

## When in Rome

In those days my dear fellow-countrymen and women were quite unadventurous regarding foreign cuisine. Some innovative souls experimented at home with exotic foods like spaghetti, which was sold in tins, the strands boiled to a pulp and four times as bloated as the native *al dente* preparation. Our compatriots insisted on heavy Irish breakfasts washed down with gallons of tea. It was difficult to convince them that bacon was not available in Italy in the summer months. Meanwhile the locals would make do with a tiny *espresso* coffee or two, accompanied by a *brioche*. They exited to the Roman heat never to shed a drop of sweat to soil their pristine collars, while the heavily-breakfasted Irish sweated profusely all morning.[5] Traditionally, the Romans were light breakfasters, their

---

[5] Even local construction workers seemed immune to perspiration. In those days such tradesmen invariably wore folded newspaper hats – a Roman version of *origami*.

main meal of the day being evening dinner, the opposite of the older Irish tradition. While the Irish enjoyed frequenting a pub in the evening the typical Roman enjoyed dining out in his local *trattoria*, especially if it were *al fresco* in those days before air-conditioning and multi-channel TV. The tradition of running family restaurants is as ingrained here as it is for families to run pubs in Ireland. The legal restrictions on the sale of pork in Italy during the summer months, legislation harking back to the days before refrigerators, were widely diffused, and lasted until the coming of autumn. As for a big juicy Irish sirloin or, *magari*, a T-bone steak – forget it. Slivers of veal sandwiched between slices of cheese and ham were the closest to a steak, at least in the ordinary restaurants. Nor do I recall in those days being served the now-popular *carpaccio*, Italy's cured beef answer to smoked salmon. Maybe it was served at the celebrated *Osteria del' Orso*, a medieval hostelry still going strong after 700 years, but its tables were beyond my purse in those days.

## Castel Gandolfo

One important event each week was to ensure that the group was brought to the Pope's summer residence at Castel Gandolfo in the Alban Hills for a Papal audience. The ecumenical John XXIII was, in his day, as big a superstar as the later John Paul II, a *molto simpatico* Pontiff, especially compared to his austere, aristocratic predecessor, Pius XII. Getting the faithful into the audience hall and keeping them together afterwards was quite a demanding logistical exercise – especially when on return to our coach the desiccated gentlemen spotted welcoming bars offering cool *Birra Peroni*. The ladies, in turn, were drawn to the perennial rows of souvenir shops like filings to a magnet.

Procuring the entrance tickets to the Papal audience was a key task for an Irish tour guide, that and securing accommodation in a favourably-located 'tribune', as near the papal chair as possible. The event was staged so that the Pope entered the front door of the building and was carried up the main aisle scattering benedictions, if not *urbi et orbi*, at least in profusion on each side of the hall. This had the advantage that he would pass everyone present within a couple of metres at the most. The more enthusiastic fans were eager to secure a place right up at the retaining barrier and, normally, the key to success was to arrive on time.

Once I had guided my charges to their designated tribunes it was a matter of waiting a half hour or so until the Pontiff arrived. This inevitably provoked a surge in the crowd, particularly by nuns, and especially those tiny Italian ladies who seemed to dominate the profession. Most of our guests were kind-hearted and prepared to defer to ladies, but if your average Irish gent had queued for an hour to see a Pope whom he reckoned other Italians could see any day of the week, he was likely to take umbrage. Yet these steely ladies had their own ideas and when it came to greeting their *Santo Padre* they could out-elbow a crusty rugby prop and woe betide you if you tried to hinder their passage. At the height of the Roman summer many travelled with black umbrellas which served as *para-soleils,* but could double as pikes. In addition, these sprightly ladies seemed uniquely equipped with sharp elbows and toes with which they gouged their way to the front line. Their elbows were usually wielded at the level of your rib cage or kidneys. Their shoes seemed adorned with stiletto toes rather than heels. Some would have made intimidating ice-hockey players. Even allowing for the linguistic difficulties, it was no use trying to convey to them you had arrived an hour before and they should remain in their place in line. At this distance in time I can ashamedly confess I devised a ruse and, on occasion, surreptitiously reached out a discreet hand in the scrum, fastening it to the end of the dangling veil of the most aggressive of these human tunnel-borers. As she burrowed forward, unaware that her headgear was now anchored, she risked a cranial striptease amid a shower of hairpins. '*Oh, scuzi mi Suora, mea culpa, mea maxima ....*'

Securing well-positioned places for our clients at the audience was one of my most important tasks. This was greatly facilitated by the fact that the ultimate boss of operations was one Monsignor Tom Ryan, who had been Pope John XXIII's secretary when the latter was Papal Nuncio in Ankara, and then in charge of the Swiss

Guards. Each week I would approach the entrance to the Vatican Palace with an envelope addressed to the Monsignor which I would show to the Swiss Guard, mumbling a few words in the appropriate German. Halberds would be stood at the vertical, staffs smartly whacked the ground and I would receive a most martial salute. A brief word with the receptionist and, in those pre-terrorist days, I would be directed towards the appropriate office, unescorted, free to wander at will amid the magnificently-marbled halls and frescoed ceilings.

## The 'Scoglio'

A visit to a lively Italian restaurant was an indispensable part of the week's entertainment. We would adjourn to a spot popular with the Irish College and Aer Lingus, the *Scoglio di Fresio*, then accepted as the unofficial Irish restaurant in Rome. Aer Lingus District Sales Manager Captain Gus Madden held court there almost nightly. It was a lively and welcoming establishment. But to suggest this was a typical Italian restaurant was like saying the Abbey Tavern in Howth, or Blarney Castle, was the embodiment of Irish rusticity. A lively quartet of local musicians circulated, serenading the admiring guests. They were accompanied by a charming local songster in the style of Mario Lanza. Once these minstrels identified an Irish presence at a table our virtuoso would bust forth with an Italian rendition of *Danny Boy*, to the delight of his audience, especially the ladies. Other Italian favourites, such as *Azzuro*, or a Neapolitan number popularised by Gigli or Caruso would follow. The vocal style was, frankly, more *con belto* than *bel canto*, but it made for a most memorable evening, especially for those ladies who had their photos taken while being embraced by Razzle-Dazzle Danny. Some even considered it redundant to make the further visit to the opera later in the week.

## Caracalla

Rome of the 1960s managed to scale the traditional Italian artistic redoubts in the field of arts, and music in particular. Ballet was performed *al fresco* in the evenings in the nymphaeum of the Villa

Giulia, open air symphony concerts were conducted by many of the world's top virtuosi in the old Basilica Maxentius in the Forum, and opera was staged at the Baths of Caracalla. For those who enjoyed opera the open air amphitheatre halfway between the Circus Maximus and the old Walls of Rome beckoned. During the summer the main opera house was closed and a central point of the vast ruins of the old baths was converted into stage and amphitheatre, with an *élan* of which only the Italians are capable. To reduce any risk of noise pollution, local street traffic was diverted. The beautiful, balmy *al fresco* Roman evenings, set within the archaeological ruins with encompassing pillars, slim elegant cypress and graceful poplars standing sentinel amid the characteristic umbrellas of the Roman pines which studded the garden landscape, provided an ethereal setting.

One experienced a certain sense of foreboding on entry as the immense walls of the old structure reared into the night sky, disbelief that such a relic of antiquity, haunted by the uneasy shades of the old imperial tyrant, could possibly serve as a setting for music, never mind an opera. Two thousand years ago these baths were enormously popular and formed a major social hub in Rome. But once the lights were extinguished, the stage illuminated and the semi-concealed orchestra struck up the overture, the audience was immediately transported into an aural and visual wonderland.

Though some opera singers were said to be reluctant to risk projecting their voices in such an enormous amphitheatre there have been performances which would rival the best of La Scala and La Fenice. No better stage could have been imagined for presentations of, for example, *Aida* or *Lucia de Lammermoor*, which demand large spaces. But the story line of other operas, especially *La Bohème*, some of whose scenes are set in an impoverished Parisian garret, was lost in the enormity of the amphitheatre. The giant stage allowed the bringing on of live camels and horses for *Aida*, accompanied by hundreds of 'Ethiopian slaves' and 'Egyptian soldiers' waving their spears in time with the music, and a multitude of torch-bearers, any one of whom would have been banned in an indoor theatre.

There were many faithful clients who returned annually to attend Caracalla. I recall William (Willy) Lemass and his daughter Maureen, Pat Cosgrave, Valerie Lombard and the charismatic Fr Peter Shields, choirmaster from Dundalk, Co. Louth, all good friends of the Dublin Grand Opera Society. Willy had sung while his wife (who had passed away in 1957) had, respectively, played the piano with the Walter McNally touring opera company which enchanted and enhanced Irish rural society before the era of the radio. It specialised in presenting such musical pearls as the 'Irish Ring': *Maritana*, *Lily of Killarney* and the *Bohemian Girl*. Willy Lemass's group, stalwarts of the Dublin Grand Opera Society, founded in 1941 by Col. Bill O'Kelly, had been attending Caracalla since 1959 and had got to know such artists as Giuseppe Forgione, Attilio D'Orazi Guelfi, Piero Cappucilli, as well as the noted conductors Maestro Napoleone Annovazzi and Maestro Morelli, from their performances in the Gaiety Theatre.

In 1963 Col. O'Kelly had arrived in Rome to seek a new tenor for a forthcoming presentation of *Rigoletto*. He set off to the north east of the country in search of an unknown debutant who was recommended to him, one Luciano Pavarotti. Pavarotti duly accepted the invitation to the Emerald Isle, to enthral audiences not just at the Gaiety but in the Belfast Opera House and in Dundalk, where Fr Peter Shields, known in Italy as Dom Pietro, was the resident impresario. The reverend Monsignor snared the emerging maestro into singing at the local church hall and rewarded him with the munificent fee of five pounds. In Dublin he was spotted by an Irish lady talent scout for Covent Garden and engaged to understudy Giuseppe di Stefano as Rudolfo. He almost immediately had his chance when di Stefano was indisposed, and his famous partnership with Joan Sutherland began.

## IATA in Excelsis

Among the problems which the Rome Representative was obliged to solve was that of clients who missed their charter flight or, for some other reason, had to return home prematurely. The 1960s represented the high noon of IATA, the International Air Transport

Association cartel, which rigorously controlled all fares and levels of services offered. Together with de Beers in diamonds it must have been one of the most overt textbook cartels of all time. It had compiled a list of fines which were imposed on airlines caught offering reduced priced tickets or free drinks to tourist class passengers. A list of sanctions was rigorously enforced, if I recall correctly US$5,000 for serving a free drink to a tourist class passenger, and something like US$45,000 if caught offering a fare reduction. The IATA cartel had their international network of plain clothes detectives policing airlines to ensure no undercutting or 'unfair' incentives were offered by any airline, especially third-world airlines, on routes such as Rome to London. Many of these companies flew aircraft with an average of ten per cent of their seats filled and would have been more than happy to fill more, even for half the official price. It was not until 1978 that US President Jimmy Carter deregulated the nefarious cartel as highly inimitable to consumers' interests and withdrew the US from its malign control. (I used to think of the number of homesick Irish emigrants who would have loved to fill one of the many empty seats if offered at a more affordable price.)

Nineteen sixties-vintage aircraft did not have the range they now enjoy and had to make far more frequent refuelling stops; most from the Middle or Far East stopped off at Rome en route to London. Since a single ticket from Rome to Dublin cost almost as much as an inclusive tour with two weeks' accommodation one could appreciate the plight of an impoverished traveller who for some reason missed the return charter flight and had to buy the standard single fare home, or was left stranded in Rome. An infringement such as offering to sell an empty seat on a charter flight to one who had not actually booked the full two weeks' all-inclusive tour would bring the full force of airline retribution down on the travel agency, which would also lose its licence to issue air tickets. One had to be very careful about offering even a close relative a free seat on a charter flight.

One means of securing a cheaper flight ticket to Dublin was to book with some airline which had perennially low load-factors and which flew the Rome–London sector. This was difficult unless one had an introduction to a consenting sales manager. The second part of the ticket to Dublin would be reserved with Aer Lingus or British European Airlines, who retained a *pro rata* proportion of the indicated, official price. Of course the major proportion of the fare was accounted for by the Rome-London part. Thus, it was very attractive to the Rome district sales managers of the airlines who flew empty seats to London to offer tickets for cash at a reduction. They presumably kept a second set of books for the purpose. Among the accommodating airlines were a number from the Middle East. Sales managers had to be very careful lest they were being set up by inspectors from IATA so it took a certain amount of time to establish one's credentials, so to speak, as an investor in more democratically-priced travel.

One airline's sales manager knew me sufficiently well to invite me to his soundproof basement office which was entirely papered with photo reproductions of the insides of a magnificent sarcophagus at some archaeological site his country possessed in abundance. I recall the inside of the door of his office was cut, or the greatly magnified photo calibrated, so that it fitted exactly the size of a large stone slab of the necropolis. I would enquire the going rate to London. As a token of his esteem for me he would start by offering a special reduction of, say, 15 per cent, 'but only for you, Signor Cardiff'. 'What, only 15 per cent? Why, Middle East Airlines are offering 30 per cent this week and I hear El Al 40 per cent.' A mutually acceptable tariff was eventually agreed. My conscience twitched for some time afterwards, though I never went to the extent of actually negotiating with El Al by trying to engage them in a spot of carpet trading. My contact would remind me he had to be very careful: 'Signor Cardiff, you will not believe it but the IATA, they are always sending their spies to catch me out, even the very beautiful ladies, you cannot believe it ... all the time ....'

In those days the airlines occupied an institutional and social standing which it is difficulty to appreciate in these days of low-cost, competitive air travel. It was a hangover from the war, and airlines were still considered to play a strategic role as potential transporters of troops. Lots of airlines were staffed by WWII flight crews who still wore military decorations on their uniforms. Also, civil airline companies offered an alternative source of employment and experience for redundant air force officers. In addition, the national flag carriers were treated as prestigious national totems, especially if they were flying jets. The offices in Rome of the major international airlines, within the Via del Tritone, Via Bisolati, Via Veneto triangle, were the most luxurious of any in the city, generally with spacious and elegant ground floor offices decorated at considerable expense. The Rome office of one British airline was located on the prestigious Via Bisolati and a parking space was reserved outside for the manager's imposing limousine, his impeccably-uniformed chauffeur usually to be detected hovering nearby. One had the impression that airline managers competed with their national embassies for the distinction of representing their countries.

The Green and Friendly Airline was relatively more modest, having a third floor office on the Via Tritone, just up the road from Bernini's beautiful Fontana del Tritone, if I recall correctly. It was managed by the genial (ex-army) Captain Gus Madden, assisted by the charming and beautifully-articulate Eilish Johnson who served also as an English-language announcer on Vatican Radio. I came into frequent contact with the said captain, a member of the DGOS choir, during my weekly visits to the Scoglio restaurant. I got the impression that he had an Italian version of a *Stammtisch* reserved permanently, as he nightly regaled potential trans-Atlantic fliers. At a critical juncture in the evening he might be observed passing across the dinner table an envelope presumably enclosing air tickets. A diversion over Dublin and Shannon no doubt resulted.

Some years later I was in a position to write policy papers on the deleterious effect of the cartel, and direct them to the attention of competition authorities. I queried why the normal rules of competition, including exemption from the competition rules of the Treaty of Rome, were accepted without question for a host of anti-competitive arrangements. It seemed that, because access to air travel was then so restricted, and its business carried out in closer proximity to the heavens than earth, application of man-made laws which constrained other *terra firma* commercial activities should

not apply to this lofty business. Of course, awareness of the deleterious effects of jet engines on the atmosphere had not yet dawned
on people.

## Driving, a la Romana

Though Rome of the 1960s already had its share of traffic and
shortage of parking places it could not be compared to the Rome of
today. The most popular private cars were small Fiats, while Vespa
scooters were ubiquitous. The standard taxi was a slightly-stretched
version of the Fiat 600, the 850. Delivery vehicles were usually
three-wheelers, their staccato exhaust sounding like a drive-by machine gun. These contraptions could ease their way through the
densest of traffic. Since the roads were generally dry, Roman taxis
were driven like outdoor dodgems, in imitation of Formula 1 expo-
nents. But their drivers had excellent reflexes and could stop within
a whisker of a competitor without causing an accident. This would
have been catastrophic for both parties since there was no compulsory insurance then. Taxi drivers were wont to expound on the
world's problems, gesticulating hands occasionally touching the
wheel, like some modern-day apparition of the peripatetic teachers
of old. Maybe it was because the tarmacadam was warmer in the
Roman summer, like simmering treacle in the sunniest spots, or the
most popular tyres included an ingredient guaranteed to screech
on cornering like a racing driver on the Imola circuit, but most
drivers seem to take enormous pleasure careering round bends. Initially, foreign visitors would turn their heads expecting to witness a
scene of carnage. But the locals were highly skilled. That's not to
say that there were no serious accidents. When the inevitable occurred great theatrical scenes would play out on the roadside, most
memorably when a bloodied passenger joined in, accompanied by
the frenzied and contradictory accounts of partisan witnesses who
gesticulated wildly and pronounced instant judgment. Such anima-
tion served only as a warm-up for the even more effusive outpour-
ings when the police arrived, which seemed to encourage new theatrical heights as the dramatic events were re-enacted. Just when
the astonished witness expected a scene of Virgilian foreboding,

*bella, horrida bella, et Thybrim multo spumantem sanguine,* the sounds of horrid battle would fizzle out, a bath of foaming blood in the Tiber was averted and the contestants drifted away, still loudly proclaiming the absolute reliability of their testimony.

I myself enjoyed the art of Roman driving, as they say, 'when in Rome...'. I figured I should partake of the pageant, or maybe it was just the inner Mr Toad who was bestirred by the excitement. There were a number of corners this now sedate driver enjoyed negotiating *come un'vero Romano,* especially when there were warm cobblestones. These produced the best tyre squeals of all, especially when one came down the Via dei Fori Imperiali to join the wide expanse of ancient cobbles around the Colosseum. The fact that there might be a bunch of tourist crossing to visit the Colosseum only added to the thrill as they fled in all directions. It sure gave them something to write home about if they lacked alternative inspiration, and certainly enlivened their stay.

There are a number of ways to learn the disposition of a town without becoming an actual taxi driver. I learned the geography of Dublin when I had an old banger as a student. Frequenting tennis club dances at weekends, I was usually importuned for transport home at the evening's end by fellow revellers and learned to negotiate all quadrants of the city. (As the evening progressed some young ladies would become ever more approachable: one had to avoid self-delusion and learn this was not necessarily motivated by any amorous attraction I exuded, but by desperation to avoid a late night taxi-fare homewards on the part of the charming but usually impecunious young ladies.) In Rome we seemed to change our hotel headquarters each year so that I got to know the Trastevere side of Rome near the Castel San' Angelo and the Vatican one year, the Parioli district the next, then the eastern side near the Via Salaria and Piazza Fiume, and so on. Since I had to direct bus drivers when returning from and setting out on excursions in all directions, and had to frequently escort independent travellers to Fiumicino Airport, I rapidly learned the back streets of the then unfashionable Trastevere area better than the average Roman taxi driver.

## Austria

It probably was a continued youthful infatuation with snow: falls of snow occasionally blanketed the Dublin of my youth, heralding fantastic new games and transforming the dull winter landscape. If the fall exceeded two inches Dublin came to a halt and school was cancelled for a few days. So when the possibility arose of spending a few weeks as a *Reiseleiter*, guiding ski vacationers in Austria, I jumped at the chance. It was difficult for an agency to find tour guides with a knowledge of German who were free for a few weeks in February. I had picked up an elementary smattering of the language having experienced some adolescent palpitations for a lady of that nationality earlier. Although already in the middle of studies at UCD I suspected something of a wheeze in the chest at the requisite time each year and, just as regularly, a medical friend provided me with a cert recommending a few weeks recuperation in the Alps. To salve my conscience, if not my mind, I inevitably brought along copies of Samuelson's *Economics*, and Louden Ryan's *Price Theory* which I carefully placed on the table top beside my bed. I may have been moonlighting, correction, recuperating, in mid-term, but at least I felt the comforting presence of a couple of peripatetic professors, one a Nobel prize-winner. Neither tome was greatly depreciated during the next few weeks, it being a bit difficult to apply oneself to wriggling microeconomic graffiti on return to quarters at 3.00 am.

## Timeo Danaos et Dona Ferentes

My route to our main base at Ehrwald in Austria was indirect and involved a train trip. At the end of January JWT had secured the contract to organise travel arrangements for the Ireland-France rugby match in Paris at the end of January and there were a few spare seats on one of our charter flights. I was delegated to fly to Paris, help with arrangements and then take an intercity train to Munich and the local train on to Ehrwald in the Austrian Tyrol, just over the border from Garmisch-Partenkirchen. My sister Maureen was then working at UNESCO in Paris on the Abu Simbel recovery program. She saw me off on the train to Munich and, as a goodbye gift, presented me with a box of expensive liquor chocolates some admirer had given her. I had arranged that on arrival in Munich the next morning I would meet up again briefly with Eva Sintenis of Pensione Fabrello days who was now married and living in a suburb outside Munich. I took a taxi from the station to her suburban residence, complete with box of fancy French chocolates or, more precisely, super-sized cognac liquor chocolates, which I intended to present. I arrived before 9 a.m., forgetting that in Germany this was not a guarantee the *Hausfrau* would be *zu Hause*. The door was opened by a lady who told me she was the *Putzfrau* (cleaning lady). I was told that Eva was in town shopping but that I should go into the living room, make myself at home and await her return. Sharing the living room with me was Eva's young baby son of possibly a year old, romping around in a playpen. We soon struck up a friendship. My new buddy offered me a loan of his teddy. In a similar spirit of camaraderie I decided to offer him something, but had naught, bar the box of chocolates earmarked for his mum. Always being a bit of a sucker for panhandlers, I eventually relented, opened the box and offered him a sample. This was immediately stuffed into a mouth that assumed a surprising proportion of his face. He initially spluttered but eventually recovered and swallowed the residue. Shortly, a wee hand was extended through the bars of his cage for another helping. Well, who can resist a sweet little kid? The procedure repeated itself for about an hour until the box was almost empty. I finally took a principled stand and refused further contributions, if only to retain proof that I had really brought a present for his mum. After a further wait I decided I would myself visit the town centre and hopped on a bus outside. I returned a couple of hours later to note an ambulance and a number of cars outside Eva's house. Luckily for me, by that stage of the medical alert the all clear had just been sounded: had I arrived half an hour earlier I might have been lynched on the spot by my good but maternal friend. Relief that the child was merely enduring his first *Kater*, or hangover, saved me.

## A Little Village in the Tyrol

My little *Bummelzug* (local train) from Munich to Ehrwald made its way around the Zugspitze, past Garmisch which was then a high-class rest and relaxation resort for the higher echelons of the US army. As the train climbed to the altitude of Ehrwald the snow became deeper and we penetrated what for me was a veritable winter wonderland. I made my way in the waning twilight past typical Tyrolean buildings as if drifting through a Grimm's fairy-tale landscape, dropped my bags at the *Gasthof* and was directed for my dinner toward the inevitable *Austria Keller*. No self-respecting resort in the Tyrol of those days seemed to lack its own Austrian Keller, with regular Tyrolean evenings of live music and dancing to the melodies of Bert Kaempfert and James Last.

I met my predecessor in the posting, Sam Lombard, who provided me with a brief review of tasks, indications as to where the guests were lodged and introduced me to the world of skis, ski boots and ski schools.

The agency had wisely invested in about 40 pairs of skis of various lengths which were leased out to the clients. It was among my tasks to size up clients and skis, allocate one to the other, show how they were attached to the ski boots and ensure they were returned at the end of the week – hopefully in one piece, especially the skis, if not the clients.

It was then the apogee of wooden skis and primitive safety bindings whose wire cable looped around the heel of the ski boots and hooked to front-fixing clips. They should, theoretically, have opened in case of a false manoeuvre. The spring-loaded lever situated in front of the ski boot would be adjusted and clipped into place. The tightness could be adjusted so it would pop open with a certain level of unwarranted force, while the rather simple technology had the advantage that one could immediately see if there was much leeway or not. (They were known in Canada as 'rat-trap bindings'.) Most accidents happened when the safety binding was set too tight and instead of opening the ski stayed in place to act as a lever to snap bones or tendons. Thus a high proportion of skiers returned home in plaster and hordes of the walking wounded were to be spied on in the streets of each ski village. The local doctor in Ehrwald would be foxed if one went to seek a cure for a cold, but present him with broken bones and he was immediately up to his elbows in plaster of Paris, like my mum when she was making the icing for Christmas cakes. Nowadays ski injuries seem mostly caused by collisions, because of the mass of skiers transported to the *pistes*, and especially between skiers and snowboarders whose techniques and manoeuvres are different.

The wooden skis of the 1960s were of compacted plywood – though an American aeronautical engineer, Howard Head, was experimenting with the first aluminium sandwich skis. It was recommended they should exceed one's height by a hand's length or so. Hence many used skis over two metres long; my first pair were 215 cm. I took a certain pride in insisting that clients look and learn how the binding worked and to leave them on a relatively loose setting, light enough that they would come open in case of an accident rather than staying attached with the consequent broken bones and torn ligaments. My argument was that it was smarter to get cold fingers refitting cold skis to boots after a severe bump than having them too tight and causing severe damage. During the times I served in Ehrwald I experienced no seriously broken limbs among my charges, though many bruised egos. But we also booked clients who wished to avail of our charter flights, yet stay at some other resort such as Kitzbuehel, Kirchberg, Westendorf or St Anton. Here they looked after themselves as regards skis and boots. Every weekend before organising transport home from Munich airport I had to phone the independents' resorts to count the casualties and arrange for Aer Lingus to have the appropriate number of stretchers installed on the Viscount aircraft. It was like the charters to Lourdes, except that the stretchers were in place only for the return journey. I recall one pilot remarking to me he did not like taking off in bad visibility with so many stretcher-cases on board in case we had to make a forced landing.

Ski boots were then made of laced-up leather, though the most elegant were a new Swiss design fitted with *Schnalen* (fancy clips). The quality and comfort of the boots is more important in skiing than the skis themselves since they transmit body signals to the skis. Leather boots would eventually stretch to fit comfortably around one's foot, but with plastic boots, if they did not fit correctly the first minute they would never fit properly.

I recall the first time I eventually got kitted out myself: I thought my feet had been nailed to the floor. I began to mentally query the intellectual sanity of sliding down the sides of snow-encrusted mountains athwart a pair of slippery planks. The planks were not only longer than is the case with modern 'carver' skis, but their sides were perfectly parallel and had a central groove running the length underneath, for greater control in a *Schuss* or straight line – so it was then believed. A regular morning chore for earnest skiers was to polish the ski base using a selection of coloured waxes, the choice being dependent on the snow temperature.

An earlier morning chore for the vacationer was to queue for shared toilet and shower: humble Austrian guesthouses may have been spotlessly clean but bedrooms offered only a hand basin for ablutions. Even in hotels use of a hot bath was an optional extra for which one paid 20 schillings; the receptionist unlocked the door, drew the requisite quantity of hot water and retreated to allow the guest to luxuriate as in a Turkish hamam.

## The Ski School Round the Corner

Ski school was another chore of the resident *Reiseleiter*, especially getting Irish revellers to school on time. One instructor of Irish beginners accepted fate and turned up first at 10.30 a.m., then eventually at 11.00 each morning. While the Germans were usually lined up in perfect formation well before 10.00, many red-eyed Irish tottered along an hour late looking like the remains of Napoleon's *Grande Armee* retreating from Moscow. Even Napoleon's lesser regiments did not look as if they had been celebrating Dionysian vigils in the Austria Keller until 4.00 a.m. Friends Joy Reid and Betty Moran mortified us once by taking a 300 metre taxi trip up to their ski class, an hour late.

Some of our clients took to skiing like ducks to water; others were just not cut out for mountain sliding and often called a halt, especially if a stretched ligament or sore ribs provided a valid excuse, like malingering troops in wartime. An injury which involved a cast was seen as suffered in the line of duty and gave a certain social status to the invalid. Depending on how spectacularly he or she fell, the story could be recounted over and over, especially if attending the popular *Tiroler Abend* session. The streets of the village were invariably peppered with the walking wounded, those more incapacitated were often to be found propped up in the local cafés and restaurants which kindly supplied reading material in the old Austrian fashion. Sympathisers were invited to sign the plasterwork like early Roman graffiti artists, and would offer a beer or glass of wine to the sufferer.

As already suggested, skiing is an activity not necessarily correlated with intellectual ability. I recall one of our guests, a genial lawyer, Daniel, let's call him. The affable Daniel had supped in said Austria Keller till the generously late closing time and, understandably, appeared somewhat lethargic when presenting himself at class later that same morning. He was consigned to the lowest beginners' class which seemed to be composed of young and impeccable female models, skiing debutantes who wanted the cachet of skiing while avoiding the concomitant risk to figure and fingernails. Daniel arrived clutching an eclectic haberdashery of driving gloves, scarf, Donegal fly-fisherman's hat, other accoutrements trailing, skis akimbo like a signal for a railroad level crossing. The instructor and the charming ladies helped upholster him, though he seemed to take almost as long to kit out as an astronaut. The instructor then demonstrated a simple *Schneepflug* or snow-plough stop, first sliding downwards with skis parallel and together, then pushing out the back of the skis while angling the outsides upwards like a ploughshare to break the movement, for all and sundry to imitate. None volunteered to repeat this simple manoeuvre except our ever-accommodating Law Library gallant.

He set off slowly at first, facing a wide, sloping apron of snow, which was deserted, except for the rotund silhouette of a distant *Skihaserl*, far removed, near the bottom of the *Alm*. Then, as if she were emitting some form of magnetism as yet undetected by cosmologists, our hero was ineluctably drawn to the snowbound siren at an increasing pace. Maybe he was then going too fast to hear the shouts of the ski instructor to *Schneepflug! Schneepflug!*, he just could not get the back of the skis to separate out to provide the requisite braking. His classmates shouted contradictory advice and encouragement at the retreating figure, such that even an astute, legally-trained mind could not absorb under the circumstances. He inevitably made violent contact with the lady and surrounding snow. They became inextricably entangled in their own private *pas de deux*, a pulsating mix of snow, skis and ski sticks. When the *Pulverschnee* whirlwind settled it was to be observed that the lady was sitting astride his neck, she unable to disentangle herself from encumbering skis and sticks despite her best efforts, our recumbent hero unable to defeat the force of the juggernaut bearing down on his neck bones, one of which was later found to have been broken. His only resort to encourage his corpulent companion to speed departure was to bite at her adjacent bottom through her ski pants, which entailed furious screams but no effective change of position. The decibel diva's high-pitched shrieks melded with his *Heldentenor* bellowing to create a dissonant duet, from which even Wagner would have recoiled. Unfortunately, neither classmates nor instructor were capable of immediate assistance as he, rather unprofessionally, joined them rolling in the snow with mirth. Eventually, another team of Samaritans arrived to the rescue, separated the entangled couple, skis and sticks, and the lady's plaintive wails subsided into tearful, tremulous whimpering.

Our heldentenor's neck was conspicuously bandaged, and with this resplendent trophy of honourable combat, was discharged from further Alpine duties. He dined or, more precisely, supped out for many a subsequent night on the story and, presumably, returned to the Four Courts and more pacifist pursuits. We never saw his consort again – though we did drink to her restored health.

## Obergurgl – Lofty Idyll

One unseasonably warm March the snow on the lower slopes of Ehrwald melted and a couple of our clients decided to venture to a distant and exceptionally high resort whose reputation was becoming known to the *cognoscenti* of high mountain skiing. This was the first time I heard of the exotic resort of Obergurgl, high up in the Oetztal Alps, near the South Tyrol border, and almost inaccessible at some 2,000 metres up a narrow and primitive road along an avalanche-ravaged valley. It provides skiing on cool north-facing slopes up to 3,300 metres. But it was a day's travel from Ehrwald, leaving on the early 7.30 a.m. Post bus.

A few years later when I travelled on my own account to Austria during another unseasonably warm March I attempted to check in to Obergurgl, to be informed that under such weather conditions every room was reserved. I booked into the nearby village of Vent, equally elevated, which specialises in mountain-touring holidays, involving trekking with combination skis and, when going uphill, placing seal skins under the skis, hairs pointing backwards (the 'nap' in case of artificial skins) so that they did not slide back on the ascent. Departure was at sunrise every morning, stopping off at the next overnight hut by midday before high avalanche time. The old road up along the Oetz river valley was narrow, rude to the point of being almost hair-raising at times, especially when car tyres began to slide. Despite the difficulties and the occasional day-long delays further down the valley when avalanches blocked the higher road, I fell in love with both of these high mountain villages, among the highest permanently-lived-in villages in the Alps, and have stayed loyal ever since.

## E Finita la Commedia

It was Shakespeare who suggested that familiarity breeds contempt: I never grew contemptuous of the city of aesthetic delirium, Byron's city of the soul, but I had a sneaking feeling that Rome, with its ubiquitous travertine masonry, impervious to earthquake, sieges and sackings, a metaphor for its timelessness, and its haunting palette of tones – sienna, umber, shades of ochre – was keeping the march of time at bay, slowly turning me into one of its own calcified museum pieces. I first noticed this when guiding my group. I found that occasionally I no longer needed to look up at a monument, such as the column of Trajan, or point out a site with the same undisguised enthusiasm as in the early days: I had begun to operate on auto-pilot. A Roman might live on top of a two-thousand-year-old palimpsest with the greatest of insouciance, his wife hanging out the washing along its sides, the city might be the political capital of a modern economy, but I still feared that Rome is essentially one great magnificent, all-enveloping heritage museum, little changing in the old *centro storico* but the models of the cars and the prices in the windows. Those who fall in love with that most magnificent treasure-house, aptly described by that marvellous storyteller H. V. Morton as the graveyard where the heart of the ancient world lies buried, risk losing consciousness of time and inexorably and imperceptibly succumb to its passage. I began to feel that inside the old Aurelian Walls one lived within a time-warp. The Greeks refer to the tradition of preserving old cities in aspic as *archaeolatreia*; I was beginning to feel I was suffering from a touch of said syndrome myself. I decided that I should quit while I was still enjoying the action, and face what destiny might offer when my days as a chronic final-year student inevitably ended.

# 4

# AD ASTRA – ERRANT SCHOLAR

*Aristotle's fear of any form of money earning, i.e. of all professional activities, goes perhaps even further than Plato's ... For Aristotle every form of professionalism means a loss of caste ... A feudal gentleman, he insists, must never take too much interest in any occupation, art or science ... There are some liberal arts, that is to say, arts which a gentleman may acquire, but always only to a certain degree ... For if he takes too much interest ... he will become proficient like a professional ... This is Aristotle's idea of a liberal education ...*

– K.R. Popper, *The Open Society and its Enemies*

*The real university has no specific location. It owns no property, pays no salary and receives no material dues. The real university is a state of mind. It is that great heritage of rational thought that has been brought down to us through the centuries and which does not exist at any specific location ... The real university is nothing less than the continuing body of reason itself.*

– Robert Pirsig, *Zen and the Art of Motorcycle Maintenance*

SOMEWHAT LIKE RECOLLECTIONS OF early education those of early years at University College Dublin are fading into sepia-tinted memories of classes and teachers, idealistic discussions and hectic chit-chat in the Main Hall and corridors of University College Dublin (UCD) at Earlsfort Terrace, especially when students and teachers burst forth enthusiastically and vocally from lecture theatres and corridors on the hour. Though I completed studies just before the start of the 'Gentle Revolution' of 1968, I certainly did not find UCD an intellectually-asphyxiating 'Catholic Boys Technical School' as have some other more illustrious alumni. I found the place in many ways quite liberating and illuminating. That may have been because I chose courses, history, politics, economics, which lent themselves to greater openness of enquiry – or because I just was not intellectually-critical enough myself - or have now become excessively mellow in the autumn of my life. In fact there was a number of inspirational teachers there at the time who left an indelible impression on all who had the good fortune to attend their lectures, individuals such as Desmond Williams, Fergal O'Connor, Paddy Lynch, Dudley Edwards and Denis Donoghue. They combined exuberance and charisma with vision and imagination, whetting a scholarly appetite while nurturing the development of the human spirit. They can be looked to as metaphors for the Irish renaissance in the pre-hubristic second half of the twentieth century.

I recall the helpfulness of the librarians working with Miss Power, the staff in the registrations office and their understanding of delayed payment of fees, and Paddy Keogh, Head Porter and an institution in his own lifetime.

There were two choices of university in Dublin of the 1960s, Trinity College or UCD. Trinity was the older, socially more prestigious, though financially-fraying entity, founded under Queen Elizabeth I in the sixteenth century, the repository of the famous Book of Kells and a depositary library for all English language books. For a couple of centuries, until 1793, Catholics and Dissenters were either refused entry or were reluctantly accepted as students only. Then, when its gates were finally opened, the natives got a bit uppity and established their own rival university on Stephen's Green.

Trinity had in its favour its gorgeous and iconic academic architecture on a prime site of a few hundred acres in the historic centre of Dublin, and had acquired that patina of old age which distinguished it from the late nineteenth century architecture of upstart Earlsfort Terrace.

Though the numbers attending UCD in the 1950s were just over 3,000, it was obvious that the five-acre site was far too small; the library was full to capacity most days, the lecturers lacked their own staff rooms, there was little office space from which to manage the institution efficiently. At the time many were envious of the comparatively enormous campus that Trinity enjoyed on a prime site near the city centre. UCD then occupied the original early Georgian residence at 86 St Stephens Green, the Earlsfort Terrace construction – faux Palladian with premonitions of Albert Speer – half completed during WWI when the funds ran out, and some outlying faculties, especially the elegant College of Science on Merrion Street. The Terrace did enjoy access to the adjacent and relatively-undiscovered Iveagh Gardens which were a source of enjoyment to students between classes.[1] The college authorities had attempted to acquire further land close by but failed so, as it was obvious that there was not enough space to expand, they sought an appropriately-sized parcel of land outside the city centre.

Despite its favoured location and renowned academic traditions Trinity too recognised it needed to change and integrate itself more into the new Free State, rather than continue as a distinguished hangover of empire. Its venerability meant that it recorded amongst its alumni many more historically-noteworthy intellectuals than its more recent rival, which acted as a major defence against any tampering with its statute. In addition to its illustrious past students, such as the mathematician Rowan Hamilton, George Berkeley, philosopher and scientist, the eminent divine Bishop James Ussher (who painstakingly calculated the Earth was created on 23 October 4004 BC), and writer Samuel Beckett, Trinity boasted a Nobel Prize-winning professor of Physics, Prof. Ernest Walton, who had helped split the atom in the 1930s. Statues of

---

[1] These delightful gardens are still open to the public but few seem aware of them and they are but rarely visited.

writer Oliver Goldsmith and the curmudgeonly father of conservatism, Edmund Burke, grace the elegant portals on College Green.

UCD could boast of James Joyce (especially when the works of that irreverent iconoclast, previously banned by the national censor, had been removed from the index and introduced into the college library) as well as a cadre of first-rate literary mentors, Denis Donoghue, Augustine (Gus) Martin, Roger McHugh, Lorna Reynolds and John Jordan, who had inspired a rising generation of young writers, poets and playwrights. The medical, engineering (Professor Timoney springs to mind) and history departments (Professor Robin Dudley Edwards) had generated a well-deserved reputation for academic excellence, comparable to the best international competition.

Both UCD and Trinity have been criticised in retrospect by historian Joseph Lee for not putting sufficient emphasis on publishing academic articles. Still, considering the modern tendency of some US academics to concentrate energies on their own publications and research rather than on teaching their students, maybe they did us undergraduates a greater service than is generally acknowledged.

Trinity in the 1960s still harboured many foreign students, especially English, some of whom had failed to make it to Oxford or Cambridge and considered Trinity a socially-acceptable alternative at the time. In the opinion of one (London) *Times* correspondent quoted by Donal McCartney in his compelling narrative *History of UCD*,[2] 'Trinity was one of John Bull's outposts ... and a playground where wealthy English students pass time in comfortable idleness'.[3]

Though identified in the public consciousness as institutions representing two different cultural traditions, it is quite possible that the rivalry evident in the 1950s and 1960s was as much about good old fashioned competition as a wish to raise the higher educa-

---

[2] Gill & Macmillan, Dublin 1999

[3] It was also wryly referred to in some circles as a temporary place or state of repose for young Alexandra College ladies in the period between leaving school and finding a socially-acceptable husband.

tional standards of the populace. One area where competition between the two institutions openly flourished was on the sports
fields, in the boxing ring, and rowing on the upper reaches of the
River Liffey.

## UCD – Founder's Philosophy

The founder of the institution which eventually became UCD was
Cardinal Henry Newman, a famous nineteenth century Oxford
convert to Catholicism, who expounded his very lofty concept of a
university in a series of talks, 'The Idea of a University'. Newman
was really more an academic than a theologian, as he is regarded in
Britain. He was a leading member of the 'Oxford Movement' who
converted to Catholicism while teaching at that university. He had
initially wished to set up a new college there with a Catholic ethos,
which was lacking among the existing colleges of the time. Aware of
the agitation in Ireland to set up an academic alternative to the perceived Protestant Ascendancy traditions of Trinity, and which would
cater for the interests of the majority community, he came to Dublin
as an alternative incubation centre for his ideal institution.

His philosophy of higher education could be encapsuled in his
belief that education is a sufficient end in itself, deepening one's
understanding of what it is to be a good human, living a meaningful and ethical life.

> Such is the constitution of the human mind that any kind of
> knowledge is its own reward. Knowledge is an object so unde-
> niably good as to be the compensation of a great deal of trouble
> of attaining....

As a pre-eminent philosopher of higher education he is recognised as the primary proponent of a liberal as opposed to a professional education:

> The process of training by which the intellect, instead of being
> formed or sacrificed to some particular or accidental purpose or
> specific trade or profession, or study of science, or discipline for
> its own sake, for the perception of its own ... highest culture is

called liberal education. And to set forth the right standard ...
this I perceive to be the business of a University.

He attacked the concept of utility as an ideal criterion of a university education. He trenchantly criticised, in particular, the utilitarian philosophy of the Scottish thinker John Locke and his followers who had earlier attacked the value of a liberal, especially a classical, Oxford education. Newman strongly defended the value of a liberal education: 'Gentlemen, I will show you how a liberal education is truly and fully useful, though it be not a professional education'.

Newman was thus the prime promoter of the role of the intellect as a perfect, admirable, noble good. Yet, as McCartney *(op cit)* argues, he also recognised the need for teaching professional subjects at the new Dublin university: he established schools of medicine, law, engineering, the useful arts, mining and agriculture.[4]

In 1929 Newman's ideals for a university were the subject of a bitter dispute, predating modern concern about too much insistence on the role of education as a vector for the promotion of economic growth. This critique was penned by a Jesuit priest in the college education department who attacked Newman for attempting to impose on post-Famine Ireland a gentleman's liberal education imported from decadent Oxford

## A Modern College on a Modern Campus

The college experienced a rather convoluted transformation from its 1854 origin with some 20 initial pupils to its present form as an effectively non-denominational university with over 20,000 students. Many of the leaders of the 1916 Rebellion, dreamers and po-

---

[4] Newman's ideal of a liberal, otherworldly education for cerebral gentlemen differs substantially from that advocated earlier that century by Humboldt in Germany who emphasised the role of the university in the creation of new knowledge as well as its diffusion, unifying teaching and research. This is the model which has been adopted by many US colleges, especially by such powerhouses of technology as MIT and Caltech. One may surmise that for Newman the ultimate scholastic Hades would be the pursuit of monetary economics at the Chicago Business School and the ethics of 'greed is good'.

ets, had studied there and it was the institution of choice for the children of the politicians, professionals, central and local administrators and ancillary agencies of the newly independent state – so much so that many referred to it as the National University.

The President when I entered was Dr Michael Tierney, reputed to be a feisty old dinosaur – not that I ever conversed with him. When elected in 1947 he was considered something of an innovator, but became increasingly conservative over time. Yet he seems to have combined both a visceral conservatism with a cerebral progressiveness, and had a cannily-perspicacious view of his responsibilities and role in promoting third-level education for a far wider spectrum of the community at large. He reputedly nursed a strong disregard for Trinity, though this may have been driven by a sense of rivalry towards a competitor institution. His one talismanic initiative and enduring legacy to the college was the energy and tenacity he expended in aggregating a number of large contiguous farms and houses in the suburban area around Belfield House, south of Donnybrook, which he envisaged as an American-style campus. Anyone who has managed to extract funding from a parsimonious financial authority or government in times of stiff financial stringency will salute his powers of persuasion as well as his exemplary tenacity of purpose.

## Adapting to the Needs of a Changing Society

At about the same time the authorities of both colleges realised their responsibility to contribute to the quality of public administration and business management, both for the public and private sector. Though Trinity remained popular with the more traditional Church of Ireland section of the community in the Republic and North of Ireland, it was gradually and successfully evolving from its original status as an Anglican divinity college, to becoming a liberal, independent-minded university. Despite its former West Briton image, the management had been prescient and made serious efforts to integrate it into the life of the newly independent state. It took the initiative in organising evening courses in commerce and public administration for civil servants – as described in

Chapter 5. This was a smart move, since at that time a practising Catholic was normally expected to seek a special episcopal dispensation to attend Trinity from the redoubtable Archbishop of Dublin, John Charles McQuaid, and the argument that the college was providing specialist courses not available elsewhere was impossible to gainsay.

Though not obvious at the time, Irish society, as was also the case with our British neighbours, was undergoing a deep seismic change at the end of the 1950s. British Prime Minister Harold Macmillan spoke of the winds of change which were blowing throughout Africa: those wafting across the Emerald Isle may have been gentle in comparison but they too heralded profound longer-term changes in attitude, especially upon handing over of the position of Taoiseach by the ascetic de Valera to the more pragmatic Lemass in 1959.

By the early 1960s UCD had some 7,000 students in total, most of whom were located at the Earlsfort Terrace building. The main hall and adjoining corridors which gave onto lecture theatres became thronged in the intervals between the end of class on the hour, and the start of next. Students and teachers burst forth from lecture rooms into the constraining passageways to the seething main hall and a frenzy of banter. Only the high ceilings seemed to prevent asphyxiation. For ten minutes after the hour it became a cauldron of chatter, the lofty hubbub of aspiring cognoscenti, oratorical gyrations of poseurs, political intrigue by embryonic politicos, furtive attempts to flirt with the opposite gender, the scrounging of loans guaranteed to be reimbursed within an improbably short deadline. Insights into football, horses, opposite-gender psychology were exchanged, the relative quality of the pints in O'Dwyer's and Hartigan's pondered, confidential whispers exchanged as to forthcoming parties. All combined to create a special atmosphere which pervaded the cramped space, and which most alumni fondly recall. The intermingling of students from so many faculties created a more eclectic ambience than the disciplinary apartheid forced by the specialist accommodation on a modern campus, surely essential to the hallowed ideal of a *uni-*

*versitas* of thinking and learning. Years later when I visited the campus at Belfield and observed the separate buildings occupied by the different faculties, I recalled that the Terrace was like the old Berlaymont in the early days of the European Commission when a majority of the services were huddled under one roof and we intermingled with and got to know colleagues from all the different Directorates General.

## Memorable Mentors

I enrolled in first year majoring in history and economics. Latin was then a compulsory minor subject for those who wanted to follow the honours stream in second year. (Until a few years previously Greek had also been a subject requisite for entry.) Those not very footsure of their linguistic ability were offered an alternative lower-level course which involved studying an inordinate amount of Roman history; instead of attempting to translate a couple of short paragraphs of Livy or Virgil they had to plough through the equivalent of Gibbon's interminable *Decline and Fall of the Roman Empire*.

First year economics was something special: over 500 students packed into a double lecture theatre to listen to the mellifluous tones of the patrician Professor James Meenan as he delivered his emollient, early morning reflections and recollections of Irish economic development, or lack thereof. He had a certain wry sense of humour, especially when he reminded students that the common laws of economics did not apply to the agricultural sector: the land and its cultivation were endowed with a special approbation from on high by the Almighty when he created the world – and policy-makers and politicians overlook this at their peril. This was before he eventually published his historic tome on Irish economic development.[5] Though the gestation was lengthy, being published well after I had departed, it was worth the wait, a most magnificent and authoritative work of political economy, with an encyclopaedic re-

---

[5] An apocryphal tale circulated at the time of a student who asked another why he did not bother to take notes, the latter replied that his father had also taken political economy and had taken careful notes.

view of background economic history. It broke new ground by including a vast arsenal of economic statistics, all presented in a most elegant style as befitted a disciple of the renowned author and orator Professor George O'Brien – were his ghost ever to excuse Meenan for descending to the level of citing quantitative data in a work of political economy.

Microeconomics was taught by more junior lecturers later in the day. The reason that Meenan's morning classes were so crowded is that they were shared by first year students of economics proper, in addition to commerce and sociology, the latter mainly of the fair gender.

The numbers following economics dropped off significantly in second year due to failures at first year exams and, more significantly, to the fact that a nodding acquaintance with elementary calculus was required from second year onwards, especially if one were to follow the honours course. There was something about calculus which seemed to spook some more thespian minds, and many opted to study law as a main course in second year instead of economics. Soon after the start of second year you knew which of your colleagues had opted for law when they discarded hacking jackets and jeans to appear in suits, ties and sporting polished shoes. The gentility of the King's Inns and the Law Library obviously beckoned.

I would have preferred to have taken history as a major in my second year but the economics faculty was not so rigorous in monitoring attendance as the much smaller history department, where one had to submit a weekly tutorial and absence from class was immediately noted. (The history department was not structured to foster student peripateia: they were unconvinced by arguments in favour of a few weeks vagabondage as a ski-bum on distant hillsides in the middle of winter term.) Obeisance was paid to developing the body as well as the mind in some faculties; Meenan was President of the UCD Rowing Club and rumour had it that he looked benevolently on any of his students who spent afternoons training on the Liffey to do battle with our competitors from College Green. If one wanted to frequent the snowy slopes in February history was

not to be selected. So the more pragmatic major of political economy, complemented by the more aesthetically acceptable minors of
politics and statistics, became my choice from second year onwards.

Second year opened new perspectives as we had more interesting if more specialised lecturers. One was Professor Patrick Lynch,
Ireland's early proponent of Keynesian economics, who had returned from Cambridge at a time when the generally accepted economic policy was for the Department of Finance to balance the fiscal ledgers and avoid any overt interference with the natural progress of the economy. The conventional wisdom was to leave the
invisible hand of the economy to guide its own self-regulating trajectory towards maximum employment and high growth if it were
not interfered with by government. Paddy Lynch, as he was univer-
sally and familiarly known, was an ex-official of the Department of
Finance, later Department of the Taoiseach, Chairman of Aer Lingus,[6] Chairman of the Irish Anti-Apartheid Movement and a member of numerous organisations in the pedagogic and development
world. He was, then, also chairing an OECD group which in 1965
produced the path-breaking report *Investment in Education*, commissioned by then Education Minister Patrick Hillery, which was to
have long-term ramifications for Irish economic development.
Though the report was usually attributed to Lynch as its editor, he
reminded us that he was ably assisted by a team from OECD, including a lecturer in Trinity, one Martin O'Donoghue, later a TD
and minister in a FF government, who executed much of the heavy
statistical lifting.[7] The following year Lynch was to produce another
landmark analysis looking at the wider implication of education
and science policy with the publication of *Science and Irish Economic Development*. He had a unique ability to integrate economic

---

[6] Former Aer Lingus Secretary Niall Weldon tells how Lynch encouraged him to
write his highly engaging history of the company, *Pioneers in Flight: Aer Lingus
and the Story of Aviation in Ireland*, The Liffey Press, Dublin, 2002.

[7] Chapter 15 on Education and Economic Progress shows clear signs of the mind of
the study's director and is probably as profound a description of education's role
in professional life as Newman's on the metaphysical.

analysis within the wider perspectives of a scientifically and technically advancing society, as exemplified by his paper 'Whither Science Policy?'. Along with a number of younger academics, especially Basil Chubb, Professor of Political Science at Trinity, he was
to make a considerable contribution to intellectual discourse and
national policy analysis.

Included on the curriculum was microeconomics. The recommended text was that of Louden Ryan, Professor of Economics at
Trinity, which was considered as much a standard text at that time
as Samuelson's in macroeconomics.

Having reluctantly dropped history at the end of first year I
greatly missed the imaginative and invigorating discourses of charismatic Professor Dudley Edwards with his magnificently unkempt
grey mane. He became quite an institution in UCD at the time,
held in awe and admired by the student body. He was ably complemented by the brilliant Desmond Williams. Williams would arrive at lectures, most of the time a good quarter of an hour late,
stroll up to the lectern with a scrap of paper on which he had scribbled a few notes, not that he ever seemed to need an *aide memoire*,
and the inevitable packet of fags which he proceeded to chain-
smoke as he spoke. He would proceed to deliver the most perfectly-
structured lecture which could have been typed up and ready for
publication without the need for any editorial changes.

Two personalities from the politics departments left a lasting
impression: one, curiously, was a highly independent-minded Dominican priest of luminous intellect and outstanding humanity, Fr
Fergal O'Connor, the other was John Whyte. Fergal O'Connor was
highly inspirational and his Socratic mode of teaching (though he
reflected the honesty and non-conformity of the master he abso-
lutely avoided his intellectual arrogance, desire to dominate and
too frequent resort to irony), constantly stimulating critical dialogue with his pupils, so popular that a considerable number of
students who were not enrolled for his course attended his lectures.
Provocative and thought-provoking as they were, it was a wonder
that he managed to survive the conservative ethos then dominant
in the ethics and politics department. As far as I can recall it was

Fergal O'Connor who first introduced me to the intellectual delights of Karl Popper, especially his treatise on the *Open Society and its Enemies*.

John Whyte's speciality was the relationship between church and state in modern Ireland, though his course may not have been so labelled. We learned later that when it came to the attention of the clerical *nomenklatura* that he was drafting a definitive exegesis on the same subject he was apparently warned off, with the result that he resigned from UCD, departed to Queen's in Belfast for a few years, only to return a couple of years later with enhanced stature, and a well-received tome to his name.

## Student Social Life

With my peripatetic lifestyle, also disappearing on occasions to check out potential hotels in promising new overseas tourist locations, I was not in a position to participate seriously in student societies, though like my other colleagues I attended the many dances organised by students in the various faculties, such as the weekly 'Ags' or 'Yerrawaddies' organised by the agricultural and engineering students, respectively. These social engagements were highly remunerative for the student clubs which organised them, entrance costing three shillings and sixpence, if I recall correctly. The commercial logic was based on the hankering of young and impecunious male students to meet young ladies, and of unattached Dublin damsels to meet up with students. There was a perceived honorific and potential about the title student, no matter how impoverished they may have been. But the status was often tarnished by some parsimonious gallants who reputedly made rendezvous with the objects of their affections *inside* the dance hall, thus avoiding the distraction of a visit *a deux* to the box-office.

Students in the different faculties seemed to have had their own ethos. Some students of the black arts of economics could appear to take themselves too seriously at times, perhaps as a result of analysing and reading about millions, if not billions. The history crowd, of which my older brother Jim and his fiancé Mary O'Sullivan were part, and which included such luminaries as Liam

Hourican, Pat Cleary (later Mrs Liam Hourican), Patrick Cosgrove and Ruth Dudley Edwards, daughter of the eponymous professor, similarly took themselves seriously, though in a more cerebral, metaphysical manner, as befitted those untainted by contemplation of filthy lucre. They could be frightfully civilised, maybe because *les esprits* were leavened by the equal presence of young, refined ladies. In contrast, some agricultural science students evoked images more of arcadia than science: one such scholar, temporarily insolvent, solved the challenge of putting food on the table for guests by hopping over the fence of St Stephen's Green late one evening to appropriate a couple of unfortunate ducks. That Saturday evening he invited some fellow cash-strapped cognoscenti for a seven course AgSci dinner – a portion of duck, *a la Parc Saint Etienne* presumably, and a six-pack, the latter furnished by the guests. The science crowd was a most eclectic grouping. Many of the friends who tolerated my company in undergraduate days were kindred spirits from the science faculty, Fred Reid, Peadar Braiden, Jerome O'Carroll, Ken Douglas, Jim Leech, Mat O'Donoghue; we regularly met at the Old Stand to discuss the meaning of life, the future of the universe and other matters of high consideration, such as the general shortage of women and the price of the pint.

## The L&H

The revered Literary and Historical Society, the L&H, seemed to have been frequented mainly by history, law, philosophy and political science students, budding senior counsels and politicians, a scattering of flamboyant butterflies, socially-aspiring Trots – and a chronic awkward squad. It convened in the Physics Theatre on a Saturday evening, conveniently so as its deliberations might be reported in the *Sunday Independent* next morning. And frequently their musings and baiting of the bourgeoisie made it to the front page. This only encouraged more intensive vapourisings and fulminations, by what Myles na Gopaleen referred to as 'the blatherers in the L&H'. Yet the same Myles was himself an adept performer at the same forum in his day, even if he had failed to be elected Auditor. It had a deserved reputation for the quality of debate: in 1959

and 1964 the discourses of Anthony Clare and Patrick Cosgrave
won it the coveted Observer Mace award. Anthony Clare was later
to become an acclaimed psychiatrist, broadcaster and writer. His
highly popular series *In the Psychiatrist's Chair* was broadcast on
BBC4 from 1982 to 2001. He emotionally engaged members of the
British establishment, softening many a stiff British upper lip in the
process. He proclaimed Freud a sham, describing psychoanalysis as
'the most stupendous confidence trick of the century' and its proponent as 'a religious prophet speaking in a secular language'.

It probably was the growing popularity of Gay Byrne's Saturday
evening *Late Late Show*[8] on the newly-established RTÉ which eventually shifted the spotlight from the L&H, and its ruminations were
no longer treated as seriously since questions of topical interest to
society could now be followed in the tranquillity of one's own living
room. Yet the L&H boasted a long and eminent pedigree in college
history as a focus of creative, even radical and eristic, thinking and
debate, as well as providing a unique forum for criticising the management of the college. Many of its attendees went on to follow successful careers in politics, the bar and journalism. It also included a
number of luminaries of mildly Wildean excess who excelled at oratorical gyrations. The Society had a history of provoking conflict with
the authorities, especially when such topics as the inevitability of
Marxism or the death of religion were chosen as topics for debate.
On a number of occasions the more conservative authorities tried to
stifle debate or change the theme selected for discussion. This would
lead to lengthy disciplinary proceedings, made the more tantalising
for the authorities when the Auditor of the Society was a sharp and
litigious post-graduate legal student. (In my time a favourite target
for debate and criticism was the conservative and autocratic

---

[8] Byrne also hosted a popular morning radio entertainment/discussion programme. By raising sensitive topics, such as the fission between outward religiosity
and inner spirituality and the abuse of women, normally hidden behind the discreet tapestry of Irish life, he probably played a more influential role than any academic or writer in opening up Irish culture and values to scrutiny. For many years
an informal conscience of the nation, he was what some Japanese would consider a
Living National Treasure.

Archbishop of Dublin, Dr John Charles McQuaid, criticism of whom could be relied upon to guarantee a few paragraphs of shock-horror publicity in one of the more conservative Sunday morning newspapers.)

One institution I recall with affection: Sunday evening films at '86' St Stephen's Green (Newman House), admission one shilling and sixpence (1/6d).[9] Not only did this appeal to the impoverished students on a limited budget, costing much less than the outside competition, the main attraction was the ongoing repartee, heckling and snappy quips from the more imaginative and articulate members of the audience. I suspect that some of the more original wiseacres had actually seen the films a number of times previously such was the wit, timeliness and sagacity of their interjections.

## UCD – Not Uniformly Conformist

As noted, a number of contemporaries at UCD have penned their recollections and it is interesting how some have criticised the dull conformity they experienced. It is possible that this was characteristic, not of the institution as a whole, but of certain faculties, both students and staff. It is possible that in some of the liberal arts faculties or law, a more conservative ethos reigned, but in economics and politics there was a greater degree of creative thinking, despite the efforts of the Church authorities to ensure an intellectual lock on the philosophy department. Although Professor of Economics James Meenan, director of a number of companies and Chairman of the Royal Dublin Society, did not come across as the intellectual offspring of a *tricotuese* he had, apparently, always been open-minded, instinctively liberal, even radical for the times. In his history of UCD, McCartney *(op cit)* shows how perceptive of developments Meenan had actually been.

Professor Paddy Lynch returned from postgraduate studies at Cambridge as one of the first Keynesians in Ireland. Although we

---

[9] Modern students little appreciate the extreme penury of many students in 1960s Ireland: there were occasions when you just had no idea where your next pint was coming from.

were not all aware of it he had already started to promote his ideas in the budget of 1950, making a distinction for the first time between current and capital expenditure. In this endeavour he was supported by Louden Ryan in Trinity, and Roy Geary, the internationally-respected director of the then Economic Research Institute. He remained a man of high principle and strict conscience all his life, notwithstanding his role in senior establishment positions. Fergal O'Connor may have been a Dominican priest, not historically the most iconoclastic of the Church's orders, but his independence of thought and forceful idealism greatly influenced his students. Maybe because he was an order priest and not a member of the Archbishop's secular clergy, he could afford to display a greater degree of independence of expression not available to the emollient and more conformist James Kavanagh. In the History Faculty both Desmond Williams, also a Cambridge alumnus, and Dudley Edwards were patently open-minded thinkers, as was the eclectic and highly cultivated agricultural economist Louis Smith in Economics. Denis Donoghue was as popular with his English Lit. students as Dudley Edwards was in the history department.

In my final BA year we were lectured in the recent history of economic planning by a young and motivated political economist, Garret FitzGerald, a lawyer who was working as a statistician and planner of operations with Aer Lingus. He was to go on to become a Senator and, later, Taoiseach, elected Chancellor of the National University of Ireland in 1998, and remains a prolific writer and pundit of considerable moral authority. It was he who confronted the daunting figure of the Iron Lady, Margaret Thatcher, and convinced her to conclude the 1985 Anglo-Irish Agreement, one of the early foundation stones of the present Irish-British reconciliation.

Lady students laboured under more stringent conditions. For example, they were not allowed wear trousers, and especially not jeans, on college premises. A determined regiment of implacable justiciars, Christina Murphy and Olivia O'Leary in the vanguard, decided to invade the halls of the Terrace in such numbers one morning that the Dean of Ladies' Studies was overwhelmed and their *fait accompli* accepted.

## Academic Outreach

We took it for granted that college professors and lecturers would occasionally appear in the spotlight of media attention. They, with colleagues from other universities and a new breed of perspicacious and original thinkers in the civil service and state-sponsored bodies, especially TK Whitaker, Secretary of the Department of Finance, were frequently cited when they expressed views as to the best policy responses to pressing national challenges, especially the scourge of unemployment and emigration. Many wrote articles for newspapers or learned journals, especially publications of the ESRI and the IPA's *Administration*, delivered lectures on Radio Éireann, contributed to government-sponsored reports and investigations and to public colloquia. In retrospect, it was the combined thrust of all these reflections which helped ease the implacable and still incomplete transition of the 26-county state from a calcified, rural outpost of a mighty colonial power to something approaching a self-confident, sustainable, small-country economy which is carving out its own unique narrative along the lines of Denmark, Sweden or Switzerland.

At the highest policy-making level, especially in the Departments of Finance, and in Industry and Commerce, the conventional wisdom as to the conduct of economic affairs, during the earliest years of the state, was still highly influenced by the teachings of Alfred Marshall: an economy was considered to comprise a mass of rational consumers willing to spend their income in the best way to maximise satisfaction; and industry was composed of a large number of competing firms desirous of making a small, normal level of profit. In Marshall's model, industry is not normally distorted by the constraints of monopoly or the demands of technological change. The role of the state was merely to ensure observance of the law by consumers and producers, and balance the fiscal books; the market mechanism can be depended on to ensure the provision of jobs and growth. If there is unemployment that is because workers and unions were demanding too high wages; lower these somewhat and fuller employment will be restored. Since in the long run supply was considered to create its own level of demand, and over-

all demand never falls short of an economy's potential, governments did not need to step in to stimulate employment creation.

Unfortunately, this comfortable doctrine was rudely disproved
by reality; it was to be intellectually undermined by the highly
original and incisive analysis of John Maynard Keynes. He argued
that financial markets are basically volatile and so is the level of
investment. He proposed that there is a difference between the way
a government may spend its income and how a family does. In
times of low effective demand which leaves many workers unemployed, the state can run a deficit, letting the financial stimulus
kick-start greater economic activity; this will even have a multiplier
effect on the wider economy. On the contrary, in times of excessive
demand and inflation the state should run a surplus to cool things
down. It was Paddy Lynch who, on return from postgraduate studies at Cambridge, promoted the new theories and encouraged escape from stagnation. (In this context it is interesting to recall
Keynes's celebrated dictum which he often cited, that ideas are in
the longer term much more powerful than practical men, who consider themselves free from intellectual influences, realise.) Fortunately the new man in Finance, TK Whitaker, had a brilliant, open
mind and embraced broader perspectives and strategic thinking.
He had already published his modest but, in the context, revolutionary *Programme for Economic Development*, which advocated
the re-organisation and efficient use of government resources to
promote economic development and export promotion, thus
stimulating demand, growth and employment. While Whitaker was
decisively opposed to current deficits he would accept capital debts
if the return would more than service the debts. Still, as the state's
most senior economic official he had to be ever-vigilant that politicians did not succumb to the temptation of allowing capital deficits
morph into current deficits.

The Programme was to prove a great success, not just economically but psychologically when the initial modest growth objectives
were not just attained but surpassed. Setting up the psychological
infrastructure was essential in releasing much pent-up energy and
drive among a host of actors within the public and private sectors,

and academia. These thinkers, policy-makers and men and women of action helped with devising an appropriate national strategy which had been lacking but which would still take many more years to hone. A new generation of students who had been educated at UCD, Trinity, Cork and Galway, and were likewise influenced by the new thinking, no longer emigrated but took up employment in the civil service, state-sponsored bodies, and private industry, helping to strengthen the quality of management and policy-making. With the setting up of the first MBA program, UCD was to further cement its reputation as a springboard for the renaissance of the Irish economy.

The external environment was also turning favourable: the Anglo-Irish Free Trade Agreement of 1965 helped condition Irish industry to face the chill winds of foreign competition in preparation for the 1973 entry into the EEC. The decision to complete the Internal Market by 1992 and the associated Cohesion Fund provided vital structural assistance to the Irish economy, especially human resource development, helped prepare the infrastructure for investment in high value-added industry and services, and reverse the brain drain. It was a long, tortuous and demanding road which achieved considerable success by the end of the millennium – only for an irrational hubris based on easy credit and property speculation to contaminate the formula. But the Irish universities and technological institutes did play the crucial role in helping build-up the intellectual and social infrastructure, key to the emerging knowledge-based society.

## UCD in the New Millennium

The college goes on to play an increasingly important role in Irish society, promoting higher education as an end in itself as Newman proposed, and as a wellspring of cultural, scientific, economic and social advance, actively contributing to the emergence of a knowledge-based economy. The 1960s building site at Belfield has begun to acquire the patina of a dignified and elegant centre of learning with over 20,000 students populating its spacious campus.

Some 150 years after it was founded it is developing into a leading European research-based institution, generating knowledge as well as diffusing the holistic education promoted by its founder. The academic structures have been completely restructured recently under President Hugh Brady: the previous structure of 90 disciplines has been regrouped into five colleges comprising 35 different schools. It reaches out from its home base to cooperate with academia all over the world.[10]

---

[10] I am also pleased to note the college actively promotes the European Credit Transfer Scheme (ECTS), developed by one of my Commission colleagues, Peter van der Hijden, as an integral tool for successful international student and academic exchange.

# 5

# Resuscitating Celtic Society – From Coma to Early Renaissance

*Something had to be done or the achievement of national
independence would prove to have been a futility.*

– TK Whitaker, *Memoirs*

*Dr TK Whitaker never said a truer word than when he re-
minded us of the thousands who had, and still have, a better
life because Michael Killeen lived to work for his company and
country ... his coming coincided with that of a handful of men
who were to make it the Golden Age of the 1960s.*

– John Healy, Political Commentator, *Irish Times*, 18 January 1986

*The day will come when all of you, France, Russia, Italy,
England, Germany, all of you nations of the continent, though
without losing your distinct identities and personalities, will merge
into a higher unity and will found the European Brotherhood.*

– Victor Hugo, 1848

WITH THE PASSAGE OF YEARS IT became obvious that alternating
the *dolce vita* of Roman guide, recidivist travel adventurer
and chronic final-year student must end and a more meaningful
career be sought, especially if such a move did not mean an end to

winter visits to the Alps and an occasional trip along some of the world's less frequented byways.[1]

My introduction to the more serious world took place when I worked for two institutions, both instruments of national purpose involved in different aspects of development. I subsequently went to Brussels upon Ireland's joining the European Community. Although I did not fully appreciate it at the time I had the good fortune to join a series of organisations, catalysts of development, each at the springtime of its establishment, the personnel still infused with a vibrant pioneering spirit, humming with imagination and a keen sense of mission. Between them they provided a window on the unparalleled historic changes which occurred in Europe before and after the breaching of the Hungarian-Austrian border and fall of the Berlin Wall. I was to work for such inspiring *chefs* as Tom Barrington, Michael J. Killeen, Jacques Delors, Giovanni Ravasio, Hywel Jones and David O'Sullivan, who were to constitute the gallery of visionaries I was to observe and serve, and who left an indelible impression on the rest of my protracted odyssey. Both visionaries and strategists, they had in common that they were all self-effacing leaders of inspiration who not only exuded the potency of ideas but knew how to turn ideas into action. Contrary to my initial reluctance to accept a full-time job, the work in all three organisations was to prove exhilarating.

First I joined the Institute of Public Administration whose objective was to improve the quality of management in the public administration of my home country, then the Industrial Development Authority which was charged with the creation of quality employment across its regions, finally on to service at the still fledgling European Commission when the original six EEC expanded to a grand total of nine members. Here I worked on the problems of development in the less-developed regions of the

---

[1] My reluctance to bid goodbye to the nomadic lifestyle evinced different reactions among friends. A kindly Japanese lady friend, reflecting the instinctive diffidence of her culture, was consoling, 'Brendan-chan, you are that rare growth, which we call a late-blooming chrysanthemum'; an Irish heart-throb was less comforting, 'typical Irishman,' she sniffed, 'a thing of beauty and a boy forever'.

Community; then plumbed the deep recesses of man's inhumanity to man when assisting development in an African land tormented by a vile and sadistic psychopath; returned to Brussels to work on improving Europe's ability to innovate and help complete free movement of goods, services, labour and capital within the internal market; finally, encouraged the free movement of ideas and students, and improve education and lifelong learning in an expanded Community of 25 Member States. I learned the value of working as part of a multicultural, multi-skilled team, of both genders, to initiate a number of original projects. I was to learn the potency of ideas and, above all, the importance of turning ideas into action, how to be both architect and builder.

I was privileged to witness the transition of a small island economy from penury and depopulation, where average income was half that of the northern continent, to a society newly confident and ebullient, wherein nearly all who want work could find it at home without having to involuntarily emigrate. This was in the happy period when the emphasis was on knowledge and skill-intensive, export-oriented activities, before untrammelled hubris set in, the infrastructure began creaking under rapid demographic growth, society became less equal and economic growth driven down a vortex of speculation and credit.

## The Vanishing Irish

As already mentioned Ireland of the 1950s and 1960s was a comatose country in urgent need of reanimation from the catalepsy into which it had sunk.[2] Life support was mainly provided by an agricultural sector whose only export outlet was the UK with its tradition of subventing its own farmers while encouraging imports provided they were at rock-bottom prices. This sector was complemented by a chequered collection of small-scale, coddled, indigenous industries and supplemented by emigrants' remittances which attenuated the poverty of many a rural household.

---

[2] Playwright Michael MacLiammóir averred that a nation was but a people in slow motion: in which case Ireland was uniquely defined as a nation.

There was a pervasive and corrosive pessimism abroad; many doubted the prospects for the new state. Independence seemed to have been a failure – it had not provided the progress some had imagined would come from cutting the imperial apron strings. Instead we witnessed the obscenity of continued emigration, a debilitating process which had continued since Ireland's own holocaust, the Great Famine. This lack of confidence in the future of the country seemed like a self-fulfilling prophesy. It was the time when John O'Brien, an Irish-American priest, published a demoralising thesis he called *The Vanishing Irish*.

The newly independent state had suffered from an implacable catalogue of calamities, a brief but cruel civil war, followed shortly after by the economic depression, creeping international protectionism, the economic war with the UK in the 1930s and the bleak years of World War II when basic supplies all but dried up or were desperately short.

One could argue that a difficult birth is oft characteristic of newly independent nations, especially when freedom has had to be achieved through violence. It is fanciful to expect that revolutionary freedom fighters can seamlessly morph into constitutionalist economic strategists and businessmen once independence has been achieved. Luckily for Ireland there were a few exceptional personalities amongst the leadership, especially Sean Lemass, veteran of the insurrection and civil war and, paradoxically in view of his later policies, in charge of introducing protectionism when the new government came to power in the 1930s. Like Jacques Delors, his formal schooling had been interrupted by national conflict. He was responsible for ensuring supplies during the critical war years and later became Minister for Industry and Commerce. Unfortunately he had to wait until 1959 to become Taoiseach.

For some years after the end of WWII the Irish temporised; farmers, industrialists and organised labour in protected sectors were opposed to radical change. Of course, they did face a dilemma: to open up the tiny protected economy to external competition would risk its collapse, triggering even greater emigration. Independent Ireland lacked the Continental traditions of manufacturing for export, killed off by eighteenth century British tariffs. Yet, in order to invigorate the lethargic structures it became increasingly obvious that the bracing wind of external competition was called for. Meanwhile, the former combatants on the Continent, with the incentive of the Marshall Plan and then their own Schuman Plan, had begun sharing vital supplies of steel, coal and coke. They were prepared to share these supplies (especially coking coal, access to which had been one of the main reasons for hostilities in previous decades) with former foes.

Though Ireland's leadership recoiled from radical initiatives, the tectonic plates were slowly moving. Under the veil of stasis lurked the growing determination of younger and more imaginative politicians, public servants and thinkers. Though Lemass had been to the forefront of protectionism he became determined to dismantle this constraint and give native entrepreneurship its head. Like JM Keynes, the highly pragmatic Lemass believed that, if policies are patently not working, they are evidently wrong, so the solution was to change the policies.

Within the civil service there was an increasing debate regarding the stifling effects of protectionism and the orthodox *laissez-faire* economic wisdom. Here Ireland was fortunate: whatever criticisms may be made of the old colonial masters they had left behind the kernel of a dedicated, honourable public service (it has been stated that some senior civil servants tore up postage stamps they had bought each time they made a personal phone call from their office.). After Independence a civil service commission was established to ensure competitive recruitment on the basis of merit. In the absence of other jobs the best of those who exited the secondary school system opted for employment in the civil service. Few had had a third-level education which might have expanded their professional and intellectual horizons, yet they were dedicated to their jobs and, given the opportunity, were mostly prepared to avail of any further educational opportunities which might present themselves.[3]

---

[3] Later, Patrick Lynch was to be critical of the Irish civil service's continuance of the British tradition of recruiting 'gifted amateurs': he emphasising the equal need

At the same time there was a number of dynamic and imaginative personalities within the wider reaches of the public service, including state-sponsored bodies, such as those for domestic energy, export promotion, industrial development, air transport, tourism. They were all fully committed to help strengthen the sinews of Irish entrepreneurship and ingenuity.

The Irish pathway from comatose kitten to economic renaissance was long and tortuous, and was further debilitated by a number of self-inflicted wounds as a result of some seriously misguided economic policy initiatives taken in the 1970s and 1980s. Many failed to realise that economic and social success is achieved only as a result of a joined-up and coherent strategy, and to appreciate the complexity of creating an infrastructure fertile for the growth of enterprise. Ireland, whose psyche was hobbled for a century and a half following the Famine, took at least another generation to change a conservative and pessimistic mindset which recoiled from innovation and risk taking. Ireland did suffer one further disadvantage: unlike Sweden, or the Netherlands, it had for generations been run mainly as an agricultural backwater of an industrialised motherland, supplying the metropolis of London with cheap foodstuffs. The repeal of the Corn Laws in 1846 reduced the cost of food for urban British workers but, unfortunately, also reduced the income of tillers of the land. The new state initially lacked the elementary infrastructure of an independent economic and administrative entity.

Amid the adversity, Ireland did eventually reap one advantage: it could leapfrog a couple of generations of outmoded heavy industry and opt for more knowledge-intensive, less polluting sectors.

It was thus my good fortune to have been employed by a number of organisations in Ireland and Europe, observing and learning from many outstanding leaders during this fascinating period.

---

for specialists who continued to update their skills, lest they lapse into 'desiccated generalists'.

## Institute of Public Administration

My first stroke of fortune was to have been invited to work at the Institute of Public Administration (IPA): it was devoted to systemic change in the public administration, just as its sister organisation, the Irish Management Institute, founded at about the same time, was devoted to improving the quality of management in the private sector. The IPA was founded by a small group of idealists dedicated to the cause of good public service. It organised training courses for civil servants and public administration in general, researched all aspects of best practice in administration, published a range of books and literature which provided a forum for original discussions, offered a professional degree in administration in the School of Public Administration and provided a comprehensive library service.[4] The Institute had been set up a few years earlier as the brainchild of TJ (Tom) Barrington, a public servant of exceptional vitality, authority and courtesy, one of a number of visionary and energetic public servants dedicated to modernising the administration of the country. His strategic objective was to introduce modern management objectives and methods, create an intellectual forum in the public service at all levels, hence the publications, research, training, and school. He was especially concerned with the structure of local administration, which then lacked coherence with diverse structures for health, industrial development, tourism, etc.

TJB and the board members of the Institute were assisted by its own team of exceptional public servants which included Kenneth Whitaker of the Department of Finance, Michael J Killeen of the Export Board (CTT) and later the Industrial Development Authority, Todd Andrews of Bórd na Móna and Jeremiah Dempsey of Aer Lingus, among others. These were supported intellectually by a number of academics, such as Patrick Lynch, Kieran Kennedy, Garret FitzGerald at UCD, with Louden Ryan and Basil Chubb at Trinity. Many of these personalities frequented the Institute to deliver lectures and share their insights at a time when such talents were

---

[4] Managed by the ever-helpful Mary Prendergast.

in short supply in the State. One would sometimes sight the tall, Old Testament figure of Todd Andrews with the chiselled magnificence of an Easter Island *moai* in the corridors, on his way to a board meeting. Though considered a force of nature when running the Irish Turf Board, and holding rather robust political views, he was the personification of a gentleman when dealing with junior staff. We occasionally noted the presence of Dr James Deeney, the unsung hero of Irish public health, as on his way to revise a history he was writing.

Probably because its ethos was set by the personality and character of its Director, so perfectly complemented by Institute Secretary Tess Higgins, the organisation was imbued throughout with a keen sense of commitment. I was to experience that same dedication later in the Commission with directors such as Jean Claude Morel, Giovanni Ravasio and David O'Sullivan. One had a sense of working *with* these leaders rather than *for* them.

I was initially posted to work in the training section under Director Colm Ó Nualláin, a good-humoured, urbane but exigent manager, to organise courses on economics and statistical techniques. The object was to teach economic analysis and statistical techniques to public servants who had not formally studied such subjects and were then in positions where they were expected to appreciate the policy-making potential of such analyses, if not their limitations. The classes were given by a number of academic economists and statisticians drawn from UCD, Trinity and the Central Statistics Office. Among these featured John Bristow of Trinity, the main mentor on the academic side, backed-up by other well-known teachers such as Alan Tait, Garret FitzGerald, Bill O'Riordan, newly-appointed Trinity lecturer Martin O'Donoghue, Sean Barrett and Antoine Murphy also from Trinity, Cathal Cavanagh from Finance and Gerry Sexton from the CSO. One of my tasks was to write up the notes of the lectures afterwards; I was thus forced by fate to finally master the intricacies of the various graphs and other graffiti which are the tricks of the microeconomic trade.

Other contributors to the IPA School of Administration were Professor Basil Chubb of Trinity who had written ground-breaking texts in the area of politics and administration in Ireland, and Dr David Thornley who also fronted the *7 Days* current affairs programme on RTÉ.[5] I also got to know Kadar Asmal, who taught administrative law, and who went on to become Minister for Education in South Africa after the universal elections in 1994. He recruited me to the committee of the Irish Anti-Apartheid Movement, for which he was secretary and, in fact, the main driving force, along with his wife Louise.[6]

After a couple of years organising courses I was transferred to the publications division of the Institute which was then managed by the avuncular James (Jim) O'Donnell, a writer with a virtuoso command of language, the author of *How Ireland Is Governed*, the annual bestselling *Administration Yearbook & Diary* and, later, *Wordgloss*, an eclectic and engagingly informative cultural lexicon. Our colleagues included Dermot Scott who edited *Léargas*, a monthly review of public affairs, and Christina Murphy who edited *Young Citizen*, the standard text for civic classes in the schools of Ireland. Christina was a ball of energy, bubbling with vitality. She had helped organise the revolt of the ladies in UCD a few years earlier against the embargo on trousers, as already mentioned. (We were all shocked some few years later when, having been a widely-regarded Education Editor of the *Irish Times* for some time, we heard of her premature death.) Denis McGowan was publications editor. Disguising a sharp intellect behind a throwaway manner he joined the European Commission in 1973 to become one of the longest serving officials from any country. He later became editor

---

[5] When he was eventually elected a backbench TD in 1969 he had to leave his IPA part-time job, as well as that of presenter of the main RTÉ current affairs program. This surely must have been a great sacrifice on the part of such a highly-active and dynamic intellectual.

[6] For a few years I served on the committee of the movement, campaigning to prevent the execution of members of the ANC, including Nelson Mandela. Delight at the successful transition in South Africa following universal voting rights has gradually given way to disillusion with the cynical comportment of the ANC government in relation to similarly-oppressed minorities elsewhere, as well as its own AIDS sufferers. The irrepressible Archbishop Desmond Tutu remains one admirable and thoroughly engaging beacon of moral authority.

of the internal newspaper of the Community institutions, *Commission en Direct*. He probably knows more individuals at all levels of the Commission than anybody else.

It is probably not an exaggeration to say that the publications section greatly helped generate a lexicon with which the public administration engaged in a more confident and articulated way, new to Irish life, with other sections of society. Its many initiatives were supported by outreach academics and a growing intelligentsia – the many books and articles of the prolific Professor Basil Chubb of Trinity springs instantly to mind – thus preparing public servants to engage in a creative dialogue with their new European colleagues and ensuring the professionalism with which they so successfully conducted their early first Irish presidency of the EC under Garret Fitzgerald from January to June of 1975.

We admired Tom Barrington, but even more so when his daughter Ruth joined some architectural students in defending an old Georgian building on Hume Street which some property speculators were about to demolish. At lunchtime Tom would proceed from his office to the site of the protest, and stride insouciantly past Gardaí lines to deliver flasks of coffee and sandwiches to the occupiers. Despite all the demands on his time he managed to publish an encyclopaedic guide to Co. Kerry to where he repaired each August.

## Devlin Report

During the late 1960s a small and distinguished committee of management, public and private, laboured away to write a monumental and innovative report on the reorganisation of the public service in the Republic under the chairmanship of Dr Liam St John Devlin and including TJB. Among the many original proposals for the comprehensive reorganisation of the civil service was that for the separation of policy and execution with the introduction into each Government department of a policy unit to be known as an *Aireacht* (literally 'ministry') to formulate overall strategy. TJB had long been concerned by the prevalent malaise whereby those responsible for strategic thinking were too involved in day-to-day activities to the detriment of good long-term policy-making. Devlin was a timely and critical analysis which fingered a major strategic deficit. Unfortunately the recommendations of this ground-breaking report were not immediately pursued, as such innovations were considered a bit radical for the time. Possibly some civil servants, especially those employed in middle management, were not enamoured at the prospect of an elite taking decisions over their heads; maybe the politicians did not immediately push for a reform which risked excluding them from the formulation of policy and evaluating progress.

Yet change was imminent, including that imposed by external developments. The new round of negotiations regarding EEC accession was under way: the implications forced a major rethink of Ireland's future development in the context of an increasingly integrated Community. The European Commission had already instituted a range of programmes and policies across a wide area of economic, social, infrastructural, regional and scientific activities, and the Irish authorities had to learn to integrate their own policies into this broader picture.

## Aireachtaí and Cabinets

The Devlin Aireacht proposal also shares some features with the system of cabinets at the European Commission, a system  inspired by the French system of party-political, personal advisors and assistants who ensure that their bosses are fully apprised of developments Commissioners and members of their personal cabinet arbitrate decision-making and recommend or reject policy proposals formulated by other commissioners and the executive staffs in the Commission departments. However, most departments have their own policy-development function, while the Commission has a separate think-tank (formerly the Forward Studies Unit, now the Bureau of European Policy advisors) of exceptional scholarship and insight, as mentioned in Chapter 7. On the basis of my experience at the Commission I believe that such an aireacht/cabinet structure has its disadvantages as well as its advantages, though it may help to speed up decision-making and increase transparency. Should the tendency arise to nominate political appointees who lack professional experience this could well have the effect of choking off good advice to ministers and demoralising the politically neutral, impartial permanent staff. While commissioners strive to maintain the vision of their theoretical impartiality and act strictly in the Community and not the national interest, it was an unstated reality that cabinets also served as listening-posts for the original six Member States. One must also remember that commissioners of different nationality and political background are likely to have even less in common with their collegial colleagues than members of a coalition government. Yet, the democratic legitimacy of the Commission is enhanced by the fact that individual commissioners are sensitive to how proposed initiatives will be perceived in, to use a time-honoured phrase, 'the country with which they are most familiar'. While many members of cabinet, though not recruited on a competitive basis, are highly experienced tacticians and negotiators, a few have had the reputation of instinctive political acuity but without a thorough working knowledge of the institutions, sometimes acting on personal initiative and a partisan bias.[7] In the world of international politics one should not underestimate the importance of having a reception/information office open to visitors from Member States who appreciate meeting with an insider within what is initially perceived as a perplexing Brussels bureaucracy.

## Parsons Bookshop

Toiling away in the publications department of the Institute meant I came in contact with that marvellous Dublin shrine, nearby Parsons Bookshop, a literary oasis just beside Baggot Street Bridge. Managed by two kindly ladies, Miss Mary O'Flaherty and Miss Mary King, it had started out as a hardware store which increasingly sold newspapers and then specialist periodicals and books. Popular at first with Beckett, it later became a second home to Brendan Behan

---

[7] In the Commission members of cabinets are recruited either from amongst permanent officials with a proven track record and a capacity for demanding work, or directly from outside, including the commissioner's home country (though there are now stricter rules requiring a mix of nationalities).

and Patrick Kavanagh, as well as Flann O'Brien, Liam O'Flaherty, Frank O'Connor, Mary Lavin, Seamus Heaney and an assortment of artists and bohemians. I once bumped into Professor Cornelius Lanczos, theoretical physicist and a contemporary of Einstein, inside. But to savour its history one should read Brendan Lynch's hagiography of the two proprietors, *Parsons Bookshop: At the Heart of Bohemian Dublin.*[8] My memories are of Miss O'Flaherty pushing the more inspirational texts, while Mary King advised on an eclectic collection of books on Irish or world politics, economics, philosophy, current affairs and history – the more iconoclastic the better. She managed to pack all of the most engaging literature into her tiny corner. (The only other store which comes near it for intimacy and wide choice of material is Kramerbooks and Afterwords Café, just off DuPont Circle in Washington DC. In a corner, not much larger than that of Mary's, they also manage to stock an all-embracing collection of works on public affairs, history, politics, philosophy, and many Irish texts.)

I used to sup at this inspirational fountain with ex-Commission colleague Tom Arnold after he left Brussels to wend his way towards the job probably best suited to his aptitudes and likes, running a development-assistance NGO. Hopefully Concern is now benefiting from the investment Tom made over the years from pursuing and perusing Mary King's recommended texts.

## Industrial Development Authority

After four enjoyable and rewarding years at the IPA I was tempted by an advertisement for a post as information officer at the Industrial Development Authority (IDA). I was interviewed by another institution of the Irish public service at the time, Michael J. Killeen, or MJK, as he was known, the Managing Director. MJK radiated energy, focus, gravitas and charisma in equal order. Resilient, relentlessly optimistic in adversity, notwithstanding bombs and shoot-outs in the north of Ireland (British servicemen being shot at as we were supplicating the British press to provide positive coverage), the clo-

---

[8] The Liffey Press, Dublin, 2006

sure of factories in towns where there was already high unemployment, he just kept pressing forward with stubborn tenacity. While he may not have challenged the standard economic idea that the invisible hand knew best to manage the economy he dedicated his efforts to cultivating the visible hand – especially successful international companies which had cornered a part of the global market for high-tech merchandise. He did annual battle with the Government for a budget which was extraordinarily generous considering the level of economic development at the time. He radiated optimism to local politicians, foreign industrialists and journalists alike. He was also a most impressive interviewee with the foreign press: although he talked up the bright prospects for the country he never exaggerated or dissimulated. Journalists are no fools so they respected him when he was honest about the difficulties to be tackled.

MJK had a track record for getting things done and, somewhat unusually for the time, harboured no doubts that an Irishman or woman could perform as efficiently and professionally as anyone else as long we set our standards and expectations sufficiently high. He could be abrasive if these standards were not met by his staff, but was, behind the perfectionism, a man of impeccable courtesy and humanity. If you goofed he would rap you on the knuckles, more egregious mistakes could involve a transfer, to get instantly fired you only had to fiddle a few pence of your expense account. He had a most charismatic and magnetic presence; people immediately noticed when he walked into a room. Years later I met him in Brussels where he had just come out of a meeting chaired by 'Stevie Wonder', Viscount Etienne Davignon, a Vice-President of the Commission at the time; MJK proclaimed that he had never witnessed such a virtuoso performance in his life. This was some commendation coming from Davignon's *Doppelganger*. Later in the Commission I was to work for an uncannily similar character in the person of David O'Sullivan.

I was delegated to work in the Public Affairs department on the overseas promotions' side. We were based in the newly-constructed Lansdowne House, just up the road from the eponymous rugby stadium and the IPA. Córas Tráctála, the Irish Export Board, occupied the top two floors of the building. MJK had previously been Managing Director of the Export Board and, on the basis of the reputation gained there, had been transferred to lead the IDA when it was freed from the suzerainty of the Department of Industry and Commerce in 1969 and made an independent state-sponsored body. On 'independence' the staff, all permanent and pensionable civil servants, was given the opportunity to return to the safety of their original cocoons. Though such pensionable jobs were rarely relinquished in Ireland of old, few hesitated following an introductory pep talk by MJK. He left his imprint on both organisations; in each morale was high and there was a great commitment on the part of the staffs. Both organisations were to serve as linchpins in the emergence of the subsequent economic renaissance based on exports of value-added production and services, mostly knowledge- and skills-intensive.

I arrived at a time when the IDA was expanding, both at home and abroad. At home the country had been divided into nine development regions, each of which was staffed by an office consisting of a regional director and specialist support staff who would advise local and foreign investors. The Authority was covering the country with industrial parks, land pre-zoned for industry and advanced factory buildings, so that industrialists who did not require custom-designed buildings could immediately move in with their equipment. Industrial investors, both domestic and foreign, were offered capital investment grants as well as a temporary tax holiday: all this was supplemented by generous labour-training grants. As a 'one-stop-shop' – national developmental portal was the posh term we used – the IDA could even arbitrate the setting up of new specialist curricula with the regional technological colleges. In the case of Galway, the local Regional Technological Institute set up new courses in information technology with the arrival of the Digital Equipment Company (DEC), computer manufacturers. The IDA has started building up a land-bank, especially near towns experiencing high levels of unemployment. Each regional manager and their small local team knew the territory like the back of their hand

and competed intensively with other regions to entice industrialists, domestic and foreign, to invest in their region.

The organisation had offices in the main advanced countries in Europe and near centres of high-tech industry in the US and in Japan. There was a research department, under the leadership of Ray McLaughlin, an Irish international rugby player, whose job it was to identify the industrial sectors with the greatest potential value-added, knowledge and skill-intensity and long-term sustainability. His staffers were highly perceptive at identifying the sectors, pharmaceuticals, chemicals, computer hardware and software, intellectual property development, which would offer the best long-term potential in terms of quality employment creation. They combed all available sources to identify the most competitive and dynamic companies in each sector of the major industrial countries, and prepared tailor-made presentations. Appointments were made with the relevant CEO, or at least with the executive in charge of deciding on new investment, especially when that executive also advised on the location of overseas investments.

The IDA cooperated closely with the departments of Industry and Commerce and Foreign Affairs in reaching a double taxation agreement with the US, so that potential American investors would not be deterred by being taxed twice on any profits gained from the Irish production facility. This arrangement was to greatly enhance the attractiveness of the country as a base for American industry to export to the EC in view of impending membership. It may be recalled that in those days even high value-added computer components were large and weighty objects, containerisation was not yet widely available, and transport costs, especially by air, were high. So we suffered a major locational disadvantage. One of our major competitors in attracting foreign investment then was Belgium, with its central location and excellent network of motorways and railways.

One of the main tasks of the Public Affairs department was to provide information for the domestic and overseas press and to prepare advertisements for the main international economic and specialist business press. A new corporate image for advertisements was decided on, all very modern, punchy and highly professional.

These won a number of international awards for their presentation. My responsibility was for the foreign press and drafting speeches for any overseas promotional trips by senior directors, the Minister for Industry and Commerce (to whom the IDA reported), or the Taoiseach. Another colleague, Padraig White, became responsible for the much more politically-sensitive domestic information department. He eventually succeeded MJK as MD on his retirement a few years later.

My first task was to help draft a speech for the Industry Minister who was about to depart with MJK on a promotional tour of the US. I drafted it in a factual, though banal, economic style, spicing it up with a few statistics indicating the outstanding growth of the Irish economy, especially that of the manufacturing sector. The recent growth of industrial exports was seen to be especially impressive. My departmental head suggested that I spruce it up further, inserting some elegiac literary and cultural references, outlining the bonds of friendship Ireland traditionally enjoyed with our American cousins. I took the elevator to the MJK's office to present this literary confection. MJ had a reputation for entertaining neither purple prose nor paddywhackery: facts, facts, and more facts, especially such favourable facts as high growth rates for industrial exports, were his forte. He proceeded to cast a jaundiced eye over the text and, in my first formal exchange as an employee, he pronounced, 'Brendan, so you wrote this lot, you're like an old parish priest saying the rosary, hopping and trotting from one mystery to another'. From then on speeches submitted to him were purged of irrelevant literary content to the exclusive benefit of factual and quantitative analysis. That's the secret of speechwriting, if you can manage to tune onto the user's wavelength the going is relatively easy thereafter, if not, look for another posting.[9]

---

[9] In my next job in the Commission I found that the stylistic demands were more complex, depending on the clientele: political texts had to be couched poetically, recommendations of the Commission presented in prose, communications to the Council in legalese, and implementation documents (vademecums) in technical jargon.

In the early 1970s the IDA was experiencing a very demanding and yet exciting phase in its development. The then 15-year profits tax holiday was a major incentive, especially to the most highly-profitable sectors such as pharmaceuticals and chemicals. Although some information technology firms had set up in Ireland, such as the aforementioned Digital Equipment Company in Galway and Amdahl in Dublin, it was a difficult job to convince others to follow. Later, in the 1990s, when the effects of major investment in Irish education and training had kicked in, the shoe was on the other foot. But the prospect of Ireland's entering the EEC was viewed as a major attraction.[10]

An ongoing problem at the time was negative international publicity generated by the mounting level of violence in the North of Ireland. Many industrialists, particularly in the US, were daunted by the idea of investing in an island where the violence might spread and engulf the whole country. Our job in the public affairs directorate was to convince them that this was not the case. A network of offices abroad had to identify the major players in the selected sectors and approach the directors responsible for investment decisions to come and visit the country. On arrival they would be presented with a thorough briefing on potential sites and benefits available, were subjected to a series of briefings and meetings in Dublin with the responsible directors and others such as bankers and lawyers, and entrusted to the care of the Regional Office Managers who knew their regions inside out.

The offices abroad also had responsibility for identifying the most influential editors, journalists, specialist correspondents, pundits, in the most important local media and invite them to visit Western Europe's latest industrialising *Wunderkind*. Invitations were not restricted to the strictly economic and technical/engineering press; many industrialists formed opinions as to the suitability of overseas locations by reading the generalised news magazines in the

---

[10] The availability of good golfing facilities often proved a deciding factor when a choice between two possible locations became otherwise too close to call.

days before CNN. So we cultivated the less specialised press, especially the major international news magazines.

I recall the story told by the American managing director of a
firm producing quality pens, sorry, 'superior writing instruments',
who had arrived to scout out Ballinasloe, Co. Galway, as a potential
production site. Like any diligent investigator he popped into the
nearest pub and proceeded to sound out the local bar-stool phi-
losophers. Asked what he did for a living he took out a beautifully-
crafted, gold-plated, writing instrument. He then enquired of his
interlocutor if it would be possible to manufacture such impressive
pens in Ballinasloe. It was closely scrutinised by the local sage who
pronounced judgement, 'by God sir, you sure could make them in
Ballinasloe, but you'd never sell any of them here'. He told that
story ten months later when they were turning the sod for building
the new factory designed to sell pens, if not in Ballinasloe, at least
to the rest of the world.

Amid all the bad news circulating worldwide about the North of
Ireland it was rumoured that a senior editor of *Time* magazine was
thinking of cancelling a proposed visit following some dire incident
in the North. Our New York office tried to convince him and his
wife that they need not bring bullet-proof vests to make the journey from Dublin Airport to the Intercontinental Hotel in Balls-
bridge. I was then considered unconstrained by domestic arrangements compared to other colleagues. (I had just been ignomini-
ously dumped by the love of my life – to my great distress but, no
doubt, the enduring bliss of the fortunate young lady.) I was therefore designated to escort the distinguished editor and his wife on a
series of visits to the great and good. They proved to be a most delightful and entertaining couple and we soon struck up an excellent
rapport. I was amazed at the extent to which the mention of *Time*
magazine would open doors to people who normally would not be
inclined to grant an interview.

At this time US President Richard Nixon's daughter Tricia got
married and a selection of her wedding presents was exquisitely
displayed with the energy of glowing colour on the pages of *Time*.
These included two iridescent pages of Waterford crystal, artfully

photographed. The incisions in the glass refracted rays of divers hues, not unlike a Gustav Klimt golden portrait, a shimmering incandescence radiated from the pages. Demand for Waterford immediately soared in the US, and ensured an especially warm welcome for us when we called on the senior executives of Waterford to inspect their facilities. In order to convince the distinguished visitors of the rigorous quality controls applied at Waterford they staged a visit to the quality control department. Two gimlet-eyed inspectors were to be seen applying a magnifying glass to a magnificent, three-foot-high vase which would have turned the head of a Ming dynasty Emperor. They suspected they had detected a tiny, residual grain of sand. Yes, they could confirm the microscopic imperfection. We were requested to retreat a number of yards; they did not want their VIP guests hit by any Waterford shrapnel. An employee of stern and determined mien arrived with a hammer and swiftly demolished a magnificent work of art which had already incorporated a few hundred hours of skilful cutting. The horrified couple was solemnly assured that Waterford did not market any 'seconds' and their quality control was of a standard to meet the approval of the most exigent American gurus of Total Quality Control. I silently reflected that most of those guys could have trodden the boards of the Abbey Theatre were Waterford ever to close its doors.

On another occasion I accompanied some important British TV journalists to meet MJK before departing with them on a regional visit. They were diplomatic, admitted it was the first time they had visited our little island and, while they would review developments with an open mind, admitted they understood the country to be basically a clerically-dominated theocracy. MJK told them that, on the contrary, Ireland was changing rapidly; there was a new generation of clergy which was unaffected by the thinking of the past. He mentioned one new bishop, Eamon Casey, who had returned from a number of years' successful social work with Irish emigrants in London, and who was now the Bishop of Kerry. Would our guests care to meet the bishop if he were he free later that week? On telling him we would be over-nighting in Killarney, having visited the

Liebherr crane factory, Scott Precision Tools and Pretty Polly Hosiery, they indicated their interest in meeting a real, live Irish bishop for the first time in their lives. MJK's assistant, Kathleen Fitzgerald, was delegated to ask the bishop if he would be agreeable. A few minutes later she confirmed that he would join us for dinner, in the company of Paul Werner of Liebherr (then churning out tower cranes for US atomic energy plant construction), John Scott of Scott Precision Tools, and Ralf DeZeyer of Pretty Polly (then one of the largest and most productive hosiery plants in Europe). The presence of an ex-Luftwaffe test pilot, an ex-member of the Dutch underground and a perfect English gentleman industrialist together with the British journalists was set to make for an entertaining evening. We enjoyed an animated dinner at the Aghadoe Heights hotel. The bishop combined a captivating personality with a wonderful repertoire of stories and insights which he shared with all, effortlessly dominating the evening's conversation. Dinner ended, Paul entreated the bishop, who also had a reputation as a songster, to entertain our guests with a few songs. Instant auditorium was formed in the visitors' lounge of the hotel, not far from the front desk and guest rooms. His Lordship was of fine voice that night, but the hotel was accommodating a group of rather elderly Irish-Americans who did not appreciate being awakened by the serenading, no matter how fine the voice or distinguished its possessor. They began to phone the reception desk using the technology the Department of Posts and Telegraphs then provided. The phone exchange comprised a machine with a series of lights, flaps and associated sockets into which the receptionist inserted the jack at the end of the headphone cable. The instrument sprang into life. The manager, Louis O'Hara, was called. He approached me as the organiser of the impromptu gig: 'Brendan, could you ever ask the bishop to stop singing, there are more lights on the phone exchange than on a bloody Christmas tree'. Thereafter the bishop often honoured us with his presence when entertaining important overseas journalists and managed to dispel at least one image of our misty island. He was a wonderful, if unremunerated, ambassador for our promotional efforts.

Other distinguished ambassadors were the highly talented and charming ladies of Bunratty Castle which we invariable visited the evening before meeting with executives of the Shannon Free Airport Development Authority (SFADCo). Although I visited Bunratty weekly for over three years I always delighted in the marvellous presentation of traditional Irish music and song these radiant choristers staged in the evocative setting of the old O'Brien clan redoubt. Though they could have fallen into the trap of serving up sentimental, saccharine tunes, the Bunratty Entertainers, as the orchidaceous ensemble was officially known, provided an eclectic menu of music and song of the highest artistic standing – recruitment to the corps being highly competitive. No matter that these talented ladies, and the odd gentleman, repeated their performance daily, they exuded an engagement with and affinity for their art on each occasion as if it were the premiere. Equally evocative was the literary and musical presentation at the hauntingly-attractive castle of Dúnguaire, anchored by the waters of Kinvara Bay, which left an indelible impression on visitors.[11] These highly innovative and entertaining shows devised by SFADCo not only made for a uniquely memorable evening for our guests but solved a problem as to how to entertain them in the Irish outback on dark and dank autumnal evenings. Such hostelries as Moran's of the Weir at Kinvara, O'Connors of Doolin, when animated by the melodious Russell brothers from Innisheer, and Durty Nelly's at Bunratty, were greatly enjoyed for their unique ambience and informality by journalists who were fed up at having to endure interminable speeches, dinners and lunches in more formal establishments.

On one occasion I was escorting a young, distinguished lady journalist from an influential French financial magazine when I met up with my colleague Brendan Bracken, who was escorting a pharmaceutical journalist on a different itinerary. We had scheduled an overnight stop at an old Geraldine castle converted to a hotel near

---

[11] Dunguaire had previously been the home of Cristobel Lady Ampthill whose love life had been the talk of London, and decision-making of the Law Lords, during the 1920s and 30s.

Tralee, Co Kerry. *Mademoiselle* found the setting, its lawns populated with elegant but raucous peacocks, enchanting but was terrified it might be haunted by stalking ghosts. We assured her that such apparitions were extremely rare. On retiring she heard some curious noises coming from the corridor outside. Cautiously inching her door ajar to peer out she discerned two writhing figures encased in white sheets emitting unearthly moans. But she maintained her integrity as a scribe by not allowing this distraction to negatively affect her subsequent report which was highly favourable.

The IDA was frequently accused of favouring foreign investment at the expense of the domestic arena. This was largely wishful thinking as there was just not enough entrepreneurial spirit in the country at the time to absorb more than a small fraction of the unemployed and those coming onto the labour market. As MJK used to argue, it was better for Irish workers to toil for some multinational at home and generate economic spin-off locally than to involuntarily emigrate thousands of miles from family and friends. Ironically, the grant assistance to indigenous industry was even more generous than that available to foreign companies.[12]

In the early 1970s the big debate was about the possibility of joining the European Community. Entry negotiations continued apace. At the IDA the promise of entry was tempered by fears that Ireland might have to drop its very favourable tax incentives for incoming companies. Together with an eager and relatively well-educated workforce this attraction comprised the jewel in the crown of incentives on offer.

Eventually word came back from negotiators in Brussels, informally, it must be admitted in retrospect, that the Commission had agreed Ireland could continue for a limited period with the tax holiday, but would be eventually required to modify it so as to correspond to a more generalised framework of regional incentives. Eventually, the Irish authorities found a neat solution: whereas a tax-holiday militated against the rules for regional development, a

---

[12] This was provided under the Small Industries Programme and the Re-equipment Grant Scheme for the larger existing firms.

differential national rate of taxation related to fiscal policy and was
not subject to regional policy guidelines and, anyhow, questions
regarding taxation are subject to unanimous decision and they can
be subject to a national veto. The old scheme was eventually replaced by a low rate of corporation tax at twelve and a half per cent.
Though low, this represented a transparent rate of tax.[13]

Years later, in early 1986, it is probably no exaggeration to say
that many in Ireland, especially in the West, were shocked to hear
of the premature death of MJK. The papers of the day ranked him
with Sean Lemass and Kenneth Whitaker as one of the outstanding
architects of the modernised community; all the major papers de-
voting their main editorials to lauding his unique role in national
development.

## European Commission

In 1972 Ireland held a referendum on joining the European Economic Community and the majority of the electorate voted in favour. We joined with the UK and Denmark in January 1973, bringing membership to a total nine. When the Commission published
posts for Irish officials I immediately applied. There still lingered
the germ of wanderlust. MJK kindly offered me leave of absence. I
had been strongly attracted by the moral and visionary impulse of
the founders of a movement dedicated to halting the stupid and
repulsive tribalism, the bigotry and xenophobic jingoism, which
had utterly despoiled the last thousand years of European history.

The interviews proceeded favourably. I was called to Brussels
and made the rounds of departments whose acronyms recalled specialised KGB departments in a le Carre novel. I was advised to try
DG XVI (it was explained that this was the code for the department
responsible for regional policy), DG III (industry), DG II (economic
and financial affairs), DG I (external relations) and others I no
longer recall. Eventually I was interviewed by an impressive French
official who exuded savoir-faire and intellectual panache, Jean-
Claude Morel, a director in the economic service, who seemed in-

terested in my former study of the economics of growth, education and science, and my industrial development background. I was introduced to another genial French head of division who was in charge of *politique structurelle*, which I at first feared might have something to do with construction, before learning that this was the eminently logical French economic expression for medium and long-term economic policy. The other main policy departments were concerned with *politique conjuncturelle*, short-term policy, which included the country desk officers who follow developments in the individual Member States, and monetary policy.

Apart from the adventure of returning again to the Continent I felt a degree of pride in working for such a pioneering and inspirational organisation and its highly motivated staff. Being culturally and emotionally attracted by the Continent I had long hoped Ireland would join the European adventure. I recalled stories of WWI as recounted by my grandmother. Her three older sons served at the front in Flanders, another in the British navy, all following the advice of Redmond to fight for Britain as the price of Home Rule. She lived in terror of a visit from the telegram boy. Those in her street who had sons at the front would freeze when they heard the *put-put* of the telegram boy's bike as it heralded a death or a 'missing in action' notice. I too was headed for Belgium, but under strikingly different conditions than my uncles, thanks to the exemplary vision and idealism of the new European culture of peace.

On starting work at the Berlaymont I attended meetings staffed by young French, German, Italian, Belgian and Dutch colleagues and silently reflected that a generation before many of them might have been in Belgium patriotically trying to blow one another's heads off. We instead were all beavering away, hoping to live up to a sense of duty and obligation as the new public servants to the citizens of the growing community.

The European Commission is the civil service executive branch of the European Union institutions. At its summit is a College of Members known as Commissioners; below that the professional civil service or executive. One of its main tasks is to make sure that the Member States observe the treaties and agreed decisions, and to act as referee or honest broker implementing policies. It is also authorised to propose initiatives and legislation, a more important responsibility than would appear at first sight. But the final decisions are all taken by the politically-powerful Council of Ministers. Nowadays most such decisions are also taken in conjunction with an increasingly important European Parliament.

The Commission is not the omnipotent institution of popular imagination: its power, and even that of the Council, can be curtailed by the European Court of Justice which interprets the Treaties, a bit like the US Supreme Court when it interprets the written US constitution. In doing its job of ensuring the treaties are respected, especially in the core competencies of trade and competition, the Commission could, for example, fine a company considered guilty of infringing free trade or indulging in monopolistic practices, but the decision can be appealed at the Court in Luxembourg and possibly reversed. The Parliament has been accorded greater powers of decision-making regarding the budget under recent changes to the treaties. In chapter 8 the setting up of the highly-popular 'Erasmus' program for student mobility is recalled: in that case the Council of Education Ministers hesitated long before giving agreement. When eventually they did they reduced the budget estimate of the Commission. Following on discussion in the Parliament the original budget request was restored, even increased. Members of Parliament are rather partial to such visionary initiatives. But, of course, they do not have to face the electorate to raise the revenue as have members of the Council.

All this may seem very complicated but on reflection it makes sense as a form of checks and balances. For a small country like Ireland it is also a much more democratic arrangement than that of the United Nations, wherein Ireland is only a second class member (not having a permanent seat on the Security Council). At the (Community) Council all members have a vote, even if weighted, and, in certain nationally-vital cases such as taxation, have the right to veto. As long as this system continues, even if the votes are slightly recalibrated to reflect better the population of the Member States, it is to the advantage of the small members: what they would have to fear would be the establishment, even informally, of a 'directorate' of a small number of influential large States, as with the UN Security Council.

## Big Pond, Small Fish

Though my first job was to work on structural economic questions, the entry of the UK and Ireland meant that all official documents had now to be translated into English. In the absence of sufficient translators in the early days I was informally asked to help out. One of my first tasks was to translate articles on the proposed single currency: I learned a lot about optimal currency areas and the pros and cons of single-currency-fits-all-economies arguments.[14] Previously at Earlsfort Terrace I had studied the complexities of introducing a single currency and optimal currency areas – however, this was no longer an ivory tower but the real world.

Our other tasks were to shadow the work of the regional development service, a politically important activity in those days as the regional development funds were allocated for various projects in the different Member States. If I thought a project should or should not be funded I had to argue the case on paper, defending my arguments up the chain of command to director general level. Despite the sensitivity, it was illuminating the degree to which good clear-reasoned economic or sociological arguments would influence decision-making at the higher level.

## Social Life in the Early Days

Social life was determined by the speed at which trailing spouses arrived, some under duress, to join partners in Brussels.[15] Most of the newly-inducted British, Irish and Danes had not yet found permanent homes, never mind squash or golf clubs or other such distractions. So, after work many of the new arrivals would meet up

---

[14] The proposal to introduce a single currency was first made in the 1973 *Werner Report*.

[15] Some years later a club known as STUDS, or Spouses Trailing Under Duress, was set up.

in the *Foyer*, the staff café and restaurant, then situated near the old Berlaymont building. After dinner there seemed little point in returning to a temporary flat with sparse furnishings so it was easy to convince colleagues to adjourn to a pub convenient to the Berlaymont. Thursday evenings in the 'Drum' were especially jovial as the Welsh Choir retired there after weekly practice. These evenings were to become a tradition, especially for unattached ladies from the institutions who could come and go without hassle.

Brussels at that time was a rather quiet city. It mainly comprised office employment and was largely residential. Contrary to its characterisation by Bill Bryson, it enjoys many green spaces, especially on the outskirts which are mostly surrounded by forest. Residential accommodation is easy and cheap to come by, axiomatically as the local legislation favours the owners of property rather than the tenants. This has ensured that a plentiful supply is available for rent.

The main centres of historic architecture in Belgium are found among the provincial cities of Liege, Antwerp, Ghent, Bruges and a host of charming little towns and villages. Brussels may not be as hectic a centre of social or cultural activity as Paris, though it can more than compete with that metropolis in the wealth of musical entertainment on offer, but it is an exceptionally pleasant, civilised and delightful place in which to live.[16] The locals can be a bit diffident at first with employees of international organisations but once one gets acquainted they make the most charming and loyal of friends. I recall colleagues who criticised certain Belgian customs vehemently on arrival who now, after many years of residence, trumpet the attractions of Brussels and its Flemish and Walloon hinterlands. One further attraction of Belgium, especially to those of us experi-

---

[16] In early 2010 a populist British MEP, leader of a xenophobic party, mounted a virulent attack on the new Belgian President, calling Belgium a 'non-country'. While it might be naïve to expect a knowledge of history, much less objectivity, from one pandering to the baser instincts of the lager-lout constituency, he ignored the fact that in 1914 the army of the non-country held up the concentrated right wing of the German Army for a month, scuppering the Schlieffen Plan and possibly saving the British Expeditionary Force from annihilation, thus considerably changing the course of twentieth century history.

encing the wear and tear of life, is the excellence of its public health service, with its multiplicity of university hospitals, specialist consultants, doctors and nursing staff offering their services at a reasonable price.

## Farther Horizons

However, my objective at this stage was not to settle down and savour the delights of Brussels. I had long hankered to avail of the opportunities offered by the Community to provide frontline assistance in one of the less developed countries (LDCs) with which the EEC had arranged development assistance. The Community was just then drawing up the new, wide-ranging and historic Lomé Agreement for cooperation with the developing countries of Africa, the Caribbean and Pacific, the ACP. I then believed the main constraint on poor country development was the level of financial aid available. I was shortly to learn a stark lesson as to the degree to which the absence of civic institutions, and equality before the law, played in the overall process. My high idealism was about to be mugged by stark, recalcitrant reality.

# 6

# DARKNESS FALLING, PARADISE LOST

*Monstrum horrendum, informe, ingens, cui lumen ademptum*
[A monster frightful, formless, immense, with sight removed]

– Virgil, *Aeneid*

*First Moloch, horrid King besmear'd with blood*
*Of human sacrifice and parents tears*
*Though for the noyse of Drums and Timbrels loud*
*Their childrens cries unheard, that past through fire*
*To his grim Idol...*

– Milton, *Paradise Lost*

*Creon: According to our laws does not the ruler own the city?*
*Haemon: By yourself you would make an excellent king, to rule*
*the desert beautifully alone*

– Sophocles, *Antigone*

THE MOST HIGH PROFILE EXTERNAL activity of the EEC six prior to 1973 was the aid program providing assistance to the world's poorest, less developed countries (LDCs), mainly French ex-colonies, under the Yaoundé Conventions of the 1960s. On enlargement to nine a number of other developing countries, mainly ex-British colonies, were invited to join the European aid program, forming the 46-plus-members of the African, Caribbean and Pacific grouping (ACP). The final agreement was reached at Lomé in Togo in early 1975 under the first Irish Presidency of Garret FitzGerald. Over three billion ecus (European Currency Units, approximately equal to the US dollar at the time) were allocated to help the ACP partners during the following five years.

Expanding the number of partner countries included under Lomé involved opening new offices to be staffed from Brussels or, in some cases, by personnel nominated directly from Member States.

Spotting an internal call for volunteers to take up appointment in one of the partner countries, I applied, was interviewed, and offered the Papua New Guinea posting by Maurice Foley, Deputy Director General. I was greatly excited by the challenge of the new assignment. I had an appointment to meet my good friend, Philip Ryan, director of the IDA Brussels office, for dinner the evening after I received final confirmation.[1] In the restaurant Philip was accompanied by a friend of his unexpectedly visiting Brussels. What I did not know was that his guest was being recalled to HQ from his Continental posting. I told Philip I had just been confirmed by the Deputy Director General and expected to be leaving Brussels shortly.

Next day at noon Philip phoned to tell me that I had lost my job. Our dinner partner of the previous evening may not have been considered effective by his superiors but had cultivated friendships with VIPs, one of whom was currently occupying a senior diplomatic position in Brussels. Following an early morning call the diplomat arranged for his distressed friend to meet the Director General for Development for interview, upon which he was offered the posting I had been promised. My request that I also be interviewed at DG level was to no avail, my complaints for fair treatment merely antagonised higher authority. I was allocated to a lesser posting, as

---

[1] But confirmation of a job in Brussels is only finally assured when you have completed a month's work and have received your first salary (or, rather, if you have irretrievably spent it).

Economic Advisor in Uganda. Shortly afterwards my competitor succeeded in swapping a job in the field, for which he really had no interest, for a more congenial posting with a newly-established agency in Brussels. My personal comedy of errors, the first of a remorseless drumbeat of vicissitudes, had started.

## Uganda

At that time the world was waking up to events in Uganda, then under the misrule of the vainglorious psychopath, Idi Amin Dada. He came to international attention having toppled another gory dictator, Milton Obote, when the latter was attending the Commonwealth Conference in Singapore, leaving the little-regarded army chief, Amin, in control of the military. Obote had pardoned Amin for murders he had committed and he seemed to have expected gratitude and loyalty in return. But Obote had many enemies in the international community, including the Commonwealth countries, not to mention within Uganda where, as a member of the northern Nilotic Langi-Ocholi tribe, he had begun to repress other Ugandan tribes, including the majority Baganda and Amin's Kakwa.

For historical reasons the Langi and Acholi were mainly Church of England, while Amin's West Nile Kakwa tribe, and their Nubian and Southern Sudanese friends, were mainly Moslem. The Baganda people - who live in Buganda and speak Luganda - are the dominant tribe in Uganda, so much so that the British had to arrange for a non-Baganda to emerge as leader on independence, otherwise their Kabaka, or King, would have taken over. The Baganda are mainly Catholic. They are a people with a keen appreciation of education and the benefits it brings. Consequently the older generation did everything to ensure that their children received the best possible start in life. Baganda elders believed that even if *they* could not aspire to becoming *mafuta minghi* (fat people, meaning rich), they hoped that, through education, their children would. Obote distrusted and oppressed the Baganda because of their demographic strength and economic power. Amin also feared their educated class, who could think for themselves and access material critical of his regime. But first he turned his ire on to the Langi Acholi whose leader he had just overthrown – the Baganda could wait their turn.[2]

Amin again came to world attention some years into his dictatorship when he expelled the Asian community from Uganda. The Asians had been brought to East Africa by the British, not as planters but as labourers, and these highly-entrepreneurial people rapidly made a reputation for themselves in commerce, especially running shops and providing services of all kinds. Their relative affluence caused great resentment among the indigenous Ugandans who could not fully comprehend the economic success of the newly arrived. Although the Asians constituted a vital element in the economies of East Africa, their monopoly of trade, and the difficulty for Africans to break this monopoly, caused great resentment, one which a populist firebrand could be tempted to exploit – especially if he thought that in the process of expelling the foreign arrivistes the locals could take over the jobs and companies the Asians had built up over the years. Houses, factories and shops presented a tempting target for the rapacious members of the tribal elite Amin had installed since taking power. And so, tapping into the wellspring of atavistic tribal resentment and to buoyant local acclaim, he expelled the Asians with little more than a few suitcases each.

Later he achieved even further notoriety when he collaborated in the hijacking of an Air France aircraft, whose mainly Israeli passengers and French crew were eventually freed, except for one elderly woman, Dora Bloch, in a daring raid by Israeli paratroops. Frustration at the underperformance of Amin's elite was taken out on the frail old Jewish lady who had been taken to Mulago hospital. She was hauled out of her hospital bed and murdered.[3]

---

[2] Later, when in Kampala, someone showed me a locked room which was rumoured to contain radio equipment that had been used to overhear radio conversations among Amin's fellow conspirators – apparently speaking Hebrew. It was alleged that old comrades of Amin in the Israeli parachute regiment where he had been sent for training assisted the coup. If this were true it would have been ironic in view of subsequent events.

[3] I was subsequently told that during the night of the Israeli raid word only gradually reached Amin's army, whose troops arrived intermittently along the Kampala-

The Israelis had destroyed the airport technical installations and, from then on, aircraft arriving, including the SABENA and Air France Boeing 707s, flew in over the lake, visually checked the wind sock's direction and then selected the preferred landing approach to the one runway. A phone call from Brussels would have already confirmed the craft had left Europe. Allowing time for stops at Nairobi, Bujumbura or Kigali en route, one calculated the ETA at Entebbe. Notification of its arrival was confirmed, not by radio or radar, but by those with the acutest hearing among the airport staff, or those keen of ken and sight.

Amin's previous martial exploits had consisted of interrogating Kenyan 'Mau-Mau' freedom fighters as an NCO in the King's African Rifles. When installed as President-for-Life and, having conferred on himself a field marshal's baton and VC, he cinematically enacted the taking of 'Cape Town', a hill near Kampala, as a putative invasion of South Africa. In seeking to re-enact the exploits of the US marines in their iconic taking of the hill on Iwo Jima the corpulent marshal just about managed to carry his humungous hulk up the hill to 'victory'. Such clowning caused great hilarity when shown in western cinemas and on TV, especially among those opposed to African independence, as well as playing into the hands of the regime in South Africa. But to conclude that Amin was a mere clown or fool was a great mistake. He was both a behemoth of malice and bloodlust – and as smart as a bag of ferrets.[4]

Amin was not inspirational: he was a petulant, bombastic rabble-rouser of staggering vanity and nihilism – yet an expert at play-acting the humorous clown. The leitmotiv of his cruel regime was the flaunting of brute force and the threat of immediate and cruel retribution for anyone who showed the least sign of disagreement

---

Entebbe road from various barracks. This road provides a panoramic view of the airport and Lake Victoria. As each succeeding corps approached within a few kilometres of Entebbe it apparently halted and began shooting indiscriminately at the troops ahead, mistaking them for the enemy. The Israelis were halfway home while a series of mini battles were still underway at the approaches to the airport.

[4] The trailer to a recent Hollywood film on Amin seemed equally misguided: it depicted him as an inspirational if brutal leader. I accidentally viewed a bare snippet on TV: I could not bear to watch the whole presentation.

or opposition to his wishes. Behind the harlequin exterior and gro-
tesque smile lurked a sadistic killer. Supremely cunning, he trusted
nobody, even relied on renegade, grovelling white gargoyles to provide his physical and medical wellbeing.

## Appointment

Accepting the position in Uganda with its infamous regime caused
me much soul-searching. Large sums of European development aid
had been earmarked by the Commission development service, in
agreement with the Member States' development ministries: the
program had to be efficiently managed locally and someone had to
ensure that European taxpayers' contributions were not wasted.
(Although not mentioned in polite diplomatic company there was a
tacit understanding that none of the funds should end up in a Swiss
bank nor be diverted for the buying of arms.)

When nominated as economic advisor to the Delegation in
Uganda I was sent on a training course which included the economic assessment of developmental projects, using a variant of a
World Bank cost-benefit type analysis. Applying this technique was
to have unforeseen results a year later.

I emptied my Brussels apartment, dispersed furnishings and
packed my suitcases in anticipation of my new appointment. The
head of delegation was already nominated, an Austrian-Italian engineer who had experience with a major Italian international construction company after World War II and had worked in Gabon as
Delegate under the first Yaoundé Convention. Otherwise, apart
from his earlier military experience, he was new to public administration. At that time many of the Commission delegates were
nominated or seconded from Member States on the basis of experience, or establishment endorsement. The third employee, apart
from the local secretary/receptionist, was the administrative officer
who had also worked for the same Italian construction company. A
thoroughly decent and capable colleague, he had been selected by
the delegate for his African work experience.

Prior to my arrival the draft program had been agreed with the
partner country, as was then the procedure. The amount set aside

was considerable, surely worth over a half billion Euros in present-day values. For some reason some ninety-seven per cent of the aid was already earmarked for a large road-building program, and three per cent for humanitarian aid. This represented a rather unusual putting of all eggs into one basket I surmised, rather than apportioning aid over a number of projects in different areas. However, that was the declared choice of the host government.

My main task was the analysis and justification of the expenditures, and overseeing that the money was correctly spent. An important point, in view of later developments, is that the Lomé Convention was signed in a spirit of *bon enfant* on both sides. In the euphoria of post-independence Africa it was not envisaged that the newly-independent states would prove anything but paternalistic and caring for all their citizens. Therefore the idea of inserting a human rights clause just did not arise. Consequently there was no legal basis for depriving a partner country in the ACP of the promised financial assistance just because, for example, it was 'ethnically cleansing', i.e. exterminating, a rival tribe. In addition, the Agreement contained no mechanism for closing down a delegation office if human rights were being trampled on. Thus, surveillance of funding at a local level was even more important.

### En Route

From the very start of my odyssey in Uganda I had entered into a surrealist world, a theatre of the absurd and tragicomedy. On arrival at Frankfurt airport to connect with the direct flight to Entebbe, I was told there was no such flight. I protested, presenting the ticket from our travel agent in Brussels. I was informed that was just a fiction. Since the Israelis had wrecked the airport at Entebbe, flights to the whimsical capital of Uganda were automatically cancelled a few hours before scheduled departure, although this could not be publicly acknowledged as Uganda was a member of East African Airlines, and formally cancelling phantom flights would mean a breaking of the joint agreement with Kenya and Tanzania. As Amin was perceived as having cooperated with the Air France hijackers, travel to his country had all but halted. So I found a seat on a flight to Nairobi, where I hung around until there was a flight to Entebbe. Departures to that destination from Nairobi were also haphazard since Amin had earlier arranged an altimeter-triggered pressure bomb on board the aircraft of a Kenyan businessman, close to senior Kenyan politicians and considered to have assisted the Israelis on their return flight from the Entebbe episode. This too was not conducive to fostering good aviation links.

I eventually secured a place on a flight to Entebbe, striking up a conversation with a couple on board, Joe and Kit Roche. Both were born in Ireland and lived in Uganda since the end of the war when Joe returned from a Japanese prisoner-of-war camp. Apparently he was in the RAF, flying somewhere in the Pacific theatre just after Pearl Harbour. The engineer of Joe's plane detected something amiss with the craft so they decided to land in Hong Kong where they could also avail of a spot of R&R while the aircraft was being repaired. Bad call. They were not the only visitors to Hong Kong that night: the Japanese invaded, so Joe and his mates ended up 'in the bag'. As a Catholic he assisted the padre at Mass each Sunday morning. They had to resort to fruit juice instead of wine and automatically after each service the padre and he were whipped for being drunk and disorderly. Joe and Kit had many friends amongst the Irish community in Uganda, especially with the Irish medical missionary nuns who ran the only working hospital in the country at Nsambia, that at Mulago being effectively out of commission.

## In Situ

I checked myself into the International Hotel, Kampala, a fifteen-story, prestige white elephant, which was the tallest building in sub-Saharan Africa outside of the Republic of South Africa. Built by Milton Obote as his own virility symbol it was taken over by Amin and his cronies after the coup. It was effectively empty, except for Soviet and East German military delegations that arrived and departed as a group, each occupying its own floor with no contact between their personnel and other guests. Due to the character and connections of its new owners, the ground floor bar was usually stocked with beer which was pretty well unobtainable elsewhere, unless one had connections or a pass to the diplomatic shop supplied by Amin's personal Boeing 707 on its return from a weekly shopping trip to Stansted.

One simmering evening I felt thirsty and decided to try the ground floor bar for a beer. Drinking water was dangerous due to the risk of bilharzia. I was the only *mzungu* there, the other clients being obviously security personnel, some the worse for wear. One started shouting his loyalty to Amin. 'Without Amin, Uganda does not exist, I'm going to kill his enemies,' etc. He turned on me. I decided it would be better not to get involved in arguing with him in English, considering his state, especially when he pressed his revolver to my head. At that stage my Russian vocabulary consisted of about twenty words. I used all of them, and even more, in the hope that I might be taken for one of the Russians servicing army tanks and MIGs. Eventually the well-connected manager was called and he quietly took the gun from the protesting drunk, to my great relief. No matter how thirsty, I never again ventured into that bar.

Since there was no tourism to the country, and practically never any commercial visitors, the hotel was effectively empty of guests. The twelfth floor was reserved for western, colonialist, Zionist imperialists; the thirteenth floor for guests from the DDR who were mainly employed to ensure public security, and the fourteenth by Soviets, many of whom were assembling aircraft and providing military assistance to Uganda. (At that time Kenya was allied with the Americans and, to balance the equation, Tanzania, whose president hated Amin, was cosying up to the Chinese, who were building the new Tanzam railway.)

The top, fifteenth floor if I recall correctly, was some kind of nightclub casino. Though I never visited it I soon came to realise that this space was animated late at night, first by the booming noise generated. I then learned it was mainly frequented by the secret police interrogators and military executioners, who would pop in after completing their night's work to anaesthetise what remained of their consciences. Night after night *Don't Cry for Me Argentina* and other popular western numbers of the time boomed out for the revellers on the top floor. I was the only guest on the twelfth floor.

Outside my door was a stairwell with broken banisters, and one could peer down to the ground floor. I was appraised later that the banister was broken when a resident German or British aid worker] was accused of having either entertained a local lady and/or had criticised Amin.[5] State Research Bureau ton-tons got him and hung him over the banisters which he gripped for dear life. To ensure he released his grip the banisters were kicked out and he fell, to the enjoyment of the onlookers, down through the stairwell to the ground floor. Some acquaintances were still intrigued later to show me the broken tiles and the traces of blood in the cracks. Nearby hung a sign, 'Welcome to Uganda', and the obligatory photograph of Al-Hajji, the Field Marshall and Life President, complete with rictus grin.

Meeting with the *Ingenere,* as the head of delegation was known, on my first morning was all of a piece with the less than happy introduction to the new posting. He told me he did not need an economic advisor from Brussels in his office and that the administrative assistant who had prior experience in Africa could do my job. He considered me redundant. This was hardly the most optimistic note on which to start a new career, especially as I had emptied my Brussels apartment and come four thousand miles bubbling with enthusiasm for my new job.

I began to appraise my surroundings. For the first few weeks I did not venture much out of Kampala. But even when visiting the suburbs one could realise why Winston Churchill called Uganda the original Garden of Eden. Situated on the equator but about 4,000 feet above sea level the climate is near perfect. In one way it

---

[5] Amin was shrewd enough to decree that any *mzungu* caught trifling with the local ladies was beaten up; more intimate displays of affection were punished by death. Since Westerners had the reputation of using their relative wealth to seduce local women this was a popular move with aggrieved local males. But in this particular case it is possible there was no lady present and this was merely a convenient excuse to blacken the reputation of a development assistant whose family and embassy would be desperate to avoid any scandal.

reminded me of Ireland: there are basically two seasons, one rainy, the other even wetter. It differed from neighbouring Kenya in a number of significant ways, but mainly because it had not been colonised by white settlers who evicted the locals from the most fertile land. No colonists had come with their herds of horses and domesticated European cattle. The reason was that Uganda, unlike the Kenya highlands, had tsetse fly which spreads terminally-afflicting sleeping sickness, *trypanosomiasis*, to both man and do-mestic beast.[6] The British army found this out the hard way when their horses began to keel over and expire, shortly followed by their riders. But indigenous wildlife had developed immunity over the ages. In the interests of discretion it is probably better not to de-scribe to the delicate reader the culinary and digestive habits of the lady tsetse fly. Suffice to say she has a relative capacity which would provoke admiration and incredulity in equal measure in Mulligan's of Poolbeg Street or the Stag's Head: she can drink twice her own weight at one sitting, except that her favourite tipple is blood. So if central Africa is still full of wild animals rather than being a tropical version of rural Gloucestershire or Westmeath it is thanks to this engaging little parasite.

Uganda must be one of the most fertile places on the face of the earth. Locals claimed it is barely necessary to hoe the land to culti-vate: one could just drop a tomato on a patch of ground and a plant would start growing within a few days. There is little risk of starva-tion in Uganda because of the luxuriant growth and the fact that cassava roots and tapioca seem to grow easily and profusely there. So also does plantain, a green banana-like fruit which is used to make *matoke*, a not particularly pleasant dish. There was a profu-sion of the most magnificent plants and flowers. A thunder storm would last half an hour, the rain cascading down like stair rods. Then it would end as quickly as it had started and the sun would break out to rapidly dry the land. But I eventually found that, frus-tratingly, there were really no seasons and, more boringly, the sun

---

[6] It should more honestly be called *writhing-in-agony* sickness, but in the early days that might have dissuaded the European immigrants.

set each evening promptly at six thirty-five. Twilight lasted a brief few minutes, during which five million bats took off from a nearby forest to make their way down to Lake Victoria for a night's gobbling of mosquitoes and midges which formed in clouds over the lake. I was to gain a great respect and liking for the dietary habits of this little creature. I dreamed of adopting a pet bat and enticing it to practise its hunting skills in my room at night when the mosquitoes were especially active. Stupidly, I did not bring a mosquito net with me; nobody seemed to use them any more despite the ubiquity of the pests and the risk of malaria. Nor was it possible to buy the old fashioned hanging sticky paper used to trap flies in the Ireland of my youth. Instead I had to equip myself with a wet washing cloth. When the buzzing of these micro Stukas near my ear became too distracting I would get up, put on the light, whereupon the latest heavily laden imbiber of Chateau Brendan would make an emergency landing on the wall behind my bed. Whack! Another big red blotch added to the existing fantailed collection. Eventually the red blotches formed a perfect distribution curve, from deep red in the centre to a mottled red and white as it splayed out from the gory epicentre like a spiral nebula. I pondered if the renowned mathematician Pearson, who had devised the brain-wracking formula for the normal distribution curve, had himself been kept awake at night whacking mosquitoes.

As night descended over Kampala there was little movement on the roads. A wary population became even more spectral with the descent of darkness; most vehicles were either the Datsuns of the State Research Bureau or army trucks. Nightlife was pretty much non-existent, apart from one Chinese-Ugandan gentleman who ran a small restaurant, and the aforementioned late-night revellers on the top floor of the International Hotel. Most foreigners, especially the tiny community of Westerners still left, tended to stay strictly at home in the evenings and, if they had access to the diplomatic shop or hard currency, cracked open bottles of gin and tonic as soon as the sun had set. There was some elementary form of black and white TV, when transmitters worked, and when there was mains electricity which could fluctuate between 160 and 260 volts.

Programs usually consisted of a series of the Marshall's latest invective and fulminations, followed by his adventures of the day, how many cordial messages he had exchanged with such other worthies as His Imperial Majesty, the Emperor of the Central African Empire, and how he (Amin) was single-handedly setting the world to rights, Uganda in particular. In singing his praises they often ran out of adequate superlatives. Hyperbole in relation to the great leader's achievements went unrestrained. Uganda was achieving supersonic rates of economic growth. Under his wise leadership the Mach index of growth was perceived to be climbing by the month – all this when the local markets and remains of shops stood empty, the latter's windows filled with empty tin cans. Of course, some of the proprietors of the stores had 'inherited' them from the departing Asians and had little or no experience of commerce beyond informal market trading.

Nor could one look to the local journal, the *Ugandan Argus*, if I recall its title correctly, for a nice relaxed evening of intellectual stimulation. The front page seldom depicted less than four photos of the Field Marshall, usually with an incandescently-braided uniform and rows of medals, meeting the great and the good of his constellation, reading exhortations, denouncing imperialist exploiters, greeting friendly diplomats and various opportunists who called to pay compliments and seek contracts.[7] It was rumoured that a previous editor had mistakenly failed to achieve the minimum number of photos required to show adequate respect on a day when Amin was not recorded as having left his lair, and paid the price for his lack of fidelity. Still, a perusal of the rag was no source of amusement, every second article contained threats as to the likely fate of those who did not show sufficient loyalty to the regime. We were constantly reminded that nobody was above 'the law', not even the Life-President's brother or mother or father. It was never suggested that Amin was not above the law. We sur-

---

[7] A friend surreptitiously suggested that Amin must have employed a full-time blacksmith hammering out medals on a regular basis. But one had to be very careful joking about the Marshall's bravura.

mised the law was merely his latest whim, caprice or grudge. In fact, Amin's definition of law was similar to that under his great mentor Hitler whose expressed whim became instant law – the Fuehrer Principle.

## Machinery of Terror

Few ventured far from home or went out after dusk since the one efficient component of local administration was the secret police. There were two or even three competing security services. We knew two of them as the State Research Bureau and the Public Safety Unit. Wearing sinister mirrored sunglasses these death-squad goons drove around in Datsun 2600 cars presented to Amin by Khadaffi for some previous OAU meeting. They were easy to recognise with their UVR or UVS registration plates and a little radio antenna on their roof. A feature of this model which made it popular was that it had a large boot, so that those arrested were just handcuffed and their shoes taken off before being thrown into it. On driving around town in daytime one often saw them malignantly staring out the windows of their Datsuns, questioning those standing at crossroads waiting in vain for a *matatu* (minibus) or truck to provide a lift somewhere, public transport being almost non-existent. They would ascertain the language and accent of those in the queue and, if one unfortunate was Langi or Acholi, would slowly step out of their car, handcuff the victim, take off his shoes and dump him in the boot. They were not in any way embarrassed about this; it obviously was an ideal means of psychologically intimidating the populace. On the odd occasion an enterprising individual would make a run for it, but mostly they froze, mesmerised like a mouse confronted by a rearing mamba.

On occasion I travelled to Kenya to buy supplies and witnessed trucks and buses stopped, some passengers taken off by the military or security services and forced to kneel down handcuffed by the side of the road to await their fate.

I was introduced to a kind, educated and relatively well-off neighbouring Baganda family, the tribal grouping which so respected the value of education. One of the brothers was, I understand, manager of the branch of a bank at Entebbe and had been arrested by State Research rottweilers on leaving the Kampala golf club. Some days later his body was left on the rubbish dump outside a police station, the relatives being eventually informed that there had been a car crash and that he had been killed while held as a prisoner in the back seat between a couple of goons. Neither they nor the car needed attention. As an example of how psychologically brain-washed even the toughest can become under such a tyranny some otherwise resilient individuals asked me if I though that was really possible. I demurred, but thought to myself that that if this can happen to such exemplary individuals how long before we all succumbed to such conditioning?

A young lady, a sister, if I recall correctly, of another friend, was scared stiff of being arrested and lived with her mother and surviving siblings in an attractive house. This in itself was dangerous: Amin's goons would arrive from their west Nile homeland and, being in service to the big man, expect appropriate accommodation in the city. The popular technique of house hunting by the secret police consisted in identifying a *des res* occupied by a Buganda or member of another tribe not favoured by the secret police. Instant possession could be assured by arriving with a group of secret police friends and arresting the occupants on the spot. From what I understand, it was often done in a more leisurely fashion: the occupants were given a few days to leave with some portable possessions. Furnishings were to be left for the new occupant and family. I heard of cases where the goons arrived to arrest a member of a family, telling the others that they would be back shortly to arrest them, one by one. Such individuals would huddle in their house, which by then had become the source of their grief, with haunted faces, awaiting the next visit and arrest. Once arrested, people did not last more than a few days in the interrogation-execution camps based in Kampala, particularly Makindi and Nakasero. I offered the lady concerned dollars for some handicraft she wished to sell and told her to try and escape to Kenya or Tanzania. But escape was difficult: Europeans do not understand that Africans, such as these, live in towns and villages and are not used to long treks across dif-

ficult countryside, through jungle and swamp. I often thought that
the educated Buganda who clung to their homes were akin to the
Jews in Nazi Germany in the Thirties, who hung on, trying to convince themselves and those who might listen, that they harboured
no antipathy to the regime and would remain loyal if only left in
peace. Amin was a big admirer of Hitler; only pressure from the Soviet Ambassador prevented him from erecting a statue to his mentor in Kampala.

When I arrived in 1976 mass killings, at least at camps in the
centre of Kampala, did not seem to have started. There was frequent shooting to be heard in the distance – which, one could be
led to believe, was target practice at the various military barracks.
(In Dublin I had lived near McKee, formerly Marlborough, barracks
and was used to such sounds.) Suspects were seen to be picked up
off the streets by State Research or the military police and, after
interrogation, their bodies were often thrown outside the police
stations or military barracks on to the rubbish dumps which traditionally fronted such institutions. A couple of Saturday mornings I
agreed to accompany a Buganda acquaintance to the different barracks. His brother had been arrested a few days earlier and they
had had no word of him. We found no bodies outside the city barracks that morning. I then accompanied him outside the city to a
forest off the road to Jinja. I left him to go in, as he only he could
identify his brother, and I was deterred by the stench which perme-
ated the area. I retched while I awaited his return, ashen-faced, to
the car. We drove back to his house in silence. Back at my own
place I remember looking at the magnificent, exuberant vegetation,
vibrant green against a cobalt sky, yet swearing that I would never
again criticise the cool, damp Atlantic wind which blew back home
over my green and chilly island; damp it may have been but the
bracing air smelt deliciously sweet.

## Angels of Mercy

With the ever-increasing oppression and savagery of the regime
personalities among the ex-pats tended to polarise too. Not that
one ever spoke out of turn on the phone in the office which was

monitored by the 'Stasi', or even at home, for fear it was bugged. Many took care talking in front of servants, *ayahs* (childrens' maids), or *askaris* (security guards generally armed with a *panga* (African machete) or a spear) in case State Security subsequently put the squeeze on them for information. Different categories of expats could be distinguished, the good, the supine and the morally-inert. There were people who were committed to doing good. Some because they had to, such as diplomats, though those from Western countries were becoming fewer as their citizens packed up and left. Others hung around because they hoped to pick up contracts, including from the military and police. Others still, such as the local managers of the international oil companies, stayed on to do business.[8]

The Americans left overnight in the mid-1970s, abandoning their embassy, leaving the keys with the German embassy as the protecting power. As a handy means of keeping the building spruced up they in turn loaned it to the Commission Delegation, with the exception of one room which was heavily locked. We wondered if it were stuffed with guns and ammunition, prayed we wouldn't have a fire in the building, but never tried to gain entry. We thus had the use of magnificent, old-style American furniture; the design of our desks suggested they had probably been selected by Secretary of State Thomas Jefferson in person. But there was only one phone, at the reception desk, and commanded possessively by the local secretary/receptionist who showed an obvious interest in the content of calls, especially those from HQ.[9] Phone calls out of Uganda required not only the number but indication of the language to be used. The exchange would confirm if there was a 'translator' present before placing the call. Straying even a few words from the chosen language meant being cut off instantly.

---

[8] In the case of one Western oil director it was whispered that back in Europe he would be hard-pressed to secure a job as manager of a roadside petrol station.

[9] On occasion, Brussels had an Irish colleague call me, *as Gaeilge,* to pass on a message from on high. This seemed to drive our local receptionist to distraction as she liked to be informed of developments. Presumably the 'Stasi' who always listened in were similarly frustrated.

*Jim Cardiff Sr, with Jim Jr.*
*Mary Agnes with Brendan*

*Jim, Maureen, Brendan*

*Holidays in Skerries*

*Fledgling nomad*

*Rome, author (second from right) with fellow guides and drivers, including Olivia Sheridan (third from left)*

*Author, IDA days*

*Sister Maureen, Unesco, Paris, working on the Abu Simbel project*

*St Peter's from the Tiber, Rome*

*Fountain, St Peter's Square, Rome*

*Detail of Hadrian's Column, Rome*

*Author at audience with HH Pope Paul VI, 1963*

*Michael J. Killeen
(photo: Hugh O'Toole)*

*Robert Schuman*

*Jacques Maritain*

*Jean Monnet*

*Prof Patrick Lynch, TJ (Tom) Barrington, Noel Whelan*
*(photo: IPA Library)*

*Bunratty Entertainers, 1970s: standing, l to r, Pearl Mulqueen, Stella Walsh, Enda McLoughlin, Gerry O'Brien, Maretta O'Hehir, Helen Barry, Adrienne McCory; front row sitting, Rosario Gallagher, harpist Marese Dolan and, on right, Anette Murphy. (Photo: Dermot Hurley, SFADCo)*

*Brussels 1993, dinner following agreement to first EC-US joint project selection with US Department of Education: Marion van Macklenbergh, Eulalia Cobb, Charles (Buddy) Karelis, Director FIPSE, author, Constance Meldrum*

*Belfield 2000, ceremony conferring of PhD (hc) on Richard Riley US Secretary for Education: Tom O'Dwyer, DG for Education, Commission, author, R. Riley, Chancellor Garret FitzGerald, NUI*

*Mary King of Parsons Bookshop with Tom Arnold, 1981*

*Author with European Commission colleagues in Obergurgl*

*Author enjoying a brief rest.*

With a diplomat they could do nothing, but if it were a private individual the indiscretion would apparently be noted for further reference.

At this stage the British and Ugandans had broken off relations but, because of the number of British needing consular service, the head of the British mission, or High Commissioner, doffed his British hat, donned a French one and transmogrified into the Head of the British Interests Section of the French Embassy. The French flag flew over the residence on Nakasero Hill, although Her Majesty's elegant portrait still graced the entrance hall.

The good guys of this story were mostly ladies – encouraging reminders of human nature at its best. They epitomised the moral values so lacking in many. Fear, generated by awareness of pervasive, profound cruelties also had the effect of anaesthetising the normal ethical impulses of the average citizen. Among the leading lights on the side of the angels were the Irish medical missionaries who ran the hospital at Nsambia. These good ladies offered assistance in accordance with the hallowed Hippocratic tradition: if sick or injured you just had to address yourself to them and, if they had the medication or equipment, they treated you to the best of their ability. Injured members of the security forces were treated as well as possible opponents of the regime, as were, of course, the great unwashed. Before leaving for Uganda I had adopted the conventional intellectual wisdom of the day and queried the advisability of European missionaries entering Africa to impose their culture and values on a free people. Development aid work is probably like warfare, the best laid plans do not survive initial contact with reality on the ground. Rather than imposing their values on the host peoples the altruism of these good ladies provided a glowing example of true humanity; theirs was almost the only medical service then available, free of charge, in the best Good Samaritan tradition, engaging directly with the locals.

There were some doctors still employed at Mulago public hospital but from what I heard they had no equipment or medication, especially since imported medicine had to be paid for in foreign currency. That commodity was of course needed by the kleptocracy for their personal requirements, such as the duty-free items imported weekly on Amin's Boeing 707 from Stansted. The nuns at Nsambia hospital faced the same crippling lack of medication and instruments but did the best they could with what little means they had. Contributions of foreign currency from Dundalk or Drogheda HQ allowed some ferrying of supplies from across the border in Kenya.

Sick Ugandans from all over the country would traipse for days to Nsambia, alone or with sick relatives and children, in the hope of a cure for their illnesses. Some would travel from the wilds of Karamoja to secure medicine for sick children. One problem the nuns faced was supplying containers to the out-patients. The one pragmatic solution was to put the word out to all their friends in Kampala to conserve any bottles they had, including corks and, especially, screw caps. I helped Kit Roche and Herma Glasby, wife of the senior British diplomat then seconded to the French embassy, to collect bottles. I once helped Herma to carefully wash with sterilised water the bottles she collected from the French and German embassy residences. National festivities in certain embassies thus ensured an increase in supply of medical containers - I have seldom felt so altruistic while helping to empty a bottle of claret. Little old Karamajong ladies might be spotted tracking back home clutching a recycled Chateau Lafite, Latour or Trockenbeerenauslese bottle full of a medical concoction for a sick child, with instructions as to how many spoonfuls recommended daily written over the label. Recycling of bottles was not unique at the time: my house servant and *askari* (guard at the gate) would carefully collect any empty beer-cans and hammer them into beautiful, serviceable mugs. We were implored not to squash them when empty. It was said that nothing was ever wasted in Uganda - except human life.

Another wonderful couple of my acquaintance (embarrassingly I cannot recall their name) practised as doctors and surgeons in Karamoja, a region in northeast Uganda which was relatively untouched by outside contact and whose population are pastoralists. Like all pastoralists, such as the Maasai further south, the Karamojong lived a rough, nomadic existence, frequently uprooting their *manyattas* to follow the rains with their flocks. One needed to be correspondingly tough to live among them, especially when they whooped it up on a Saturday evening. Although these two angels of mercy were of Italian origin they had acquired Canadian citizenship. Ministering to the Karamojong was not the easiest of medical vocations but they were dedicated. Monday morning was apparently the busiest day of the week as it followed the festive Sunday when the locals celebrated, lubricated by *warragi*, a type of banana moonshine whiskey. Lots of surgical sewing was required in their clinic that day.

Every few months the couple came to Kampala to visit friends, the Guandalinis. They provided me with a puppy, half Alsatian, half Doberman: it was the friendly rump of the litter. Luckily, as at six weeks old he could give a playful bite which would nearly take one's hand off. He was nurtured initially on milk made from powder bought in the local market and marked 'Aid for Ethiopia'.[10] (Dogs played a vital role as house-guards as they would bark when *kondos* (burglar gangs) came to visit in the middle of the night, allowing the occupant time to reach for the automatic rifle.) We all had a great admiration for this couple considering how rough life was in Karamoja and the huge demand for their services considering the meagre number of medical practitioners in the whole province. I was greatly saddened later to hear that the valiant lady had contracted AIDS when she cut herself accidentally during an operation, and died some years later. I understand there was a Canadian film about her life, but never managed to track it down.

I kept their dog, which I mistakenly named *Chui* (leopard) meaning to call him *Duma* (cheetah). I eventually had to give Chui to Joe and Kit Roche since I lacked enough food for us both. I had bought a chunk from the carcass of an animal which had been surreptitiously slaughtered (though I suspected it might have committed suicide when I first tasted it). Since I am useless in the kitchen

---

[10] On the road up from the port of Mombasa the trucks delivering aid were checked regularly by the army on the lookout, they claimed, for 'smuggled' goods and 'contraband'. Inevitably, some containers were left on the side of the road when the army cleared the driver, who had no 'dash' to bribe them, to continue.

some good friends helped me chop it up into suitable morsels and I deposited these in the freezer compartment of my wheezing, ancient fridge. Buying and selling meat on the black market, the only functioning market, was then punishable by death (decreed by the Economist-in-Chief as a means of reducing inflation).[11] I negotiated for it behind a bush, in great secrecy, on the outskirts of the city for 40 shillings a kilo. Supplies had completely dried up at the controlled price of 15 shillings per kilo. In order to arrest my depleting waistline I would take a small portion of meat out of the freezer-box in the morning and place it in the regular compartment. That evening I would prepare to don the white hat. By then the portion had disappeared. I would call in Musa, my steward (one no longer called servants houseboys), and ask if he had seen the missing portion. 'Give to Chui' was the usual reply. I would look at Chui, he would return a doleful gaze and I would note that we both seemed to be losing weight. I pretended to give out to Musa but the poor man, as well as his wife and child, were as hungry as I was. Besides, Moslem Africans in particular do not condone giving food to dogs while humans are in need. I could appreciate his predicament, yet I needed a dog to bark at night if the *kondos* came a-calling.

Herma Gasby was another unflinching heroine as she regularly visited Commonwealth and other prisoners in the Kampala jails, bringing food and providing pastoral assistance. Visiting Amin's jails was not an enviable task and even those fortunate enough to be able to leave after their visits were usually physically shaken.

When the level of butchery became sickening, so did the cynicism of those who supported the regime or were cravenly hanging around looking for armaments or engineering contracts. The example of these idealistic ladies provided a reassuring antidote to cosmic despair at the human condition.

---

[11] In this regard he was unconsciously imitating a like tyrant, the Emperor Diocletian, scourge of Christians, whose 301 AD maximum price edict, to eradicate hyperinflation, decreed that prices be reduced by half, and set maximum prices for over a thousand items. Likewise, Diocletian decreed the death sentence for violations, but his microeconomic initiative was just as unsuccessful. Blood was shed but supply and the markets just evaporated.

## Theory and Practice

Working in the area of development one meets many idealists: I uncharitably thought most were well-intentioned dreamers. They passed through for a few days, shared their insights and solutions to the country's problems and then departed. One was a most kindly but rather naïve British PhD student who consulted me on his thesis. Genuinely committed to the development of Uganda, he diagnosed the roots of the country's problems not as a result of looting the public purse by the ruling kleptocracy, nor the extermination of the educated class who might pose a challenge, rather it was due to the exploitation of Uganda by multinationals. At that time the only multinationals present were the European and American oil companies – the last props on which the economy precariously balanced.[12] I understand the academic assessors were pleased with this deep intellectual insight which conformed to their preconceptions of the problems of African underdevelopment and awarded the degree. Subsequently, I am somewhat sceptical when I hear simplistic solutions to developments problems, even those proposed in earlier times by such celebrities as the Blessed Bob and Bono – though, in fairness, they have begun to realise the intractability of the challenge as their exposure to the problems has deepened.

## Practical Experience

Shortly after my arrival I was invited to attend a meeting with the Ugandan official responsible for Lomé assistance, a government minister. We first engaged with opposite junior numbers from the ministry and from the Board of Works, which would be responsible on their side for implementing the road renovation and construction project. The minister then joined the meeting, wearing an impeccable uniform suitably encrusted with decorations

He sauntered into the room with evident self-assurance, exuding charm, extracted his revolver from its holster and deposited it

---

[12] In fact, a couple of years later, when the US Congress called on their oil companies to withdraw, the economy effectively collapsed and, as a diversionary tactic, Amin invaded north-west Tanzania.

on the table, leaving its business end facing in my general direction. Whether this happened by accident or design I don't know. It may have been purely accidental, his way to feign an amiable, relaxed pose, but I suspected it could also have been a calculated tactic to strengthen his negotiating position. The minister's boss may have been a ruffian but he himself appeared a pretty shrewd operator and negotiator. Still, he had been poorly briefed, since he seemed to think that the earmarked funds would be automatically transferred, and it was only a matter of pressing us bureaucrats to speed up the processing and hand over the cheque. His team did not seem to have been fully informed that Lomé assistance was intended to help a country's citizens through agreed projects, that it was provided by European taxpayers and there were people like myself whose job it was to ensure the monies were spent to fulfil their originally-stated objectives.

## The Fungibility of Aid Finance

My work started slowly as the primary data with which to justify the relatively large project was being assembled by the Ugandan Board of Works. Perhaps as a result of arresting the best and brightest locals such offices had to be staffed by suitably-qualified outside experts from the UN, with some very capable and dedicated Indian officials seconded to undertake the work. Their task was essentially to provide me with raw data to show that there was a continued increase in the level of traffic and that the roads earmarked for renovation and upgrading should be treated immediately, or else bottlenecks would appear to stifle traffic growth and commerce. I would have to manipulate this data to show that the enterprise would contribute to the expansion of the wider economy, especially that of the regions linked up to the new transport network. What I was not aware of initially was the effect the expulsion of the Asians, and the significant reduction in traffic movements this had on the data as it had happened prior to my arrival. Meanwhile my economic evaluation was under pressure from my own boss, the engineer, who was in turn being pressurised by Amin, who wanted the work to start, and *subito*. But I had to wait for the UNDP–Board of Works statistical input first.

I was concerned that aid to Uganda at the time was not always handled efficiently. We read in the local newspaper of a little local difficulty regarding aid provided by Saudi Arabia. On being promised that the largest mosque south of the Sahara would be built in Kampala, were funding available, the Saudis provided a very substantial amount – up front. Two years later all there was to be seen of the mosque was a series of trenches, a couple of rusty cement mixers and a depleting supply of concrete blocks. Apparently all the funds were by then exhausted on the most expensive foundations in Africa. The Saudis were not happy, expecting to realise their dream mosque. The solution was ingenious, and thought up by the man the Western world took for a fool; he may have been mercurial but certainly not mad. We read in the local paper that he had appointed a board of enquiry to determine what had happened to the evaporated funds. Since those with the best insight were the original overseers of the project, these same eminent individuals were appointed to conduct the investigation. I recalled Juvenal's enquiry many years earlier (implicitly criticising Plato's idealised guardian class) *quis custodiet ipsos custodes?*

I was also informed that engineering projects in developing countries could be very fungible, there being plenty of room for the contractor to skimp on expenses and compromise the quality of the work by failing to dig sufficiently deep and robust foundations, and by skimping on the quality and quantity of materials for the surface of the roads. This could reduce the originally-estimated and agreed costs very considerably, allowing the difference to be pocketed by the unprincipled. Skimping on materials would mean that within a year or so the road would disintegrate and need rehabilitation again shortly. But certain individuals' Swiss bank accounts would be agreeably supplemented. I am not saying that skulduggery would have happened with our earmarked funding, but I was employed to ensure that aid was efficiently and honestly dispensed and felt I should keep an open mind.

There was one other ingenious approach the authorities could adopt in the face of an inconvenient tendering procedure, especially the submission of a more competitive proposal from other than the envisaged contractor. I was told that such a tender could result in a visit from the gentlemen with the mirror sunglasses to check the validity of the impudent entrepreneur's residence permit: a rational businessman interested in his and his family's continued good health would immediately withdraw from the competition.

## Room Service, State Security Style

It goes without saying that the regime was paranoid about security; this was regularly reflected in the daily paper wherein the populace was ever exhorted to be on the look out for Western spies and saboteurs. And even the main hotel in town, taken over by the *nomenklatura*, was not spared. Each room had a tiny balcony. Given the poverty in Kampala it is no surprise that there were attempts to burgle the guests' rooms but, considering the few clients staying there, and the fact that the majority presence, the Soviets and East Germans, came back from work each evening in a group, it was easy to spot intruders. Still, it was possible to believe that one desperate enough might try to climb from balcony to balcony to enter rooms. This obviously provided the security services with a smart idea.

One evening I was sitting on my bed reading a book when a knock came to the door. A couple of men presented themselves as security guards, told me a burglar had been spotted climbing from balconies into rooms and insisted on checking the room for my greater security. I told them there was nobody there. They suggested a *kondo* may have entered earlier and could be hiding in the wardrobe. I hesitantly let them in and they searched the wardrobe, under the bed and in the bathroom. Nobody was found, I thanked them for their consideration and efficiency. This happened on a number of other occasions. I suspected this was a ruse, and was glad that I had not been in the same situation as the aid worker already mentioned who had been thrown from the balcony for having an African lady, not his lawful wife, in his room and/or possibly criticising the regime. Or I might have followed his trajectory, the short cut down to the ground floor.

On another occasion I left a book in my car. The lifts in the hotel had been broken for a few days and I had to use the stairs – twelve floors down and up again in the Kampala heat – air-conditioning having been either broken down or non-existent. Normally I was never rude to African staff, but on this occasion I firmly but correctly remonstrated at the price I was paying for my room with such a service, out of my own pocket (especially as I was not changing money on the black market) and it was thus costing me the equivalent of over a hundred dollars a night. I insisted that at that price the lifts should be working or, if not, they should reduce the price they were charging in their multi-starred residence. Shortly afterwards there was a knock on my door. A man stood outside with a flask of what he claimed was filtered water, so that *bwana* would not contract bilharzia or amoebae.[13] He offered to refill the container of drinking water left by the room cleaners. He took the flask that had been placed on the table that morning, opened the door to the bathroom and emptied the contents into the loo, returned to fill the flask from the one he brought. It was only when I had passed him a few shillings gratuity for his most unusual consideration at that late hour that I noticed the smart suit and what looked like Oxford Street footwear, rather than the bare feet of the usual room staff, and realised that the room and, especially, the bathroom had been rather subtly checked out.

A couple of months later there was a photograph prominently posted on the front page of the local newspaper: a large group of room staff from the main hotels of Kampala and Entebbe had completed a training course in seeking out spies and infiltrators. It went into some detail of the various skills they had acquired to detect impersonators and saboteurs, how to open bags and suitcases without leaving a trace. Although the photograph was indistinct some faces looked rather familiar.

---

[13] I later learned I could have provided the Tropical Medicine Institute at Antwerp with sufficient samples to last them for years.

The secret police with their Datsuns were especially active at night. Though few ordinary citizens ever ventured out after dark, I was determined not to spend my nights alone so I regularly went to visit friends. Both on the way to and from friends' houses I would be followed by a Datsun with the UVR or UVS plate. They were about the only vehicles ever seen on the roads after sunset.

Driving in Kampala during the daytime was subject to unwritten rules of the road. One, of course, gave way to secret police cars. Military trucks were to be avoided, mainly because they were bigger and more degraded than our models and the drivers more reckless. Where armed troops were being transported in the open back of a truck – who were prone to waving their weapons about – we kept a respectful distance. After that, right-of-way was accorded to the more beaten-up vehicle; beaten-up-bangers, in turn, gave way to others on the basis of relative size and speed of approach.

Avoiding being mowed down in Kampala was a dicey business for pedestrians, particularly at night. Non-drivers presumed the strong headlights of cars illuminating the surrounding area at night time meant the drivers could see them equally well. But as there was no street lighting and the locals usually wore little clothing and often of a dark colour, one could easily miss them, so one had to drive carefully. This I usually did but it also gave me the opportunity to disconcert the ton-tons following aggressively close behind. When I had to break hard, I observed a number of waltzing manoeuvres in my rear view mirror – even the ton-tons were respectful of their own new cars. Maybe they thought I was just a bad driver since I was never pulled over for such driving. Maybe it was because our plate number was CD 94, up there with the OAU, the PLO and other new arrivals on the international scene, and not down numerically at 1, 2, 6 or 8 with the US, British, French or Germans.

Having so-called diplomatic status at that time in Uganda was not a universal palliative. I heard, whether true or not, that on one occasion another Commonwealth country in West Africa had voted against Uganda for a breach of human rights at the UN. Amin was none too pleased with this departure from continental solidarity as he saw it. A couple of days later the High Commissioner of the offending country was being driven in his car when it was pulled over by an unmarked car, a few goons got out and he was severely beaten. Taken to hospital and patched up, he was visited by a swaggering Amin, complete with posy of wilting blossoms. A photographer was on hand to record it for posterity, or at least the front page of the local journal, as a broadly grinning Amin, exuding commiserations, handed over the blooms to the doleful, spread-eagled mummy, limbs akimbo, frozen in a scaffolding of traction, like a giant, upended and bleached tarantula.

## Terror Intensifies

Early in 1977 the level of shooting intensified; it rent the night air in particular. I presumed it was the usual target practice in the local barracks or those tribesmen kicked out of the army by Amin using the forests and woods around Kampala to mount guerrilla attacks on the new army and security forces. For some stupid reason I did not suspect it was the sound of executions, nor do I recall anyone suggesting such, at least in late 1976 or early 1977. Maybe this mindset was the result of a refusal to accept reality or a false hope that nothing was amiss. We were aware of the disappearances but did not suspect that mass killings were taking place, at least not in the army barracks in the city.

I was eventually rescued from my hotel accommodation (my boss had been desultory about agreeing accommodation normally provided) by a thoroughly decent fellow I had met at the French embassy; officially he was head of the British interests section, since the British had broken off diplomatic relations. He was appointed when the previous representative had been relieved after a number of trying years.[14] In seeking a replacement the British Foreign Ser-

---

[14] This had included the taking hostage of Denis Hills, the Makerere University lecturer who had been naïve enough to write in his diary what he really thought of the Field Marshall. Dr. Hills had to be rescued by the personal intervention of Foreign Minister James Callaghan who was treated more as a hostage of Amin than a guest. Amin let it be known that he was no great admirer of the Vienna convention on diplomatic relations.

vice presumably scoured its files for the psychologically toughest
and most morally-robust member in its ranks. And they made sure
to pick an individual whose wife was similarly gutsy and dedicated.
They were not only the type of people who would have been great
neighbours if one had been marooned on a desert island: they were
among the few who provided a moral compass in the ossuary of late
1970s Uganda.

They heard of my accommodation plight and suggested a very
welcome terrapin building on land near their own residence, situated on Nakasero Hill, the former Vice-Regal lodge in colonial
times. As such it was situated next door to a military barracks.
Since independence the barracks had been handed over to the new
government, the old residence was turned into the new embassy
and the two separated by a high wall.

My cabin and, hence, the bed inside was no further than ten
metres from the wall. One night after I had been installed I was
awakened by the blast of machinegun fire. Not the *rat-a-tat-tat-tat*
sound of fire you hear in films of the Second World War, but much
more compressed stuff – *praaaaap*. I had been advised earlier in the
game that if there was gunfire it was best to get down below the
window to avoid being shot through the glass. So I hit the floor,
wondering if civil warfare had broken out in the adjacent garden
and hoping the good guys were winning. Next morning we agreed
it had been contained within the barracks.

This performance continued on other nights, to the extent that
I grew accustomed to grabbing my pillow and sleeping on the floor
under the window shortly after the firing had died down. Then we
learned from an embassy friend and his wife who lived on the other
side of Nakasero Hill, near the exit from the barracks that, within
an hour or so after the gunfire ceased, army trucks would drive
slowly out of the barracks, without lights. This was not normal
practice for Ugandan army drivers who seemed to have been
trained in the dodgems, so something was afoot. The number of
army trucks which left the barracks, presumably heading for the
Nile, varied each night, so one could roughly estimate the number
of persons executed. We did not have to jump out of bed anymore,

but from then on I found it impossible to sleep for hours after the shooting died down, thinking of the poor bastards who had been dealt with, while I rested so comfortably in my nice room a few metres away from the carnage. I oft wondered if they were socialist supporters of Obote, shot down by the latest Soviet machine guns he had ordered.

Western diplomats in Kampala were professionals and psychologically tough but one could detect that they were sickened by what they observed or learned. In one embassy residence, situated near the reception area of a barracks, the ambassador and his wife had to turn up the volume on their hi-fi to drown out the screams of the interrogated being tortured in the cells close to the roadside.

There were many foreigners living in Kampala who were glacially indifferent to, or did not want to know or care to know, what was happening on their doorsteps. I challenged one invertebrate couple about this. Their reply was that if Africans wished to slaughter each other that was their own business, one could not reform the world overnight. This confirmed my belief that there were three categories of Europeans, the good, the supine and the bad.

During Carnival week of 1977 the shooting, especially within Makinde and Nakasero, reverberated around the city. A number of Europeans short of social activities had made considerable preparations for a fancy dress party to be held at the substantial residence of the director of an Italian construction company. Some acquaintances decided to cancel as travelling the streets was likely to be dangerous, with road checks all over the place, others considered it unseemly while these killings were taking place. But many wives revolted, complaining that they had made great efforts to produce the fancy costumes. Most of the spouses then acceded to their demands. A couple I knew dressed as mercenaries and gaily passed all the security services' controls; obviously any *mafuta mingis* and *mzungus* going out to party under such conditions must be on good terms with the boss or may have even been seen as acquiescence in their efforts to eliminate the local opposition once and for all.

What we did not learn until much later was that there were also execution sites at a number of the residences used by Amin on a random basis each night, to thwart any assassination attempts. Here the method was more refined, at least in its gruesomeness, the preferred instrument being the sledgehammer rather than the rifle – the modern version of being broken on the wheel. Apparently some morally-inert architect had even designed these execution sites specifically for such a use. Later when I lived in Kololo, not far from another highly-defended bolt-hole of the dictator, I did not realise I was living near yet another tailor-made execution centre, specifically designed for death by sledgehammer, which occasioned less sonic disturbance but was unnervingly close to where these horrifying deeds were carried out by the ghoul himself.[15]

## Weekend Parole

Although there was indigenous food available in the local market, especially matoke and cassava, I did not go there to buy supplies but relied on the boxes of canned peas, beans and mushrooms I bought occasionally across the border in Kenya.[16] This was quite an expedition, especially as one had to get written permission from the Foreign Ministry without which we could not go through the military checkpoints or cross the border. Even with the appropriate papers crossing the border was difficult and would take over an hour of hard arguments and threats. Again, along the roadsides we witnessed prisoners who had been taken at checkpoints, handcuffed and forced to kneel down in a row – one can only imagine their fate when we were out of sight.

Although Kenya shared the same topography, crossing the border provoked a feeling of euphoria that a weekend pass must evoke among convicts. One could buy international newspapers in Kenya and even write and post letters abroad without their being checked by the military censor. Visiting stores in Eldoret or Kisumu I obvi-

---

[15] I was told later that one temporary next-door neighbour in Kololo, whom I never met, was Frank Terpil, a renegade ex-CIA operative who was reputed to be advising Amin on security.

[16] This was not very smart as I did not then know that tinned food lacked vitamins necessary to ward off infections.

ously stood out as a country bumpkin – especially with my Kampala soup-bowl haircut. I recalled asking an Asian shopkeeper for a bar of soap and a tube of toothpaste. Then I sheepishly asked if I could possibly have two or even three, please, as I had some friends who were desperately short. He looked sympathetically at the obvious blow-in from across the border: I was informed that depended on my having the necessary moolah, in which case I could buy the whole store. Such bounty was almost unbelievable and psychologically unnerving after the penury of Kampala. So I would load up with supplies.

One occasion I dropped colleagues off at Kisumu on Lake Victoria, and decided to visit some Irish friends, the McGraines, who lived in Eldoret a hundred or so miles away. Taking main roads involved travelling first to the Ugandan border and from there the road to Eldoret. I noticed on the *Esso* roadmap a thin blue line which wriggled directly between Kisumu and Eldoret. I recalled my school days, one side of a triangle is shorter than the sum of the other two, or so they assured us. That may have been true at St Paul's, Brunswick Street, Dublin, but not necessarily in the African bush. A few miles outside Kisumu the metalled road became murram, and then split into three or more mud tracks, until they too disappeared. I was not sure I could even find my way back, so I directed the map to the north, looked to the position of the sun at that time of day and proceed on my first solo safari across wild terrain by Land Rover. As the French say, it rained cords; the car slipped and slid about like a conger eel in a barrel of oil. I had been warned that the local tribe had a capacity for stripping any car they would come upon in record time, removing the seats to bring back to their *manyattas* being a speciality. Word had it that they were particularly addicted to cutting up car tyres for sandals. I became concerned lest the Michelin radial-ply cross-country variety was in fashion with the Samburu or Turkana *murran* (young warriors) that season. I was even more concerned that no marauding Somali *shiftas*, poaching for elephant tusks or rhino horn, would come upon me. These gentlemen have a well-deserved reputation for ruthlessness all across East Africa.

Many hours later I arrived at Eldoret, found their house and was magnificently wined and dined by Eddy and his charming wife Anna. This was the first real meal I had had in a long time, apart from a snack in Kenya. I had barely finished the main course when I felt something amiss in the combustion chamber. I excused myself and went to the bathroom where the contents of the beautiful repast were deposited. I did not have the heart to tell my hosts what had happened. I hasten to add that it was the result of unscheduled excess for a retracted tummy, not the charming hostess's cooking. For once I returned to Uganda hungrier than when I had left.

On another occasion we visited Kenya for the Easter weekend to buy supplies and chill out. En route, travelling towards Mount Elgon, at the higher altitude, and with the rain pouring down, we were stopped at a military roadblock. The glassy-eyed gladiators showed all the signs of being sozzled on *warragi* – banana moonshine. But they were not so much out of their minds that three of them demanded to be transported back to their barracks from whence their expected shuttle service had not arrived to collect them. Their destination was over 50 miles out of our way. 'Sorry gentlemen', we replied, 'but that's not on our route, we would love to but unfortunately... no doubt your guys will eventually turn up, insh-Allah'. AK 47s were brandished in our faces. This is disconcerting enough under normal circumstances but especially so when their wielders are woozy on jungle juice. We immediately decided that indeed we could arrange to drop our new-found friends off at their desired destination. On reflection, it would be our great pleasure. They got inside, complete with automatic rifles, spare clips and grenades. Between the orbiting vapours of the *warragi* and obvious lack of local dry cleaning facilities, we were delighted to impose an arsenal of cigarettes on them: they generated clouds of the required incense. Our bibulous buddies alternatively laughed, argued, and shouted, all the time gesturing with the automatic rifles. Could we not go faster? 'Yes, Lieutenant'. Faster, still? 'Indeed, Major'. They spied our supplies, as fellow travellers they considered they should be invited to share, '*Hakuna matata,*

Colonel...'. We feared that when we eventually arrived at the bar-racks the troops who were supposed to relieve them would require a lift back to the same checkpoint. Luckily, they were not to be seen or were waiting elsewhere; we decanted our wobbly warriors and were regally saluted on exiting the gates.

We arrived late and without reservation at a Kenyan country club, high in the Aberdare Mountains. It was full. Realising we were 'refugees' from the austere delights of Amin's necropolis all efforts were made to accommodate us. First we were escorted to the res-taurant to have a meal. On finishing, private rooms were made available for us. I was allocated the room of the owner's daughter, she having found alternative accommodation. I found myself in an obviously feminine room, very much Laura Ashley, with a big warm eiderdown, fluffy pillow, window partially open and the highland rain still lashing down outside. Lights out, I quickly fell into a deep sleep. I was awakened later, having the impression something was moving on the bed. More precisely something relatively heavy was crawling across the bedclothes, over my legs. But, not to worry, it's probably only a puff adder or cobra come in from the cold to shed its old skin in the warmth.[17] 'Well, goodness gracious me...', or something more cryptic, I hissed. A good Africa hand should just go back to sleep and let the visitor do its thing. But I was made of much weaker stuff. I just could not sleep. Eventually I slowly raised my hands from under the sheets, and swiftly threw the covers over the intruder. I jumped out of bed to get to the light switch and out the door. But in the dark I tripped over the bedclothes. Two bodies tussled with Ms Ashley's refined threads. No being an habitué of the room I could not initially find the switch. Eventually the light went on. I stood by the door and watched the tussling under the bedclothes. Eventually one of the largest cats I ever saw freed itself and jumped out the partially-open window. So large was the cat I suspect his mummy must have had a furtive entente with a civet from the nearby forest. Back to sleep only to be awakened again.

---

[17] I've been told a king cobra can do that over a sleeping baby without causing any harm.

This time I had a reassuring feeling of being protected from any intruding serpents by my new friend. A truly symbiotic bonding.

Too soon, it was time to get up and return to Tombstone City.

## An Anglican Martyr

I received a call early one morning from the Foreign Ministry instructing me to present myself immediately at Nile Mansions, the president's official residence at Kampala. On arrival I noticed a large army and police presence. On the main lawn, almost the size of a football field, there were a good number of chairs set out, which were occupied, seemingly 50:50, by ecclesiastics in purple cassocks and civilians in suits.[18] Nearby was a rostrum mounted on a platform with microphones and loudspeakers. Facing those seated on the chairs was a tribune full of army personnel in uniforms. On the fourth side near the entrance to the Nile residence, was a space to which I was directed. I recognised many of the faces there as being from the diplomatic corps. There were the French, German, Chinese and Soviet ambassadors and the Papal Nuncio. Near where we were placed were some local VIPs, amongst whom was the vice-President, Moses Adrissi. Mooching around were a couple of men who had been previously identified to me as from State Research or Public Safety. A short, shifty European seemed in command of technical arrangements, acting as a ringmaster. I had first noticed his presence weeks earlier shuffling around solo at official receptions, glass in hand, not drinking but staring at guests. I had already heard of Bob Astles, one of a small number of Britons who had stayed on in Uganda after the end of the British Protectorate, Amin's weaselly consigliere, if not enforcer, who supplied the four Englishmen who had been forced to carry Amin on a palanquin some years before. The photograph of this event had been published worldwide, provoking much amusement in other African

---

[18] I did not immediately understand the significance of the presence of the ecclesiastics, but afterward recalled that most of Obote's Langi tribe were Church of England. It is probable that a couple of Northern Irish bishops were present that morning, to be deported shortly thereafter.

countries in particular. Because of his closeness to Amin he was feared among the expatriate community. He was reputed to be in charge of a senior security unit which protected Amin since the latter did not entirely trust even his own fellow-tribesmen. Apparently the scene in Nile Mansions was also broadcast on local TV: when word went out that something of importance was to be screened any locals who had sets watched and they later confirmed to me it was Amin's close collaborator.[19]

Astles started by escorting an obviously shaken individual to the podium. If I remember correctly he was from the Ugandan Institute of Public Administration or similar agency. In stuttering English he started to read a long prepared statement. We were provided with a copy. From what I can recall, or wish to recall from the disgusting episode, the poor chap was forced to describe the preparations he had made with his fellow accused to organise a revolt from Tanzania with the help of Julius Nyerere and the Chinese. They intended, of course, to sabotage the economy, blow up infrastructure, rape innocent females, butcher women and children who were not Langli Acholi, and commit other detailed atrocities. Frequently the unfortunate prisoner would break down and have to be helped to his feet and provided with water so he could continue his confession. This performance seemed to last an eternity. The Western diplomats and Nuncio appeared visibly disgusted; the Soviet and Chinese maintained the inscrutability of professional diplomats. When the official completed his confession other equally shaken prisoners were directed by Astles to the podium to make similar confessions.

My breakfast that morning had consisted of the usual two cups of tea or filtered water so I began to feel dehydrated standing in the African sunshine. I noticed a white-jacketed orderly approach with a glass and bottle of Cola. He delivered it to the Soviet Ambassador who was standing near me. I was sufficiently thirsty that, for once,

---

[19] Apparently 'Major Bob' has argued his role was merely that of Amin's Anti-Corruption Czar; given the exalted level of civic mores aspired to under the Life President such a title, with its cynical conflation of irony and menace, is characteristic of the surrealism of that demented period.

reticent Brendan decided to follow the orderly back into the Nile Mansions residence and to the bar to which he returned his tray. I asked for a Cola and was prepared to pay any asking price. But no, it was free! (Presumably the barman thought that any mzungu not in chains must be a friend of his master and that hospitality was to be provided.) I immediately took a swig from the bottle, to my great relief. Wandering slowly and reluctantly back towards the outside and the macabre Roman circus, I noticed an elderly gentleman, in a bishop's purple robes, reclining on an armchair breathing uneasily. I presumed he too was dehydrated, although he did not seem to have been served a drink. I pointed to my bottle and made a gesture to him, meaning did he want me to get him one also. He put up his hands and signalled no. I hoped that I had not made a gaffe, offering a bishop a drink from a bottle. I returned to the outdoor theatrics.

The show trial was drawing to a close. Astles handed a mike to the Vice President (Moses Adrissi, if I recall his name correctly) who was apparently acting president of the kangaroo court, reminiscent of the newsreels of Vyshinski during the Moscow show trials or Friesler after the 1944 attempt on Hitler. He spoke, or more correctly roared, face contorted with rage, in what I presumed was Kakwa. Evidently he was asking the soldiers, who constituted the jury, just as the mob attending the Roman Circus exercised the same right, to condemn the accused. Unanimously, they jumped up to roar their approval, baying for blood, repeating a tribal word which I was told meant 'death, death, death'. The half-conscious prisoners were roughly frog-marched past us as each death sentence was recorded, to meet his fate. It is possible that a few were preserved to provide the spectacle of a public execution by firing squad at the clock tower in the centre of the town. Those preserved for mere shooting were probably the lucky ones.

Next morning we opened the local journal to be informed of the latest events in our godforsaken corner of the globe. In the centre of the front page was a photo of the Anglican Archbishop Luwum. It declared he had been killed in a car crash early the previous morning near Nakasero Hill. I looked a few times at the photo and was pretty certain it was the face of the bishop I had met the previous day, but that had been just after midday, not early morning and some miles away. I shared my suspicion, if not conviction, with other European diplomats. I knew they had better systems of communication than the single phone at the reception desk of our offices, whose calls abroad were monitored and frequently cut off by the 'Stasi' controllers.

## WaBenzis and Non-WaBenzis

Two days later, if I recall correctly, the big meeting of the ACP countries opened in Kampala. This was the high-level (mostly heads of government) meeting of the recipient ACP partners who wished to discuss their strategy before the joint ACP-EEC meeting later. Both the timing and venue had been decided on years in advance and it was probably accidental that it occurred immediately after the outrage recorded above. As a strictly ACP preparatory session no Community or Member State representative was invited to the working sessions. I was one of a number of European residents invited to the cocktail reception and purely ceremonial opening the evening before the official event.

I arrived at the gates of the imposing mansion at the indicated time – driving a modest two-door Fiat 127. I was stopped by security at the entrance. My invitation, and vehicle, were scrutinised by a sceptical soldier. He returned to his hut to phone, while another couple of soldiers with guns at the ready stood nervously beside the door of my car. I was examined carefully, my plebeian transport even more so, and hesitantly informed 'invitation no good'. I replied that I did not wish to force the matter but had been sent an invitation which I had accepted. They checked again. Behind me a fleet of ambassadors and their diplomatic staffs approached, mostly in individual Mercedes, and were immediately waived past to the parking area. But they were the *wa-Benzi*, as the Mercedes-Benz-transported classes were then known. Brendan, presumably, belonged to the mere *wa-Fiat* and that just did not seem to cut ice. The zealous guardians may not have had a bike between them but they were critical assessors of fine transport and perceived social/political status. A caravan of Mercs from dozens of embassies rolled majestically past my miserable Fiat. Finally, after a lengthy standoff, a perplexed senior official (you could tell by the suit and crease in the pants) arrived, checked my card against a list and hesitantly allowed me to enter.

I had already attended a few receptions and knew that at a certain stage someone would call for a toast to the Life President. On previous occasions I just left my glass aside. Later I just refused any drink until toasts were over. I did not believe I had volunteered service in Africa to toast this bargain-basement Hitler. Nobody could accuse me of racism since I had been Membership Secretary of the Irish Anti-Apartheid Movement for a number of years.

Multiple fawning and oleaginous toasts completed, Al-Hajji, the Life President and Field Marshall, proceeded to address the assembled audience. Most of those present were heads of government from the African, Caribbean and Pacific countries, and their development ministers, except for a few leaders from East Africa such as Nyerere who had stayed away from Kampala out of principle. The genial host shared his world vision with the audience, blustering and cajoling, switching on all the animal attraction he possessed. He came alive when ego-massaging a receptive audience; it was a superb pantomime performance.

We were informed that the Ugandan economy was expanding at supersonic speed despite all the efforts of the West, and Britain in particular, to destroy it. He went on to mock Britain whose BBC World Service had accused him in the previous hours of orchestrating the death of Archbishop Luwum. Did the British not have any road accidents? Did nobody ever die on British roads? Maybe we should buy more of these wonderful British cars which never crash, they must be so ingenious. He had most of his audience rolling around with laughter.

As ever with Amin, lupine charm was mixed with an underlying menace: he went on to accuse the EC countries of being too tight-fisted and mean in their sharing of wealth. The EC was rich because it had exploited colonies.[20] He would urge his fellow presidents to insist on a much more substantial budget for the ACP at the next joint meeting.

I switched off mentally after a while, recalling the events of the previous days. The performance may have been fascinating, but even to a student of politics it became intellectually and morally repulsive. Nor could I understand those who would confidentially denounce Amin and all his works yet cravenly rush up to shake hands with him when the opportunity occurred.

Although I personally have no proof, it is possible that Amin was present the previous morning at Nile Mansions, observing proceedings from an upstairs window. Although none of the bishops was forced to join the condemned as they were frogmarched out, it was obvious what their fate was to be in time under Amin. I heard afterwards, although the account is purely hearsay, that he had personally confronted the Archbishop, threatened and insulted him, and in a fit of rage killed him. I was told a smashed car was towed out to the road near Nakasero and photographed as evidence of a crash. This was all theatre so that he could put a face-saving cover on before his continental peers during the prestigious international event to be played out in Kampala days later. I was desperately sorry afterwards that I had not been able to do more to assist the Archbishop (for I'm sure it was he) in his final hours of separation from his family and friends. I tried to console myself that maybe my gesture had, at least, been the last friendly signal from another human being.

Amin had re-enacted a version of the Roman Circus; as in the Colosseum it had its complement of martyrs, cynics, the emotionally-anaesthetised and sadists, as well as a small cohort of the virulently-disgusted.

## Censorship

In keeping with similar dictatorships the degree of censorship seemed to intensify in proportion to the level of repression. There

---

[20] At this point a certain Irishman had to restrain himself from making a verbal challenge – I did not regard myself as being contaminated by colonialist baggage.

were three sources of information or, more precisely, misinformation: the sole newspaper, the *Uganda Argus*, a radio service and an embryonic form of TV whose programming was pretty haphazard. Other sources of information were strictly repressed.

All letters were censored and marked by the Military Censor before being eventually delivered.[21] Even the rare perfumed *billets doux* with delicate feminine handwriting were scrutinized, stamped by the censor and forwarded, weeks later. Under the Lomé agreement communications to official offices on either side were specifically allowed to pass freely without any control of contents, yet they opened all letters which did not arrive by diplomatic bag – and there were indications that even this was interfered with at the airport.

Foreign newspapers were unobtainable and those posted into the country subject to special scrutiny. Few ever got through. We had a subscription to the weekly *The Economist* but, with a substantial delay, received about three copies in the year. On one occasion I phoned the post office to inquire why copies were not being delivered. I forget now the exact sequence but I was eventually referred to another phone number to get more precise information. I spoke to an individual of undetermined position and asked why our magazine was not arriving regularly. I was told that they had to prevent misinformation and false rumours being spread by hostile foreigners as this could unnerve the populace and cause unrest. He insisted that *The Economist* was printing racist, anti-African and anti-Ugandan articles. I argued that one might disagree with a lot of what *The Economist* wrote, it was inclined to moan a bit, but it was never racist, it frequently and trenchantly criticised the regime in South Africa and, I emphasised, it opposed the death penalty. I was then provided with the additional observation that *The Economist* had to be checked out as it was full of mistakes and inaccuracies and it would mislead readers. It was a bad magazine and would be very bad for my brains.

---

[21] It reminded me of old letters my family in Ireland had received from abroad during the Second World War.

Armed with these insights I dreamed of writing a stiff note to the recalcitrant editor, pointing out his shortcomings and suggesting he and his writers pull up their socks in future, but knew such a gesture would have been futile – they would have censored that letter too. I was not successful in having any further copies released; such people were not used to being argued with. In the land of the surreal one must learn to put up with such little trials and tribulations.

## Lies, Damned Lies and Statistics

The Office of Public works finally presented me with the data required to justify the major road-building project which was the crown jewel of our proposed assistance. The Indian experts from the UN had laboured mightily: a mass of statistics indicating road traffic flows for years past along all the road networks we were to have refurbished or build, was presented to me. I approached it with a positive but open mind, hoping that the proposal would fulfil our expectations and conditions. As already indicated the key to a successful justification for financing the proposal was that we could show an inexorable increase in traffic and a consequent need to upgrade the system.

Then, a quick perusal of the statistics indicated something odd, or not so odd, considering the condition of the economy and its trend-line. The long-term trend for traffic had declined significantly for a number of years, beginning some years earlier. My interlocutors reminded me this would be consistent with the expulsion of the Asians who had accounted for most of transport use in happier days. I pointed out that, as a direct result, my calculation would necessarily produce a negative rate of return on investment and there would be no way to justify the project. Jaws dropped. The significance of what I said sank in. They quickly retrieved the sheaf of documentation they had prepared for me and promised to have another look at the data. In those days there were no photocopiers available in Uganda, and certainly not in our office. So the originals disappeared with the departure of our collaborators.

The experts returned a week later with another sheaf of tables. This time the data provided a perfect basis for calculating a positive result. I protested that they must have switched the statistics around. They told me the previous listings were erroneous, had been rechecked and these were the correct calculations. No more discussion was necessary. The EEC now had the necessary data with which to justify transferring the promised sums.

I sent a factual report back to Brussels, explaining that due to the absence of a photocopier I could not show the contrasting calculations. I noted that on querying the first set of data these had been taken back, revised and ameliorated. I said I had no confidence in the new data. As the delegate was still on vacation I had to send this information back to HQ myself. He returned to Kampala a couple of weeks later but I was not invited to further discussion with him. He was an engineer and saw the future of his favoured engineering project delayed or in jeopardy. I was the economic advisor and financial controller and, for my part, considered I too had a fiduciary obligation to do my appointed job.

I learned from friends that on his return the delegate had been immediately summoned to Amin's office, that the President-for-Life expressed his displeasure and demanded the immediate transfer of the funds. The Field Marshall, whose patience was reputed to hang by a delicate thread, was apparently not swung by the cogency of my reported analysis. I heard indirectly and confidentially that it had not buoyed his humour, nor was he enamoured of its lowly, nitpicking Irish author, with whom he was not best pleased. The delegate was requested to have my opinion reversed in the shortest time possible.

## Dénouement

There was then the likelihood that the project would be stalled for the indefinite future, not least because I could not in all honesty back down as to the validity of the data provided and my analysis which I suspected might have proved pivotal in Brussels. It was my duty as economic and financial advisor to evaluate whether the project would have been socially effective as well as being in accordance with the regulations; it would have been a dereliction of duty to have exercised but vestigial oversight and not to have reported honestly. I considered that I had executed my stewardship correctly, even if I could be accused of halting or holding back the major project wished by the host government and the prospective contractor. But I was not the one who had suggested putting almost all the development aid eggs in one basket. And public funds would not be wasted: Brussels could find many more deserving projects, especially when some unexpected (and unfortunately all too frequent) natural catastrophe occurred elsewhere in Africa.

Since my boss was no longer pleased with me and I was mainly twiddling my thumbs I decided to retire from the posting. My health was not improving living mainly on tinned food and I had contracted some bugs only identified years later (coincidentally by a Ugandan Asian specialist at Erasmus University Hospital who had been expelled ten years earlier by Amin). I was warned by friends to change my timing and route to the office each day lest I experience an encounter with an army truck. I have no idea if this was a false alarm or an exaggeration, but in Uganda at that time one listened to advice from friends and tended to err on the side of caution. My departure was speeded up by a phone call from a close Belgian lady friend, Anne, who had married my good friend Philip just ten days earlier. On honeymoon on the island of La Reunion he had had a fatal accident. They had intended to spend a few days in Kampala with me on the way back.

I then decided to bring forward my resignation and arranged to immediately return to Dublin for the funeral. My good friends Mary McGowan and Paula Casey met me on arrival at Zaventem National airport. When I first arrived in Brussels in 1973 I had taken one look at that airport, a glass and steel construct with all the creativity of a biscuit tin, mentally compared it to Collinstown of fond memory, and feared I could never accept it as my hometown airport. Arriving from Uganda it now seemed like a long-lost home.

The Aer Lingus flight from Brussels next morning was delayed by three hours. I have to admit that I was not sorry to have missed one of the most harrowing and grief-stricken funerals witnessed in Dublin, especially by our colleagues in the IDA. My great African adventure had ended on a far sadder note than it had begun.

## Postscript

Having retired from the development service I slowly let slip memories of Uganda, though I remained horribly upset when reading of the ongoing terrors visited on that beautiful land – and a cloying sense of frustration and guilt at my failure to have helped as I had originally dreamed. The Irish press tried to contact me on return but I could not be interviewed as I was still an acting official of the Commission; also, reports of criticisms filtering back might not have been welcomed by friends left behind.

Later in Dublin, after I had left that service, I was invited to dinner by my friends Mary and Michael Killeen. Naturally I was quizzed about my experiences. As it happened, shortly afterwards they were entertaining a group of Americans. I learned that these were US congressmen, visiting Ireland to encourage investment. Apparently two or more of them had been promoting an act of Congress which would require American companies, fuel suppliers in particular, to cease propping up the regime in Uganda. Michael seems to have later shared my experiences with them. I have no idea if it had any bearing on subsequent events but shortly after that Congress passed the act which required the three US oil companies to withdraw. Apparently this had a major effect on an already nose-diving economy. As a diversion Amin invaded the Kagera province of Tanzania, and proceeded to bring down defeat and exile on his own head.

He retired to spend his fortune in the accommodating climes of Saudi Arabia, and I hoped his retirement conditions were not enhanced by any diverted aid money.

Some years later, long after I had left the development service, I read in the press that the ACP partner countries were objecting to a demand from the European Parliament and human rights groups that a human rights clause be included in the successor to the Lomé II Agreement. From my home address I sent in a letter to the service responsible for development, recalling the revolting events I had been officially forced to attend years earlier. Someone phoned me subsequently to discuss my letter. While being signally understanding of my arguments, he was nevertheless subtly sounding out

if my intervention was altruistic or as a result of resentment of experiences past. I assured him of the former: I was still completely in
favour of promoting solidarity with the less fortunate of the world,
but I was equally committed to human rights. I argued that my objective was to support the rights' promoters and that including human rights clause in the new agreement would only enhance it
morally and politically in Europe, as we would not be legally constrained to assist any dictatorial regime which came to power after
commitments had been undertaken. If they wished they could use
my testimony during the negotiations as evidence that a human
rights clause was needed. Such a clause was eventually included,
and became standard in all subsequent Community agreements,
with developed partners as well as undeveloped.[22]

One unalloyed positive development brightened my year of falling darkness. On departure to Uganda my Commission director
Jean-Claude Morel and colleagues had organised a goodbye *pot*, as
was the tradition. I introduced a good friend of mine, Cathal
Cavanagh, who was a Senior Economic Advisor in our DG, to a fellow colleague, Nicole Tricot, who was working in our unit. She had
been posted to Foreign Affairs on Stephen's Green during the first
Irish presidency. I subsequently received the occasional post card
from Brussels and other points, duly stamped by the Kampala cen-
sors, signed Cathal and Nicole, later merely C&N. Two years later I
attended their wedding at Kimmage Manor in Dublin.

---

[22] The insistence by the Community of such a clause in the draft agreement with
Australia, and the refusal of the then Prime Minister to accept this, was to cause
me grief some years later since I had invested much effort into designing an education co-operation agreement with that country.

# 7

# THE EARLY COMMISSION – THE POTENCY OF IDEAS

*Under your [Jean Monnet] inspiration Europe has moved closer to unity in less than twenty years than it had before in a thousand ... You are transforming Europe by the power of a constructive idea.*

– President John F. Kennedy

*Cecily, you will read your Political Economy in my absence. The chapter on the Fall of the Rupee you may omit. It is somewhat too sensational. Even these metallic problems have their melodramatic side.*

– Oscar Wilde, *The Importance of Being Earnest*

I RETURNED FROM UGANDA TO A middle-ranking job as an obscure but frontline worker, again in the long-term policy-making department of the economic service. Good Belgian nutrition followed by a spot of skiing ensured return to full health. I managed to shake off an early bout of TB which was then endemic in central Africa, especially, my Congolese-Belgian doctor said, among those who had subsisted on tinned food. One other little tropical bug has proven more persistent. Yet I continued to harbour guilty feelings, my dream broken, despondent and ashamed that I had abandoned the traumatised people in Uganda while escaping to the comforts of benign Brussels; a haunting feeling of helplessness and frustration that repression continued apace while I could do nothing about it. It was a wound which festered unassuaged, to be cauterised only on the fall of the Amin regime.

## Commission with a Mission: Springtime of the New Community

The late 1970s Commission was increasingly getting its act together and addressing new challenges; the end of the heroic beginnings when everything had to be invented from scratch. The place bubbled with a sense of purpose and creative energy, striving to translate lofty vision into earthly achievements. Yet it was a very tight-knit and convivial organisation, still coming of age in the springtime of the Community. Most of the directorates general (hereafter services) were still concentrated in the old Berlaymont building.[1] Administration and most of agriculture were located on the nearby street, while the competition people moved out to new offices across the Cinquantenaire Park – they preferred their own separate building in the interests of greater security for their sensitive dossiers. In the cafeteria near the Berlaymont one could share a table for a quick morning coffee-break with a dozen colleagues from a good half dozen different services. This was particularly useful to me as my work was one of lateral liaising with a number of other services such as regional development, industry, research, innovation, external relations and trade. If you did not immediately know who to contact in another service it was always possible to phone a coffee-time acquaintance and be referred to the competent colleague. I knew colleagues from more services in those days than, 30 years later, I knew among my own service, which then occupied a number of buildings.

Though the Commission was slowly expanding its role this was still limited to certain areas. The agriculture service had a high profile; in fact, I often considered it the glue that kept the Community

---

[1] Some claimed the old Berlaymont consisted of 40 per cent steel, 20 per cent concrete, 20 per cent glass and 20 per cent asbestos interior walls.

together during those doldrums years between the ending of General de Gaulle's boycott of the Council and the decision of states in the 1980s to opt for majority voting. The competition people were being taken ever more seriously by firms, especially those who were not fully beholden to the ideals of free and undistorted competition. The industry service was increasingly regarded as relevant, as was re-search.[2] The internal market people were heroically struggling to eliminate a host of barriers to trade in our so-called Common Market – but making little progress. The Community had still to implement the limited objectives of the founding Treaty of Rome (free move-ment of goods and services, labour and capital); yet it was also build-ing up like a coiled spring waiting for the right legal basis and politi-cal leadership.

Commission President Francois Ortoli bore himself like a cere-bral, aloof, hieratic academic from the prestigious *Grande Ecole* of which he was a graduate: neither he nor his successors, Roy Jenkins and Gaston Thorn, seemed to seek or enjoy the high profile achieved later by that unfettered force of nature President Jacques Delors. But Delors was fortunate to inherit the results of the la-bours of less celebrated predecessors: the decision of the Court of Justice, as described later, to strike down the most egregious exam-ples of technical barriers to internal trade; the decentralisation of decision-making regarding technical standards which greatly re-stricted inter-member trading; the decision by Member States to move to majority voting in many policy areas. These initiatives combined to ensure he arrived at an auspicious time. But it takes one with energy, vision and determination to make the most of auspicious moments. President Ortoli had taken up office during the dark days of the energy crisis of 1973 and the economic stagna-tion known then as Euro-sclerosis. His perceived lack of charisma meant he was less recognised as a leader with vision than Delors a decade later. One can be in the right place at the wrong time: as that highly perceptive commentator of Community policy John

---

[2] This was despite the lack of a sound legal basis in the Treaties for research at the time.

Palmer has pointed out, Ortoli was quite human behind his apparent aloofness. Few of us seemed aware that the elegant and patrician figure had been a successful resistance fighter against the Japanese in the jungles of Asia during WWII and had been highly decorated. Palmer recalls[3] Ortoli's love of all things Vietnamese, including music and cuisine; he recounts that he was once invited to Ortoli's home to be greeted by the Commission President wearing a Vietnamese chef's uniform to a background of Vietnamese folk music.

I was initially surprised at the greater degree of bureaucracy compared to a small organisation such as the IDA where everybody knew everybody else and many decisions were taken orally or by phone. The Commission was much given to paper. If, for example, one wanted to make a proposal to an equivalent level official in another service the memo had to be signed off by one's own head of unit, passed up the administrative ladder via the director to land eventually on the director general's desk, who then signed before passing it to his equivalent in the external service, where a similar procedure started in reverse. One traditional way to short-circuit or speed up the transmission maze was to informally post a carbon copy to your colleague and let them start preparing a reaction, in the hope that the superiors might not revise the original too much.[4]

For the next few years I was to serve as a middle ranking administrator gaining a view over a number of fronts as to how the Com-

---

[3] *The Guardian*, 10 December 2007.

[4] The personalisation of computing in the 1990s subverted this bureaucratic procedure. The old system of requesting visas from one's superior continued in theory, but in the early 1990s many of the higher officials, especially those politically rather than professional competent, just could not handle the new system of electronic visas and editing, and there was a gentle easing out of old wood. PCs, and the 1990s move to suburban offices, meant that the old tradition in the economic service of shared Berlaymont offices, pens, paper and venerable codices, doors (except those of senior management) invariably open with easy accessibility for face-to-face discussion and the exchange of ideas, has been replaced by officials cloistered in individual offices seeking enlightenment and sharing insights with a disembodied, flickering screen.

mission operated. For just over a decade I was to help amass information and assist in drafting proposals and suggestions for the Member States for their consideration. I also had to draft speeches for my own director general (and the occasional contribution on economics destined for Commissioner Peter Sutherland, an intellectual omnivore with a voracious appetite for absorbing recondite information, though at that time more proficient in law than in economics). Later on, for a decade, I was responsible for setting up and managing a number of academic cooperation programs. Though only a middle-grade minion,[5] I was fortunate to be allocated interesting, occasionally influential jobs, mainly devising policy. Fortunately it was during the early pioneering period of the Commission's history when creativity and imagination were welcomed, even actively encouraged; in the economic service you were only considered as good as the latest policy paper you were drafting. It had not yet become a mature administration managing, if not submerged in, the processing of a huge *acquis* of accumulated legislation. Much of my tasks were undertaken as a player in a number of interdepartmental teams set up to tackle a range of challenges. These teams were composed, on average, of a dozen or so specialists from different departments with varied professional, gender and cultural backgrounds, almost always imbued with a sense of mission. After a few brainstorming sessions, and vigorous discussion, we generally bonded to come up with some convincing proposals for our superiors. (Some little vignettes are given below.) To that degree I was privileged to have occupied a second row seat at some defining moments. But I was to learn that it is far easier to come up with bright ideas than to give them wings, between policy and delivery, mission and reality, especially when this requires agreement of many sovereign Member States and the European Parliament. It was not enough to identify a problem: one had to devise concrete steps to solve it. I certainly did not witness an all-

---

[5] I was not interested in being promoted to a grade which would prevent my taking two weeks skiing in the Alps every February.

powerful Commission which could issue *fatwas* to the Member States for their unqualified acceptance.

## A Rural Sabbatical

Shortly after my return from Africa I volunteered to spend a year in the economic analysis section of the agricultural service. This was not without interest, especially as agriculture accounted for about seventy per cent of the Community budget at the time.

The job involved interpreting the regular farm surveys, masses of statistics describing output by category – tillage, milk production, livestock, wine production, farm size, farm income, etc., for the Member States and their regions. It all provided an intriguing insight into the performance of the various sectors in the different regions. The results were referred back to the ministries and examined with considerable interest to assess how well their regions were succeeding in maintaining standards of income, in the formulation of policy and, not least, influencing the subsequent carve up of the next year's financial pie. The results were eventually helpful for reform of the CAP as they clearly showed that the bigger farmers were getting the lion's share of the assistance. This old strategy was based on the encouragement of output rather than supporting the income of the smallest and most deserving farmers.[6]

Another colleague from the economic service was invited to look at the overall economic efficiency of the common agricultural policy, the CAP. Following an analysis of the statistics available he concluded that the CAP considerably benefited another unexpected stakeholder – the American farmer producing grain feedstuffs for cosseted European cattle which spent months indoors in the winter, rather than the *al fresco* grazers in more temperate Ireland. He even proposed the heresy that the CAP was detrimental to Ireland whose

---

[6] For a most readable review of the history of Community agricultural policy *vide* the chapter by Tom Arnold, 'Europe and the Revolution in Irish Farming', in M. Callanan (ed.) *Foundations of an Ever Closer Union*, IPA publications, Dublin 2007.

temperate climate favours specialisation in beef and mutton production than is the case with more northerly Community producers.[7]

The CAP has rightly been criticised for inequities of distribution of income, supporting output rather than the smaller family income. The unintended effects of subsidised exports on competitors from the developing countries are also to be deplored. Yet, during the late 1970s, I often thought agriculture was the main show in town as completion of the internal market was effectively and frustratingly stalled due to a litany of non-tariff barriers to internal trade in goods and services.

The agricultural service is oft accused of being excessively influenced by French thinking and policy. Yet if one allows for factors outside the untrammelled whim of market forces one could appreciate the French concern with the maintenance of their rural communities, and their fierce pride and loyalty to local *terroir*. One has only to travel around certain depopulated parts of the UK, the US or Canada, bereft of farming families, but punctured with oligopolistic hypermarkets, and compare these to the lively and charming villages in France or Italy, with their multiplicity of specialist shops and open-air markets selling the freshest of local produce – epicurean delights which are the essence of diverse regional culinary specialities – to realise that there is more to the assessment of rural communities than the unfettered, invisible hand. This is not to argue a return to the days before the overturning of the old Corn Laws. The French are deeply committed to the *art-de-vivre*, the

---

[7] The CAP was run as a sort of *sui generis* club at the time and excessive criticism by external experts, suspected of scepticism regarding the humble tillers of the earth, was not encouraged. Most economists were considered far removed from any form of contact with the soil and, as *laissez-faire* agnostics, were to be distrusted. I recalled (UCD) Professor James Meenan's maxim that the economic analysis of the agricultural sector was by nature different from any other form of human enterprise since cultivation of the soil had been conferred with the unique approbation of the Almighty Himself – toil in factories and offices being strictly man-made. And much earlier Virgil opined in the *Georgics* that farmers were such a fortunate band, they should realise their good luck.

character and quality of food and wine produced and consumed locally, and the social security of rural areas.[8]

As a result of changing climatic patterns, concreting over of the rural landscape, diversion of the US maize harvest to biofuel, growing demand in China and India for dairy and meat products, could now result in a dramatic surge in prices. We in Europe might then learn to appreciate the CAP for having helped maintain a viable rural infrastructure and guaranteed supplies at reasonable cost on highly-productive small farms, its *raison d'etre* in the first place.

## Back to the Economic Drawing Board

My year with the rural brethren ended, I returned to the confines of economic analysis, or more correctly, the unconfined area known as *politique structurelle*. The directorate for structural policy was in many ways the most interesting as it provided scope for a considerable degree of initiative and imagination in the analysis of long-term challenges the evolving Community faced, especially competition with the US and Japan – then being regarded with the same degree of commercial concern as China is now. Loss of competitiveness in such sectors as textiles and clothing was causing hot-spots of unemployment in regions which then specialised in such production. It was accepted that it would be extremely difficult for Europe to compete with the US in certain technological sectors where the Americans had gained dominance; it was also becoming apparent that Europe was inexorably losing out to Japan and other dynamic emerging economies of Asia in certain sectors in which we were traditionally competitive. Europe was being caught in a pincer between American technology and quality Asian labour competitiveness. The Asian tigers may only have been kittens then, but early extrapolating of the trends was beginning to give cause for

---

[8] About the same time the US Secretary for Agriculture, Earl Butz, was expounding his philosophy to family farmers: 'get big or get out'. He encouraged the growth of corporate factory-farms, to the benefit of the fast-food industry and food-processing sector. He seemed unaware that in 1962 Nobel economist Amartya Sen claimed he had discovered an inverse relationship between the size of farms and output.

concern. Yet, when I first broached the rapid advance in competitiveness of the Japanese, in particular in the auto sector, some
French colleagues dismissed them as being capable of producing
reliable but ungainly replacements for the Citroen 2CV (*deux
chevaux*) – but not for top-of-the-range models dominated by the
Europeans. They were to soon learn how capable the Japanese were
at forcing the pace of incremental innovation, *kaizen*, and inexorably mounting the technological ladder.[9]

Europe's growing trade deficits provoked sufficient concern that
the authorities paid for a then-celebrated guru of international
competitiveness to lecture us on the rise of Japan. The central thesis of this generously-upholstered pundit consisted of the old trick
of joining two points on a graph which bookended a high growth
period in Japan; he then extrapolated the trendline into the distant
future using a straight line. Japan was shown on the point of overtaking the EC, while the Americans too had reason for grave concern; his calculation showed the Japanese overtaking them toward
the end of the 1990s to become the new world superpower. I recall
his dire prophecies when nowadays I read palpitating articles of the
imminent economic superstardom of China and India.[10]

The Commission went on instead to build up its own internal
expertise in strategic analysis, by recruiting candidates with a
broader range of expertise, who had the intellectual bandwidth to

---

[9] Some time later the Director General for External Relations, Sir Roy Denman,
achieved a degree of notoriety in Japan when an internal note he wrote was leaked:
he defined our esteemed trading partners as workaholics who lived in rabbit
hutches. For a while afterwards Japanese cartoonists had a field day depicting
buck-toothed fellow-countrymen peering out of hutches. But he did provoke a
lively debate on working conditions in that country.

[10] Some years later we were exposed to the pearls of wisdom of another celebrated
prophet of the business world, this time a 'lateral' thinker. Though I tried to filter
some nuggets of wisdom from his exposé, I recall few except for a rather detailed
enumeration of the many prestigious international companies and world leaders
which paid handsomely for his advice and how they would send corporate jets half
way around the world to pick up this *éminence grise*. I later commiserated with the
much-beset citizens of certain Eastern European countries, especially Russia,
whose new rulers swallowed the neo-liberal shock-therapy theories of reform from
celebrity consultants after the fall of the Berlin Wall.

detect strategic possibilities and make recommendations, and by expanding the embryonic Forward Studies Group, the internal think-tank.

## Whirlwinds of Change

My earliest tasks consisted of acting as correspondent on the economic side for the textile, clothing, automobile sectoral working groups, as well as the general process of technological innovation.

As mentioned earlier the Commission works as a 'college', all the Commissioners and their corresponding departments are supposed to work together and take decisions as a group, collegial consensus, thus ensuring a coherent, joined-up strategic approach. So each service nominated officials to track policies of importance to their service, but for which it is not directly responsible. These serve in joint working groups and networks. Questions regarding textiles, clothing or the automobiles, were particularly sensitive as they affected employment, especially as many such sectors were, historically, concentrated in certain regions or cities. So the locally-elected members of national parliaments would pay close attention to recommendations made by the Commission in world trade negotiations. It was one thing for the Commission to argue we needed to specialise more in knowledge-intensive sectors and leave the more labour–intensive to newly-industrialising economies, but many politicians represented thousands of constituents still specialising in traditional activities and facing mass unemployment. Retraining and setting up investment in higher value-added sectors take a lot of time.

Each inter-service team met frequently to discuss strategy. Thus, with the clothing sector, the industry service acted as the lead and other services, such as external relations, trade, employment, economic affairs, or regional policy, would meet to discuss strategy. The regional affairs people might, for example, propose a simple solution to the problem (usually more regional aid), while the trade or external people would recall existing international agreements and commitments (hence no subventions). The industry service tended to be somewhat protectionist by instinct, so the economic affairs representative would have to present the rational, if occasionally counter-intuitive arguments, such as the inevitability of structural change under intensifying global trade and the need to encourage a move towards more knowledge-intensive employment. Social affairs would emphasise the need for retraining of workers. Despite intense debate such meetings generally ended with agreeing a rounded solution which could then be presented to the Commissioners and their personal advisers who assess proposals from a more political perspective.[11] The results of their deliberations were next forwarded to the Council of Ministers for their decision. But, as ever, the final decision remained with the Council of Ministers and Parliament.

## The Commission to the Rescue – An Example

It is part of the conventional wisdom to regard bureaucracies as slow-moving operators when faced with new challenges. On a number of occasions I recall the Commission swinging into action when called upon to come up rapidly with a coherent strategy. Once the chairman of a working group had been selected there were always enthusiastic colleagues among the services to ensure a useful roadmap was swiftly drafted. Sometimes the leadership was provided by the 'Forward Studies Group', the small but influential internal Commission think-tank. One typical case occurred when the environment was identified as a crucial policy area, prior to its inclusion in the first revision of the treaties. No specialist service had yet been established but a policy document was required urgently for Monsieur le President. An inter-service team meeting was called. A particularly hard-driving and cerebral British colleague with a track record of producing quality results in record time was nominated chair of the working group. He first circulated

---

[11] Of course, harmonious agreement was not always achieved: trade-offs between the industry and the environment services on vehicle emissions were generally fraught as one concentrated on employment in the auto sector and the other equally tenaciously defended the environment. Such impasses then had to be arbitrated at the higher political level by heads of cabinet or as a lively discussion at the weekly meeting of Commissioners.

a preliminary text. He proposed we meet every Friday afternoon for the next few weeks. The procedure was that he would distribute a revised draft by Tuesday; we could use the new-fangled fax machines to send on our comments which he would take on board in his new draft for discussion the following Friday. He reworked the text each weekend. Representatives of about eight or so concerned services were involved. (We met around the historic but by then decommissioned old table used by the first Commissioners of the Community of six.) Following six or seven meetings the work was completed and a very professional text sent to the weekly meeting of the Commissioners for approval and imprimatur. Less than two months after starting work the printing presses were rolling.

If ever there were a policy area in which the EU can play a major global role it is almost certainly that of catastrophic climate change and the environment. Environmental degradation is a prime example of what is known as market failure, the environment being a public good rather than a private one. This is an ideal area for inter-regional and international cooperation since most pollution, especially atmospheric, where noxious vapours released into the air and unconstrained by borders, can poison from afar. Virtue in this case can sow the seeds of its own rewards. The imposition of standards for atmospheric pollution, which ultimately affects all countries on a global level, has stimulated German industry in particular to specialise in the production of cleansing equipment, providing a useful specialisation for the future.[12]

The recent carbon-emissions trading scheme may have faults but it acts as the spur for other large polluting nations, the US, India, and China, to tackle global warming. Only the combined power of the EU states, far outweighing the sum of the individual members, which pooled their sovereignty to achieve internal agreement,

---

[12] Likewise the imposition of high standards for vehicle-exhaust emission standards in California enabled 'first movers' in that state to achieve a global competitiveness in catalytic converters for cars.

could have succeeded in garnering enough international votes to endorse the Kyoto Agreement.[13]

When the realisation of anthropogenic climate change, drought and flooding, and the health effects of atmospheric pollution eventually strikes home to the average American, especially member of the US Senate, Chinese, Indian, Brazilian, they too may finally realise that global warming is a grave threat to all who live on the planet and agree to cooperate as responsible neighbours in promoting clean energy. The inspiration and leadership of Europe in the areas of environment and energy might well become as strategically important in the early twenty-first century as its contribution to peace in our previously strife-torn corner of the globe in the latter half of the twentieth century.[14] In combating global warming the combined influence of the 27 Member States must again be called on to redress the irresponsibility of many member of the new G20 grouping in vetoing progress at Copenhagen in 2009: only a reinforcement of effort and the determined, persuasive power of the Union can garner enough support among other conscientious countries to save our fragile planet from environmental degradation. As long as ideologues gridlock the US legislature, preventing agreement on carbon emission levels, the US will remain a hobbled giant denied a position of leadership or partnership within the global community, leaving it to a grouping of responsible medium and small states to take a principled initiative.

## The New Industrial Divide

Until the early 1980s the dominant thinking among industrial management was of economies of scale based on specialisation, as first proposed in the eighteenth century by political economist Adam

---

[13] I can understand that supporters of the political extremes of right and left will oppose Community initiatives but cannot understand why some Green Party supporters in my home country find it opportune to do so, particularly when it is organising an international coalition of small and morally-concerned states especially to confront the large and irresponsible.

[14] The British government's chief scientist recently warned that global warming represents a far greater threat to our future wellbeing than episodic terror.

Smith. Costs of production and, subsequently, prices charged would be reduced by ever-greater specialisation in the use of labour, while the introduction of more specialist capital equipment would replace most tasks performed by craft labour. This conventional theory suggested that semi- and low-skilled workers would be progressively sidelined. And with the exploitation of economies of scale the producers with the greatest employment of capital equipment could expect to achieve a high degree of efficiency and competitiveness. The accepted theory also decreed that the world was implacably divided into capital-intensive developed countries and poor, labour-intensive developing countries.

But our world was perceptibly changing: theory and practice were diverging. It had become obvious that we in Europe were losing our competitive edge, not only to the US and Japan, but to Hong Kong, Taiwan and Korea, especially for the type of goods which involved a degree of applied research, a qualified labour force that could produce and command a higher price, especially if protected by patents. These competitor countries were far removed from our markets so, obviously, distance no longer played the role the theory dictated.[15] It was obvious that there was more to changing international competitiveness than the accepted theories of international competition were still emphasising: they did not adequately and informatively explain what was happening.

As usual, when a new problem was identified, the Commission set up working groups in the areas of science and technology to address shortcomings. One of the most insightful initiatives was that of the innovation service led by Raymond Appleyard as Director General.[16] They set up inter-service teams to encourage Member States urgently to improve European innovation, stressing the fact

---

[15] I recalled memories of the sectoral research units in the IDA which tried to identify the most promising new products and service sectors with high value-added, increasingly desired in high income markets, and which were not raw-material or energy-intensive. Such goods were mainly characterised by the introduction of new technology, either embodied within the products or in the equipment and processes used for their manufacture.

[16] Dennys Watson was his energetic assistant.

that expenditure on R&D (invention) was not at all the same as successful innovation, which creates jobs in the knowledge-economy. We highlighted the reasons for the lack of innovation in Europe compared to the US and Japan.[17]

At that time the European economic experts had difficulty in explaining exactly how and why research (the addition of knowledge) and education (the diffusion of knowledge) contributed to economic advance, though it was accepted by most specialists that technology (the application of knowledge) played a part in growth. We had nothing resembling the excellent reports of the (US) National Science Foundation, and their National Academy of Science, which tracked and analysed progress in the area. We lacked the excellent structures the US had put in place to make venture capital available to budding innovators. To prove the point I attempted to put a figure on the EC's success relative to the US and Japan. I calculated the intensity of high-tech products in EC trade compared to that of the US and Japan. The result was a series of simple indices which could be presented in graphic form and showed the long-term decline of Europe, the fluctuating performance of the US, the rapid rise of Japan. This illustrated very clearly the need for Europe to take remedial measures. These summary results became a god-send to speech writers and pundits, including the exceptionally dynamic commissioner for industry, Count Etienne Davignon.[18]

---

[17] I submitted my opinion as to the reason for Japan's rapid advance in the high-tech sectors, not as a result of inward investment as was the case in Ireland, but as innovated locally or reverse-engineered from European or American prototypes. I argued that it was because they had thoroughly prepared their physical and human resource infrastructure to cater for such frontier industries. I coined the expression 'absorption capacity' which was appreciated and adopted by Mr Appleyard and entered into use.

[18] A German research institute cited the decline calculated for Germany's performance, calling for much more spending on R+D. This rebutting of Germany's presumed prominence as a bastion of high-tech wounded certain egos and provoked a row in the Bonn parliament. Commission officials are not supposed to provoke political disputes in the member parliaments. I was informed, asked to substantiate my calculations, and stuck to my guns. Instead of being hauled over the coals I was invited to Bonn as a guest of the German authorities, requested to recite my

Another interdepartmental team chaired by Raymond Appleyard stressed the urgent need for Europe to recognise its backwardness in the use of information technology and its role as a *pervasive* technology which affected the performance of almost all industrial and service sectors. We worked hard to produce a professional and convincing proposal for action. This was sent to our political masters in the Council requesting the launch of a major EC effort to catch up. The Council temporised, some countries did not wish to increase budgets; others were not convinced of the need. One Prime Minister in particular thought it no business of the Commission to become involved in such a policy area: any such initiative must be left to private industry to take the initiative. Shortly thereafter we read in the financial press that a prestigious firm in her native land won an order for jet turbine engines to pump gas along the Siberian pipeline, only to have their export vetoed by the US on the basis they contained microprocessors included on a list of high-tech items and prohibited for export to the Soviets. Almost immediately, if I correctly recall, the Research Council allocated an ecu billion-plus budget for IT research – later known as the ESPRIT program.

I subsequently regretted this seeming success: like all organisations allocated a big budget it attracted a substantial increase of staff to handle the new high-profile project. The project became so important managerially it tended to swamp the innovation intelligence-collecting and diffusion-of-best-practice activity. The service was subsequently recognised more as the ESPRIT program rather than as the innovation policy service.

Despite our success in numerous areas – mobile telecoms in Europe would not have become so competitive in the absence of agreement on the GSM standard – the role of innovation and entrepreneurship in Europe still needs far greater understanding if we are to be speedier in adopting knowledge-industries. Too many people in Europe still think of innovation as the logical, automatic

---

party piece, fed, watered and accommodated, then invited to inspect that delightful 'little town in Germany'.

conclusion to a continuum which starts with basic research, continues with the development of technology which is then expected to be successful in the marketplace. Europeans continue to believe in an oversimplified view of research and development: pour R&D funding in one end of a pipeline and, they assume, out the other end must come successful innovation. Europe is too committed to the science-push model of innovation; Japan and the US recognise the greater importance of market-pull.

## Come Fly with Me

The 30th of January 1981 was a fine day in the quiet and leafy Brussels suburb of Tervuren. I'm not normally so precise with dates but, for once, I scribbled a short note that evening on my return home.[19] My stroll had been rudely shattered by a screeching aircraft which had just taken off from nearby Brussels National airport. It was a tri-motored Boeing 727, already well past its sell-by date. The B-727 had three slim, jet motors mounted on the rear of the fuselage. All the air sucked into these ancient burners was forced through the core of the engine causing far more noise that the later wide-fanned jets then installed, for example, on the B-747s, and which are effectively encased propellers that force a sleeve of cool air around the hot core and muffle the exhaust noise.

My argument was that Boeing was too tied up with the development of the B-757 and B-767 and had not yet written off the development costs of the B-747. Lockheed had previously produced the large twin-aisle, tri-motored Tristar, which was not selling, though it was technically a good aircraft. McDonnell Douglas, a year late, had tried to catch up with Lockheed with a somewhat similar body. To save design time they stuck the third engine in the middle of the vertical stabiliser of the DC 10. Unfortunately, in the rush to market it had a flaw with the locking mechanism of the

---

[19] I had at that time arrived at the conclusion that if you want to change things in the world there's no use proclaiming nuggets of wisdom over a pint while balanced on a high stool in Smoky Joe's; you must put the idea on paper and try to get it into the right hands.

cargo doors which could blow open in flight. This caused the pressurised passenger floors to collapse locking the hydraulic controls. A couple of fatal crashes signalled the collapse of sales of that craft.

At that time Airbus was proposing to build a competitor to the Boeing 747 Jumbo, which I though very risky. My suggestion was that Europe should cooperate to build a more simple bread-and-butter, 150-seat, single-aisle, medium-range, twin-engined, advanced-airfoil-and-navigated craft as the replacement for the B-727, even if Airbus disagreed.

I presented the note arguing the case to my British director. He found it convincing, but told me that since the Concorde fiasco any proposal to build a new aircraft in Europe with British participation would be as welcomed by his ex-colleagues in the Treasury as the proverbial flatulence in a space suit. Still, I distributed a few copies to colleagues, including a roommate, Paul Rutsaert, who had just left our service to work in the cabinet of high-powered Vice-President Davignon, responsible for Industry. I then forgot about my wonderful brain-wave.

Months later I received a phone call. A lady asked if I would be free to take a call from Commissioner Davignon. I suggested to her that the V-P did not know I even existed. No, she replied, he read your note; it had your name on it. I then snapped to, took the call, to be informed that he had discussed its contents with the head of Aerospatiale and had received a favourable response. They subsequently decided not to build a competitor to the Jumbo but opted instead to develop and build the medium-sized Airbus 320, selecting a brilliant French test pilot to design the revolutionary digital fly-by-wire control systems.

I have no idea what relative influence my note had but harboured a certain feeling of paternity towards this model ever since. I get upset on board if there are any unusual vibrations or the engines and activators for the flaps sound less than refined. On one occasion I found myself rubbing shoulders with the pilot of an Air Chile A320 whose take-off was delayed at Ushuaia, and in casual manner inquired what he though of the craft, his personal opinion – 'crap'. During the subsequent highly turbulent flight I tried to convince myself he was just having a bad 'air day – and was a lousy pilot anyhow.

## High Standards to Replace Low Practices

As mentioned, the main tactic of those who promoted European unity was to lock member countries together economically in such a way they would never go to war with one another again. Yet up to the early 1980s the whole Common Market exercise seemed bogged down in agriculture, regional development, social policy, while struggling with the Member States to achieve its main *raison d'etre*, a single market for the trading of goods and services. Member States were blocking competing imports from partners using spurious technical excuses. The Commission tried desperately to get agreement on the common definition of the products being blocked so that they could be traded unhindered, but at that time unanimity was required for any decision and any one state could veto agreement. Europhobes and tabloid jingoism declared it was all about busybody Brussels bureaucrats harmonising sausages, beer, chocolate and pasta. Then the 1985 Single European Act with its majority voting was proposed and accepted while, simultaneously, a couple of decisions of the European Court broke the logjam.

Though all of this now seems extraordinarily bureaucratic it is easily forgotten how different national standards and regulations were used as a protection against imports from other Member States.[20] Technical regulations regarding safety standards and public hygiene, particularly when used for public procurement-type testing and certification, were all resorted to in order to protect the home market from neighbouring country competition. At first the Commission tried to harmonise technical regulations for products: these tended to be excessively detailed and could be held up by the veto of one interested country. Few standards were ever agreed by the Council, while a raft of new standards was being introduced

---

[20] The experience could prove of value to mooted common markets in Africa and Latin America.

unilaterally in the Member States. The market was actually fragmenting rather than freeing up.

In order to cut the red tape the Community agreed in 1983 on a so-called 'new approach', that the Commission be informed before any new standards were introduced, and be authorised to freeze the action if necessary. Then it was agreed that, instead of opting for detailed technical descriptions, the strategy would consist of harmonising the basic objectives only (e.g. a toy should not be so small that it could be swallowed by a child) while the details could then be worked out by the national or European technical standards institutes. Again, if this seemed bureaucratic, it was estimated at the time that different standards increased the costs of European machinery by fifteen per cent.

The greatest breakthrough came with the famous *Cassis de Dijon* decision of the Court. The Germans would not allow this liqueur to be sold on health grounds (*mar dhea*, delicate Teutonic tummies) and the French manufacturer took the case to the European Court. It decided that if a product were legally allowed on the market in one Member State then another could not ban it. Vitally, this judgment created a broad precedent (was *erga omnes* in legal language) so far as it affected all similar restraints to trade. This greatly strengthened the principle of mutual recognition of standards. Later decisions were taken regarding the German Beer Purity Law (the ancient 1516 *Reinheitsgebot* law) and the Italian prohibition on importing pasta not made from durum wheat.[21]

The new article in the 1985 Single European Act revision of the original treaty which allowed for qualified majority voting (in less than nationally-vital policy areas) was a further nail in the coffin of hidden protectionism. The practice whereby one or two countries could indefinitely stall decision-making on the most spurious of grounds became a thing of the past.

---

[21] I underwent a deep personal conflict of interest regarding dilution of the beer purity law, but there was no problem: German devotees were not about to abandon their excellent beers for Irish/British/American dishwater beers just because they were legally available.

We were surreptitiously encouraged when a colleague returned from exploring the internal market experiences in Canada and the US to report that they often had as many barriers to internal trade. He reported the case of a citizen in one Canadian province who noted that paving stones being laid on a public pathway were made in another province, and duly protested. Eventually they had to be ripped up and replaced by local products. Bad and all as Community failings were we had not encountered such extreme measures in Europe.

In the lead-up to 1992 the Single Market program was severely criticised, and not just the usual suspects: respectable journals, US business and trade associations accused the program of being a furtive *Festung Europa*, a new Fortress Europe. In fact the project represented a major freeing of international trade by the world's largest trading entity, since opening markets to internal partners implied an *erga omnes* opening up to external partners as well.

## Louvain

In the early 1980s the prestigious old University of Leuven (ex-Louvain), with its hallowed connections to Ireland, offered a well-structured MBA course to national and international students. It hosted many American and Asian students. Most of the subjects on offer were oriented towards business and management, but there was a considerable number of other interesting subjects, such as international trade, industrial organisation, and managerial economics (really old-fashioned microeconomics). This was especially interesting for a person who had been somewhat of a dilettante at studying basic theory in UCD. With colleagues Tom Arnold, Colm Larkin and Denis McGowan, I inscribed one evening in the magnificent old fifteenth century Aula Maxima of Leuven University.[22]

---

[22] Some years previously, during the Belgian linguistic dispute between the Flemish and Walloons, the local authorities within Flanders, where Louvain-Leuven is located, insisted that the official language of the university be Flemish rather than the traditional French. So one of the world's oldest universities was split in two, along with its equally ancient library, or what had survived Wehrmacht visitations in 1914 and 1940. The French speakers were hived off to a new campus 20km dis-

MBA tuition was provided in English and lasted two years for part-timers, with an additional year to write the thesis. The Commission had promulgated the ideal of lifelong learning for its staff and, thankfully, did not refuse us permission to attend. Possibly they noted that some of the classes started at a most uncivilised hour on a Saturday morning (operations research at an ungodly 8.00 a.m.), while others were scheduled for late evenings, so we would not be absent too much from our desks. Anyhow, they seemed genuinely interested that some of their staff were going to expose themselves to the latest ideas and thinking in economics and monetary matters. My superiors in the economic service seemed particularly interested in my access to the latest literature and research in the area of customs unions, monetary matters, industrial organisation and international trade. They realised how rapidly the technical literature had progressed since the days when most of us had completed our studies.

I found the experience of returning to academia greatly energising. Also, study when there is no vocational pressure whatsoever is at once liberating and engaging, especially if the teachers are pronouncing theoretically on an area where one is professionally involved. I was especially interested to hear of the latest thinking in the area of international trade theory, industrial organisation, as well as boning up on some econometric techniques. In view of work demanded shortly afterwards by Jacques Delors in the achievement of the internal market by 1992, the studies on industrial organisation were particularly useful as I was frequently asked by colleagues in the Commission to advise them as to the latest writings in the professional literature.

For my thesis I decided to further develop the topic I had already started exploring in the Commission, the relative competitiveness of the EC, the US and Japan in the area of technology and innovation. This was to prove particularly interesting back in the office. It also benefited from the fact that the university allowed us

---

tant over the linguistic border in Wallonia, where a new Francophone university was built. This resembled the UCD Belfield building-site campus in the late 1960s.

use a faculty computer which was programmed to do econometric calculation and, in the early 1980s, such calculations were time-consuming. Had we to pay commercial rates for this facility it would have cost a fortune at that time.[23]

The result of my input was a few metres of paper and lots of interesting results, not to mention two kilos of punched cards. But they never sent a bill.

## Uncle Sam's Innovation Archipelagos

Maybe someone in the US embassy noticed the publication of an article and that I was serving on the US-EC High Tech Group, still, I was surprised and very pleased to be offered one of a number of coveted invitations the US Mission's Fulbright Commission issued annually. With three colleagues from other services I was invited to visit the US for over three weeks visiting policy agencies in DC, science parks and research centres all over the country. The general theme was the potential contribution of information technology to industry, especially manufacturing.

In Washington DC we were introduced to the State Department, National Academies of Sciences, NSF, National Standards and various other agencies. Then we took off to visit the science parks at Carnegie Mellon and Ann Arbor, Boeing in Seattle, Washington, finally to Silicon Valley and Stanford Research Institute in the big dream machine which is California.

I was amazed at the general frankness and openness of the Americans in displaying and informing us as to their latest advances in key areas of technology, including some areas highly sensitive at the time, and to our intrusive questioning. The Americans

---

[23] Our professor of econometrics (whose other job was as an actuary for a major Belgian life insurance company) reminded us that in the early 1970s he had completed his PhD in the US and had chosen for his subject an econometric forecast of the demand for competing agricultural products. Calculating the result for a number of variables involved inverting a matrix, a tediously-long calculation in the days before computers became available. It had taken him and his research assistants months to complete the calculations, despite being able to use certain little mathematical shortcuts and tricks. Nowadays a powerful pocket calculator can invert a relatively large matrix in a matter of seconds.

have a tradition of academic and scientific openness but in this case they were exhibiting some of their latest technologies. Of course the US was then afraid that, as a result of Euro-sclerosis, as it was then known, Western Europe might implode, just at a time when the Soviets were flexing their military muscles with new medium-range missiles. What was particularly impressive was the exposure to many centres of excellence, and archipelagos of research all round the country. One got the impression that the Americans are much more open to ideas, at least in the areas of science, technology and innovation, than their European counterparts. The visit tended to confirm to me that most Europeans, including senior policymakers, have little idea of the intricate skein of links between intellectual brilliance in research labs, innovation-welcoming manufacturers and highly-discerning risk-capital providers, which ensure American pre-eminence in the area of high technology.

As a quid-pro-quo we had to write up our thoughts on completing the visit, which of course provided the Americans with an insight into our own thinking. I wrote a report developing the idea that the introduction of the new technologies, especially where they led to flexible manufacturing, would have a profound effect on the relative size of and competitiveness of firms, their location, job creation and qualifications. I was barely finished with the first draft when new Commission president Jacques Delors arrived and I was asked by my boss to draft a conceptual framework for analysis of the potential benefits of completing the internal market, or more precisely, 'The Costs of Non-Europe' as it was initially entitled.

I circulated my conclusions drawn from the US trip and believe its distribution in the Commission, especially in the regional policy, industry and research areas, provided some inspiration for others, and even triggered a number of lucrative contracts to outside research consultants.

## Soviet Technology

In the 1980s the Commission was a very introverted institution. The main focus was still on the internal twelve members' concerns. But the external people were getting increasingly involved in relations with other corners of the globe, mainly driven by trade questions. A colleague from the economic service was recruited as one of the first desk officers at the new Soviet desk. Since I had included the technological competitiveness of Comecon countries in my latest analysis, he co-opted my assistance and in turn showed me some OECD analyses of the economic performance of the Soviet Union and Comecon partners. They proved a revelation: if we in Western Europe were losing confidence in our abilities to innovate and compete, the economic authorities in the Comecon countries were facing immeasurably greater problems. Almost all the economic trends were negative, declining demographics, falling investment, productivity and output, mounting budget and trade deficits and increased hidden unemployment. Yet this was at a time when many commentators were still prepared to believe in the long-term success of the communist model.

I drafted an opinion piece in which I suggested that the US system of innovation was far superior to that of both Western and Eastern Europe. Also, spending by the US on the so-called 'Strategic Defence Initiative' might, intentionally or not, compound Soviet economic difficulties. There was little leeway in their economy, whereas the US benefited from the manic-Keynesian economic spurt given to their economy by President Reagan's military and space spending, and how their manufacturing industry certainly gained from the spin-off effects of the dual-use technologies developed at taxpayers' expense.[24]

I recall reading in some American or British science magazine that Soviet scientific publishers had unexpectedly ceased publication of research articles on directed-energy radiation. Apparently it was this which woke the Americans up to the fact that the Soviets must have considered such research sensitive, potentially applicable, and thus embargoed its further publication. Reports at the time suggested that this was what induced the US defence research

---

[24] For example it did not take a James Bond to realise that the navigational systems developed for missiles could be put to good use on an automobile factory assembly floor which required binocular vision of robots to supply parts to the production line.

community to look into the matter and suggest to President Reagan that the new-fangled lasers were of strategic importance. He bought the idea of the Strategic Defence Initiative (SDI) which the local wags immediately dubbed the Star Wars initiative. If correct, it would be ironic if scientific censorship by the Soviets, and their installation of fancy new missiles, eventually led them to an impossible level of competition with the extraordinarily polyvalent US research infrastructure, and act as the economic straw that broke the camel's back. The American science and technology community had lots of absorption capacity, the Soviets, presumably, little or none.

Visiting Moscow as a tourist at that time I pondered if the ubiquitous queues did not knock quite a few percentage points off Soviet productivity, while the numbing tedium of queuing must have germinated a terminal disbelief in the superiority of the workers' paradise which inexorably enfiladed the wider public.

It would also be fascinating to know to what degree the gradual deepening of Community integration, and the perceived success of the intensive build-up to 1992, led to a loss of confidence within the Soviet system.

## Enter Monsieur Delors

Towards the mid-1980s it was again time for the heads of government to nominate a new president of the Commission. In keeping with a tacit understanding it was the turn of the French to nominate the successor to departing Luxembourger Gaston Thorn. The Brussels bookmakers were at that stage taking bets on a list of high-profile Europeans. An august and patrician socialist, Monsieur Claude Cheysson, like President Ortoli an *enarque,* a graduate of the prestigious university ENA, an ex-EC Commissioner and government minister, was heading the list. We then read in the papers reports that he was considered too exquisite a personage for one quite practical-minded Head of Government. She insisted instead on the then French Finance Minister, who she perceived as a kindred spirit. Because of his resistance activities in WWII, he had not completed his *Bac*, never mind attending the prestigious ENA. On the insistence of this pragmatic lady the French eventually agreed to nominate M. Jacques Delors instead, and the proposal was endorsed by all other Member States. In view of his unrelenting energy, vision and strategic leadership history will, no doubt, record this as a most far-sighted intervention on her part.

Delors fitted in perfectly with the ethos and culture of the Commission whose leitmotiv those earlier years was, I believe, much more shaped by idealism and a moral vision than managerial capacity and procedures.

His whirlwind arrival provided a bracing gust of renewal in the corridors of the Berlaymont. He started by touring the Member States to learn what could and should be done to revitalise the ossifying Community. His hosts told him the so-called Common Market was far from being a proper market. He therefore decided audaciously to set a target date to achieve completion of the Internal Market. Various dates were discussed: 1989 or 1990 were considered too close and not realistic, while a longer term target such as the year 2000 would not be taken seriously and no progress would be made. Therefore, 1992 was selected as the ideal timeframe. For ages we did not even know if that implied a January or December deadline – neither, probably, did he.

As with a successful general, luck and good timing were also on his side. Reforms of Council decision-making mentioned above, and those of the Court, were about to provide the institutional basis for dramatic progress. The industry service then financed a series of studies, including almost all the industrial activities in the overall economy, from outside consultants and industrial and economic research institutes. These were instructed to outline and estimate the effects of the creation of an open market among the twelve members. Such a large number of studies arguing for achievement of the internal market, and being published at the same time, should have had a major impact, but the likely diversity of styles and presentations risked diluting the overall effort. Monsieur le President had a keen sense of strategic direction and was not one to opt for 30 minor bangs when he could organise one big boom which would reverberate across the Continent. He contacted the economic service and requested us to help pull the whole exercise together. He may not have been a physicist but he sure appreciated the notion of critical mass, especially when it was designed as the driving-force of a far-sighted geopolitical strategy.

Because of my MBA studies at Leuven, including access to the latest thinking in the areas of industrial organisation and international trade, I was asked to prepare a paper to serve as a framework, providing the techniques which would allow us to pull the results of all the diverse studies together, and provide seminal arguments to justify the whole, highly risky initiative.

The most obvious source of economic benefit would be the well-known economies of scale as a result of exploiting a continental-sized market. At that time economists had been intrigued by the fact that smaller economies were further penalised by some other factors, difficult to detect, presumably resulting from a lack of competition characteristic of large, continental-sized economies. They investigated this overlooked aspect of competition, the so-called mystery *X-inefficiencies*, as they were then called. Removing intra-Community trade barriers was considered the key to eliminating European lack of competitiveness. A larger market, equal to that of the US, was considered to force industrialists to up their game; this would be further augmented by 'dynamic' gains. The idea was to try to estimate these deficiencies and calculate the potential economic benefits. We initially called the study *The Costs of Non-Europe* since it calculated the loss resulting from fragmentation. A newly-arrived and hard-driving director, Michael Emerson, decided to set up a small team, each member would then track a batch of sectoral studies, so as to cover the overall macroeconomic picture. I was assigned telecommunications equipment, the even more important telecoms services sector, automobiles and air transport.

In the case of telecoms services I was given a fiery baptism since I initially knew little about the complexities of their organisation in the individual member countries, nor of the pricing tactics employed. I was delegated to track the drafting of a specialist consultant who had been awarded the substantial contract, an impressively bright individual and one of the very few in Europe who knew anything about this complex and evolving sector. But he was working on a number of other projects in different countries at the same time and there was no realistic chance he could come up with the results by the specified deadline. Such a delay risked holding up the entire exercise. I had already drafted a paper influenced by an IBM study which argued that the linking of computers was being greatly affected by the extravagant cost of long-distance telecommunications charges, especially in Europe. We developed this idea a bit further to propose that European call rates be changed – *rebalanced* became the buzz word – so that long-distant call rates better reflected the tiny extra costs of electricity used compared to local calls. This idea fitted well into the overall strategy developed in the telecoms services paper. It was to influence major restructuring in the telecoms industry when taken up later, including the hiving off of certain ancillary services up to then undertaken only by the states' telecoms services.

In working on the telecoms report with the consultant I again appreciated the potential of fax machines. I would write a crude draft, fax it each evening to the specialist who seemed to be holed up at a different hotel in a different country each time. He would make handwritten changes and fax it back overnight. I would work this up the next day, and so on. I sweated it out with my demanding director constantly breathing down my neck, but gained a swift insight into the economics of telecommunications. We managed to meet the Delors deadline. As the result of the different sectoral studies filtered in we totalled the individual benefits to estimate the potential gains for the Community as a whole. Emerson had the mental capacity and drive to be also a good macroeconomic accountant, as he totted up a listing of almost all the manufacturing, services and other sectors. These eventually accounted for some ninety-eight per cent of all economic activities in the Member States.

The results forecast the creation of nine million extra jobs in the ensuing four years, half an extra point in GDP growth per annum, investment up by one-third between 1985 and 1990, as well as a major reduction in the amount of bureaucracy at customs controls.

The 1992 proposals were a far bigger gamble than admitted at the time, but a great success. They involved major economic restructuring, especially for the small, less competitive economies. Had our political and business leaders, trade unions and citizens not taken the proposals seriously and accepted that a radical initiative had to be taken, the doom and gloom of the 1980s would certainly have deepened. But Delors was the right person at the right time. Two of his main lieutenants in galvanising the Commission and the Member States to take the strategy seriously were Commission members Lord Cockfield, in charge of the internal market dossier, and Peter Sutherland, in charge of competition, who worked closely together to ensure success. Working on the programme inside the Commission was an informative exercise in devising and promoting a global vision, convincing the politicians, businessmen and unions to accept the risk, and designing an effective mechanism to get it successfully operational. I began to learn the difference between devising policy and delivery of results.

When it was realised that the main direct beneficiaries of opening up trade would be the business sector and owners of share capital, pressure increased to provide some *quid pro quo* to the labour sector as well, since workers would have to pay a price for the inevitable rationalisation. It was agreed by most Member States that a social dimension should be introduced in the interests of social solidarity. This was to cause political resentment in some countries later. But it had major long-term benefits for the countries and regions that were targeted by the associated Cohesion Fund.

An interesting postscript to the publication of the technical study *The Economics of 1992* was the decision to produce a popular, paperback version edited by two eminent *Financial Times* journalists, David Buchan and Nico Colchester. It became known as the *Cecchini Report* after the senior official who commissioned it. It was eventually translated into over twenty languages and became a bestseller, chalking up sales of a quarter of a million copies worldwide. We were chuffed that a report written by our oft-disparaged bureaucracy could become such a hit.

## Cohesion Assistance

The 1992 project was a particularly risky undertaking for small countries and less developed regions. The concern was that the increase in competitiveness would disproportionately benefit the bigger companies in the larger economies who would gain from comparatively larger economies of scale. To compensate the smaller countries, such as Ireland, from the stiffer winds of competition, Cohesion Funds were established to help strengthen their commercial structures. Physical and social infrastructure, especially human resources, research and innovation, were all targeted for support. This initiative was strongly supported by Commissioner Peter Sutherland and the Irish authorities. It took some time, almost a decade in Ireland's case, for the effects of this solidarity assistance to show results. As mentioned below, this involved the imposition of certain conditions vital to the successful outcome.[25]

The experience gained from the completion of Europe's internal market should surely stand as an example to other regional groupings in South America, Africa or Asia.

## Delors' Swansong

Like all statesmen Jacques Delors decided to leave a final testament before retiring and ordered what was to be a definitive and forward-looking strategy for the twenty-first century. His valedictory White Paper was eventually called *Growth, Competitiveness, Em-*

---

[25] Some years later I read in the press of developments in Mexico during their NAFTA negotiations. This arrangement seemed inspired by the success of the Community initiative, but it was not accompanied by any cohesion assistance to less developed regions to attenuate the resulting structural adjustment. I was surprised that the Mexican negotiators did not learn a lesson from the experiences of the smaller European economies as they were all in the public domain, even becoming the subject for discussion in financial and economic journals. The Mexicans might have sought similar assistance for their infrastructure as the price for agreeing to integration with their more affluent neighbours.

*ployment* and was published in 1994, just before he departed. I had transferred by then to the education and training service which I represented on the drafting group. I argued the case strongly for recognising the importance of human resources in the long-term strategy. Normally there would have been no problem with this as some policy documents can resemble a patchwork quilt; they can be decked out with all the refinements requested by the interested parties, research, entrepreneurship, innovation, education, etc. To this extent they lack a clear strategic thrust. I did not want education to be treated as another bolt-on policy. My point was that Europe had to create a knowledge-intensive, high value-added, environmentally-friendly economic structure for the twentieth century. I cited the historic Irish efforts to stimulate growth, competitiveness and quality job-creation by investing heavily in education and training. I kept nagging everyone about the importance of human resources, how it must be considered an integral component of organic growth. The theme was properly taken on board, and for the first time a major economic strategy paper integrated education and training by including a chapter arguing their combined role as a major catalyst in creating the knowledge economy. The paper acknowledged that 'in a society based far more on the production, transfer and sharing of knowledge than on the trade in goods, access to theoretical and practical knowledge must play a major role'.

This may read like bureaucratese but one should never underestimate how intensely Community documents are discussed at all levels in the partner countries before they eventually receive the green light. This commitment to reform educational and training systems in the Member States and, especially, to emphasise the importance of lifelong learning, was agreed following much discussion around the national capitals. The fact that such decisions were taken in a supranational context rather than on an intergovernmental basis (such as the case with excellent OECD studies) meant they were taken much more seriously in the national capitals and will have a long-term influence well after they have been forgotten. But one must admit some countries, especially the Scan-

dinavians, are more effective in following through these commitments than others.

The Community was very generous in the provision of assistance to the smaller Member States. Transport infrastructure and
industrial development were assisted, as well as funding for lifelong
learning and training, especially in Ireland. I recall much anecdotal
evidence of lonely Dublin housewives whose kids had departed the
nest taking up offers of computer courses with their coffee-
morning friends, little thinking they would eventually convert their
new skills into actual employment. Shortly thereafter the economy
began its spectacular boom: they found jobs, sent the kids abroad
on Erasmus or Leonardo courses, and never looked back.

Wisely, Cohesion assistance to less affluent members such as
Ireland was not handed out without conditions. The insistence on
'additionality', that the Irish government should make a parallel
contribution, was to have profound implications for the success of
this initiative, and development policy in general. This successful
strategy merits being addressed again later when looking at development in its wider, international context.

# 8

# MINDS ACROSS (FORMER) MINEFIELDS: EUROPE AS A LEARNING COMMUNITY

*At a high level of economic development ... these educational processes may be economically more valuable which far from inculcating social conformity, rather accent and provide scope for the differences in individual talents and interests, as being perhaps a necessary step in stimulating the production of new knowledge and new products.*

– OECD Report, 1965, *Investment in Education*

*If you think in terms of a year, plant a seed; if in terms of ten years, plant a tree; if in terms of 100 years, teach the people.*

– Confucius, *Analects*

*Looking back from the great civilisations of twelfth-century France or seventeenth-century Rome, it is hard to believe that for quite a long time – almost a hundred years – western Christianity survived by clinging to places like Skellig Michael, a pinnacle of rock eighteen miles from the Irish coast, rising seven hundred feet out of the sea.*

– Kenneth Clark, *Civilisation*

OVER TIME THE TREATY OF ROME was seen to suffer from many lacunae, including a lack of a solid legal basis for cooperative actions in the areas of scientific research, environmental policy and educational cooperation. Many types of research are too costly for even the largest Member State to conduct on its own so cooperation makes sense, as it does in the area of the environment since pollution is no respecter of national borders. Our gloriously diverse Community was so atomised by a multiplicity of languages and educational systems that most third-level students more readily crossed the Atlantic than European borders. We justifiably celebrate the rich cultural heterogeneity of Europe but the very diversity of languages and educational structures creates considerable barriers to any kind of student and teacher mobility. In medieval times, when Latin was the lingua franca, there was greater mobility of teaching and learning than during the twentieth century. The graduate of the medieval universities, Bologna, Paris, Padua and Oxford, received the *Licentia Ubique Docendi,* literally a licence to teach anywhere in Christendom, especially at another university.

Within the early Commission a science, research and development service had been in existence for some years conducting useful research over a wide area of disciplines. For example, after the 1973 energy crisis it was decided to cooperate on a Community basis on the developments of nuclear fusion energy as a clean alternative to fossil fuel or nuclear fission-derived energy.[1] A host of other projects covering the spectrum of science and research is now under way: fighting climate change, securing alternative energy and food sources, preventing diseases, data banks in genomics and imaging systems. Research infrastructures are becoming increasingly

---

[1] This is the means the sun has been using for a few billion years. Cooperation made sense due to the colossal costs of building and developing a fusion torus, a doughnut-shaped tube within which hydrogen particles are induced to collide with each other to create helium. It takes a massive amount of earthly energy and temperatures higher than those on the surface of the Sun just to get the process going, so it made good sense to share the cost among all members who would benefit in the distant future. The great advantage of fusing hydrogen to make helium is that the process is carbon-free and, unlike the splitting of large atoms such as uranium which leaves a lot of radioactive debris, is almost entirely emissions-free.

complex and expensive, often placing them beyond the reach of a single research group, region, nation or even continent. The sheer size of such projects, generally hundreds of millions of Euros for construction and tens of millions for operation, requires a joint effort by several European countries. Small Member States thus gain access to a wide R&D infrastructure they could never hope for on their own, assisting them to scale the ladder of higher value-added employment.

However, research projects outside the domain of the Euratom Treaty were initially undertaken in a rather dubious legal vacuum. To set this to rights a working group was established to chart out a proper legal basis. I did not participate directly in this exercise, but was asked to come up with economic arguments as to why a Community role in common research could be justified.

I thus learned an interesting lesson regarding the inclusion of a new activity in a revision of the original Rome Treaty. Some years later when I was working for the Education and Training department I proposed to Hywel Ceri Jones, the Welsh-born director and expert navigator of the corridors of power, that he consider pressing to have our education co-operation activities formally recognised in the next revision of the Treaties (which was later to become known as the Maastricht Treaty). He needed little prodding. Training was implicitly covered in the original Rome Treaty as a support to the movement of labour, but not education. Hywel proposed to Jacques Delors that there should be a clear legal basis. Delors was already conscious of the popularity of the Erasmus programme, as well as the new programmes set up with Central and Eastern European countries (CEECs) to help structural reform following the fall of the Berlin Wall. He was very reluctant to overload the new draft treaty, whose main focus was completion of the internal market, yet was highly conscious of the need to provide the Community with a human face. The wily Frenchman asked HCJ, 'mais, Monsieur Jones, est-ce les esprits sont mûrs? 'Hywel immediately informed him that the spirits, and Hywel's colleagues, were more than ripe.

With the help of his intuitive and deft legal advisor, Sarah Evans, he eventually succeeded in getting education incorporated legally in the new Treaty, the Maastricht, the second revision of the original treaty, following much discussion with Member States and the Parliament.

## To Do and Not to Do

There was one interestingly new feature of the two articles which provided the basis for cooperation in education and training. Education and training are politically sensitive policy areas which can be managed at a regional, federal, even local level, depending on the degree of delegation of decision-making. The Community has a philosophy regarding the sharing out of power at the different levels at which decisions should be taken: basically this is at the lowest and most decentralised level practical, as close as possible to the citizen. This admirable principle is described by an old seventeenth century term which, curiously, comes from the Swiss Calvinists philosophy for devolving social assistance decisions down to the parish level, *subsidiarity*. Though hardly a buzz-word likely to set the world aflame, it helps to determine at what administrative level policies on education, training, health, environment protection are decided.

The two new Treaty articles on education and training are unique in that they outline what the Community should not do, as well as what can be done, in the context of such cooperation. Both articles specifically outlaw any attempt to harmonise rules between the different states. The main objective of cooperation was identified as supporting Member States' actions, while fully respecting the responsibility of the states for the content of teaching and the organisation of education systems and their cultural and linguistic diversity.

The articles specify the sort of activities considered suitable for promotion at the Community level, such as the mobility of students and teachers, cooperation between teaching establishments, exchanges of experiences and cooperation with non-member countries.

## Europe as a Learning Community

As noted already the Treaty of Rome proposes four freedoms of movement – those for goods and services, capital and labour. Since he first arrived at the Commission, Hywel Ceri Jones (assisted *inter alia* by ex-IPA colleague Denis McGowan) regretted the absence of another freedom of trans-border movement, that of ideas and learning.  I have read that in medieval times there was greater freedom of movement of scholars and teachers and it was agreed that scholars alone were to be permitted to travel freely across political and jurisdictional borders, their books, viands and liquid refreshments tax free.[2] Hywel came up with a plan for encouraging trans-border higher educational cooperation and mobility. He adopted the name Erasmus after the Enlightenment scholar and humanitarian who had spent part of his life in Brussels.

Hywel was both the inspiration and the driving force in this and other successful programs for intra-European cooperation. He was to be assisted in this imaginative enterprise by others who recognised his vision: rectors of universities; a host of voluntary bodies, including those of students, members of the European Parliament, etc.[3]

Yet, the Erasmus program for higher education cooperation and mobility of students and teachers had a long and difficult birth: it was much contested, including by ministries of education who protested the lack of a legal basis prior to the Maastricht reform. It was eventually given the all-clear by the Court of Justice on the basis that education had a vocational as well as a metaphysical objective, and was justified as facilitating the movement of qualified labour within the Community. One institution was to provide a most valu-

---

[2] Apparently this incited a noticeable increase not only in the number of travellers citing scholarship as a reason, but of the quantity of liquid deemed necessary to prevent scholastic desiccation.

[3] A comprehensive account is provided in the study by Ms Luce Pépin, published in 2006, *The History of European Cooperation in Education and Training*.

able support, the European Parliament, which greatly appreciates such imaginative initiatives.[4]

It did not take long for universities, research and technological institutes and their faculties, teachers and students, to catch onto the possibilities offered by the new programs and for them to become exceptionally popular in academic circles. So much so that when the Berlin Wall fell one of the first actions the ministers proposed was a programme similar to Comett[5] and Erasmus for the CEECs, later for Russia and the Commonwealth of Independent States (CIS). Whereas it had taken the ministers of education years to agree to the Erasmus programme, Tempus, specially designed for the East, was agreed to by Heads of Government over a weekend at Paris. The following Monday, Hywel, with the assistance of a newly-recruited David O'Sullivan, who had earlier cut his teeth in Peter Sutherland's cabinet working on the Comett initiative, had the draft legal document ready.

Work I had done in the area of technology and innovation had come to Hywel's and David's attention so they offered me a position in their newly-created Task Force for Education and Training. I was at first reluctant to leave the intellectually-challenging economics service. I had worked for three years with a genial and talented colleague, Silvano Presa. In addition my ex-director, the exceptionally capable Giovanni Ravasio, was about to take up his position as Director General.[6]

Difficult as it was, I decided it was time for a change. I departed my economics service colleagues to take up responsibility for the Comett university-industry program under the leadership of David O'Sullivan. Since I had had the good fortune to visit science parks

---

[4] Two members of the Committee for Education and Culture who were strongly supportive of our cooperation with North America were Daniel – Danny the Red – Cohn-Bendit MEP, a leader of the Paris students' protests in 1968, and Mrs Mary Banotti MEP.

[5] As a matter of history the Comett programme, for trans-border cooperation in teaching new technologies, was actually established shortly before Erasmus.

[6] Giovanni later applied his penetrating intelligence and drive to play a major role in helping usher in the Euro.

across the US, I was also asked by David to help set in motion a new initiative agreed by the Heads of Government under the 1990 Transatlantic Declarations to cooperate also across the Atlantic with the US and Canada. This sounded very interesting and challenging. I learned how challenging when I realised that the busy Heads of Government had not followed-up by pressing its merits upon their own education colleagues. It was to prove demanding to get the education ministers to agree to implement the idea. I was reminded that a joint declaration by heads of government is but a good intention and does not constitute a legal basis. I was to learn that there is a major difference between coming up with an idea, getting legislative approval and setting up a good organisational mechanism for implementation – willing the end but not the means. Turning lofty aspirations and good intentions into earthly achievements takes a considerable amount of perseverance.

## Towards a Community of Ideas and Learning

Since the Communities were set up Europe has, for the longest period of recorded history, been spared the cycle of destruction and slaughter which peaked with the horrific wars of the first half of the twentieth century. Total warfare, during which science and technology were perverted into the service of slaughter, called into question the very notion of a European civilisation. The routine savagery caused a chasm to open up to almost engulf a long tradition of science and learning. The plumbing of the intellectual wellsprings had been the hallmark of Europe as an incubator of civilisation, learning and culture. Then the rise of totalitarianism in the 1920s and 1930s provoked the exodus of a generation of the brightest Continental minds, some to the UK, many more to the congenial campuses of American universities and research laboratories.[7]

A further and more prosaic social challenge arose towards the end of the century: the previous link between economic growth and social progress was rent. Not only was Europe failing to create suf-

---

[7] Two of the brightest, Erwin Schroedinger and Cornelius Lanczos, came to the Institute for Advanced Studies in Dublin.

ficient high value-added, knowledge-intensive jobs, we were also losing those which traditionally absorbed the less-qualified workers. Employment not being lost to the US was leeching out to South East Asia. The social cohesion which had been so laboriously built up after the war was unravelling.

This is one of the reasons that Jacques Delors had promoted the idea of social justice to complement the gains owners of capital were likely to make from the completion of the internal market. Increasing competition was likely to squeeze employment levels. The growing level of unemployment, particularly among the young, forced policy-makers to address the social question as an equally valid objective of European construction, *pari passu* with that of economic growth. Social affairs ministers agreed that an initiative to reinforce social justice be introduced as a quid-pro-quo for the dislocation caused by market integration. It was agreed that the providers of education and training, in particular, would have to adapt their horizons to the new demands of the jobs market. Education leads to self-fulfilment, but people only reach their full potential when they become gainfully employed in some activity which contributes physically or aesthetically to the improvement of civil society. Community initiatives were designed to complement and reinforce national actions by promoting improvement in the quality of teaching and learning over a lifetime, mainly by sharing experiences and best practice, and promoting more and better life-long educational and training systems. These initiatives coincided with the historic introduction of *Perestroika* and *Glasnost* in the USSR by that great twentieth century liberator Mikhail Gorbachev.

Discussions during ministerial meetings at the Council considered initiatives to assist the restructuring of the societies released from the bonds of Marxist orthodoxy and Soviet hegemony. In the area of education much of the work of the Education Council was taken up with discussion of efforts to assist reform of education and training structures in the CEECs and the CIS, and the possibility of their cooperation with and integration into the scientific, educational and research initiatives of the Community. These efforts were detailed, technical and time-consuming, news of which was not likely to enhance sales of the popular press; it was a silent revolution of intense effort which was to lead to a major redesign of the political and intellectual landscape of the Continent. Recently some commentators have criticised the US and Europe for not doing more to help Eastern Europe in the years after the fall of the Berlin Wall: my recollection is that it was a time of intense if little publicised cooperation.

## A Hallowed Tradition

The tradition of intellectual exchange is far older than the Community programmes, the scholarships generously offered by American philanthropists, or even Erasmus himself. After all, the canon of western literature and science is a palimpsest of European, Arab, Indian, and Chinese know-how and know-why. Alexander the Great disseminated Greek culture and literature in Central Asia and India in the fourth century BC, providing channels for subsequent reverse filtering of learning. Early Islamist teachers eagerly sought out Greek learning – in medicine, geometry, philosophy, astronomy – and preserved much of classical civilisation in their magnificent libraries. While the Romans were practical people and good engineers they were not renowned as deep thinkers. Roman numerals were almost useless for calculation, unless one used an abacus, while it was the Arabs who provided us with a system for calculating large numbers, aided by the Indians who contributed the concept of zero.

In addition, China provided Europe with important advances in technology: paper, porcelain, woodblock printing, silk and gunpowder. The Europeans positively snapped up these new Oriental innovations. Later, European exploration and colonisation depended on being able to sail upwind, which the Portuguese caravel (inspired by Arab dhow designs) first allowed, thus fostering sea routes which became the sinews of the new maritime empire.

After the fall of the Western Roman Empire most classical learning was lost except for repositories in Arab libraries in North Africa and Andalusia, in monasteries in Ireland, Scotland, northern

England, and Byzantium,[8] as well as in some remote monasteries in the Fertile Crescent (Syria, Iraq and Egypt). Irish and Scottish monastic schools preserved portions of Greco-Roman literature, and later helped to reignite the flame of classical learning in Continental Europe. In addition to copying the sacred texts the Irish scholars are also reputed to have copied many pagan philosophical texts. And the importance of exactitude when copying by hand should not be underestimated, many classical texts being considerably corrupted over time.[9] Peripatetic Irish teachers who fanned out to dispel the Dark Ages across the Continent had their efforts championed by Charlemagne who commenced his great European educational renaissance at Aix-la-Chapelle, modern day Aachen.

During the later medieval period Continental scholars began to travel to Moorish Spain, Al-Andalus, to explore the treasures of Islamic libraries. Although one could dispute just how much or how little the Islamists assimilated from Greek, Persian and Indian learning and culture, as opposed to religious belief, they were sufficiently open-minded to conserve and diffuse a considerable amount of Greek natural science, geometry, medicine and astronomy which they had rescued from destruction or oblivion during earlier wars of conquests. They themselves added considerably to the sum of scientific knowledge, especially in the areas of astronomy and mapping the stars.[10] In most cases the original Greek edi-

---

[8] The Byzantines of the Eastern Empire preserved many Greek learned texts and welcomed Greek scholars to their centres of learning until the near disastrous battle of Manzikert in 1071, and to a lesser extent until the fall of Constantinople in 1453

[9] In Ireland teaching in the monasteries was based on the *quadrivium*, mathematics, geometry, astronomy and music. This would suggest that some of the texts of classical science must have been preserved in Irish monasteries, not only in Muslim libraries in Spain. Incidentally, monastic reproduction gave rise to the first recorded judgement regarding copyright. When studying under St Finnian in the sixth century the student Colmcille surreptitiously copied a book of psalms, the property of Finnian, who took him to court. High King Diarmuid offered the following adjudication, 'to every cow its calf and to every book its copy'. The copy was duly returned to Finnian and is now housed at the Royal Irish Academy.

[10] Though we in the west like to claim that the universities of Bologna and Paris were among the very earliest, proto-universities had been established in Baghdad,

tions had been lost and only Arabic translations were available. A veritable cortège of European scholars descended on Spain: those who had no Arabic depended on local Jews and Spaniards who had. Following the *reconquista* the results of such study spread to centres of learning in other parts of Europe – some historians argue that it provided the initial creative spark for the Italian Renaissance.

Up to the thirteenth century European centres of learning were based within monastic or cathedral schools of theology and philosophy. With the expansion of the economy in the late thirteenth century there was an increasing desire amongst the laity for learning, including the vocationally-directed and, more and more, this was provided by the new universities, initially centres of teaching or guilds for teachers, often attached to centres of church learning.

Medieval student mobility was also driven by the need for aspiring students from poor regions to seek education at the nearest centre available, frequently in another state or principality. With the coming of the Renaissance the search for knowledge was driven more by humanistic, cultural and intellectual, as well as professional and vocational considerations. Italy was particularly popular and students from all over Northern and Western Europe crowded into centres of learning at Bologna, Pisa, Siena, Perugia and Florence. By the middle of the sixteenth century a high proportion of students in northern Italy came from across the Alps. Such mobility was greatly assisted by the fact that Latin was the *lingua franca* of learning across the entire Continent.

But the comings of the Reformation and subsequent religious wars, and provisions of the Treaty of Westphalia, were to throw up all types of barriers to student and teacher mobility. The increasing introduction of books published in languages other than Latin, the growth of introverted nationalism in the nineteenth century, and the recruitment of civil servants who had followed a statutory national curriculum of studies, were to further dissuade students from

---

Samarkand, Fez and Cairo centuries earlier. The beginning of the end of Islamic scientific learning came about with the destruction of Baghdad by the Mongols in 1258.

following the hallowed *peregrinatio academica.* The grabbing of power by ideological dictators in the inter-war period of the twentieth century was but the final nail in the coffin of trans-national intellectual interchange, though a most effective catalyst in encouraging Europe's best to cross the wide Atlantic.

Post-war revulsion against the bestiality of total warfare and the obscenity of Marxism and Nazism, and the historic declaration by Gorbachev in 1988 that the people of each country had the right to decide on their own system of governance, provided the incentive to promote cooperation between neighbours, and what better a domain than that of learning and teaching, the very wellspring of the older and more hallowed tradition.

## A Palette of Programmes

In addition to third-level education a number of other areas for cooperation were identified by Hywel, mainly because of an obvious need for specially-targeted programmes addressing specific needs. Some, like those for distance learning or lifelong learning for adults, were identified as part of a strategic review of human resource needs and the possibility of exploiting the latest communications technologies. Others, like Comett for high-tech training, to complement the research programs, and Tempus, for cooperating with the CEECs, were introduced on an *ad hoc* basis. Some of the older programmes such as Comett and Tempus were acronyms for their objectives whose full titles are now rarely used. Others, such as Force were coined from the French for *formation continue*, or lifelong training.[11]

When the Erasmus third-level mobility and cooperation programme was proposed to create a genuine European higher education community, there was very little intra-European student mobility. Most were transatlantic endeavours with European postgraduate students undertaking PhD work at US universities.

---

[11] Again, those interested in a detailed history of all these initiatives should look to the comprehensive work of Ms Luce Pepin, *op cit.*

When working in the economic service I mentioned to an academic contact that we expected to secure a tiny part of the new R&D budget for economic research, and that this would involve some trans-border cooperation within the EC. He seemed highly perplexed, declaring that the only form of trans-border cooperation possible in the area of economics had to be transatlantic. He was convinced it would be impossible to get European economists to cooperate if no US universities were involved, and could not possibly imagine what intra-European cooperation could contribute. The programme was set up, publicised and finance was offered for innovative proposals. Once the money was on the table it was amazing how many European economic researchers suddenly had a spark of imagination and recalled colleagues they had met at conferences past who would join in some interesting transnational project.

## Deterrents to Mobility

Foreign travel and accommodation costs represent major impediments for a student, but the primary deterrent to international mobility is that of time. If the student does not have the semester or year abroad recognised at the home college, this amounts to a huge lost investment for a usually impoverished student. This called for the establishment of a system of student credits, so that time spent in the partner institution counted. Setting up such a system for accumulation and transfer of study credits acceptable across the Continent involving the range of faculties was to prove a massive exercise in consultation and design, but was critical to the success of the Erasmus exercise, and later to that of Tempus with the CEECs. A proto-system was initially introduced in straightforward areas such as engineering, architecture and commercial law, where teaching modules were relatively similar across borders. A great amount of work and dedication was needed to ensure its gradual acceptance in different faculties. This European Credit Transfer System, ECTS, was eventually extended to almost all fields of lifelong learning in Europe, and even adopted by other geographic areas, such as Asia, which was also willing to encourage international cooperation. ECTS was a major instrument for ensuring European academic cooperation and was critical to the adoption years later by an inter-governmental grouping of European education ministers for the harmonising of higher education structures under the 'Bologna' process.

Initially the unofficial target for Erasmus student mobility was ten per cent of all higher education students in the Community and associated countries.[12] But the number of students in higher education has rocketed in recent years (now totalling over 17 million students and 4,000 universities) and it was realised that the authors were aiming at a rapidly expanding and moving target. In the last number of years well over one million students have spent a semester or year in another partner country institution for which transferable study credits had been arranged. Hundreds of thousands of teachers and thousands of institutions have been involved. Based on anecdotal evidence among the children of friends, I have often noticed how frequently our efforts to link minds across frontiers had also linked hearts.

## Training for Technological Change

As noted above, Europe of the 1990s was still capable of outstanding scientific and technical advance but the Americans and Japanese had taken the lead with innovation and, hence, they employed considerably greater numbers in such high-value-added sectors, both industry and services. European inventors are comparatively far less capable of converting the fruits of their creative breakthroughs into quality, knowledge-intensive jobs, innovation as opposed to invention. They lack such imaginative conduits as the plentiful supply of risk capital and active panoply of back-up firms, not to mention the greater willingness of Americans to hear out someone with a bright new idea. With the setting up of the major research and information technology programs mentioned above, it was soon realised that just succeeding with the research and technology would be of little avail if the advances were not ac-

---

[12] The EFTA countries and Switzerland joined subsequently.

companied by the training of workers in the specific skills. Without the new skills on the factory floor as well as in management and marketing it would be impossible to ensure the diffusion of this pervasive technology across the Community's industry base.

As a result, the Comett program was set up. It was based on three main pillars: it was designed as a transnational action with a number of states necessarily involved in each project; it had to involve both enterprises and universities; and it had to involve new product or process technology. It could also involve services; for example, one project involved cooperative banks in Austria, Germany and Italy combining efforts to achieve the economies of scale needed to introduce new information technology systems. These small local banks simply lacked the extensive financial resources of the large commercial banks. Another project involved over one hundred universities and business partners in the designing of a new curriculum for the teaching of biotechnology. Hundreds of such creative and innovative projects were set up, to the envy of some overseas industrialists who lamented the lack of such a facility in their home countries. For once Europe had created an innovative structure that many Americans came to appreciate and envy at that time.

By the time I was involved in the mid-1990s the programme had supported some 3,000 projects, helped some 200 university-industry partnerships, arranged some tens of thousands of transnational exchanges of students and enterprise personnel and developed thousands of training courses. I recall one French motor manufacturer introducing a new and technically-advanced model. With the help of Comett the company developed a multi-language CD for the use of garage personnel which was interactive and explained all the requirements for the repair and maintenance of the new model.

The diffusion of technology can prove rather complex, hence the complicated structure of the Comett programme which never caught the public imagination as Erasmus did. Yet it fulfilled a valuable, if little-heralded, role in establishing the nerve endings of cooperation among innovative industry and technical institutes across Europe. It included the twelve Member States and EFTA. Organising so many projects, regional university-enterprise networks, thematic networks (biotech, lasers, CAD-CAM, etc.), student, teacher and researcher mobility, with associated credit transfers, involved an immense amount of managerial and secretarial work. The University-Enterprise Training Partnerships, despite their cumbersome title, UETPs, played a significant role in the success of the programme since the regional ones, which complemented sectoral-specific ones, eventually covered most regions of the community. Based on a lead institution they linked up technical institutes and innovating industry on a local basis, so helping to bring new technology to outlying regions. In all this the Commission was immeasurably assisted by the efforts of a technical assistance office (TAO).[13] In the context of the new challenges facing the Irish economy and the need to restructure Irish education towards greater innovation and creativity, rather than rote learning, the lessons of Comett could prove of considerable value.

## Changing the Guard

In addition to the programs mentioned, there were others, less well-know, such as for adult and distance learning, LINGUA for languages, PETRA for youth training, COMENIUS for schools co-operation, an information network, etc. These were all designed to terminate in 1994 so as to allow a reflection on their future in the light of their track record. They had all been designed to address specific challenges and lacunae in our education systems, and were perfectly simple and logical to stakeholders in the different areas, but their number meant that outsiders who were not conversant with needs in specific areas of education thought they were too prolific. It was decided to streamline: this effort was driven by our new Commissioner, Professor Ruberti, an ex-Minister for Education

---

[13] All programs had their own specific TAOs. The Commission just did not have enough personnel to manage the programs. The Director of the Comett TAO for most of its life was one Ed Prosser, a dynamic Scotsman. He was assisted by a highly competent and motivated team of some 60 co-workers.

in Italy, who determined to reduce their number to two. Hywel Jones, who by then had left our service to take over management of the social affairs service, pleaded that their number could not logically be reduced below four, or at least three, otherwise many of their essential attributes would be diluted and lost. Prof. Ruberti and the Council committees for education and training discussed the renewal at length and delivered their informed opinion. I feared that Comett would suffer the most from streamlining, and fought hard to prevent its incorporation into a more generalist action, but the oracles were of another opinion and it was decided to standardise on two major new programs: one, Leonardo da Vinci, for training, and Socrates for education, with a new and separate programme for schools. Erasmus was subsumed into Socrates.[14]

I believed that it was a great pity to have incorporated the unique actions of the Comett program, which cut across the distinctions in certain Member States between universities and technical institutes, and broke down barriers between education and training, into the overall programme for training. To many the new twin structure was simple and logical, and locating Comett with vocational training and away from higher educational research institutes represented the Judgement of Solomon. I ruefully reflected that in this case the eminent judges had actually proceeded to chop the baby in two.

As mentioned, a weakness of European policy-making, except for the Nordic States, is a failure fully to understand the intricacies of innovation. The success of such large economies-of-scale technology projects as Ariane, Airbus, the TGV, are to be celebrated but we are not sufficiently aware of the potential of small-scale innovations produced by lonely inventors. With only a few exceptions (especially GSM for mobile phones) Europe does not properly appreciate the economics of technical standards. It is difficult to convince policy-makers as to the difference between invention and its

---

[14] Erasmus's unrelenting director, Domenico Lenarduzzi, guardian of the flame, tenaciously fought to retain the popular brand name – and succeeded. In this he was strongly supported by newly-appointed director general Tom O'Dwyer.

successful commercial introduction as innovation. Innovation is often assumed to be merely part of a continuum automatically resulting from R&D spending. The absence of an experienced venture-capital industry to support the commercial success of breakthroughs made in laboratories by individual researchers, the ludicrous absence of a real European-wide patent system (all because of a linguistic dispute), bilateral exchanges between lab and workshop, the absence of an entrepreneurial mindset, are all underestimated. This weakness and a failure properly to develop the instruments necessary to increase the success rate for innovation must be overcome if Europe is to tackle the looming horrors of the current financial meltdown. The reduction of structural unemployment will not be assisted by the reawakening of the long-dormant giants China, and to a lesser extent India, with their ancient heritage of culture, education and craftwork, as they cast off the fetters of feudal bureaucracy and patronage which have so long constrained their natural potential and embrace meritocracy.

## External Cooperation

In the run-up to 1992 some pundits latched onto a new buzz word, Fortress Europe. The education and training programs of the Community could never be described as representing such a redoubt. Early on they were opened to the EFTA countries. Though some countries, such as Switzerland and Norway, had decided against joining the Community there were many people in these countries who favoured cooperation in certain areas. It was considered that the friendly spirits should not be excluded from such popular actions as Erasmus and Comett. So it was agreed, as with non-members of a golf club, that they could pay green fees and play when they wanted.[15] In addition, the pre-accession countries were generally keen to get their feet in the door via such internal programs as R+D and education. It probably is not well known outside the world of officialdom the degree to which links have been estab-

---

[15] They had to pay special 'green fees', since their countries were not paying into the common budget, so they paid *à la carte*.

lished in the research and education area with neighbours who extend from Galway to Vladivostok, from Helsinki to southern Mongolia.

As mentioned the Tempus program was the first to formally involve the CEECs, late in 1989. It was based on a combination of the best bits of Comett and Erasmus and it had special features to ensure mutual respect between the interests and special challenges of the new partners. One of the main objectives was to help with the structural change of higher education in the former Warsaw Pact states. Thematic areas such as law, economics, health, agriculture, the environment, were popular subjects, addressed at filling lacunae in academic curricula. In some of these institutes, especially in Russia, the standards of instruction and learning in such areas as science, engineering and maths were of the very highest, though there was a desperate lack of modern computers.

Projects were solicited on a bottom-up basis, in other words, faculty members who wished to submit a project proposal did it directly to the Tempus secretariat, and these were scrutinised and selected on a merit basis. This process, which allowed the most junior lecturer in his faculty with a promising proposal to submit it directly to the programme secretariat, have it assessed and selected on merit by impartial peer review, was something which caused a considerable degree of bafflement, if not consternation, in ministries which had hitherto exercised complete control over anything that moved in the area under their remit. We were allowing, even encouraging, ordinary citizens to bypass the *apparatchiks*. Proposals could be submitted without the previous dozen rubber stampings, each of which had to be beseeched, even remunerated, preferably both. There were a number of very memorable reactions in certain countries.

The main types of project favoured were Joint European Projects, JEPs, involving a number of institutions in the partner counties in cooperation with institutions in a minimum of three EC states. By designing the project in this fashion a small, inexperienced grouping in a new partner country could tap into the experi-

ence of a wider Western grouping and gain greater leverage.[16] This
European emphasis was on the projects, not on scholarships, which
was the main instrument used by the Americans with their Fulbright program. We did offer a number of associated scholarships
but these were only supported if seen to underpin overall objectives. We did not wish to encourage a sudden brain drain; it was
considered better to leave the brighter students at home where
their presence was considered supportive to the quality of teaching
and learning.

Tempus also financed the setting up of computer labs which
were in great demand at that time. Some of the colleagues who
were helping out *sur place* would return to base with stories of eager, aspiring east European 'geeks' desperately signing on to share a
computer at 3.30a.m. on a Sunday morning.

## Sharing Insights across the Atlantic

With the fall of the Berlin Wall and the break-up of the former Soviet Union, the CEECs reacted by looking westwards. Academic institutions cut off from contact with the West were especially desperate to re-establish the old contacts of generations before and set
up new faculties in the areas of law, business, politics and philosophy. The EC and US responded by sending experts to visit ministries of education and institutions, many of which were desperately
short of local, never mind foreign, currency. The EC had little experience in this area, the US even less, though the US had shrewdly
pioneered offering scholarships to their best universities to top
flight Soviet students, including the eager children of the *nomenklatura*. The US had their own ideas as to how to cooperate – they
were also prepared to learn from others. Hearing of the success of
the Erasmus programme officials from the USIA, which ran the
Fulbright exchange program, and the US Department of Education,
USED, called to Brussels to learn what they could of the Commu-

---

[16] We had wished to encourage trans-border cooperation among the citizens of the
Eastern bloc but it was not politically acceptable, they all wanted to have their
own specific share of the financial pie, apart from other difficulties.

nity experience, especially the new Tempus action. Contacts with USIA, USED and the Commission resulted in an agreement to share experiences and avoid duplicating efforts. During this halcyon period of goodwill and enthusiasm we enjoyed a most congenial cooperation with our new East European partners as with US programs, both governmental and private. Complementary actions became the order of the day – mostly, if not always.[17]

These exchanges were facilitated by the fact that in 1990 the Heads of Government in the EC, the US and Canada signed up to the Transatlantic Declarations.[18] In this they agreed to a number of areas for cooperation, including education.

When we tried to implement the agreement we were met with considerable reluctance on the part of some EC educational ministries. Not that they were opposed to cooperation with our transatlantic friends, but in some countries any funds allocated to international education activities are deducted from the existing education budgets.

The Americans were very keen to start cooperating with us. Initially they wished to join Erasmus but Hywel had to explain diplomatically that Erasmus had to reject many applicants due to lack of funds and it would not be politically astute if the disappointed read that American students were accepted and they were excluded (though the Americans were more than ready to pay their share of costs). Hywel and David believed we needed a specially tailored action. Our external relations colleagues were also keen that we fulfil what had been promised, especially when agricultural trade negotiations with the US reached a testy stage. We beseeched the Education Committee of the Council to provide funds to match what the Americans were proposing and were eventually authorised to start an experimental action. This was on the condition that

[17] Unfortunately, influential consultants managed to convince the Russians of the superiority of big-bang structural changeover to Anglo-Saxon neo-conomics, paving the way for the rise of the oligarchs.

[18] Considering the unilateralist instincts of President George W. Bush, the earlier period under his father must be reflected on wistfully as a golden era of international cooperation.

it did not duplicate anything Member States were already doing, that it somehow presented a special Community dimension and would offer a balance of benefits to both sides. This was eminently sensible and we went for it. Next task was to convert these guidelines into specific lines of action, and then try to convince our transatlantic partners to accept the value of the model.

The Member States, insofar as they had bilateral cooperation programmes with the US, such as the German Marshall Program, based these on the provision of scholarships for student exchanges. With our experiences of Erasmus and Tempus we were interested in setting up something innovative and appealing to young students, not costly bilateral student exchanges, but to provide seed funding for original forms of transatlantic cooperation. We believed these should be based not on universities as such, but organised at a faculty level, such as curriculum design for new subjects such as biotechnology and the environment.

Agreement was arrived at whereby the EC side accepted a minimum of three European partners in each cooperative consortium while the US, not used to such cooperation (their universities declared themselves to be in competition with each other), insisted on a minimum of two partners. Funding was to be provided for three years, while projects were to show signs of sustainability in the long run.

The model was to prove very successful at promoting sustainable transatlantic links between university faculties. Although there was only a very limited number of student and teacher exchanges these visitors did have the effect of establishing good contacts, which eventually led to much *virtual* mobility with the use of the new e-mail system. A combination of faculty cooperation and a limited amount of personal exchanges created the infrastructure for a multiplicity of informal contacts and exchanges proving the cost-effectiveness of the consortium cooperation model.

I occasionally caused American eyebrows to be raised in surprise when I argued that the reason for the success of our programs was that we were not so hung-up on students' exam results but on their overall ability to integrate socially, culturally and intellectually abroad, not just at the academic level. Personal ability, drive and emotional intelligence entered the equation more on the European side.

## Canada

The Canadians were very keen on a similar agreement. I had been advised to proceed slowly due to staff shortages.[19] I consulted with the small staff, including Marion van Mackelenberg whom I had recruited from the Comett program, and decided that with a bit of good will and extra effort we could progress with Canada *pari passu*. Tom O'Dwyer was fully supportive.

It is one thing to get legal agreement to the general format for joint action but quite another to work out the many practical details and mechanics, which must include a joint call for tender, explaining to potential candidates exactly what topics should be proposed, how the proposals should be presented, arranging peer review and for final joint selection, as well as managing the project over a three-year life. For our internal programmes we had a quaint old name for such a blueprint: the *Vademecum* (literally 'go with me'). Within the Community such a document often needed months of discussion among Member States' stakeholders to get final agreement on all sides.

Luckily I had on my little team an extremely experienced Scots lady, Constance Meldrum, who had years of experience organising Erasmus in British universities and later working for the Erasmus secretariat in Brussels. She thus had invaluable experience with the submission of applications as well as assessing them. (I occasionally teased her that she was an ex-poacher turned gamekeeper.)

We drew up the vital document which outlined the nuts and bolts of organising joint consortium projects first with the Canadians. Work started in Ottawa one frosty January morning, a start which was far from auspicious. The first item on both French and

---

[19] With the departure of my two former bosses, Hywel and David, I was acting head of section for almost a year until a reorganisation and a new Director General, Tom O'Dwyer, was appointed.

English radio channels was of a major row which had just broken out between Canada and the EC. Apparently the Canadian coast guard had arrested an overzealous Spanish fishing trawler off the Newfoundland Banks in what our Community colleagues considered international waters, but domestic by Canada. Canadian public opinion reacted as if the Armada had been reconstituted and was invading their northern fastness. The Spanish position was defended vigorously on radio and TV by the newly-appointed and feisty Italian Commissioner Signora Emma Bonino, responsible for the fishery policy. She stated her position clearly and uncompromisingly: *c'est de la piraterie* (it's piracy) in her best Italian-French accent.[20]

Constance and I got down to work with our Canadian counterparts from the Foreign Ministry and the Education Department. By that Thursday evening we had wrapped up drafting the document: Constance reminded me that with each Erasmus cycle it had sometimes taken months of discussions with all the interested parties to arrive at the final outline of such a complicated arrangement. We succeeded mainly because we devised a very useful method of working together. Each morning we would meet for late breakfast and discuss the draft; by midday we had it revised to our satisfaction and faxed it up the road to the ministry. We would then take a leisurely stroll along the deeply-frozen Rideau Canal with its ice-skaters so reminiscent of scenes from a Breughel painting. During that time our interlocutors would discuss the draft and suggest changes to the text. Joint discussions would commence at 2.00 p.m. and continue until the evening, when we would call a halt. Next

---

[20] John Beck, Head of Delegation, Frank Deeg, the local Commission Science and Education Counsellor, and senior Canadian officials were all very pleased that we continued to negotiate as it showed a partner country could have a disagreement with the Community in one area yet continue dialogue in another. This was not the only time that the Community had a serious trade argument with a foreign country and was happy to continue dialogue in the less sensitive areas of education and culture. At about the same time Commissioner MacSharry was involved in intense negotiations with the US on a major international trade round involving reform of the agricultural supports.

morning we would have received a fax from the Canadians and the process would continue once more.

The Canadians appreciated the three-partners-by-three formula, though we had not yet fully convinced our US colleagues of its inherent value. For the Canadians one considerable attraction of this innovative model was that it was the first time they had instituted inter-provincial cooperation between Quebec-based colleges and those in Anglophone Canada.

As a further example of exemplary international relations we agreed to hold joint annual review meetings with all North American partners, including Mexico,[21] alternately in Europe and North America. The experience the EC had gained in the area of credit transfers was especially valuable to success as each consortium was allowed a limited number of transatlantic student placements for the second and third years.

The real success of the programmes lay in the many intangible activities undertaken, such as developing new teaching curricula in academically-advancing, multi-disciplinary areas of study (such as the environment), or in the design of new teaching materials.

Our activities were later subject to scrutiny by outside external evaluators. They discovered that an additional benefit was the promotion of 'virtual' mobility. It was estimated that in each of the participating institutions about 60 students engaged in some form of transatlantic virtual mobility using the web or e-mail.

Our initial applications *Vademecum* totalled eight pages: a couple of years later some of our participants took some administrative shortcuts and we were forced to stiffen conditions to protect public monies: the document ballooned to over 30 pages.

## Involving the Regions

One additional benefit from the multi-partner consortium model for cooperation was that it achieved a good regional spread. We

---

[21] The US and Canada later decided to set up a similarly-designed action with Mexico in the context of the NAFTA Agreement.

were initially concerned that the majority of applications would only come from the UK, Ireland, the Netherlands and France. The objective of the program was to ensure participation of all Community members and regions. In fact what happened was that the lead partners had already considerable experience cooperating on a bilateral basis; with the coming of the multilateral model these pulled in additional partners from other countries, especially from institutions in the distant regions of Europe and North America. Faculties in less advanced regions which had wanted to set up international cooperation, but had no hope due to the lack of money and manpower, were thus able to join in and many of these became extremely active when the work progressed. I recall a visit of a French lady professor from a prestigious Haute Ecole who told me she had first set up contact with a US Ivy League college. The venerable US partner initially objected to any form of cooperation with another US college. He recalled that his was a prestigious college which did not have to cooperate with any other US college, while they considered all other Ivy Leagues as their competitors. OK, he was told, in that case you cannot participate at all. Reluctantly he recruited as partner a state university from the mid-west, with its traditional public service role. The French lady told me these newcomers were so happy to become involved that they were even more impressive and committed partners than the Ivy League people.

The regional spread was such that in one case five of six partners were situated north of the Arctic Circle in Finland, Sweden and Canada. It was a trans-polar consortium designed with the idea of setting up a University of the Arctic which could cater especially for indigenous Inuit-Sami people.

The topics for cooperation ranged from mathematics, engineering, agriculture, biotechnology, forestry management, nursing, coastal development, child abuse and protection, curricula for deaf persons, tele-detection from space, and many other innovative proposals.

By the time I handed over that activity in 2002 there were many hundreds of US, Canadian and European colleges cooperating on hundreds of different topic areas.

## Working with the North Americans

The honesty and professionalism of the Canadian and American colleagues were very impressive. We were at first concerned that each side would seek advantage for themselves, especially during the final bilateral selection of projects. The US team from FIPSE proceeded with the same high professionalism that the US research community employs in selecting competitive R&D projects, using peer review. They sent out the proposals to professors around the country for multiple reviews. In Brussels we convened a meeting of 24 independent experts from the Member States. Each proposal was given to three separate reviewers to assess and rate. If anybody was in any possible way likely to be compromised by knowing an institution or teacher, that evaluator would withdraw himself or herself. We bent over backwards to ensure the honesty and objectivity of the selection. Eventually, having made the initial selection on each side and established short lists based on the total of the three assessors' marks, we then met our transatlantic partner for the final joint selection. Though initially wary, both sides soon accepted that there was no point in pushing for a project which was unlikely to succeed. Neither side would benefit. This procedure was necessary as we always had far less money than we wished, and could not finance more than thirteen or so project groupings with the US, and about six with Canada.

No matter how successful we were at reaching the final listing we always felt sad for the unsuccessful candidates, some of whom spent months putting together their proposals. Due to the Freedom of Information Act in the US the unsuccessful candidates had to be provided with copies of the US evaluations. We were concerned on our side that that this procedure would cause European evaluators to soft-pedal their assessments. So, in a spirit of transparency, we would verbally provide the unsuccessful candidates on our side with a full feedback as to the evaluator's assessment, though without disclosing their identity. It was thus possible for a candidate to review and improve the submission for a further round, including the bringing in of new partners from outlying regions – though selection was still decided on the basis of competitive merit.

I recall my colleague Constance's observation that the consortium model is both democratic and cost-effective, while she considered transatlantic scholarships-for-the-best-and-brightest to be 'a limousine service for the fortunate few'.

## Institution Building in LDCs – A Suggestion

If the above recital reads somewhat detailed and bureaucratic the experience gained from such multi-partner cooperation projects could surely be used to a far greater degree in assisting vital institution building in developing countries. Granted, it is much more labour intensive than the more straightforward formula of offering scholarships in the hope that the fortunate scholars will eventually return to their home countries, accepting lowly salaries, bringing know-how and insights.   The Community has not been nearly as successful as it might in helping fragile and failed states, despite an extremely generous aid budget. If, as argued later in the addendum on development, the EU is to make a greater contribution to institution building in Third World countries, or if the advice of the European Council on Foreign Relations were heeded and the EU set up a 'European Institute for Peace' then, instead of hiring expensive consultants, the *acquis* is there already in the experience of the education cooperation service – especially in their tried and trusted vademecums.

## Policy Wonk

The year 2002 witnessed major changes of organisation and personnel, and the Director General kindly allowed me to choose a new arena. After ten years of rewarding programme management I returned to the guild of policy wonks. I threw in my lot with a highly capable and dynamic Greek lady, Angelique (Kiki) Verli, who also handled our relations with the Council. This was the unit which was to develop strategy, draft policy papers and speeches for the Commissioner, and pursue with the Council the follow-up to the Lisbon Agenda. The objectives of Lisbon are now somewhat embarrassing to cite: the strategic goal was that Europe should be the most dynamic and competitive knowledge-based economy and society in the world by 2010, capable of sustainable economic growth with more and better jobs and greater social cohesion. Our task was to use our long experience to encourage the Member States to raise their game in the area of lifelong learning and achieve the challenging vision proposed by Lisbon.[22]

My main tasks were to represent the policies and priorities of the education service and interact with ideas and policies coming out of other proactive services.

The formal acceptance by our overall political bosses, following the Lisbon summit, that the diffusion of knowledge was as important as its creation and application, provided me with an opportunity to join an exceptionally creative and active team. We were then working for a Community of twenty-five partner countries, shortly thereafter to become twenty-seven, up from the nine of 1973.

The Lisbon Agenda was named after the initiative of the Portuguese Presidency in 2000 which decided that the only future for Europe lay in specialising in knowledge-intensive, high value-added activities.[23] I felt that the pigeons had finally come home to roost. Having studied the economics of education and science aeons ago at UCD I was about to approach retirement harping on about the same theme. I had to prepare a paper for Education Ministers which boiled down, in clear, convincing language, the complexities of economic growth theory, the latest thinking as to the sources of economic growth, and concrete evidence as to the returns to investment in education and training. These new ideas represent the contribution of education and scientific progress as integral components of the growth process. I tried to highlight the contribution of lifelong learning as an organic component of the

---

[22] Some members, especially the northerners, made the effort and were pretty successful; there was stiff resistance to change from others, especially students and teachers who went into the streets to protest in some capitals, and reform was blocked. Still, as a sportsperson will tell you, you have to set the bar at its highest if you want to succeed.

[23] It was proposed by the eminent Portuguese, Professor Maria Joao Rodrigues of the Institute for Strategic and International Studies (IEEI), who was advisor to the Prime Minister.

growth of an economy, and to eliminate the traditional mental barriers erected in Europe which compartmentalise science, research, development and education.

There is nothing like an idea whose time has come. Having been endorsed by the Heads of Government we now had a visa to push the importance of education. I spent my last two years assisting my colleagues to promote these ideas and ensuring they remained highly visible on the Community policy radar screen. With the evolving economic meltdown and the need for a radical transformation of economic structures in countries excessively dependent on property, construction and finance, the importance of lifelong learning should be increasingly appreciated.

It proved very rewarding personally that the team in which I spent my last years worked so well together.

The experience in my last posting was of working within an active, creative and cooperative team.[24] Our individual and collective endeavours all benefited from such cooperation, it alleviated pressures and stresses of tight deadlines and made for a most productive and beneficial environment. I was very fortunate to work with such a wonderful team and reluctantly retired on this high note.

## Swan Song

I retired the last day of September 2004.[25] I joined over 100 colleagues and friends I had worked with over the preceding 30 years for a most memorable valedictory party. Mike and Anne Hamell

---

[24] Roger O'Keeffe, a wordsmith with a consummate drafting style in a number of languages, would cast a critical eye over my inelegant drafts and burnish them; Luce Pépin, editor of the guide to Community programmes referred to above, would gladly assist, despite her overwhelming office and maternal workload, to suggest the legal and political references which give that professional finish to an early draft.

[25] Just before official closing time I received notice from the Secretariat General that my last contribution had been formally accepted. I carefully guarded a souvenir copy.

dropped me home after midnight and I felt a terrible sense of final-
ity and foreboding as I closed my front door.

Next morning, Friday, 1 October, I awoke at the usual hour. But
not in the usual form: my normal matinal lassitude had been replaced by disorientation. I knew I had a free pass to listen to the
morning news on the radio and adapt to a Saturday morning routine. I had thought that when you retired every morning would
morph into a Saturday. At nine-thirty I could stand it no longer; I
phoned Kiki, reminded her that I had taken early retirement and
that she had entreated me not to retire so soon. Could she please
tear up my resignation paper and I'd be in the office in a few minutes? 'Désolée', she replied, as a result of the new desiccated communications technology my resignation was irretrievably registered
by the administrative system, my phone and PC already discon-
nected. If I wanted to return I'd have to await the next *concours*
and apply all over again. She advised me to learn to relax and confront my new dawn.

My respite lasted but a couple of hours. Retirement, I decided,
is a time for rediscovery. I booked a berth with Lindblad Expedi-
tions-National Geographic on a boat with reinforced hull and prow
scheduled to ship out of Ushuaia, early January, down the Beagle
Channel, across the Drake Passage of the Southern Ocean, through
the bergy bits and growlers, to the Land of the Midnight Sun.

But, as the old *seanachai* said, that's another story ....

# EPILOGUE

SUCCESS OF THE REAL IRISH ECONOMIC renaissance, achieved by the end of the 1990s after the long and manifold vicissitudes which beset the emergent 'Free State', was not simply the result of the 'luck of the Irish', or financial transfers and tax breaks, valuable as these were. It arose out of sustained effort, endurance and meticulously thought-out strategy. Such organisations as the IDA, CTT (Irish Export Board), Irish Management Institute, schools, regional technology colleges, universities, and a host of other state and private institutions played the leading role – nurturing not luck. The strategy was to prove a resounding success until the turn of the millennium when the Greenspan credit and property bubbles, fuelled by a simplistic belief that markets are self-regulating, seduced imitators in the UK, Ireland and Iceland; a vaunting euphoria set in, leading to the hubris of the unfortunately-labelled 'Celtic Tiger'. The government recoiled from removing the punch bowl during the height of the hooley. The pursuit of a balanced, productive, export-oriented economy with a reasonably egalitarian social fabric was gradually forsaken for the siren call of Anglo-American untrammelled financial markets and light-touch regulation. Boston not Berlin became the mantra. The temptation of easy gains, not from consistent effort but from speculation and profligacy, proved too hard for many to resist. Credence in the myth of an omnipotent tiger economy only encouraged greater hubris. But behind the hype it was but a pneumatic feline fated, like all balloons, to burst. In fact the rot, which metastasised slowly, had arguably set in much earlier and more insidiously with the arrival of some foreign financial outfits offering risky off-shore financial services. The injection of thousands of new, highly remunerated financial service jobs helped cause an inflation of house prices and the cost of living for the local population. Financial contagion eventually spread to the other domestic financial institutions in our excessively concentrated banking system. The last rites were administered when property prices boomed, one-fifth of national income and employment was generated in the property sector, stamp duty increasingly financed a bloated public budget, leading to a seriously lopsided economy. An unsustainable level of credit and consumption fuelled inflation which led to further loss of international competitiveness and employment.

To aggravate matters the level of investment in education faltered. Educational standards slipped while grades were inflated. Jobs in high-tech international plants began to seep away to more competitive countries. Worst still was the loss of national credibility; painfully built-up reputational capital was also compromised. The real economic renaissance, based on effort, was subsumed within a bubble based on ease. The model productive economy morphed from paragon to pariah.

A crucial tipping point was reached when those who shared a genuine concern about some clauses of the Lisbon Treaty were joined by an esoteric coalition to vote 'No' in the 2008 referendum. Ireland risked being isolated on the periphery of Europe to be possibly joined in 2011 by a xenophobic and Eurosceptic Britain. Lisbon, essentially a legal housekeeping treaty, drafted mostly in stodgy juridical jargon under the chairmanship of French ex-President Giscard d'Estaing, that Irish politicians, commissioners, diplomats and representatives of civil society had painstakingly helped put together over a number of years, was rejected. Some genuinely believed it would involve an irrevocable loss of sovereignty to an authoritarian, militaristic, federal super-state. But the 'No' side was motivated by greater passion and commitment, were more shameless in taking poetic licence in the content of their eye-catching campaign posters and literature than the 'Yes' side, and carried the day. The low turnout on the 'Yes' side showed that the electorate should never be taken for granted.

The scene was to change during the more fevered 2009 campaign when the 'Yes' side was galvanised by a more committed civic partnership, especially in view of the clarifications and guarantees received from other governments regarding taxation and neutrality. For this emphatic decision the Irish also owe a debt of gratitude to the cerebral scribes of British tabloids who so generously allowed us to tap a rich vein of wisdom, as they shared their counsels with the under-informed natives. And the 'Yes' side was probably helped significantly by the eruption of the unsavoury UKIP into the national debate.

The greater turnout and decisiveness of the result indicated how seriously the electorate took their engagement as responsible citizen-guardians of the constitution. The intensity of the debate proved to be an excellent exercise in participatory democracy. For this the enviable commitment of the 'No' side in particular is to be commended for stimulating an admirable exercise in awakening national consciousness, contributing significantly to the national dialogue. The very intensity of the debate the second time round meant that it was focused on the Lisbon Treaty itself and not, as in 2008 in Ireland and earlier in France and the Netherlands, used by the electorate to vent mid-term frustrations at the government – always a risk with plebiscites. Civic involvement led to civic responsibility. While it is usually the Irish who are considered indebted to our British neighbours for their contributions to shaping our cultural dynamic and national destiny, in the wake of the vote the Irish arguably made a significant contribution to redefining British long-term international relations.

The draft treaty is rightly criticised for being excessively detailed, an indigestible legalistic potpourri stuffed with institutional minutiae, leaden enough to roof the Berlaymont, and lacking the brevity and elegance of the lauded US Constitution with its imaginative hankering after life, liberty and the pursuit of happiness. Yet we forget that the same brevity and inexactness cost the US a horrific civil war to resolve the question of slavery, another hundred years for full civil rights for blacks and Native Americans, while it has not yet resolved such basic issues as capital punishment. Nor does it allow for a state to withdraw from the Union as is proposed by Lisbon.

The ongoing economic implosion will take longer to put to rights and some tough decisions need be made by politicians and social partners. There will be a quadrupling of unemployment, honest and profitable firms will go under due to a lack of finance and customer demand, dream houses with nightmare mortgages will be surrendered, livelihoods destroyed and communities shattered. Youths leaving education eager to take up an appealing career may well vegetate despondently, the ladder of opportunity broken, the creativity of a generation of youth lost to a renewed haemorrhage of emigration.

However, there is little to be gained by letting post-tiger melancholy fester, indulging in a sterile introspection on past failings – except insofar as they teach us lessons for the future. The September 2008 financial meltdown could have led to Armageddon in the real economy, a depression even worse than that of the 1930s, but for the lessons economists learned from past failings. It had taken the US well over a decade and a ramping up of wartime production to eliminate unemployment provoked by the crash of 1929. Ireland also endured traumatic days in the 1950s and 1980s, but reflected on shortcomings and devised solutions, emerging more resilient on each occasion. It might prove some consolation to recall that it is the same country which showed it could change a deep-seated culture when it pioneered a national ban on smoking in public places, eliminated plastic bags almost overnight, finally shook off an ingrained tradition of driving home from the pub with copious pints on board and doggedly stuck with the Northern Ireland peace process. The country of uninspiring suburbs deprived of adequate social infrastructure, except for a proliferation of supermarkets, is also the country which pioneered the admirable Tidy Towns Competition which radically improved the appearance of so many towns and villages across the country, all at the voluntary initiative of civic society. There has been an enviable revival in culture, design and the arts, especially literature and theatre.

To avoid a long-term return to mass unemployment and emigration the country now needs a new vision, decisive leadership and a resetting of the nation's ethical compass. Hopefully the present sense of trauma will encourage a fundamental revaluation of national ethics; a new ethos might emerge from the feckless rubble of the Celtic bubble. It may be some consolation to note that we are immeasurably better placed to confront the challenges than during previous recessions: we still have a relatively educated and trained workforce, a significant proportion of youth with third-level education, far greater technological and entrepreneurial know-how, energy and vitality. Though many are facing a dire future, there remains a considerable private enterprise sector, creative and innovative, which did not exist in the 1980s. Our reputational capital may be damaged but not destroyed. National morale may be severely dented but for the sake of the new generation we just have to regain a sense of renewed national purpose. Fiscal retrenchment and the overhang of national debt means that the social fabric will be stretched to the limit for many years. There is an urgent need to restore competitiveness lost to Asia and Eastern Europe.

Above all, the Irish national psyche needs to mature and finally cleanse itself of the pervasive clientelism syndrome induced by the proportional representation electoral system, and the sneaking regard for the fixer of public affairs. Southern Italy indulges in an equally self-defeating *furbo* mindset. It probably is no coincidence that in both territories the dominant social mores suffer from a hang-up about sexual transgressions (one recalls with horror the appalling treatment of the Magdalene laundry young women) while the principal architects of the prevailing moral standards, especially the church, preach little of the need for greater rectitude in the body politic. In charting a way out of our current difficulties we could well learn a lesson from Scandinavia in relation to standards of public probity, integrity and political culture.

Ireland must pursue a diversified and balanced economy far less dependent on the financial and property sectors. Growth must be encouraged by investing in lifelong learning, retraining for an innovative economic architecture, wide diffusion of advanced broadband networks, expansion of the talent pool, emphasising knowledge-based domestic investment in post fossil-fuel technologies, especially small, innovative business start-ups, eco-friendly farming and agri-food, and new services. Risk-taking, but not gambling, should be encouraged and rewarded. The financial sector requires more effective supervision and there must be a thorough rethinking of corporate governance. Manufacturing should no longer be looked upon as a sector worthy only of the Chinese and Indians: both production and products can embody the fruits of insight, and design and technological creativity. Financial services must be regarded as the lubricant of the economy not the driving force.

The Germans have shown the way in cultivating environmentally-friendly products and processes. The Scandinavians demonstrated the potential of innovative, new technology sectors, though it takes time to replicate the innovation absorption capacity of their historically collectivist, social democratic societies. Top school and college graduates may once again seek to work in productive sectors which had been crowded out by finance in recent times, thus cultivating flair and enriching culture and the quality of life. Much of the knowledge-infrastructure built up over recent decades remains, thankfully, in place. With global recession there is now less risk of a brain-drain. Hopefully more ethical and astute long-term policies and values will emerge. Despite all the gloom the attitude of the younger generation has changed from the ingrained pessimism of the 1950s to a self confidence and creative impulse which should eventually weather the severe buffeting this has received in recent times.

Years have passed since the celebrated political economist Kenneth Galbraith published his perceptive reflections on the enduring paradox of private affluence and public privation. During the boom years the Irish landscape, too, has been blighted by vistas similar to those he described. Some of the most scenic regions have been ruined by an architectural straightjacket of little or no artistic merit – drilled rows of semi-detached, back-to-back suburban awfulness, tacky trophy homes blighting bucolic landscapes. The former glory of my dear hometown's main thoroughfare has been blemished by a series of fast food outlets and tacky trinket stores, the faux-jewel in the crown an aesthetically lobotomised steel lamppost of improbable elevation. Many low-income neighbourhoods are deprived of public space and civic amenities. Construction standards are still as we inherited them from our former colonial masters and are noticeably inferior to those of the North Europeans. When policies are eventually adopted to re-fire the economy a start could be made with new planning and building standards, social and environmental infrastructure, the construction of ecologically-efficient houses and offices, within socially-conducive public spaces. We could learn from Belgian usage where many communes insist each house should be built to a different design: this would not just restore employment among architects and experienced builders but enhance the aesthetics of the landscape. The Belgian practice, whereby young persons can rent accommodation at a reasonable cost rather than committing to the major investment of their life when they can least afford it, could be emulated: after all the lauded tax breaks offered in Ireland merely hike up the price of housing. We could also benefit enormously by emulating their marvellously efficient health system.

Certain problems call for regional and global solutions. Acute anthropogenic climate change is the greatest challenge the world faces: it will affect some countries worse than others. The poorest countries, those with the smallest carbon footprint, are facing the brunt of the damage. Pollution is no respecter of political frontiers; the atmosphere is a global good but treated by many as a dump. Ireland must continue to play a determined role in the EU, and the EU in the G20 and other fora, just as the EU took the lead in pushing global partners for agreement to the Kyoto protocol. All responsible countries need to commit themselves to internationally binding targets; there will also need to be agreement on a compliance mechanism to enforce agreed standards and commitments. Unfortunately a UN treaty needs unanimity, which means the agreement of the US. Hopefully, the US Senate, where the big energy corporations enjoy immediate and influential access, will, after years of inaction, accept the principle of responsible sovereignty, recognising the international effects of measures applied domestically, atmospheric pollution in particular.

It would appear that the new G20 grouping of major developed and developing countries will now assume an ever more central role as the generator of geo-economic policy. Unfortunately, as evidenced by the unfortunate breakdown of the Copenhagen 2009 climate meeting and recent trade talks, this new entity may not initially inject greater equity and realism into global policy making. Some of the prickly new G20 members share a culture of grievance and resentment towards the former masters of global governance, exude a new-found assertiveness and are likely to frustrate initiatives for global decision-making promoted by members of the G7/G8.[1] Nor is global governance likely to be aided when the negotiating remit of the US President is hobbled by a gridlocked Congress. It may be premature to consider disbanding the G8, while there may be a convincing argument to reinvigorate the highly experienced and authoritative OECD. This is not to propose that all countries must necessarily mirror western democracies but that they should adhere to a number of basics principles of free societies and public good as outlined in the UN Declaration on Human Rights.

Within the EU, individual members will continue to design their own national narrative, while the union should provide a framework for thinking about common long-term challenges, not as a centralised superpower, carefully avoiding what is best done at the Member State level. This will inevitably involve resolving differences through give and take, a careful balancing of the interests of the large and smaller partners, while each will retain a veto over interests considered vital.

If we can help design an enlarging Community as a voluntary partnership of civilised values, we can more effectively address such challenges as global warming, energy security, demographics, medical needs of an aging population, mass migration, integration

---

[1] Before one goes on to condemn the irresponsibility of the newly-promoted global decision makers it is salutary to recall the approach of such developed countries as Japan, Norway and Iceland regarding the hunting of whales and fishing of bluefin tuna.

and the pernicious downside of globalisation, especially the haemorrhaging of jobs which are not being replaced. The Community should evolve as a 'soft power' force for good in the world.

The Community could, for example, based on experience of co-operation with the CEECs after 1989, take a lead in encouraging establishment of an Open Society Forum, leaving the execution to voluntary organisations, think-tanks, and academic researchers within the EU and among wider international partners of like mind. That way Europe could share with the wider global community its commitment to certain core ethical values with a more diverse world community, plus other such values as the lesson of burying past conflicts with neighbours. In the Balkans the prospect of joining the Community has led to an attenuation of extreme nationalism and stabilising of peace through democratic and economic restructuring. If France and Germany, loyalists and republicans in the North of Ireland, can bury the axe of historic grievances so surely can protagonists in the Middle East and in Asia.

For the last half-century the Community has been an unparalleled if somewhat imperfect (too many lobbyists in Brussels, failure to stand up to national fishery pressure groups, excessive deference to Third World potentates) force for good, consolidating peace, stability and prosperity, extending membership to new partners some until recently ruled by dictators, while helping strengthen democracy in Central and Eastern Europe and the Balkans. We can surely feel proud of our record and hopefully, with Ireland a committed member, face the future with even more confidence in the values of tolerance, a caring society, with concern for the global environment and the less fortunate of the earth. The Lisbon Treaty is eloquent in declaring its respect for human dignity, the rule of law and respect for human rights, a society in which pluralism, tolerance, justice and equality between men and women will prevail. As President Mary McAleese noted on a visit to Luxemburg in 2009, the European project is a 'collective bulwark' against the triumph of darkness to ensure the triumph of light, as a centre of principled gravity, guided by human rights, egalitarian democracy, the rule of law and human solidarity.

# Appendix 1

# THE ANATOMY OF DEVELOPMENT: WINNERS AND LOSERS IN AN INTERDEPENDENT WORLD

*(Because of the demands of space the following article is but a resumé of a more detailed original. Readers wishing to consult the full version may contact the author.)*

One of the most defining hallmarks of civilised society is its humanitarian impulse, a commitment to justice and sense of collective solidarity with our less fortunate neighbours: altruism rather than selfishness. It is an ethical motive probably best described by the timeless injunction 'do unto others as you would have them do unto you'. Despite innumerable wars, slavery and lapses into the abyss of totalitarianism, an underlying humanitarian instinct has remained resilient during the most brutal of times. A belief in the common good and in assisting the less fortunate as a moral imperative has evolved as a pillar of foreign policy of the most advanced societies.[1]

---

[1] The dismissal of weak-kneed altruism has not entirely died out: Ayn Rand, the best-selling American author of *Atlas Shrugged* (over 6 million copies of her ravings sold), standard bearer of a purer libertarian, laissez-faire capitalism which she called 'rational self-interest' or 'rational selfishness', would apparently argue that altruism is the real source of evil, while money is the source of all good.

Not only are world leaders under pressure to address the challenge of equitable development in their own countries, there is also a growing pressure to tackle the obscenity of fellow humans dying of starvation or curable disease in a world which celebrates ostentatious consumption. The distinguished political commentator Hugo Young pointed out after Bob Geldof's 1985 'Live Aid' concert[2] that the one issue on which governments of the day felt free from moral and political pressure was Third World poverty. 'Geldof's achievement,' according to Young, 'was to call the bluff of governments with an event of highly political significance; he showed how the public all over the world did take famine relief seriously and they gave generously. Public opinion could be galvanised in a worthy aim', he wrote. Yet the urge to just do something can often prove ineffective or even unintentionally counterproductive in the long term, if we attempt to impose our nostrums where the social topography is significantly different from that at home. Aid to less developed countries (LDCs) can serve to consolidate venal regimes, militating against the wellbeing of the mass of the population, if badly or cynically administered, benefiting only elites and corrupt administrations in the recipient, and commercial interests in the donor, countries.

In our interdependent world economic and political upheaval in failing states can spill over frontiers and spread collateral damage to neighbours and the wider region, leading to an uncontrollable exodus of desperate migrants, if not of vengeful insurgents. Bad governance, inequalities, hunger, destitution and humiliation are the main incentives for terrorism and fanaticism. Depredation is compounded when bad governance leads to environmental degradation; pollution of the atmosphere is no respecter of international frontiers. In an interdependent globe environmental challenges are increasingly coalescing with developmental policies to define sustainable development policy. Climate change is threatening to destabilise the planet, making a fifth of its population homeless. It is a threat multiplier which exacerbates existing trends, tensions and

---

[2] *The Guardian*, 18 July 1985

instability, and will encourage an increasing level of environmental migration.

Yet, prescribing a solution is complex due to the wide and inchoate diversity of instruments, actors, cultures, politics, local conditions and requirements. Many like to believe in a model of development assistance whereby finance is poured into one end of a converter and successful development automatically appears out the other.

The character of donor institutions is also complex: they include development professionals and volunteers who have toiled *in situ* in underdeveloped lands and have gained a practical experience of problems on the ground, consultants committed to provision of valuable advice and sharing knowledge of best practice, philanthropists and *pro bono* activists unable to participate in the field. The architecture also includes politicians and diplomats who may pay only lip-service to human rights, high cost consultants who spout corporatist jargon and representatives of venal regimes in the developing world. Academics inspired by outdated ideologies feature among the more articulate. The cast is complemented nowadays by celebrities who are genuinely committed to making their contribution to a better world – while not being averse to an extra bit of accompanying publicity.

Their varied prescriptions are implemented by a wide range of agencies, national and inter-governmental, and a host of NGOs. While the national and international agencies tend to provide assistance on a top-down basis, i.e. to governments in the LDCs, the NGOs tend to assist on a bottom-up basis, empowering citizens at the grassroots level to tackle a host of problems.

Many countries we hypocritically refer to as LDCs are, in fact, regressing. Halfway to the 2015 target year for meeting the UN Millennium Development Goals (MDGs) for eliminating poverty, no African country is in line to meet the objective.

Many post-colonial societies have as yet to achieve the full promise of their independence movements, their liberation-struggle veterans reluctant to abide by earlier promises of liberty, democracy and the rule of law. In many post-colonial societies the cancer of crony capitalism, *rentier elites* and totalitarianism has leeched into the sinews of government to debilitate the vital organs of society.

African living standards are but a fraction of those recorded in South and East Asia, despite both parties starting from the same low level a generation ago. Over half of Sub-Saharan Africans still subsist on less than a dollar a day, whereas the number of poor in Asia has fallen dramatically during the same period. The World Bank estimates that, since 1960, income in East Asia has risen 34 times faster than in Africa. Different investigators have estimated that, since the end of the colonial period, Africa has received vastly more aid than Europe did under the iconic Marshall Plan.

Africa, in general, has evidently failed to deliver on independence promises. The record has improved somewhat in recent times, but much of the growth has resulted from demand for raw materials (the so-called curse of natural resources) rather than manufacturing or farming.

In addition, Africa is especially plagued by diseases: bilharzia, AIDS, malaria, TB, sleeping sickness and river blindness. Droughts and natural calamities have repeated themselves with a depressing regularity. What is most disheartening to the outside observer is the persistence of so many preventable diseases (300,000 AIDS suffers died in South Africa alone under the obtuse leadership of Thabo Mbeke). Although not politically correct to say, the plight of many countries results not from plagues and malign forces of nature, but from irresponsible governance, mismanagement and cronyism, so that social conditions have actually deteriorated since their independence was declared.

The rate of growth in Africa in 2007 was estimated to be just over six per cent, slightly up on 2006. Unfortunately, because of population growth Africa needs to grow by over seven per cent annually to halve poverty rates in order to meet the MDGs. From the donors' perspective, it seems unlikely that the developed countries will meet their UN-agreed target of 0.7 per cent of GDP by 2015. The UK and Ireland are, or were, progressing slowly in that direction, though still well behind the level of the Nordic countries. Aid from the US, France, Germany, Japan and Italy is either less than that promised or falling.

Yet, in spite of this despondent litany, one major source of encouragement is the fact that the ordinary people of Africa and Central and South America, especially the womenfolk, display an admirable resourcefulness and resilience in the face of adversity, and a hunger for betterment. Most inspiring of all are those young children who have lost their parents to AIDS and go on to lose their own childhood while rearing their younger siblings – one cannot but admire the heroic stoicism of pre-teen girls striving to feed their ill and starving brothers and sisters. They, above all, give the lie to the characterisation of Africans as feckless.

Development professionals recommend a number of overlapping instruments: debt relief, trade openings, financial aid and good governance.

There are those who favour debt relief to remove a major impediment to development and growth. The argument is that countries heavily weighed down by servicing debt overhang at punishing rates are not in a position to adequately invest in their future.

Most recommend the removal of trade barriers and entry into the multilateral trade system, citing nineteenth century Britain, the GATT members and the Asian Tigers. They point to the negative example of highly protective and semi-autarkic economies such as Egypt, much of Africa, North Korea, and, until recent years, China and India. There is a school of thought which advocates a very gradual removal of tariff and quota protection of local industries, citing the infant industries argument. Joseph Stiglitz and Andrew Charlton figure among the prominent supporters of the trade route as presented in their recent work *Fair Trade for All: How Trade Can Promote Development*.

The main policy instrument for assistance favoured by the development community is the provision of financial aid.

The aid argument was summarised by Alan Beattie, the World Trade Editor of the *Financial Times* (8/9 July 2006), when he commented:

Firmly on the sceptical side of aid is [Professor] Easterly, a re-
pentant World Banker. Easterly has developed a dominant
market position as one of the chief critics of aid, his analysis
given weight not just by his academic heft – a member of New
York University's increasingly star-studded economics faculty –
but because he has worked in development all his life. He and
his frequent sparring partner Jeff Sachs, celebrity economist
and aid cheerleader at Columbia University, have started a 'yes,
aid works – no it doesn't' debate. To me [Beattie] the centre of
gravity on this debate rests around the proposition that well-
directed aid can help growth and development but is not sufficient, may in fact not be necessary, and in any case is not the
most interesting question.

A more recent contributor to the conundrum of aid policy is the
Zambian economist and ex-World Bank consultant Dr Dambisa
Moyo. Her book *Dead Aid* argues that aid is demeaning and bad for
Africa. She recommends cutting off aid within ten years. She be-
lieves Africa should follow the development model of China and
India. She is apparently not fully convinced of the relevance of democracy to African LDCs but would appear to advocate governance
by a benevolent strongman. While her analysis is lively and provocative her contribution to the debate seems to combine some
common sense with a failure to recognise that a rejection of western democracy and hankering after 'big man' leadership is the main
cause of bad governance in Africa. While aid may be demeaning it
is probable that an African parent dying of AIDS would rather be
ministered to by the denigrated Bono or Bob than the sceptic
President Mbeki.

The argument in favour of good governance is widely presented
by many commentators, especially Professor Easterly in *The White
Man's Burden: Why the West's Efforts to Aid the Rest Have Done So
Much Ill and So Little Good*, and Robert Calderisi's *The Trouble with
Africa: Why Foreign Aid Isn't Working*. The latter's work is especially relevant considering his lengthy experience of African development. He realises that the great majority of Africans are hard-
working and resourceful, but their efforts are frequently frustrated
by corrupt governance which borders on the criminal. He refresh-

ingly challenges the silence of those who witness bad governance and corruption but remain mute.[3] Promoting good governance is also the main goal of philanthropist George Soros's 'Open Society Fund' which gained considerable experience at promoting transparent civic structures in the CEECs after the fall of the Soviet Empire.

In order to learn lessons from the past it is useful to cite successful regions and countries. Two interesting examples spring to mind: Italy and Ireland, both with contrasting records in their northern and southern regions. The former agrarian south of Ireland has witnessed an economic dawning which contrasts with the relative economic decline, almost *pari passu,* of Ireland's former economic and industrial heartland of the north-east. The recent meltdown of the Republic's overheated economy also provides valuable lessons in how hard-won success can be squandered.

An original investigation of governance was carried out by a trio of academic researchers following the reorganisation of regional government in Italy in 1970. Over a period of 20 years Professor Putnam and colleagues scrutinised how successful a sample of regions were. The findings were published in *Making Democracy Work: Civic Traditions in Modern Italy* (Princeton University Press, 1992). Their conclusions appear highly instructive for students of development, though they make rather discouraging reading for those who think they can easily induce representative democracy in countries which have no such traditions. Their main conclusion is that the most successful Italian regions in the early 1990s were those which had enjoyed a long legacy of civic constructs – since the early Middle Ages, no less.

They learned that for ten centuries the north and south of Italy have followed different destinies. In the north, they found that:

> norms of reciprocity and networks of civic engagement have been embodied in tower societies, guilds, mutual aid societies,

---

[3] Bono is on record as telling ministers from developing countries to their faces that corruption is as detrimental to development as AIDS. Maybe Bono and Geldof should organise a new concert called 'Make Corruption History'.

cooperatives, unions, even soccer clubs and literary societies. These horizontal civic bonds have under-girded levels of economic and institutional performance generally much higher than in the south, where social and political relations have been vertically structured ... this ... suggests that *both* states *and* markets operate more efficiently in civic settings. In less civic regions, political and social participation was organized vertically, not horizontally. Mutual suspicion and corruption were regarded as normal. Involvement in civic associations was scanty. Lawlessness was expected. People in these communities felt powerless and exploited.

One main lesson from their research was that 'social context and history profoundly condition the effectiveness of institutions'.

After independence in 1922 the Irish state, an underdeveloped periphery lacking the infrastructure of an independent country, had to carve out its own distinctive economic strategy. Its experiences, including the later temptation of delusional hubris, could offer lessons for colonies whose independence came later.

At the turn of the twentieth century the north-east corner of Ireland (within the UK) was one of the most developed regions of the world. As mentioned in Chapter 5, progress in the independent Free State (Republic post-1949) was frustrated by an incessant drumbeat of calamities: civil war, the great depression, international trade protectionism, the economic war with the UK, WWII and the innate conservatism of the new post-independence leadership. One success of the new state, often overlooked by historians, was the peaceful and successful transition in 1932 of political power (some supporters of the first post-independence CnaG government being initially suspicious of the enduring commitment of the successor FF party to democracy), a key step many post-colonial independence movements in Africa have failed to emulate.

With the end of WWII the government in the Republic remained committed to protectionism of domestic industries, inefficient firms enjoying an existence inoculated from the rigours of competition-induced efficiency. Cosseted industrialists, big farmers and trade unionists favoured maintenance of the status quo. The most enterprising, educated and skilled took to the emigrant ship and contributed their skills and energy to the development of the British and, especially, American economy.

Luckily, as mentioned in Chapter 5, a younger generation of civil servants, academics and political leaders was becoming more active and influential in public life. The same pragmatic minister who had introduced protectionism during WWII set about a radical reversal of policy. This new generation of political leaders, assisted by perceptive policy-makers, introduced historic initiatives for economic development and, later, multi-annual programs for economic growth.

The transition from an introverted, agricultural and import-substitution economy was hard fought and involved sustained engagement. The Industrial Development Authority (IDA) introduced a range of grants, incentives and an export-profits tax-holiday to encourage both domestic and quality overseas investment.

The efforts of the IDA were complemented and strengthened in the longer term by the decision to provide free universal post-secondary education and technological training following the 1965 OECD report 'Investment in Education'. The decision to sign a free-trade agreement with the UK in 1965 was also timely. The attractiveness of the country as an investment location was greatly enhanced with prospective entry to the European Economic Community in 1973.

But it is important for those wishing to draw a lesson from the Irish experience that their eventual success was not merely the result of luck and subventions from Brussels but from a combination of many factors, especially the enlightened and far-sighted strategy evolved by the new generation of politicians, dedicated civil servants, managers in state-sponsored agencies, academics and perceptive pundits.

In contrast, the record in the six counties of Northern Ireland has proved to be less exemplary, probably because those in the rest of the country had to pull themselves up by their bootstraps. The northern establishment did not react sufficiently vigorously to the structural competition affecting their traditional sectors. They could rely on generous transfers from London.

Ireland did indeed benefit from the very substantial transfers of Community structural assistance from Brussels, especially those provided by the Cohesion Funds in preparation for 1992. These funds insisted on *additionality* as a condition for assistance. To achieve sustainable growth the Irish had to provide matching funds themselves. There was no question of providing budgetary substitution assistance, as some now propose in the case of underdeveloped counties.

Later, when discussing the merits of financial aid provision, we might keep in mind parallels with East Germany, the Mezzogiorno and many dependency-habituated ex-colonies in Africa, and ask ourselves if relative economic stagnation in states and regions which have received generous economic transfers leads to the conclusion that aid is not necessarily beneficial in the longer term in all cases.

The generous Marshall Fund provided a lifeline to the devastated countries of Western Europe and was a landmark initiative in saving them for democracy. But even in its ravaged state Europe had the residual human resources, including management, administrative and technical expertise, and political commitment; all that was needed was the finance. Many developing countries have received substantial infrastructural assistance but have not been able to exploit this in the longer term due to a lack of social and human capital and institutions. It is possible that, when structures are oriented more towards accepting aid rather than creating the conditions which galvanise initiative, enterprise and a capacity for self-organisation, this may merely encourage a long-term dependency syndrome.

Successful European experience strongly suggests that the creation of honest, transparent civic structures, responsive government and a modern infrastructure involving brain-power rather than brawn-power, commitment to hard work and entrepreneurship, are key to successful development. The Irish experience also highlights the importance of changing outdated mindsets and cultural attitudes.

It is arguable then that the most important basic ingredient of long-term development lies in the ability to improve social capital and the community culture. Once a country or region has evolved democratic institutions, impartial administration of justice, efficient systems for lifelong learning, cultural attitudes supportive of enlightenment and horizontal social networks, then the basic infrastructure for an enterprising and innovative society will have been laid.

At a lower level of development the changing of mindsets and practices is also vital in areas such as sanitation, prevention of contagious diseases, irrigation, better health standards, and provision of education for girls. It can be surprisingly difficult to convince poor people that improving sanitation habits can eliminate childhood diarrhoea, amoebiasis and bilharzia. Major advances in welfare can thus be achieved at little or no cost by sharing experiences of best practice.

Closely related to mindsets in importance is the evolutionary state of the civic institutional structures and of democracy – the ultimate source of legitimacy. It may be possible to witness a high rate of economic growth in 'catch-up' economies without honest, representative government, but a solidly-entrenched civil society enjoying democratic accountability and justice can only be guaranteed by honest civic structures, freedom of information and expression, and a rule of law applied equally to all by an independent judiciary. States in which corruption spreads its poisonous tendrils are unstable in the long-run.

Education and training helps the individual realise his/her full intellectual and emotional potential and elevates the human spirit. It strengthens the potential for self-fulfilment and self-dignity of the individual and enhances the cultural and social infrastructure of civil society. The provision of skills and qualifications prepares the individual for a rewarding life by improving employability and combating exclusion. Access to vocational education encourages youth and adults to develop core economic and social skills and develop more active citizenship capacities. The concept of lifelong learning is of particular interest to developing countries: it covers the spectrum from early childhood development to second-chance basic education for adults. Where parents are mobilised in support of their children's education they can help break the intergenerational cycle of underachievement, school dropout and poverty. Training for enterprise, or for the creation of rural or urban cooperatives, the training of trainers and managers of educational institutes, contribute to the formation of a virtuous circle strengthening development. Training and education provision can also ensure that results of successful pilot projects can be diffused among the broader society.

The effects of a brain drain are complex, though probably not as negative in the long run as normally assumed, especially if some return later to mentor within an expanding economy with new insights and experience. Innovation involves a spectrum of tacit knowledge and is best fostered with legal, institutional and cultural systems which may be lacking in an individual's home society. Thus mobility of students, teachers and workers can play a major role in diffusing vital know-how from a more innovative to a traditional society where the main hindrance may be ingrained mindsets.

In addition to the human cost of poor health there is the greater social cost of disease and malnutrition. Diseases such as AIDS not only rob a society of its most productive people but ill-health and lack of nutrition set to nil efforts to provide education and skills, especially to children who must travel great distances to school. Often parents have to prioritise health provision for children, thus depriving them of access to education.

Hygiene, including that of preventative tropical medicine, and the provision of clean drinking water and adequate nutrition, is also linked to that of health in general.

Natural riches can skew economic and social policy thereby debilitating the rest of the economy, as happened initially in the Netherlands with the discovery of natural gas, provoking the so-called 'Dutch disease'. The solutions adopted by the Dutch and later by the Norwegians stand as an object lesson in how to develop the resources sector without unbalancing the rest of the economy and society, especially those who will not share in the resultant prosperity. The inordinate profits some government elites acquire from exporting natural resources all too easily stifle attempts at reform which might undermine the status quo.

Food aid is the most urgent requirement in the face of a famine. But in less extreme circumstances the provision of free or cheap food, which competes with local suppliers, depresses demand from local markets and impacts on local farm producers' income, if not driving them out of business altogether. Only when no local alternative is available should food be brought in from developed countries.

Irrigation is crucial to the sustainability of small rural farms; with increasing droughts in certain countries, such as Ethiopia, effective irrigation systems can prevent mass starvation caused by repeated crop failure.

Development assistance to the education sector should be rigorously monitored to ensure that there is equal provision for both sexes, especially if provided as a form of sectoral budgetary subvention to the recipient's education department. LDCs may feel a sense of entitlement and resentment at foreign interference with their cultural traditions: donors are equally entitled to believe there should be some conditionality.

It is difficult to generalise when it comes to the best mechanisms for the provision of assistance. Should it be provided directly government to government as top-down aid, or by NGOs which is usually bottom-up? Most recipient country governments favour top-down aid without conditions or interference.

Some of the most successful aid programmes are provided by local NGOs at community level, usually financed by overseas donor agencies which monitor progress with implementation.

Trade measures designed to encourage LDCs to manufacture for export probably offer the greatest potential long-term benefit. The examples of Hong Kong, Singapore, South Korea, Taiwan and, more recently, China, Vietnam and India, provide a convincing, but not complete, lesson. The multilateral system of trade wherein concessions offered to one are automatically offered to all partners, and trade need not be balanced on a bilateral basis, is in the best interest of the smaller and less economically powerful nations. As a general rule bilateral deals favour the mighty.

Aid-receiving countries should be encouraged to gradually remove growth-retarding protectionism, while at the same time protecting infant industries, especially textiles and clothing, and local financial institutions, until they can achieve international competitiveness. The problem with protectionism is that, once introduced, it not only leads to cosseted local firms which are not pressured to innovate but it can also create a corrupt class of licence-holding barons.

Debt relief, by removing the burden of servicing the overhang, can lift a seemingly impossible economic handicap from a poor country. But relief should be granted under strict conditions, structured to ensure additional productive investment and not send out a signal to unscrupulous leaders that they can merrily borrow for consumption expenditure in the hope that special pleading in the future will result in further cancellation of illegitimate debt.

The provision of financial aid by rich countries is commendable and justifiable, presuming that the recipient country can effectively use it, otherwise it can be argued that too much aid is worse in the long run than too little. If aid breeds a dependency syndrome, negatively impacting initiative, entrepreneurship and good governance, then it is bad. Financial assistance is vital to saving lives in the short term following natural catastrophes, such as famine or earthquakes, especially if it saves lives while stimulating local markets and employment. The quid-pro-quo should be that aid is used productively and equitably, in which case it can speed up the process of development and elimination of poverty and human misery.

As a general rule care should be taken with the provision of top-down aid, especially budgetary subventions to entire sectors, for example, education and health. If such sectoral aid only subvents what would have been undertaken in any event, it is merely an exchequer transfer. In order to ensure that assistance is given to the most deprived of society it would seem logical to channel it directly to the needy via NGOs, especially those in the partner countries operating at local community level. The implementation of this type of bottom-up aid would assist the evolution of vital social infrastructure central to the creation of a culture of development.

Where key infrastructures are targeted for assistance care should be taken to provide adequate follow-up to ensure long-term success: this could involve 'ring-fencing' future finance.

Aid should be targeted to where it can be profitably and honestly used for the benefit and empowerment of the most deserving of the population. Grotesquely expensive infrastructure projects can facilitate corruption. In line with the Human Rights chapter in all EU agreements, aid should not serve to reinforce authoritarian regimes. In the case of grievous human rights abuse, especially the practice of work-bondage or slavery, financial assistance should not be provided to the elites and, again, aid should be channelled through NGOs to assist the deprived on a bottom-up basis, privileging humanitarian assistance.

Efforts should be made not to encourage and institutionalise a long-term aid dependency mindset. Aid should be subject to conditionality, and there should be regular monitoring of its use.

The principle of *additionality* should be applied whenever possible to encourage and energise the poorer partners, provide a greater degree of leverage and encourage a self-help mentality.

In order to assist developmental partner-countries restructure and build new civic institutions, aid could be provided to finance joint cooperative consortia with a number of participant institutions from public administration or university faculties in the EU and partner country, or grouping of countries to develop a specific theme, e.g. independent judiciary, free press, political party structures, public administration, agricultural and industrial management, etc. This could be organised along the lines of the joint consortia so successfully set up by the EU after 1989 for cooperation with neighbouring countries, especially the CEECs.

It must not be forgotten that efficient institutions are the key to absorbing and maximising assistance. Many countries are badly governed, not because they are underdeveloped, they are underdeveloped because they are badly governed.

Calibrating a judicious balance between the public and private sectors is difficult, as the economy advances. Markets and public initiatives are not mutually-exclusive and can prove mutually-complementary. Some years ago the telecommunications network seemed to be an example of a 'natural' monopoly: nowadays entrepreneurs and farmers can exploit mobile telephony to empower themselves and dynamise the regional economy.

Those responsible for allocating assistance must be on their guard against diverting an excessive share of aid directly back to the donor country when employing consultants. It has been estimated that half of the US$15 billion aid provided to Afghanistan has been spent on consultants from Western countries. Advice from experienced and dedicated professionals can prove of the greatest long-term value, especially if they share their insights and best practice experience freely with embryonic public policy institutes in the developing partners, and are subvented at a reasonable rate.

The EU should review its tax laws to encourage more philanthropists to assist development in LDCs. This can also be provided by celebrities, such as Bono and Sir Bob, or by the late Sir Edmund Hillary who dedicated himself to the provision of education and healthcare in Nepal. It has been suggested that celebrity endorsement can lead to donor fatigue and cynicism, diverting aid from other development agencies. Yet, the immensely popular global profile of such individuals means that calamities often hidden from public scrutiny, think Darfur, will be effectively highlighted, and potential donors encouraged to provide aid. One should not underestimate the hankering of world politicians and global decision-makers to be photographed rubbing shoulders with such celebrities, providing an ideal opportunity for a humanitarian-minded mega-star to apply moral pressure. Undoubtedly, those suffering in a distant blighted land will hardly object to their distress being broadcast, even if it serendipitously provides welcome publicity for the celebrity. The tussle-haired Geldof practises a directness of speech more likely to bestir the average well-disposed TV viewer than an emollient diplomat could; he can make pertinent remarks to dilatory ministers that professional aid workers are dying to say but cannot, and stimulate the latent idealism of otherwise jaded youth. Efforts to make poverty history may not have greatly stimulated long term growth but have undoubtedly saved thousands of lives in the short term when they targeted starvation and health.

We live in an ever-more intertwined world. In the interests of equity and humanity the developed world must continue its altruistic traditions and provide a helping hand to the less fortunate of our world. A balance is needed between the position of the cynics who would claim all aid is wasted, that there are still many impoverished at home, and idealists who believe that the solution is to advance unconditional finance to administrations which lack the absorption capacity.

The EU should be able to forge mutually advantageous cooperation with a selected number of committed and deserving world partners along the lines of the existing neighbourhood partnership programmes, using the above-mentioned consortia models. There are countries dedicated to advancement but which are constrained by weak institutions, insufficiently trained management and poor administrative structures. This could be introduced as a pilot action to provide a template for future best practice. Success of programs with such countries would surely act as exemplars and provide a more effective force for change than the simple provision of aid. The European Council on Foreign Relations concluded in 2009 that the Union badly lacks the ability to launch global nation-building and institution-building missions. Yet it has had considerable experience and success in assisting universities, vocational and policy-making institutes in the CEECs post-1989. Emphasis should be placed on capacity building, strengthening the public service, democratic institutions, independent judiciary and restructuring of educational, health and commercial structures within the partners. It would surely be commendable if some such mechanism could be set-up to share restructuring and institution-building with the least fortunate of the world's fellow citizens.

# Appendix 2

# QUO VADIS: TEN POSTCARDS TO WHET THE WANDERLUST

*I met a traveller from an antique land*
*Who said: Two vast and trunkless legs of stone*
*Stand in the desert...*
*Nothing beside remains. Round the decay*
*Of that colossal wreck, boundless and bare*
*The lone and level sands stretch far away.*

– P.B. Shelley, *Ozymandias*

*Magical days of frost and sunshine.*

– Pushkin

A CONSEQUENCE OF BEING A FORMER tour guide and a recidivist vagabond in later years is to be oft consulted regarding favourite destinations. It's easy to offer advice but each inquirer has his/her own preferences: some would rather relax in the same spot for the duration; others opt to keep moving or prefer shopping to studying ancient ruins, history and heritage. There are those who prefer poolside lassitude to scuba diving, or perpetrate lowland golf to waltzing down the snowy slopes on a pair of skis; others would rather sip *caiperinhas* on Ipanema beach than hack through the muddy, penumbral undergrowth and endure the bloodthirsty leeches of the rain forest. Some prefer to explore novel vistas while others frequent the same friends and location year in, year out.

I tend to suggest that there is a list of 'definitely-to-be-visited' places and add a dozen or so favourite spots, many now lost worlds, from which to send a postcard. Among the 'must-be-visited-in-a-lifetime' are obvious destinations like Rome, Florence, Venice, the Amalfi Coast, Athens and the Upper Nile. Of course, there are other great cities such as Paris, London, Barcelona, Granada, Krakow, Budapest, Prague, Dubrovnik, St Petersburg, Kyoto, San Francisco, Vancouver, Samarqand, not to mention great train journeys, such as the Trans-Siberian, the Trans-Andean, and Canadian Rocky Mountaineer.

A further problem which arises when offering travel advice is that one may have visited places years ago when political circumstances or the level of tourist development were very different. There are certain destinations where only hardy travellers visited forty years ago but which are frequented by busloads of tourist nowadays. One could travel Ethiopia in reasonable security in the 1960s and 1970s, but not in the 1980s, while those of us who now hanker after a journey through the Khyber Pass or Persepolis may nurse regrets for having opted for the *fleadh ceol* in Ballybunion in the halcyon days of the 1960s. Some provinces of the Yemen have become less safe in recent times. The byways of eastern and southern Turkey of the 1960s required fortitude but some modern Turkish resorts now resemble the Costa Brava. Others, the Seychelles, Polynesia, Obergurgl, have adopted the strategy of relative conservation, avoiding excess growth and the race to the bottom to attract the mass market.

So, depending on one's interests and energy, and to whet the appetite, the ten destinations below might form a useful starting point, though circumstances may have changed considerably since this old, footsore nomad visited. Some may appear daunting but cheaper airfares, improved roads and accommodation, and the possibility of booking local guides, drivers, even mules, by internet, means that trips which would have previously proven impossible for reasons of cost, duration and risk, are now realisable during a two- or three-week vacation period. We may bemoan the 'massifi-cation' of travel but cheaper communications have also democra-tised access to places hitherto the exclusive domain of the rich and privileged. The Duke of Wellington was remarkably prescient when he remarked that one unfortunate result of building railways would be to encourage the lower orders to wander aimlessly about.

## Yemen – Arabia Felix

It was probably a subliminal recollection of twin paintings in our old front room in Dublin depicting romantic scenes of Araby the Blest which tempted me to visit the fabled land of frankincense and myrrh. They enticingly depicted camel caravans laden with exotic spices, unguents and incense, camped by a lush oasis of date palms, sparkling pools of crystal water, all under an enveloping canopy of turquoise, the surrounding sands stretching towards a mysterious horizon. On sombre, damp days I ventured into our little-used *masrakh* to conjure up such exotica in my childhood imagination. Later I read that they had discovered oil in that corner of Arabia: I feared that the old Arabian Nights' architecture of the Sa'ana *me-dina* and *suq* would succumb to the bulldozers like the Georgian squares of old Dublin. My good friend of Ladakh memory, Christian Andre, and I, organised another trip and we contacted an agent in Sa'ana who arranged Land Rovers and drivers, and a *Bedu* escort to take us through the *Rub al-Khali* (Empty Quarter).

For once my fears of a disappearing landscape were unfounded: UNESCO has declared the old medina of Sa'ana as a site of historic importance to be preserved.

Yemen is one of the oldest inhabited countries in the world. Not only was there considerable agricultural production in the more watered mountainous parts but it was ideally situated on the earliest trade routes, when frankincense and myrrh, as well as cin-namon, pepper and other exotic spices, were shipped overland from Dhofar, now in the modern state of Oman. At one stage the largest and richest city in the world was Baraquish, on the edge of the fearsome *Rub al-Khali*, the Empty Quarter, and halfway be-tween the Indian Ocean and Red Sea. Dhofar was the source of the small trees or shrubs of the genus Boswellia from which the prized Frankincense for the religious and ceremonial markets of the ancient Levant comes. It was the most desired ritual perfume for the altars of Damascus, Jerusalem, Babylon, Thebes and Petra. (A funeral in those lands not perfumed by incense was akin to a wake in Ireland not lubricated by traditional dark creamy-crowned brew, or golden distillate.) Frankincense is the sweet smelling gum resin from these shrubs, the better quality being found further inland. As it exudes from the bark like milk juice it hardens on exposure to the air. Myrrh, also an aromatic gum but from a shrub of the genus Commiphora, was used mainly as an ointment, the everyday aspirin of yore, as well as an embalming fluid.[1] Frankincense grows mainly on rocky ground along the Arabian Sea coast of Yemen and Oman, myrrh mainly along the Tihama coast of the Red Sea. The wealth generated by the Incense Route ceased when the Ancient Egyptians discovered the benefits of the trade winds and transported the merchandise, as well as pearls, muslin and silk, by boat. Later still, the Egyptians were in turn trumped by Vasco da Gama's voyage around the Cape of Good Hope into the Indian Ocean. The Yemenis regained their commercial advantage later when the Turks accidentally introduced the Austrians and then other Europeans to the delights of Arabica coffee exported from the now silted-up port of Al Mokha.[2]

In ancient times in the fertile area near Baraquish, the waters of the Wadi Adana were dammed to give rise to a sophisticated system of agriculture, helping create the wealthiest kingdom on the Arabian Peninsula, centred on the ancient city of Ma'rib. Once again that *femme fatale*, the Queen of Saba (Sheba), makes an appearance. In fact the old history of Yemen is replete with the story

---

[1] Myrrh was also mixed with cheap wine and offered as a tranquilliser to prisoners on the point of execution, such as in the drink the Roman soldier offered Jesus during his last moments. He was buried in a shroud containing myrrh and aloes.

[2] Recently most coffee bushes of the highly-productive Yemeni highlands have been grubbed out to grow the more profitable narcotic *qat*, which the local males masticate incessantly within an awesome dome (developed over years of masticating the herb) puffing out one cheek.

of how Bilkis, for that was the lady's maiden name, was invited by King Solomon (or Suleiman in Arabic) to spend a romantic week-end in Jerusalem. She must have been one smouldering *allumeuse* since this involved pre-empting the attentions of HM's 700 wives and 300 concubines. Miss 1001 was such a hit she is mentioned in the Old Testament and Christian Gospels, though referred to as the Queen of the South (Arabia)... '[W]ho will rise in judgment of this generation for she came from the ends of the Earth to listen to Solomon's wisdom...'. She also manages to be mentioned in the Ko-ran in a number of *suras*. Since Yemen was often conquered by an-cient Abyssinia, just across the Red Sea, it is understandable that both states should lay claim to this formidable lassie.

Millennia later the British fought to have a base at Aden, at the vital entrance to the Red Sea, especially with the opening of the Suez Canal. But, despite having a protracted history over the last thousand years, the country was closed to foreigners, except their Turkish overlords, and it is only in the last few years that travellers could visit.

Explorers of the early twentieth century brought back stories and photos of a magical, enchanting land, straight out of the Ara-bian Nights, with breath-taking scenery, extraordinary architecture, a wealth of archaeology and a people shut off from the outside world since medieval times.

To arrange our itinerary we contacted a Sa'ana agency which mapped the most interesting routes for a three-week trek around the country. We started from Sa'ana, headed east to the old frank-incense transit city of Baraquish, to the Old Kingdom City of Ma'rib with its ruins of the palace of aforementioned Queen, then 650 kms across the Rub al-Khali to the lost Manhattan in the Desert, Shi-bam, on the edge of the Wadi Hadramaut in the south east. Our *safar* then led to the old Sultan's capital city of the Hadramaut, Se-yun, and nearby Tarim whose architecture is heavily influenced by travellers and merchants from Islamic Indonesia – the East Indies of old. We then hacked down the Wadi to the city of Al Mukalla on the Arabian Sea (gorgeous from the distance, but less so up close), continuing on to Aden on the southwest corner. We departed our

Aden hotel – the reception area was blown up two hours later (rumour had it that some of the rather curious US guests were not regular tourists) – and made our way via Ta'izz and Ibb to the Red Sea coast, past the old deserted port of Mokha into the desiccated costal zone known as the Tihama. From there we ventured up the sides of the western highland mountains whose fertile land is watered by the monsoons from the Red Sea, further up the mountainous northern provinces visiting ancient walled cities whose gates were locked at night, such as Tawilah, Kawkaban, Attawila, Al Hajjarah and, clinging like a barnacle against the towering mountain face, Tiblah and Jawila. The roll call of medieval towns ended at Sadd'a, near the Saudi Arabian border, with its even more phantasmagorial, Turkish, if not Gaudiesque, architecture. Somewhere along the way we visited a village called Zahid, which was the birthplace of the mathematician Al Jabr who, locals claim, subsequently took off to the House of Wisdom in Baghdad and gave his name to the eponymous scourge of childhood, Algebra. All told a safar of over 8,000 kilometres over some tarmac roads, but mostly desert with a wide variety of sands, up *jebel*, down *wadi*, to the excruciatingly rough, boulder-strewn, execrable tracks of the western mountains.[3] Everywhere we were met by friendly faces and welcomes, except perhaps in conservative Sadda, but this was provoked by a young French lady in our group whose rule regarding couture was to shed it with the intensity of the sunshine. (A lack of consideration of local mores by some European visitors is one of the few occasions when travellers meet opposition in that otherwise hospitable land. We even animatedly engaged with the locals about the popularity of posters depicting Iraqi dictator Saddam Hussein, provoking heated argument but not animosity.) Of course it is difficult, almost impossible, for the male of the species to establish rapport with the local ladies, one must not even point cameras at them, at least, not without asking permission, *mumkin sura*?

---

[3] During one especially enervating stage I opined our frankincense route was no myrrh trail, and was threatened with exclusion from jeep and forced march if I chanced any more such wisecracks.

## Bonding with the Locals

We even managed to overcome the difficulty of getting to know the locals in their own homes. This was due to the enterprise of the ladies in our group who took the initiative of knocking on local doors. We men would stand back. Inevitably the little grill in the door would squeak open and the ladies would attempt a conversation in Arabic. Gestures were exchanged. Then the grill would be closed while negotiations were conducted with the Masters of the Universe. Finally, the lady members would be invited in to the *diwan*. Then some men would come down the stairs and invite us stragglers upstairs to the *mashraq*, the upper room where the local boyos discussed the state of the cosmos, puffing on their *nargiles* and feeding their distended left cheeks with leaves of the ever present *qat*. Since we invariably had our local guide with us to translate, the conversation was lively and we would stick around, trying the qat and the odd puff on the shared hubble-bubbles, until eventually one of the ladies, shrouded like a mobile roll of black cloth, entered our holy of holies, deposited a tea tray and respectfully departed.

Our intrepid ladies managed to learn sufficient Arabic to identify the spices and condiments which were laid out in beautiful geometric designs in the stalls in every local *suq*. It was interesting to note that the streets, and even rural landscapes, were polluted with discarded plastic bags and cigarette packs, and the streets of medieval towns littered with squashed plastic water bottles. Yet the interiors of the homes, though some looked troglodytic from the outside, were spotlessly clean, thanks to the ministrations of the local ladies whose managerial roles started once over the threshold. The main exceptions were the blankets and pillows in the highland *funduqs*, local inns where we spent some shivering nights. Granted, there were no dry cleaning facilities for a million miles but, interestingly, it was men only who ran the funduqs. Faced with the choice of freezing on the cold stone floor or sleeping under a covering which had never been washed in its entire life, we reluctantly opted for warmth.

At breakfast our first morning in Sana'a we ordered some of the excellent Arabica coffee for which Yemen is renowned. We could not drink it. In Yemen they don't follow the Turkish custom of roasting the coffee beans, and green coffee was not to our liking. The waiter apologised and announced he knew exactly what we required. He repaired into the kitchen to return with a jar of Swiss Nescafé. And I had always associated the wonderful aroma which pervaded Grafton Street from Bewley's Oriental coffeehouse with the glamorous, biblical scenes in our front parlour paintings.

Ancient Sana'a did not disappoint, with its totemic architecture, windows surrounded by white plaster to scare away insects, window arches surmounted by glass fan lights which would be the envy of Georgian Merrion Square, each building is a work of art in itself. There is a warren of different *suqs* or markets for clothing, copper, silver, the *suq al djambias*, or iconic curved daggers, where specialists make steel blades, hilts, scabbards and belts on the spot, the spice suq, where merchants offer tempting technicolour displays of all the exotic spices and unguents that ever travelled the silk, spice or frankincense routes.

## Crossing 'The Sands'

While it is possible to avoid the epic trek across the desert to the magical architecture of Shibam by flying, it is far more interesting to experience crossing one of the most formidable deserts in the world - the one which attracted the masochistic peregrinations of Wilfred Thesiger. The *Rub al-Khali,* the Empty Quarter, is a real desert's desert. It stretches across the bottom of the mighty Arabian Desert from Yemen in the west, through southern Saudi, to the *djebel* ramparts of distant Oman.

We arose at four bells, drove out of Ma'rib along a dark, rutted dirt-road until it petered out at the edge of the desert. We half deflated our tyres and, in the still chilly night air, awaited the arrival of dawn. The first golden rays hesitantly gilded the distant horizon, and from the recesses of memory I recalled the serenading of the mellifluous maestro John McCormack 'Morning was gleaming with roseate light ...'. The roseate light radiated like a celestial searchlight to unveil a resplendent vista: the shadowy outlines of dunes uncoiled sinuously to the distant horizon. With our two Bedu guides, each in charge of a battered jeep, keeping a sharp look out for Saudi patrols (since the border is disputed), we headed off into the magnificent desolation of The Great Sands. The landscape resembled a scene from Mars or the primordial Earth at the dawn of creation, before water flowed or life stirred. Chilled by night the sands turn searingly hot well before midday. The Bedu have an uncanny feeling for the consistency of the sand and an innate sense of direction. They laughed at the idea of even glancing at a map, and diverted around obstacles invisible to us novices. We just did not have the natural instinct of the Bedouin trackers for the wide range of terrain which makes crossing the desert so complicated. The surface ranges from hard heavy sand (which is easy to drive on), gravel, salt and gypsum plains, the occasional light brittle shell surface through which wheels can sink twenty centimetres, to the lightest sand with the consistency of talcum powder, all resulting from the different structural geologies as they break up under the combination of the intense heat of the day and the sudden drop in temperature at night. Most difficult to navigate are the ultra fine deposits which form dunes tens of metres high, some even over a hundred. The easiest sides to climb are the windward sides where rocks can be bared by the wind; the most difficult are the lee sides, filled with soft, shifting sands.

The landscape and colours changed constantly with the angle of the sun and the underlying geology. We admired a palette of hues: rose-tinted in the early morning light, when the oblique light cast shadows over serpentine dunes, grey as the heightening sun and shimmering haze leached out colour and relief, and russet with the onset of evening.

Midday we halted at an artificial refuelling oasis, minus palms and babbling brook, one with stocks of soft drinks buried in the sand and covered by awnings to protect patrons from the 55° Celsius dry heat of that fine December day. Since it was Christmas Eve I was not only feeling a bit *brónach* for the special ambience and watering holes of my shivery Liffeyside hometown, but the haunting strains of the traditional Handel's Messiah occasionally repeated themselves as if on a gramophone in my mind.

*Young school girls, Jibla in the Tihama highlands, Yemen*

*Ta'izz, at the Al Ashrfiya Mosque*

*Palace of the Rock, Wadi Dhar, Yemen*

*Shibam, the Manhattan of the desert*

*Typical highland town, Yemen*

*Young Yemini ladies, Sa'dah*

*Fanlight detail, Palace on the Rock of Wadi Dhar, Yemen*

*Monk in Ladakh*

*Market on Dal Lake, Kashmir*

*Mogul Gardens, Shalilmar, Kashmir*

*Houseboat on Dal Lake, Kashmir*

*One of our transport trucks
Srinagar-Zanskar-Ladakh*

*Monks enjoying summer sunshine
outside Rangdum gompa, Zanskar*

*Gompa library, Zanskar, Tibetan language manuscripts hundreds of years old*

*Souvenir lady, Urubamba Valley (Sacred Valley of the Incas), below Machu Picchu*

*Machu Picchu from Inca Trail*

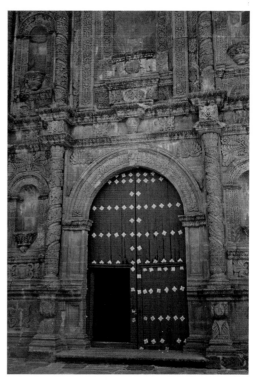

*Old Spanish church, Arequipa, Peru*

*Afternoon scene at Machu Picchu*

*Prow of Totora (balsa) reed boat of Uros people who live on the floating islands, Lake Titicaca, Peru/Bolivia*

*Market day, Chincheros, Peru*

At one stage Bedu driver Hamid spotted a rare desert fox. He reacted as all true Bedu would, grabbed his ever-present Kalashnikov, hopped out of his still-moving 4x4 and blasted away at the waving tail. This ill-treatment of a poor lonely fox was not appreciated by a lady of our group who launched a rugby tackle on the crouching marksman. She upbraided the unfortunate hunter, while the savvy fox, tail teasingly flailing, scampered behind a nearby dune.

At times we made good progress across flat surfaces, featureless stony plains with hard, gravelly sand, then a roller-coaster of undulating dunes which resembled a seascape during a violent storm, except that the waves had been suddenly and catastrophically frozen into silent immobility, like a snapshot fixed in time. Often the most dramatic formations were composed of the most pliable sand so that our progress consisted of rushing to crest the wave, then tracking down the other side in controlled low gear, while landing like an ungainly ski jumper at the trough, to repeat the process for the umpteenth time. We were occasionally stuck in soft sand: so we heaved and dug out frustrated wheels which ungratefully showered us with sand till our impregnated garb took on the consistency of sandpaper.

We were fortunate: we had jerry-cans of water even if our jeeps were not air-conditioned. The daring travellers of yore needed weeks to complete the hundreds of miles of the safar from Wadi Hadhramaut to the caravanserai at Barraquish without the benefit of revitalising wells or oases. Their lives and that of their camels depended on the robustness and impermeability of goatskin water containers, often given to perspiring. Our Bedu guides boasted that they could last a week in the desert without water – their camels a month.

We arrived at the outskirts of Shibam after nightfall, paid our guides, who happily turned round to face the 650 kilometre trip back to their Ma'rib encampment. We unloaded at our creaky desert guesthouse. My bedding was somewhat basic but, unlike the more primitive funduq, was separated by a plywood wall from my next door neighbour, a German lady. I settled down to a brief rest, *tuirseach, traochta*. Then, almost magically for this nostalgic nomad, from my neighbour's room there emanated the glorious and majestic opening bars of Bach's Christmas Oratorio from her cassette player. It was a tradition in her family to listen to the successive movements over the Christmas period. Feeling a bit homesick for the ambience of Dublin at Christmas, and Handel's more traditional notes, I was rhapsodically transported by the Leipzig lady's improbable transmission for most of an hour.

Having explored the attractions of Manhattan-in-the-Desert, with its nine and ten-storied mud-and-straw-bricked buildings ornamented with ibex horns set in decorative plaster, we set out along the Wadi Hadhramaut, arriving unannounced at a local restaurant. They did not intend to turn good customers away, and confirmed that lamb was on the menu. Unfortunately, when the offer was made the poor animal must have been grazing nearby, innocently unaware of commercial developments....

Arriving late on Christmas evening at a real hotel, though bereft of bar facilities in that arid landscape near Al Mukalla, and built to accommodate oil exploration geophysicists, I saluted a lone and lonely American. I invited him to join our company for Christmas dinner, warning that it was mainly Francophone. Had we been speaking Mongolian he would have accepted with equal alacrity. I ventured that unfortunately we had only a few secreted bottles of Bordeaux's best for our group. He replied that if we provided the company he could provide some of Kentucky's best. Amazing what surprising elixirs exploration engineers in prohibition lands stumble upon amid the equipment shipped in to aid their searches for liquid gold ....

### Kashmir/Tibet – Om mani padme hum

Oliver Cromwell's lieutenant general in Ireland, Edmund Ludlow, is reputed to have described the Burren countryside in County Clare as having 'not enough water to drown a man, wood enough to hang one, nor earth enough to bury him'. That endearing gentleman could also have been characterising the landscape in what is culturally Tibet, just over the Himalayas from the Vale of Kashmir and sandwiched between them and the Karakorams. The Himalayas are so high that they cause almost all the rain from the monsoons to fall before the winds reach the Tibetan plateau. There may appear to be plenty of snow in 'them thar hills', but because of the cold at that altitude it melts but slowly, cutting off the valleys of Ladakh and Zanskar to land access for eight months of the year.

In their wisdom the British colonial authorities, or the surveyors they sent out to map their territories, included a large chunk of land populated by Tibetans in the territory they designated as India. A large portion of this became part of Pakistan on partition and, in 1960, the Chinese came calling and took another two parts of the territory, high up in the Karakorams. Still, India retains control of a large chunk of old Tibet with its many ancient *gompas*, or Buddhist monasteries, and their invaluable inventories of old Tibetan artwork, religious paintings, *thang-kas*, and libraries. All gompas in Tibet itself[4] were ransacked by the Red Guards at the time of Mao, though many have been built anew. But those in Ladakh and Zanskar are the real thing, decorating the otherwise desolate landscape like jewels in an otherworldly crown.

There are many reasons for choosing to trek or travel round the northern Indian state of Kashmir: the sublime, almost feminine beauty of Srinagar, Dal Lake and the nearby Mogul and Shalimar gardens, the majestic moonscape of Ladakh and the towering, overwhelming, Martian landscape of Zanskar. Despite the overarching sense of silence and loneliness when travelling in a largely unpopulated countryside the people you meet in the remote villages are exceptionally hospitable, kind and honest. In the wilderness there are so many reminders of local friendliness, from prayer flags to *chorten* (religious statuary) and the odd, cryptic (Indian army) reminders to slow down when approaching bends along the vertiginous switchback route where, a thousand feet below, the valleys are strewn with the carcasses of less fortunate vehicles.

Anyone considering travel in this area, which is far less equipped to deal with travellers and trekkers than Nepal, should decide if they want to walk or travel by jeep/truck, and choose a

---

[4] Except the Potala which was considered as much a political as a religious centre, possibly because it contains a massive quantity of solid gold statues.

reliable local travel agent. But the distances are so vast and the roads so rough this scribbler preferred the relative comfort of an Indian Army (Tata) truck – after all, the main route from Srinagar to Leh, the capital town of Ladakh, was only built by the army after the Chinese invasion of 1960. The track off that route down the Zanskar Valley gives the impression it was carved out over the aeons by goats and yaks. If at all possible start the trip at Srinagar instead of spoiling the experience by flying into Leh – which is like arriving in Machu Picchu (see below) by rail instead of along the Inca Trail and through the appropriately named Gate of Heaven.

Srinagar was the most desired resort for the higher echelons of the old British *Raj* who wished to avoid the stifling summer heat of Delhi. However, its remoteness meant that most had to settle for the relatively more convenient resort of Simla – poor dears – which served the British army and colonial civilians based in Rawalpindi. Located at the foothills of the majestic Himalayas and surrounded by glorious, refreshing lakes fed by the Jalum River, Srinagar was considered by the old Mogul Emperors as the nearest thing to heaven. Hence they built magnificent palaces and planted enchanting gardens here. It is reminiscent of Venice, albeit Central Asian style, with *shikaras* (similar to Venetian gondolas) and lakeside houses. But the town goes one further by organising its markets on the idyllic lake itself, the fresh vegetables arriving by shikara, and the best hotel accommodation is found in the sumptuous, intricately-carved, cedar-wood houseboats on the waterside. Apparently in the nineteenth century the local maharajah refused the colonials permission to build on land, so they resorted to these historic houseboats. Excursions can be made by motor-powered shikara to the maze of backwaters and channels with their traditional domestic architecture, to the floating islands on which vegetables such as melons and cucumbers are grown, or to the nearby Mogul and Shalimar Gardens. These gardens, intersecting the bottom slopes of the Himalayas and the lakes, resemble an exotic Tivoli gardens, with rectangular flower beds and cascading water. The hinterland is one of rice fields watched over by lines of sentinel poplars, interspersed with almonds and spices.

There has been tension in recent times between the mainly Muslim population and the Hindu authorities which has disrupted tourism and caused some of the houseboat owners to close shop on occasion. If possible, one should use the town as a base from which to visit the majestic Himalayan hinterland. Apart from the beauty of the local countryside there is the possibility of shopping for shawls, Kashmir carpets, silks and artwork. The famed *pashmina* shawls are woven from the exceedingly delicate underbelly fleece of the Kashmiri (strictly Chang Tang) goats which populate the nearby mountains and plateaux, and are considered superior to those which come from Mongolia or other parts of Asia.

The little group with which I travelled had arranged to hire two sturdy army trucks, drivers and assistants (called *sherpas* locally), tents, water, food and cooking utensils. Comprising mainly French-speaking colleagues from Brussels and Luxembourg we brought along our own refreshments with which to complement the vagaries of the local nightlife. Apart from rice, tsampa (oatmeal for porridge) and other foodstuffs our two sherpa chefs brought two large woven baskets containing two dozen chickens and a couple of live lambs. The chickens provided fresh eggs for our morning breakfasts, though the quantity diminished and the level of cackling was reduced as the trip wore on, and more chicken soup was served for dinner. This smacked of gross ingratitude: it reminded me of the Antarctic explorers who regularly topped and ate their ponies along the route. Quite obviously I was not cut out for the heroic age of travel. At least we were spared the sight of the chickens but the two lambs were highly visible and petted by the group, especially the ladies, while our cooks, much to their amazement, were under strict instructions not to touch a hair of them. The lambs were the only ones to make it back to Srinagar without being emaciated, though this may have sealed their fate when we parted company.

With a great grinding of gears we set off from the lush and fertile fields of Srinagar for the foothills, then the wide-angle, arid landscape of the Himalayas proper, along the army supply route, direction Leh. This road had previously been a mule track, hastily upgraded during the short 1960 China-India war to allow army supply trucks to get through during the summer months. Many are the reports of travellers negotiating the slippery, stony ledges cut into the steep sides of majestic mountains, bereft of any protecting fence. Often we passed through walls of compacted glacial snow which had been cleared by snow plough or bulldozer, like the old road up to Obergurgl and Vent in the Tyrol. The only restraining wall was psychological, seeing the remains of broken trucks many hundreds of metres below in the ravines and valleys, bolstered by safety instructions on the roadside to restrain any army truck drivers who fancied themselves as formula one drivers: 'Death lays his icy hands on speed kings'. We made our way at about six kilometres per hour seated on wooden benches designed to teach young lowland recruits the delights of sacrificing oneself for Mother India. We competed for a place in the observation box above the driver's cabin, where the view was immeasurably better, if more intimidating, and the dust levels were marginally less than inside. The track was so narrow that it was better not to reflect on whether the outside wheels were touching the surface or hanging in mid-air. Riding in the observation post one felt that it might be possible to jump clear if the truck threatened to join the many vehicular corpses on the valley floor below. We witnessed proof of the old saw that the Alps are related to the earth while the Himalayas are related to the heavens. It was bad enough when the rear wheels of the truck began to slide hair-raisingly close to the edge, but worse when we encountered another truck, which was invariably a military one. Considering himself on a vital errand the army driver usually insisted on being given precedence and we had to back up a few hundred metres while the rear passengers noisily guided the driver who was reversing without the benefit of a rear view. All the while clouds of dust were thrown up which alternately blinded and choked us. Our dust-encrusted clothing began to feel like sandpaper. A few ladies, showing the eminent practicality of their gender, had thoughtfully brought along scarves which they draped around their heads like Tuareg raiders, to partially fend off the all enveloping-particles. The dust was to remain our faithful companion until we returned to Dal Lake two weeks later.

One town en route is Drass, a collection of white stone dwellings which, because of its elevation and remoteness from any modifying ocean breeze, is one of the coldest towns in the world, its winter shiver index competing closely with Yakutia in the north of Siberia.

## Zanskar

Arriving at Kargil, the last Muslim town on our journey, we decided to hack on, though late in the day, turning left down the Zanskar trail. Those who have a hankering to travel to Mars at some future date but fear that time and tide may not favour them, should note this route. In fact, the scenery is much more awe-inspiring than Mars would ever be; after all, space navigators usually select a relatively level landscape for landing. Here the mountain sides soar up into the heavens, daubed with a kaleidoscope of colours as the sun peers through the jagged peaks to light up snow-covered peaks, glaciers and dark, foreboding valleys. The only life we saw, apart from hovering vultures and hawks, were marmots that scampered over the rocks. In the empty vastness of this spectacular panorama it was easy to believe that the abominable snowman existed.

We passed the 7,000 metre-high peaks of Kun and Nun, and the Nun Kun glacier, bumping and grinding our way past Rangdum Gompa, a thousand-year-old lamasery whose monks are cut off from the outside world for eight months of the year – and who give the impression they are not greatly inclined to travel any further during the balmy few remaining. We passed over the 4,400 metre-high Pensi *La* (pass), heading for the bright lights, or rather oil lamps, of Padam.[5] With twilight deepening we called a halt at a rare patch of level but rocky ground, beside a gurgling brook and  not far from a small collection of inhabited stone huts which reminded me of a deserted cluster of *botháns* abandoned in Co. Kerry at the time of the Great Famine. We set about erecting our tents while

---

[5] In some Arab countries they go on a bit about their djebels and their wadis; in Tibet they presume such features to be the normal dispensation, their main topographical concern is for the local *la*.

our sherpas began preparing the evening meal. This was not as easy as it seemed but our chefs were experienced: at that altitude water boils at about 85° centigrade, so cooking rice or eggs takes far longer than at sea level.

In all such communities deprived of electricity the practice is to hit the horizontal at sunset and rise before sun-up. We savoured a few glasses of carefully conserved Bordelaise while marvelling at the clarity of the bitingly-clear night sky in the gratifying lack of urban light-spill. The moon was bright as a Camembert and had what appeared to be a halo around it. It seemed as if one could reach out in the starry canopy of the sky and snatch a handful of stars. We adjourned to our Indian army tents for the night. I found that they obviously do not cater for six-foot draftees since my tent was at least six inches too short. I stuck my stocking-clad feet outside - which was not the brightest idea. This immediately attracted the attention of the Tibet mastiffs the villagers use to safeguard their valuable Kashmiri goats corralled behind low stone walls from the attentions of wolves or snow leopards. Feet retracted, the hounds withdrew, till I was awakened a second time to hear the dogs snarling at the half frozen toes again protruding. At least my undercarriage had been spared a pedicure from a snow leopard, though that might have made for a good story had I been subsequently interviewed hobbling down Grafton Street. Just what is it about animals in different corners of the globe which are respectful of a body as long as it is enveloped in a millimetre of tent cotton?

Next morning the natural instinct was to wash and shave in the nearby brook - except that it was no longer babbling, having frozen over during the night. What to do? Let nature take its course and avail of a good excuse to grow a beard. At least the children from the local huts did not object to our hirsute appearance, especially as the strangers were distributing biscuits, biros and balloons. And during daylight the hounds transmogrified into poodles.

We visited the monks of the *gompa*, were given a guided tour and treated hospitably to mugs of yak-butter tea. Footsore and weary from an afternoon's trekking we retired for a late afternoon rest while the sherpas prepared the evening repast. We awoke feeling cold and quite damp: in the late afternoon the sunshine briefly kissed the snow on a nearby mountainside and our campsite was swamped by its melt water. Maybe that would have been the ideal time for a wash and shave.

## Kargil

After a few days exploring the rugged charms of Zanskar valley we headed back to the military road and the bright lights of Kargil, a town three-quarters Muslim, quarter Buddhist. Our departure was temporarily deferred by the fact that the diesel fuel had jellified during the night. But our drivers were up to the challenge: they lit rags which they held on sticks to the undersides of the reluctant diesel tanks until the contents had sufficiently liquefied. Fearing an explosion, which would have happened had it been petrol, I hopped onto the lorry to extricate my camera and flea bag.

In Kargil we booked into a hotel whose notice board proudly informed intending guests that it was nothing less than a seven-star establishment and came highly recommended – by the owners. We found that the as-yet-to-be-inaugurated establishment needed some further fine-tuning to live up to its stellar designation – such as the provision of door handles and locks, doors in some cases, and running water in almost all. My room was situated right over the town's diesel-powered electricity generator. This should have been no problem as they switched it off at about 9.30 p.m. But then they switched it on again just before midnight, and again at three in the morning to provide power for the local mosque from whose minaret the muezzin called the faithful to prayer every three hours. I have always considered the muezzin's call of the Faithful to prayer as an evocative and resonant characteristic of a visit to the Lands of the Prophet, especially if he is endowed with a nice baritone voice and his invocation of the Compassionate and the Merciful is scheduled no earlier than 6.00 a.m. But there is a limit to such endearments when the antiphon consists of a generator a few metres from one's room and the subsequent serenading is amplified from what resembles an intercontinental ballistic minaret encrusted with omni-directional boom boxes.

Still unshaven, complete with hennaed beard, though now generously scented of diesel aftershave, sun- and sand-blasted of vis-
age, I set my own alarm clock for well before the decibel diva got
going again at 6.00 a.m.

I had left the group for a day or two and was travelling on my
own on the daily public bus to Leh. The hotel concierge arranged a
sherpa to carry my bag to the bus at 5.00 a.m., where I was advised
that an offering of baksheesh would ensure a seat reservation as it
was bound to be crowded. Sitting drowsily awaiting the bus to fill
and depart, I was fascinated to note a group of little boys playing
what obviously was a game of cricket on the nearby parking lot. No
doubt some long-forgotten District Officer in this most remote outpost of the Raj had introduced the game here many moons ago. It
may not have convinced me as to the merits of empire-building but
sure raised my appreciation of what one stalwart player of the Great
Game, possibly an ex-internee of Eton, had achieved in his own way.

## Leh

The military road to Leh, capital of Ladakh, may be rough but it
leaves one of those indelible memories which etch themselves onto
one's consciousness. The epic day-long journey passes the giant
statue of the Maitreya Buddha sculpted out of a hillside at Mulbekh
in the eight century, and the enchanting vista of the Lamayaru
gompa, a kilometre off the roadway and set against the towering
mountains, looking like a mini version of the majestic Potala at
Lhasa in Tibet. The bleak roadside is frequently relieved by iconic
*chortens*; these are religious structures, up to ten metres high, consisting of a square base like a mini pyramid, a round structure like
an inverted bun surmounted by a bronze or stone circular column
and crowned by a moon holding a sun.

All over, especially near villages or gompas, were the ubiquitous prayer flags and inscriptions of the auspicious mantra, *Om
mani padme hum* (praise the jewel at the heart of the lotus).
Which is a lot kinder and more reassuring for visitors than, say,
'kill all infidels', or 'death to the Great Satan', while the idea of
prayer flags, whose every flutter signifies a prayer for you, seems

much more efficient than the repetitious reciting of individual beads on the rosary.

Leh is no Himalayan Florence, although the inhabitants, Tibetan, lowland Indian military and a sprinkling of Kashmiri Muslims, are very friendly, especially if they are involved in providing services to tourists. Its most outstanding feature is an old palace, now abandoned, and innumerable stores of dubious architectural merit, mostly catering for the tourist trade. But it is a base from which to visit the magnificent old Tibetan gompas and their treasures within a radius of a hundred kilometres or so, some bordering on the Chang Tang plateau which gives its name to the eponymous pashmina-haired goats. These include eleventh century Alchi with its beautiful frescos; Spituk, also eleventh century, and situated beside the embryonic Indus River; Phyang, with its many magnificent stone-coloured *thang-ka* paintings (depicting with calligraphic precision details from the life of the Buddha), libraries and highly decorated wooded pillars; Shey, with its many chorten and two imposing statues of Buddha; Thiksey, with its wonderful view of the valley below which rewards the demanding climb to the top floor; and, Hemis, one of the largest with 500 monks and founded in 1602, with its exquisite paintings, frescos, statues of Buddha and bronze figurines.

After a while the roll call of gompas morphed into one another, but I will ever retain a fond memory of the extraordinary gilded portals leading to their exotic interiors, the scent of incense, the butter votive lamps, the mani mantra stones, the hanging thangkas framed with silk, the locals wearing traditional stovepipe hats with gull wings, and the hospitality of yak-butter tea.

## Machu Picchu, Lost City of the Incas – Sublime Enigma

There are few more magical sights to enchant the weary traveller than the vista suddenly unveiled on reaching the *Intipunku*, Gate of the Sun, along the high Andean Inca Trail. Approaching Machu Picchu from along the Inca Trail, 60 tough kilometres from the depart point at 'Stop 88', descending the last of many high passes which exceed 4,200 metres, one gains this first spectacular sight of the Lost City of the Incas. On a bend in the trail the Gateway frames the sublime vista of the silent stones, some five kilometres distant. This is the ceremonial city never discovered by the Spanish Conquistadores in all their searches for *El Dorado*, nor by later treasure-seekers along the forgotten, jungle-shrouded trail to the lost, last Inca city of Vilcabamba.

Time, the ravages of weather and the encroachment of the jungle may have stripped away the finer paintwork and wooden roofs of the ancient city, but the solid foundations, the fine carvings of the more important buildings, testify to a culture and architecture which specialised in dressing stones more elegantly and precisely than the old Egyptians or Romans. The ruins stand proudly as an evocative reminder that this was the last major civilisation to be discovered and conquered by the expanding West. They had not devised the rounded arch of the Romans but, unlike the Greeks who were without exception 90 degree designers, they did develop trapezoidal doors and windows whose sides lean inwards on the rise, providing far greater stability in that earthquake-prone region. The delicately tapering ruins imitate the surrounding peaks, enveloped usually in a blue, misty haze. This was a culture which, like their Mayan cousins, could calculate precisely celestial movements but had not invented the wheel, except for children's toys. Of course, the rugged, gruelling mountainous nature of their Andean kingdom, stretching thousands of kilometres from modern Ecuador and Columbia to Argentina and Chile, dictated that feet or hooves would be the sole means of transport on the great highways, more stairway than roadway, which joined up their immense Empire. Not having developed an advanced system of writing, though they had devised a system for recording physical accounts, the main record of their ancient civilisation has only been transmitted to us through the perspective of their conquerors.

The great Empire was only a century old, being founded about 1430, when a period of internal strife coincided with the arrival of a fearless, gung-ho, double-crossing buccaneer, Francisco Pizarro, from the new Spanish territories in Panama. A cross between Genghis Khan and Machiavelli, amazingly his 'army' merely consisted

of 183 men, mostly hardy ruffians from the desiccated plains of Ex-
tremadura, armed with metal weapons and 37 horses (horses being
then unknown to the Incas). Of course a hidden weapon was later
unwittingly unleashed on the Incas: European diseases to which
they had no resistance. These intruders must have seemed like ex-
tra-terrestrials to the poor Bronze Age Incas. Pizarro succeeded in
crossing the desert coastline, climbing the steep Andes towards
Cuzco, and defeating the Inca Empire, much as Cortez had done to
the indigenous Mexicans and their leader Montezuma. A weakness
of the otherwise collectivised, agriculture-based Inca society was
that it was structured on a hierarchical, class-ridden fashion, each
of the main tribes having a leader, but with the Inca Emperor in
overall charge. There seems to have been a labouring class, hard
worked although not enslaved, but whose loyalties, when the test
eventually came, could be swayed by the Spaniards.

That agriculture was highly important is evidenced by the complex system of agricultural terraces and irrigation noted, inter alia,
in the ruins of Machu Picchu. Their main food was Indian corn – or
maize as we know it. In the outlying regions of Empire, probably in
modern day Bolivia, the potato was cultivated, although it could
also have been grown on the terraces of the lost city. Archaeologists
still dispute the original role the mountain city played: it could not
have contained more than 1,000 inhabitants and may have been
mostly devoted to ceremonials. Like all Inca towns there are ample
storage facilities for agricultural produce and shelters for their lla-
mas, as well as defensive positions and ceremonial buildings, including the Temple of the Sun, and the nearby *Intihuatana*, the
Hitching Post of the Sun. The real political centre of their world
was higher up the Urubamba Valley, at Cusco, where the four corners of their Empire came together at the *Qosqo*, the earth's navel
in old Quechua.

Within twenty years or so of the arrival of Columbus, the Spanish had conquered Mexico and arrived at the Isthmus of Panama.
Under Balboa they managed to cross this narrow, jagged, jungle-
covered, disease-infested barrier to access the South Sea (the Pa-

cific Ocean) to establish the town of Panama. This was achieved by Balboa and not, as Keats suggested, by

> ... stout Cortez, when with eagle eyes
> He star'd at the Pacific – and all his men
> Looked at each other with a wild surmise –
> Silent, upon a peak in Darien.

Among Balboa's men was Pizarro. No doubt he learned a lesson from the glory-stealing Cortez, since he went on to double-cross not only the Inca but his own companions in conquest. Setting out by boat to explore the coast south of Panama he eventually came across an Inca balsa trading raft carrying much silver, gold and precious stones. Some Incas sailors jumped into the sea to escape, others were released on land to spread the story of the kindly Signor Pizarro, while three were shrewdly held to learn Spanish and act as interpreters later. The more gold and silver the Conquistadores saw the more it whetted their appetites. The entrepreneurial, illiterate, yet ruthlessly courageous Pizarro then returned to Spain to seek finance from a contemporary 'venture capitalist'. Back in Peru in 1530 he made his way inland with his newly-financed men and horses, encountering almost incredible challenges. He eventually managed to convince part of the Inca army to come unarmed to meet him, massacred them, fooled the Inca general once again, trapped the Inca chief Atahualpa, ransomed him for an enormous amount of gold and jewels stripped from the temples of the great Inca city of Cuzco, then refuse to release him. On capturing Cuzco he cynically executed the cruel but naïve Atahualpa in the central square.

Some years and much Inca grief later, the Conquistadores hunted down the last rebel chief, Tupac Amaru, who was then burned at the stake in Cuzco. Leaving a garrison in that great city Pizarro carrying much of his looted treasure, artwork, gold decorations and icons from the temples, melted down for convenience of transport, returned to the new coastal city of Lima. Some years later his gory past caught up with him: his brother Hernando had executed Pizarro's earliest companion, Diego di Almagro, whose son and followers were seeking revenge. They achieved this when, at his Governor's residence in Lima in 1541, he was assassinated. His other main partner in plunder and villainy, de Valverde, now promoted to Bishop, took off on hearing the news, and was captured and eaten by natives en route to Panama. Which seems to prove there is a just God after all![6]

Although the conquerors later managed to find silver mines, enslaving the locals in the process, the outlying Inca towns fell into decay as their citizens were decimated from war, massacre and disease. However there was no deliberate program of extermination as practised later in North America and Argentina. The old towns, settlements and trails were soon swallowed up by the jungle, yet the legend persisted that before his capture Tupac Amaru, last chief of the Inca, had managed to stash away much treasure in his secreted redoubt, Vilcabamba. The hunt began for this lost city, but neither it, nor the then unknown Machu Picchu, was found by the Spaniards.

Among those who came seeking Vilcabamba was a young, intrepid archaeologist from Yale University, Hiram Bingham. In 1911 he was following a newly-opened path cut through the Urubamba Valley from Cuzco to assist transport of that much-sought after, valuable commodity, rubber. He asked some locals if they knew the whereabouts of the lost city and was directed to a nearby hillside. The further he climbed the more he came on abandoned agricultural terraces, then on the more impressive masonry of the ruins, until the quality of some stonework, rivalling that in Cuzco and the nearby fortress of Sacsayhuaman, convinced Bingham that he had indeed found the lost city of Vilcabamba. In fact, earlier on he had been nearer than he imagined to the site, but Machu Picchu, meaning the old peak or bump, gloriously situated near the saddle of two mountain peaks, its twin being Huayna Picchu (Young Peak), captured his imagination and he was not to be gainsaid.

Yet the enigma of Machu Picchu continued: what exactly was it, a ceremonial, administrative or commercial town? An agricultural settlement to provide high quality coca leaves to the temples of Cuzco?

---

[6] This fascinating story is eloquently recounted, and in greater detail, by John Hemming in his book *The Conquest of the Incas*.

And the deeper enigma: why did the Spaniards never hear of it? After all, they had methods to encourage the locals to talk yet there is no evidence the locals knew of it at the time of the Conquest. So, it must have already been abandoned to the jungle, maybe because local resources were exhausted, it had been devastated by an epidemic, or the local jungle tribe had wiped out its inhabitants.

With the help, initially, of Yale University funding, the site was gradually cleared and explored by archaeologists. Recently discovered archaeological sites nearby are helping to shine a light on the exact role it played in Inca history and may even eventually explain why it had been abandoned and forgotten. More recently experts have discovered the ruins of Vilcabamba along the overgrown Inca Trail, 100 kilometres further down the Andes in the direction of the Amazon.

Potential visitors should, ideally, if they have the time and energy, take the Inca Trail to get a real feel for the landscape and local colour. It takes three or four days of sometimes hard trekking from 'Stop 88'. Local porters, with lungs twice as large as our sea-level versions, can carry heavy backpacks over the passes to the next overnight halt site while the tourist travels with a light knapsack. Best consult a good travel guide in advance. Those arriving by train from Cuzco to Agua Calientes, especially on an organised circuit, should try to book a trip which involves an overnight stay at or near Machu Picchu. Most visitors arrive on the morning train from Cuzco at nine or ten, dash madly round the ruins for a few hours midst a crush of other tourists, have lunch at 1.30 p.m. and return to the train, leaving the site to those fortunate enough to stay on till the following morning's repeat invasion. Staying overnight allows a leisurely reconnaissance of the site, an exploration of the Inca Trail in comfort and a visit to Intipunku to watch the sunrise over the majestic site. It also gives one a second opportunity of seeing the ruins with their evocative mountain backdrop if, as sometimes happens, it has been covered in cloud on day one.

Since the gateway city of Cuzco is located at 3,700 metres, far higher than Machu Picchu at only 2,800 metres, it is a good idea to make a graduated change from the costal city at Lima by visiting the beautiful old city of Arequipa at 2,800 metres for a few days en route. Towering over the city is the foreboding, rumbling volcano El Misty. As well as the gorgeous old cathedral it is worthwhile visiting the spacious convent of Catelina. While in the university museum rests the well-preserved, serene mummy of the poor little Ampato Maiden, probably only twelve years when she was ceremoniously marched up to the top of the mountain of that name to be sacrificed to the Sun god and buried in the high, permanent snows. Her haunting remains were only recently discovered by archaeologists.[7]

On arrival at lofty Cuzco it is highly advisable, as in Lhasa, to rest up on the first day. At the airport and in the hotel there are flasks of oxygen available for the temporarily weak of limb. The old Temple of the Sun is only one of the many wonders to be seen. Not to be missed is the famous 12-angled carved stone along the Hatunrumiyoc laneway, nestling perfectly amid a lapidary jig-saw puzzle of artistic masonry. The Calle Loreto and others maintain the old Incan stone walls, some incorporated Roman-style as palimpsests upon which newer structures have been superimposed.

A visitor can stay most comfortably at the charismatic old Hotel Monasterio, carefully converted, as its name implies, from an old Spanish monastery, with many rooms overlooking the interior atrium garden. At reception one is welcomed in traditional mountain style with a samovar of boiling water, goblets and coca leaves, loose or in dainty tea bags, provided to dispel any potential altitude sickness, a tonic resorted to since time immemorial by the locals.

There is a wealth of ancient monuments and colourful towns within a short distance of Cuzco. The market town of Chincheros, like nearby Pisac, is delightful on market day, like a Peruvian Chichicastenango, as the local vendors don their finest traditional gear to sell fresh foods, naturally-dyed wool, handicrafts and artwork to locals and visitors alike. At nearby Ollantaytambo are walls composed of inter-joined monoliths weighing up to 50 tons and carted, one knows not how, from the facing mountainside.

---

[7] National Geographic has made a very touching film of her final days.

The same station which provides the train to Machu Picchu also hosts the TransAndean train to Puno, high up on the altiplano, beside Lake Titicaca at 3,800 metres, with floating islands and totora reed boats. Nearby beckon the ruins of another ancient culture: the older and ever more venerable Tiwanaku on the high road to La Paz.

## Easter Island, or Rapa Nui – Magnificent Isolation

Apart from Pitcairn Island there are few places on Earth as remote as Easter Island, or Rapa Nui as the original inhabitants call it. A quiet, peaceful 30 kilometres long volcanic speck, lost in the boundless wastes of the Pacific Ocean, it is five hours travel from the Chilean coast - by jet aircraft, not by boat. In the other direction Polynesia and Hawaii are also hours away by jet. Yet all the evidence is that the original colonisers were intrepid and extraordinarily-professional Polynesian navigators who arrived in large, open-ocean, double-hulled canoes and who brought plants and livestock with them. These were men, and their ladies, who could navigate across the vast distances of the Pacific without any compasses, depending only on their innate skills, super sharp reading of certain indicators, such as the direction of a flight of birds returning with sea food to feed their young, or vegetation floating on the surface. (There are those who claim that Polynesian sailors can smell land 50 miles away.) They probably arrived about 400 AD, long after their people had colonised Hawaii and New Zealand (*Aotoaroa* to them), so that those three lands comprise the triangular limits of the Polynesian conquest, enclosing a large proportion of the Earth's surface.

The indigenous people account for about half of the population of approximately 2,700. As a result of their keen sense of navigation they don't greet one another with a cheery 'hello', or *Dia dhuit*, but *kihe koe*, meaning 'where are you heading?' in Rapanui, a language related to the Maori of Cook Islands.

All the archaeological evidence, supported by modern research methods, indicates that when they arrived the island was covered in forest and dense vegetation, with a limited amount of fauna, including the bird-life which survived their accidental introduction of rats which had travelled in their canoes. Though semitropical, the island is a little too far south of the equator to sustain coral reefs with their wealth of marine life, so the newcomers cut down trees to provide the wood with which to build a range of specialised fishing boats adapted to the local deep water conditions. There were many types of tree growing on the island when first occupied, the most outstanding being the giant Chilean wine palm which grew far taller than on the distant mainland of South America.

The historical evidence suggests that their founding community was divided into two main tribal groupings under a king. These included a number of social strata, such as priests, aristocrats, workers and slaves. They adopted the typical Polynesian practice of constructing outdoor stadia for religious ceremonies but added large stone platforms, the *ahus*, near the coast, with statues, called *moai*, representing important ancestors, placed on these. The statues faced inland to emphasise that the gods were important to the local faithful, not some sort of disinterested deities looking out to sea. With the passage of time these platforms, the most sacred parts of the stadia, became *tapu* (taboo) to all except the priests. To emphasise the importance of tribe and family and, in the spirit of one-upmanship, these became progressively larger and larger. Later, to enhance the size and importance of the statues, large red stones or *pukao*, weighing up to ten tons each, were placed like top hats on the heads of the statues.

The characteristic style of the statues themselves was probably based on old Polynesian wood or fishbone carvings, some of which may well have been brought with the original settlers. They included the head and upper body of both men and women though, surprise, surprise, mostly of male ancestors. The defining characteristic features of these mystical and iconic sculptures are the protruding chin, long, stubbed nose, fine and joined lips, prominent angular cheekbones and long ears. One of the largest completed is almost 10 metres tall and weighs some 70 tons. When erected and about to be ceremonially inaugurated there is evidence that eye holes were carved and coral or whale bone used for the white of the eye and scoria rock or basalt for the iris. Those few which have been restored, and which include these peering eyes, have an eerie effect on the observer – one can imagine the profound impression on the original onlooker.

Almost 1,000 moai were completed at specialist quarries; only one-third made it the distance to their ahus. Many were abandoned at the quarries or en route to the intended seaside location. Others lie unfinished, one of the largest being El Gigante, an enormous 21 metres high and weighing, had it been completed, between 160 and 180 tons. The statues were sculpted horizontally either out of tufo (volcanic tuff) rock or tougher basalt using even harder tools of black obsidian. Many of the chisels and specialist tools used were found near the uncompleted statues in the quarries. The most productive quarry was that of Ranu Raraku where the rock is tufo,[8] a softer form of volcanic stone which is ideal for sculpting.

One reason why there was such a mystique about the strange statues was the early European voyagers could not understand how such massive objects were transported miles from the quarries to their shoreside destinations on an island where there were no longer any  trees to use as rollers, nor hemp to make ropes. It appeared even more enigmatic than the question of how the huge stones used in the Egyptian or Mexican Pyramids, or at the Inca fortress of Sacsayhuaman, were transported. One eminent scribbler even suggested it was proof that extraterrestrials had visited the Earth. It is now agreed by archaeologists that they were rolled on tree trunks to the altars, and poor husbandry eventually led to the disappearance of trees on the island. Not only did this spell an end to their fishing fleets but the lack of root systems allowed rain to wash away the topsoil, and undermined tillage and bird life. For a fuller account of the mystery of Easter Island consult Jared Diamond's book *Collapse: How Societies Choose to Fail or Survive*. He devotes a chapter to the implosion of Rapa Nui, from its internal tribal rivalries, to its excesses in exploitation of a limited land and

---

[8] It seems similar to the type of rock through which the early Roman Christians tunnelled the catacombs.

coastal environment, the consumption of the last chickens and wild bird life, with the ultimate descent into cannibalism. For him it is a lesson we should all take to heart because of the strong parallels with today's threat worldwide to our own limited earthly resources.

If the mystery of the statues was solved by the realisation that there had once been trees on the island, one final enigma remains which resists the sharpest minds: the deciphering of the Rapa Nui *Rongorongo* script. It is one of the few writing systems which are still undecoded, along with Etruscan, ancient Nubian, Minoan linear A from Crete, two ancient scripts from Mexico and one from the Indus Valley. But of them all Rongorongo is the most beautiful, using mainly some 120 symbols, based on plants, fish, birds, and some geometric shapes. Most of the rare examples left are found inscribed on pieces of wood, including battle staffs. But with the cutting down of the last trees no further wood was available apart from driftwood and all examples are now held in collections abroad, with nothing remaining in the local museum at Hanga Roa.

As a result of the disintegration of the island old beliefs in the ability of the priests to deliver *la dolce vita* were swept away, statues of tribal altars were destroyed and a new religion, the Birdman Cult, was introduced. In order to climb the promotion ladder in this new creed stalwarts had to swim through shark-infested, choppy waters to the nearest offshore island to fetch whatever birds' eggs were in season – the Rapa Nui version of swimming from the Kerry coast to Skellig Michael and back. However, by that time the population had been further decimated: famine, smallpox and other diseases brought by passing sailing ships took their toll; Peruvian slavers abducted half the population in the late 18th century and, when Chile took possession of the island formally in 1888, vast herds of sheep and goats were introduced which stripped the island of anything edible that was left.

An interesting historical footnote is that just after the outbreak of the First World War the Admiral of the German Pacific Squadron sailed to Easter Island for supplies of fresh water and victuals, and paid the British rancher who supplied the lot with a cheque drawn on the German government. Cut off from the rest of the world and without radio, the islanders were unaware war had broken out, and the admiral remained *shtum*. But after the war was over the punctilious Germans eventually redeemed the cheque.

Most of the remaining moai were destroyed by the locals between the time of the first Dutch naval visit in 1722 and Captain Cook's arrival in 1774. What remained of the ahu and moai, especially at Aku Tongariki, the largest with 15 moai on its ahu, was swept inland by a tsunami in 1960, following a powerful earthquake in southern Chile. The eminent archaeologist Claudio Cristino assisted in its restoration in the 1990s, with the help of a crane he entreated and finally charmed from its Japanese manufacturer. Even with the help of this advanced lifting device it was only with the utmost effort that the final statues and pukau hats were returned to their original position. The tsunami had swept these giant blocks almost a kilometre inland from the coast and most were broken into pieces.

Although there is an enormous gap between the more affluent Chilean settler society and the descendants of the indigenous population, the latter are now beginning to acquire political and economic status. The massive herds of sheep and goats were finally removed by the mid-1980s, allowing replenishment of native and cultivation of new flora to the island. An attempt was made to reintroduce the Chilean wine palm from the Chilean mainland but the land and the soil on Rapa Nui have changed so much that it just would not grow there anymore.

Some years ago NASA built a long runway in case the Shuttle had to make an emergency landing in the middle of the Pacific; this is now used as the local airport with twice-weekly Air Chile flights from Santiago and Tahiti. Since the climate is very mild, and there are a number of sandy beaches across the relatively small island, a visit combines the best of adventure with comfort. It is one of the destinations which has improved in recent years as a result of access by air, the presence of a few modest though pleasant hotels and restaurants, and a considerable number of restored ahu and moai. The fact that it is so far away and air transport correspondingly expensive means it retains a sense of isolation and serenity, with an unsophisticated and friendly people, and where one can still enjoy freedom from the stresses and demands of modern competitive life.

A visit to the anthropological museum is a must to gain an understanding of the people and their culture. At the Taha archaeological zone, within walking distance of the main town Hanga Roa, there is a fully restored moai, complete with scoria top hat and restored eyes. A few miles away lies Ahu Akive one of the first restored ahus with the characteristic seven statues on top. Nearby are the Te Pahu lava tubes (volcanic caves) which were used by the people in dire circumstances during the worst of the civil strife. Another 'must' is a visit to the Rano Raraku quarries where the majority of the statues were carved and El Gigante lies semi-entombed and semi-completed in its rock embrace. Nearby are picnic facilities under the trees. The most impressive of the ahus is that of Ahu Tongariki with its iconic fifteen-statue altar.

The hilltop Vinapu ceremonial centre is fascinating as the stone constructions are somewhat similar to those found near Cusco in Peru, which convinced the maverick adventurer and archaeologist *manqué* Thor Hyderdahl, mistakenly, that the natives were originally Amerindians who had arrived from Peru on totora reed or balsa wood canoes. Though it was probably a wasted effort, he made a name for himself as a great adventurer, especially in Hollywood, by making such a trip himself, and no doubt had lots of fun into the bargain. Further along the dirt track lie the Rano Kau dormant volcano and caldera and the Birdman Cult's ceremonial village of Orongo, from which the Birdmen dived into the ocean to bring home, if not the *en primeur* Beaujolais,[9] but the season's earliest and freshest Sooty Tern eggs to a hungry and grateful populace.

A stroll around the lively but decidedly non-hectic town centre is to be recommended by day as well as by night.

A visit to the anthropological museum is essential to complete one's picture of Rapa Nui culture and history. There is a fine souve-

---

[9] A long lost wine variety, Carmenère, 'the lost grape of Bordeaux', was rediscovered there about 20 years ago. It had probably been introduced by thirsty missionaries two hundred years earlier.

nir shop beside it with plentiful documentation, history, anthropology, geology, zoology, etc., and sale of local handicrafts. The nearby church is also worth seeing with its unique statuary in the Polynesian style, the most unforgettable statue being a unique depiction of the Holy Ghost, displaying the considerable imaginative process of the artist. By the altar are a Mother and Child, with baby Jesus in profile, as some irreverent locals suggest, like a cross between a moai and a Mussolini.

A most memorable experience is to rouse oneself well before dawn and take a horse or taxi to Ahu Tongariki as the sun rises on the ocean side, directly behind the majestic statues. A wonderful silhouette can thus be recorded as the first golden light of dawn breaches the black ocean horizon and a kaleidoscope of colours plays out among the clouds – or, as Homer more elegantly put it, 'when primal dawn spread on the eastern sky her fingers of pink light'. I once had the good fortune to witness dawn in the company of Claudio Cristino and an eclectic American geophysicist Dennis Marks and his wife Patricia; in the minutes before dawn Dennis pointed out the different planets and star formations as seen from the austral hemisphere. He then discussed with Claudio the likelihood that a certain constellation resembled markings on a petroglyph near the Birdman ceremonial centre. Archaeologist and geophysicist began discussing the inscriptions and agreed that that could well be the meaning of the strange markings.

One question was left enigmatically unanswered: who was the genius so reckless that he chopped down the very last tree, turning the indigenous inhabitants into boat-less prisoners?

## Brazil – twixt wood and water

Among its many superlatives Brazil boasts the largest marshland and river in the world. The Pantanal, in the Mato Grosso (thick forest) south of the country, is considered a marsh although it is strictly a giant, flooded, alluvial plain of 130,000 kilometres square, which spreads another 100,000 over the borders into Bolivia and Paraguay (in comparison, the whole of the Green and Misty Isle is a mere 84,000 kilometres square). It is fed by the Paraguay, Parana

and Cuiaba rivers. In the wet season some two-thirds lie under water, in the dry season about one-third. The Amazon is the second
longest river after the Nile at 6,400 kilometres, but the largest in
the world; with its headwaters way back in the Peruvian Andes, it
passes below Machu Picchu as the Urubamba, goes through many
more names changes, including Solimoes, to officially become the
Amazon once it meets the Rio Negro at Manaus. From there it is a
mere 1,600 kilometres to the Atlantic. Ocean-going ships can navigate its bounteous waters from Belem at the Atlantic mouth right
up to Iquitos in Peru, some 3,600 kilometres in total. It drains some
40 per cent of Brazil, the fifth largest country in the world – as well
as large portions of Peru, Columbia and Venezuela. It is said to contain some 20 per cent of the world's supply of freshwater. In between these two mighty waterways lies the thick, steamy and exotic
Amazon jungle.

These woods and waters account for a vast selection of superla-
tive flora and fauna, much of it unique to the region. The Amazon
forest is of interest to the visitor mainly because of its abundant flora
since fauna are difficult for non-experts to spot, while the Pantanal is
noted for its exotic fauna, especially amphibians, hosting the greatest
concentration in the New World. Other, less adventurous, travellers
are more attracted to Brazil's coastal ecosystems, especially such delightful resorts as Ipanema and Copacabana beaches. All told they
constitute a magnificent, unforgettable photo safari, although being
equipped with binoculars will prove even more rewarding.

### Pantanal

The Pantanal consists of a complex intermingling of land and water, of forest, islands, rivers, lakes, bays, channels, creeks, and
ponds – an ocean of fresh water under boundless skies. The border
between land and water is undefined, constantly changing with the
season. During the wet season (October to March) many of the
low-lying islands are completely submerged. During the rainy season the territory is composed of an archipelago of islands, but in
the dry season is intersected by *boreens* used by the local cowboys
and stockmen as they herd their white humpbacked *Zebu* cattle to

fresh grazing. There are estimated to be over 300 species of fish in
the waters and 600 species of birdlife. But the most memorable and
dominant image of the Pantanal is one of waterways infested by
alligators, called *jacares* locally. The adults of this prehistoric species are at the top of the food chain, they survive mainly on the
abundant fish life, especially the catfish and piranha. The jacares
share their watery world with anacondas, *sucuri,* which are the
largest snakes in the world. Boa constrictors are also to be seen
sliding nonchalantly through the grasses or wrapped around
branches in trees. Among the myriads of birds, including storks,
herons, spoonbills, the most characteristic is the *tuiuiu* (pronounced too-you-you), the *jaburu* stork, a good metre and a half
tall supported on skinny stilt-like legs – an underwater camouflage
to unwary fish as they look like swamp grass stalks – and equipped
with a prehensile, scimitar-like beak about a metre long which can
effortlessly grab the most ferocious of the 20-odd species of piranha. Its body is covered in white feathers while the black beak and
neck are separated from the rest by a bright red collar. These incredible creatures can actually fly. They become airborne by grace-
lessly legging it a certain distance and, at maximum speed, they
flap wings and withdraw spindly undercarriage, somehow achieving
lift-off, reminiscent of the converted DC4 Carvairs Aer Lingus used
as air ferries back in the fifties. Among the land-based animals is
another unusual creature: the *capybara*, weighting up to 65 kilo-
grams and looking like a large dog supported on rat-like legs, which
is not surprising as it belongs to the rodent family. These innocent-
looking creatures feed entirely on vegetation and spend much time
in the water, which is why their noses, eyes and ears are positioned
on top of their over-sized heads. When resting on land they look
like contented sphinxes, their noses constantly twitching. Their
main predators are the anacondas. One adult capybara for lunch
and an anaconda is apparently satiated for over a month.

I was innocently strolling down a *boreen* one day when I noticed a very agitated tuiuiu in a channel jabbing furiously at the water with his beak. Thinking it was one tough piranha putting up a
final fight I noticed that there seemed to be a long fire hose rising

up and down like the Loch Ness monster, except that this one was exceptionally thick and colourful. I then realized that it was an anaconda attacking from underwater, trying to encoil the tuiuiu's stalky legs, which would have been fatal. The tuiuiu retreated on its spindly pins, constantly jabbing at the anaconda's head with its giant beak. Then the tuiuiu did a quick pirouette, splashed off onto the marshland and managed lift-off, disappointing a rather ruffled, and possibly injured six or seven metres of anaconda which slithered by me. I don't know if he saw me but carried on anyway: maybe he had had enough for one day – or was a discerning diner. But I was told they prefer to attack from underwater where they are far more agile, their bodies are a bit too heavy for manoeuvring on land. Apparently if the anaconda can suddenly coil its body around the jaws of an alligator, which has powerful closing muscles but almost no opening power, the poor old croc is done for; but if it fails to clamp the jaws then the anaconda is in trouble.

Our *fazenda*, a time-warped ranch-style guesthouse, organised motor-powered canoes for us to tour the waterways and watch the unfolding drama of wildlife stalking for prey, feeding and resting. The alligators basked in the sunshine preferring to hunt underwater, mainly at night. Herons caught fish in their beaks, expertly tossed them in the air and swallowed them headfirst, while avoiding spiky dorsal fins. Trees, colonised by myriads of birds, were silhouetted against the sky. There were many tuiuiu, twenty or more to a tree, together with young. We made as little noise as possible passing these as a sudden sound could startle them all into flight and many of the baby birds, unable to fly, would fall into the water or on the land to be gobbled up by hungry predators. We sighted a few human inhabitants, eking out an existence in temporary huts, a few zebu cattle in the background. At one point our motor broke down and the boatman pulled over to the bank, by a tiny *bothán*, for repairs. This gave us the chance to engage with a family of locals. The *bean a' tí* was busy de-scaling piranhas she had caught, ready to cook *sopa de piranha* lunch. We shared drinks: we gladly accepted her coffee, while she and the kids enjoyed chilled colas from our icebox. The *fear a' tí* was busy cutting up a cow hide to made reins. The kids were playing at the water's edge; occasionally mama cautioned them not to swim near the group of alligators, tennis-ball eye sockets and snouts protruding from the water, in the nearby channel. In fact that was normal, since, over a few hundred years, the jacares have somehow developed a live-and-let-live accommodation with invading caballeros and cattle, and prefer to hunt catfish by night. I asked the man of the house where we were. He replied that we were nowhere, but if we kept going in our boats for an hour in a certain direction we would arrive at a place with a name. A sound man with a clear sense of no place.

Motor repaired, we continued our fascinating sightseeing for another 60 kilometres until we arrived at a picnic spot on the banks of a creek to which the fazenda had sent a chef and barman to prepare our aperitifs and BBQ lunch. We started with very welcome *caiperinhas*: limes crushed in a tall glass, shredded ice added, then liquid cane sugar and *cachaca* cane rum. Perfect for the time, location and temperature. A couple of bored-looking jacares, each a good three metres long, crawled close to observe our antics. Jaws gaping, they remained at a respectable distance.

That night we took the boats out again, complete with torches to catch the reflection of the jacares' eyes, like coals glowing in the darkness. An overhead moon supplied sufficient light for our boatman to navigate, while our lamps picked out literally hundreds of the reptiles. Unfortunately for them this is how the poachers hunt them for their hides, killing between one and two million annually over the whole Pantanal. I had a torch in my hand leaning over the side of the narrow canoe just above the water when I noticed that silently, and without even a ripple, my torch was being escorted by a pair of tennis balls, encased not in yellow cotton but expensive-looking Gucci hide. I resisted the temptation to tickle his back; not knowing how crocs take to uninvited neck massages from perfect strangers and, anyhow, I feared that a lash of *caiman crocodilius yacare's* tail would capsize the canoe, and we would be suddenly in his environment. Later our lamps spotted a jacare exiting the water with a huge, flailing catfish in his jaws, his idea being to suffocate the fish on land. Caught on our torch beams the jacare became alarmed, ran around in circles on the muddy bank before sliding back into the water to wait our departure.

One day we abandoned canoes to set off with our guide through a marsh in search of a breeding spot for female anacondas. One of our little group balanced himself in the slippery mud by grabbing a liana for support. Unfortunately there was a hornets' nest in the tree and his rocking the cradle was not appreciated by the insects that attacked one innocent member of our group and almost stung him to death. We beat a hasty retreat.

Our fazenda was situated in the marshes some distance from Pocone, the gateway town to the northern Pantanal. We had flown in to the nearest airport at Cuiaba. Outside Pocone we visited a biblical scene, a deep crevasse created by *garimpeiros* or gold-diggers. Their gallery narrowed to about four metres far below ground, where hundreds of loin-clothed men slaved away in steaming humidity in search of the magic metal. Their only connection with the land above was by lengthy, rickety, ramshackle ladders improvised from the branches of trees. Sometimes the entire cuttings would collapse, burying alive the garimpeiros below. In washing out the gold they use lots of mercury, which is now seeping into the groundwater, spreading across the entire Pantanal and poisoning, first, those bottom-feeding fish at the base of the food chain, later, the birds and alligators which feed on them.

The first evening in my fazenda room I noticed what seemed to be a boldly coloured frog or lizard on the wall near the bed. Taking a piece of paper, since some frogs secrete poison on their highly-coloured backs and must be handled with care, I tried to catch the little chap in a paper towel, intending to throw him outside. When I approached him he effortlessly popped onto the opposite wall. Another attempt and he was on the ceiling. I then recalled that there are some little creatures called *geckos* which share a symbiotic relationship with humans who attract mosquitoes around their beds at night. The gecko jumps past you, flicks out its tongue en route to catch the mossies. The little creatures are a boon for anyone who is disturbed at night by the mini-buzzsaw-raspings of mosquito wings near one's ears. When I was packing to leave the fazenda I was tempted to catch my new friend, put him in a cigar box and bring him back to Belgium where the mosquitoes can be a nuisance on summer nights.[10]

Luckily, the flooding of the wet season which causes the waters to rise by up to three metres makes it difficult for humans to undertake permanent, intensive grazing, otherwise the Pantanal as we now know it would rapidly disappear. But the former system of light, extensive grazing by a small number of peasants and Indians is being jeopardized by the arrival not only of the gold miners but of land-grabbers and their hired guns, the *pistoleros*. They are attempting to cut down existing forests and reseed the islands with imported grasses to produce more cattle for the making of hamburgers. There have even been discussions and proposals to drain the general area in the interests of intensive agriculture and inland navigation. The depredations of the poachers and hide-smugglers continue, with only a handful of park guards to protect an area the size of France. One can only hope that ecotourism will provide sufficient employment opportunities, and the protests of concerned nature lovers the world over will convince the riparian states to protect this unique ecosystem for future generations.

### An Inland Ocean

If the Pantanal is mainly landscape and sky the dominant perspective of the Amazon forest is of an almost claustrophobic intermingling of plant life bounded on high by an impenetrable canopy. The Amazon itself is so wide, almost like an inland sea, that apart from the odd fresh-water dolphin, the bounteous forest is just a fringe on the riverside. My old Bradt guidebook explained different ways of capturing the feel of the place by taking cargo boats up from Belem to Manaus, providing useful advice regarding etiquette, if not survival skills, aboard. No doubt later editions provide up-to-date advice.

---

[10] A colleague of mine, Katherine, who worked in the Commission Delegation in Vietnam, and normally not an admirer of creepy-crawlies, adored these little creatures and would greet her fellow lodgers with a 'GECK *kow*, GECK *kow*', to which they would reply in kind. Presumably this is how they originally got their name.

Again, being short of time, we flew from the Pantanal to Manaus. Our small group hired a river boat which ferried us three hours up the Rio Negros. The trip reminded me of Conrad's morose description of sailing up the Congo River in *Heart of Darkness*. 'Going up that river was like travelling back to the earliest beginnings of the world, when vegetation rioted on the earth and the big trees were kings. An empty stream, a great silence, an impenetrable forest.[11] The air was warm, thick, heavy, sluggish. There was no joy in the brilliance of sunshine. The long stretches of the waterway ran on, deserted, into the gloom of the overshadowed distances.'

We reached our lodgings for the next few days, a forest-tree hotel – a form of Treetops-in-the-Amazon. It was grafted onto three large mahogany trees, 'emergents' which soared some ten metres above the canopy, in an *igapo,* or permanently flooded backwater, just off the main Rio Negro. The first tree comprised the floating pontoon deck and above that, approached by ladder, the reception area and desk. A wood and rope walkway linked that to the next tree, which housed the restaurant and bar, built round the huge tree trunk. A further walkway linked this with some twelve bedrooms built round the trunk of the third tree, like slices of cake leading out from the doorways. At the outer perimeter of the rooms was a tiny toilet, hand basin and shower. This was open to inspection by all the local fauna, but if any howler monkey, bird or tree boa decided to pay a social call, it was prevented from doing so by tough mesh netting. In this equatorial zoo we were the caged ones. Looking through this in daytime I could see the canopy of the jungle and, lazing in the river below, at least one decent-sized black caiman.

As we were on the Rio Negro I was delighted to hear there were no mosquitoes to bother us at night. The mighty river flows fast over old rocky terrain and, with no humus to break down leaf material, this turns into black acids. Hence there were no mosquitoes nor, unfortunately, giant Victoria lilies. Since my childhood I had

---

[11] Conrad was obviously writing from the perspective of a sailor: had he spent the night in the forest his description of the sounds to be heard would have been rather different. But the Congo is as wide as the Amazon and one might as well be at sea.

seen these growing inside the implacably steamy, hot, palm house in the Botanical Gardens at Glasnevin, Dublin, and had wanted to see them in their natural habitat. Both proliferate on the other branch of the river, the muddy yellow/brown Solimoes which meets the Negros at Manaus before their waters eventually intermingle a good 20 kilometres downstream. At the top of the middle and highest emergent (tree) an observation tower had been built. Since it rose some fifteen metres above the jungle canopy, it was an ideal spot from which to sit and watch all the comings and goings of the jungle. We were at one side of the Negro; the other bank was about 10 kilometres away – an inland sea, as the first conquistadores who accidentally found the Amazon, called it.

*Jungle Chorus*

Sleeping in the middle of the jungle is a wonderful experience. Although relatively quiet by day at night the noise, yea the almighty cacophony, raised first by rasping cicadas, equipped by nature with miniature football rattles, to be joined by tree frogs, birds, howler monkeys, gibbons, and thousands of other species, presumably advertising their wares during prime night time listening, or screeching in terror while being hunted, is an experience not to be missed. I lay awake for hours just enjoying the melodies of raw, primal nature. The background throb of the cicadas, whose vespers peaked about sunset, was joined by the hooting, tooting, chirping, aarg-aarging, screeching, wheooing, wheet-wheeting, cawing, warbling, whistling, and general serenading of our discordant forest orchestra. Some birds even resorted to a version of the whih-wheeooing we had emitted when passing ladies of gentle breeding during our rude Dublin adolescence. An eclectic selection of voice boxes competed, each to its own tempo and key, major and minor, from adagio to allegro to prestissimo, occasionally maestoso, but always sostenuto, to warn off, attract, court, maybe even to entertain and amuse the potential audience. Night-time auditioning in my high mahogany loggia was tempered by trepidation when a tropical storm erupted, complete with enormous flashes of lightning and crashes of thunder. As flash and bang almost coincided I reckoned I

*Rapa Nui (Easter Island) Dawn arising over ocean behind Ahu Tongariki (the 15 moai were restored after the 1960 tsunami).*

*Ahu Tahai, restored moai with pukao top, whalebone eyes and obsidian pupils*

*Vinapu Ceremonial Centre, carving of these stones, somewhat similar to those in Cusco, gave Thor Hyderdahl the mistaken idea the inhabitants descended from Incas*

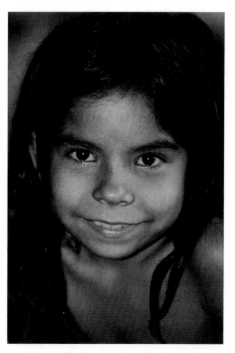

*Young lady, Acajetuba hamlet,*
*Amazonas, Brazil*

*Jaburu stork (tuiuiu) on takeoff,*
*Pantanal, Brazil*

*Early morning on the Amazon delta*

Borneo, resident of longhouse repairing longboat (canoe) used for travel on the river Skrang.

Tending pepper crop, Borneo

Longhouse headman practicing poison dart blowing

*Ethiopia, Gondar, Falasha (Black Jewish) villagers selling local handicrafts
(note moldings of crowned VIP couple in bed)*

*Debre Barhan Selassie church by Lake Tana, ancient frescoes on ceiling*

*Fallen stele (obelisk) at Axum,*
*legendary home of the Queen of Sheba*

*Classic Ethiopian stele*

*Tissisat (Watery Smoke)Falls on the Blue Nile*

*Namibia: Deadvlei, Sossusvlei, fossilised tree against a typical sand dune*

*Kudu, Okavanga Delta, Botswana*

*Uganda, White Nile scene just below Murchison's Falls*

*Hohe Mut run, Obergurgl, Austria*

*January 2005, ...through bergy bits and growlers to the Land of the Midnight Sun*

had a ringside seat – or bed. I began to imagine my noble mahogany tent-pole taking a lightning strike, both of us mightily singed and little old *moi* ending up as a snack for the big black caiman I had spotted earlier, loitering with intent! Next day I was informed that, theoretically, there is no risk to a tree rooted in water, as lightning travels directly to it.[12]

During the next few days we explored the forest on foot, visited Indian or *caboclo* (half-Indian) villages. We used motor-powered canoes to tour igapos, many of which seemed the size of Lough Neagh, stretching as much as 30 kilometres from the main course of the river, and went swimming. Our guide told us a good swim would cure an irrational fear of piranhas that only go for humans in the dry season, when no alternative grub is unavailable. We went out by boat again at night with lamps looking for caimans, our jungle survival expert even capturing some young ones, which we released, gingerly avoiding their jaws. She showed us how to judge their age by counting the number of plates on their backs.

## Floral Warfare

In the following days we explored the forest with our Indian guide. This, the largest tropical ecosystem on Earth, exudes both extravagant fecundity and an air of foreboding. Flora and fauna are locked in an incessant, unrelenting battle for survival. With most plants it is a race from the penumbra of the forest floor, through a convoluted lattice of growths to breach the labyrinthine canopy and expose eager chlorophyll to the brilliance of the now blinding tropical sunshine, like giddy Nordic maidens released unto Mediterranean beaches in early summer.

Although the floor of the tropical forest is poor in humus the action of slime mould, bacteria and insects breaks down fallen leaves and encourages the growth of fungal filaments just below the

---

[12] Theoretically! Which was only a little reassuring during the following nights, when I prayed the theory was right and Karl Popper's conjecture that all theories are basically ephemeral, true until they are eventually proven wrong, was itself a mere conjecture.

surface; these in turn succour the roots of the forest giants, recycling food back to them. But the reign of the victor is ephemeral and precarious. The relentless fight to survive continues apace with the inexorably aggressive, lethal advance of other and less benign greenery, especially the contorted embrace of parasitic growths, the sinuous vine with its deadly coils and tendrils, and the liana. When leaves pass their optimum evergreen prime, or are partially eaten, the tree simply sheds them, knowing that the bugs on the forest floor will quickly recycle them to their root system.

The bounteous vegetation and fruits provide sustenance for a vast variety of species of insect, bird, and beast, especially monkey and leafcutter ants. Birds, bats and monkeys help fertilise the next generation and disperse the seedlings further afield, to ensure the rich diversity of species. Occasionally a momentous event occurs as an aged, weakened forest giant gives up the ghost to come crashing to the forest floor, bringing in its wake many arboreal neighbours and all their interlocked latticework of vines and creepers. This abundance of dying vegetation is the signal for a feeding frenzy on the part of those who convert the detritus of the previous generation into the nutrients of the next. Insects and fungi swiftly get to work as the relentless Darwinian cycle of death and life accelerates to consume the remains of the fallen colonnade. Light now floods the stygian darkness, as if opening the curtain of some giant natural theatre. The growth of seedlings and plants accelerates as they take their place in the sun and shoot up to close the breach in the towering canopy. Fratricidal and inter-species combat erupts, like gladiators in the Colosseum, as neophyte plants thrust their leaves at the life-giving sunlight; parasitic competitors are fought off until a few dominant species replace the fallen warrior. For every possible niche there is always some specialised growth to exploit it: those which prefer proximity to the canopy produce shiny leaves which restrict transpiration and are shaped to shed rainwater which would only encourage the growth of fungus; the higher emergents have tougher leaves as the rain is quickly burnt off by the intense sunlight. Some plants even send out small leaves to catch the scarce sunlight on their way up, to eventually produce magnificent, enormous specimens when, like successful corporate moguls, they succeed in making their way to the top.

On high the intertwined canopy hosts a fecund cornucopia of birds, insects, reptiles and animals who, in a complex biological ballet, evolved over millennia to ensure the reproduction of their hosts' species at the same time as their own. Exotic epiphytes, glorious orchids and bromeliads, all colonise the middle reaches to attract pollinators. Water-tank bromeliads can store their own water supply which attracts another array of opportunistic visitors, including mosquito larvae. The pitiless internecine combat continues as untethered vine or strangler fig seedlings germinate on high; lacking an independent nutrient supply, they send tiny aerial roots to the ground far below, to suck up water and reveal their deadly character as vegetative constrictors, as deadly as their reptilian counterparts, to encircle and eventually garrotte their hapless hosts. When the host is eventually suffocated it is possible to come upon an empty sleeve of knitted vines, each thick as a man's arm, like a giant, abandoned chimneystack.

We followed an elementary forest survival course conducted by a few forest dwellers, the leader being an instructress with the Brazilian army, who teaches jungle survival techniques. They plucked selected leaves, encouraging us to chew them, a rich pharmacopoeia of cures for innumerable ailments, and showed us which plants to avoid – most plant leaves contain defensive toxins for their protection. The leaves of *strychnos toxifera*, for example, are not apparently conducive to longevity. To me, somewhat colour-blind at the green-brown part of the spectrum, they looked almost the same in the faint twilight below the shading canopy. We were invited to chew some bark of the fever tree – quinine: interesting, but I still prefer to ingest the prescription at sundown, Brit-style, in liquefied form, with a genever mixer, and on the rocks.

I read in the enthralling book by Catherine Caufield, *In the Rainforest,* that the French originally took their quinine mixed with wine. In the chapter on Fever Bark she recounts the history of quinine as an antidote to the dreadful scourge of malaria, then considered to be caused by bad air, *mal aria.* The first European to learn about it from the Indians was a Jesuit based where the modern borders of Peru and Ecuador lie. News of his magic potion was initially ignored in the capitals of Europe. Another Jesuit, possibly looking for brownie points at malarial-stricken HQ, brought back some of the powder, now known as *Jesuit's Powder*, to malaria-plagued Rome, located by the as yet undrained, mosquito-infested Pontine Marshes. It arrived in time for the Papal conclave of 1655. Normally, during summer conclaves, a number of attendees succumbed to the mal aria, but not this time: it was the first recorded summer conclave at which no death from malaria was reported. On the contrary, in London the Jesuit/Papist cure was repulsed as part of a plot to exterminate Protestantism. In 1658 Cromwell died of malaria rather than submit himself to the dreadful papist poison. More than 250 years later the British were to make up for this earlier prejudice when one of their own made the vital link between the *anopheles* mosquito and malarial plasmodium.

Our instructress explained the difference between creepers and lianas. She showed the best lianas to cut down to quench a thirst; with machete she reached up to chop through a thick liana, then a second clean chop a metre and half further down. Out flowed the sweetest water I ever tasted, better than a G&T at that time of day. She showed which little snakes and frogs to avoid. In fact she had to search for these; I doubt we would ever have found any on our own. She pointed out leaves which were in fact perfectly camouflaged butterflies and insects. Still, I would not care to spend the night lost and alone in the darkness of the rainforest floor, sharing my improvised bed with leafcutter ants and certainly not with the larger, fiery ones she advised us to avoid at all costs. But the risks of being gobbled by a jaguar were slim as they have been mercilessly hunted, she informed us there were some still in the forest but they shunned humans.

Due to the gloom of the forest *res-de-chaussee*, deep down in the shadow of the impenetrable canopy, little vegetation grew. To collect nutrients and support the towering trunk some plants establish huge buttresses which stretch out to taper off a hundred metres away. Between termite mounds grow ferns and bushes which can thrive although almost devoid of sunlight – ideal for sur-viving in the gloom of European houses during the dark winters. Yet the forest floor is remarkably infertile: it seems to act as a mere foundation stone for the forest giants, an arena for the deadly struggle between various plants for sunlight, and as a source of wa-ter for the creepers and lianas which drop down from the canopy. Leaf-cutter ants can be seen marching in their thousands, each car-rying a portion of leaf to their nest. There they void themselves on the leaves to stimulate the growth of fungus for a queen who enjoys mushrooms while, coincidentally, encouraging some vital, though limited chemical activity, in the humus-impoverished soil. Yet all is not predation, some useful friendships are formed: there are spe-cies of ants which depend on excrescences from certain trees for nourishment and in turn defend the tree from the attacks of other parasites and moulds which would otherwise kill them.

It is only recently that scientists started to explore the high canopy, some 40 metres up, with the odd specimen piercing the skies even higher. Some say we knew more about the surface of Mars a few years ago then about the complex cycle of flora and fauna life, and the role of avian pollinators, in the high rainforest canopy.

An interesting feature of almost all such forests is the dispersion of species to prevent attack by insects or disease, and to prevent too many plants with the same nutrient requirements fighting over the same area of poor soil. I once asked why they did not grow rubber in plantations in the Amazon, as their competitors did in Malaya, once they succeeded in smuggling out seedlings of the wild rubber plant. The answer, apparently, is that there are bugs which will at-tack rubber plants in the Amazon and in the Congo, but the planta-tions in Malays are artificial and the specific bug is not endemic there, so the concentrated Malaysian plantations flourished while the natural, dispersed growths of the Amazon around Manaus could no longer compete, leading to the economic eclipse of that fabled town with its iconic opera house.[13]

Exploring the igapo backwaters and the myriad of tributary rivers was enchanting as we made our way by canoe through elevated root systems, thickets and water plants to enter another gigantic lake of black, reflective water. I regretted not having a mask and snorkel to suss out the underwater life since the piranhas don't attack before the end of the rainy season, though the black caiman has a reputation of being far less tolerant of visitors than the regular jacare. We encountered a number of 'Indians' in canoes offering fish and handcrafts for sale. The little ladies were especially able and convincing sales personnel. But in fact they are not always pure Indians but *caboclos*, resulting from the intermingling of Indians and prospectors over the centuries.

Back in Manaus we visited a craft centre run by Catholic missionaries which sells genuine Indian handcrafts and artwork from distant villages visitors are not advised not to frequent for fear of spreading diseases. It seemed a simple way to provide support for these poor indigenous peoples who have suffered so much from exploitation by white settlers and colonial elites over the ages. Hard as it is to believe, in the early 1960s the agency charged with the protection of the indigenous peoples deliberately introduced European diseases to exterminate forest tribes so their land could be taken over by land grabbers and their pisteleros. In fact the problem in Brazil seems not to be one of overpopulation but of the egregiously unequal distribution, or expropriation, of land. The impression we got of Manaus is that of a city trying to restore the economic glories of the past when its opera house (built in the 1890s) attracted stars from Europe and the local *pezzi grossi* sent their laundry to Paris. The glories of the primeval rainforest and its denizens are held in little esteem by some modern Brazilian politicians who look forward to the days when the forests are bulldozed to be

---

[13] I recently viewed the extraordinary scenes in the BBC film *Planet Earth* showing something I had not previously known; a type of contagious fungus attacking the ants in their turn, decimating and dispersing these otherwise invincible armies, said to weigh more than all other forest fauna put together.

replaced by cattle stations to produce beef for hamburgers and the growing of soya to feed the cattle. One prominent populist politico has fashioned a reputation for himself by making outlandish anti-ecological statements claiming, inter alia, that the forest trees are riddled through with woodworm and should be chopped down. One has only to fly over swathes of barren soil which, until recently, supported magnificent vegetation to appreciate the truth that there is little or no soil on the forest floor. Burn down the forest and the ashes will provide nutrients for a limited time before the top-soil is washed away by the tropical downpours. What is even sadder is the fact that once destroyed there is no way of restoring this highly complex ecosystem of flora and fauna, especially those oft-overlooked but all-important little bugs which pollinate and keep diversity alive.

To add to the list of jeremiads, rising levels of global warming are expected to reduce rainfall in the Amazon region, the roots of the trees will slowly dry out, adding to the risk of forest fires. Increasing local droughts will fuel a further vicious circle of less critical mass for 'homegrown' rainfall from the drier forests. Trees will die and great chunks of the rainforest turn into savannah. It is feared that even a 2°C rise in temperature could cause up to 40 per cent loss of forest, while a 4°C rise could result in an 80 per cent loss. Instead of acting as one of the greatest carbon sinks on Earth the Amazon could end up as a source of carbon release, intensifying global warming significantly.

One encouraging development was the recent decision of the Brazilian Supreme Court to defend the rights of Indians living in the Raposa Sena do Sol reservation in the north of the country. It decreed that the land is for their exclusive use and disqualified encroaching loggers and rice farmers. Hopefully, this may set a precedent for similar decisions to benefit other indigenous tribes attempting to hold on to their lands.

## Borneo – It's an absolute jungle out there

The brooding primeval rainforests of Borneo are the oldest in the world; a hundred million years of continuous evolution created their rich diversity of fauna and flora. Although parallels can be drawn with South America and Africa, both equally damp, dark, fecund and cruelly competitive, there are also many differences. The tree canopies seem to be even higher and the forest floor darker, probably because the canopy is more often covered by brooding, leaden storm clouds, alternating with a gun-metal grey sky. While forest elephant, rhino and tiger once proliferated here, the most remarkable animal to be found now is the *orang-utan* (Malay for man of the jungle), although even this primate is hard to find.[14]

Also noteworthy in Borneo is that, until recent and more conformist times, some of the inhabitants practised the quaint hobby of headhunting. Since the relatives of those who had been topped would, inconveniently, come looking for retribution, if not to retrieve the missing appendages of their loved ones, it was deemed sensible to live with your fellow huntsmen in a defended longhouse with a ladder capable of being drawn up (used also by the monks in Erin of yore when the Vikings came calling). The possibility of retaliation and, no doubt, the presence of jungle rats, creepy-crawlies, snakes, leeches and bacterial fungi, dictated that residences be built on stilts high off the ground. The arrangement also provides ventilation and added coolness. As there are no roads in the jungle, and travel is by river, many longhouses are constructed by the riverside, but high up on the bank since river levels can rise by metres within a few hours. Apart from a lingering attachment to cranial collecting the locals are very kind and hospitable.

Borneo Island is ten times the size of the Emerald Isle and even moister. It consists of three separate states: the tiny but oil-rich Sultanate of Brunei, Sarawak-Sabah ruled by Malaysia, and Kalimantan ruled, if not managed, by Indonesia. The magnificent forests and ancient bogs of Kalimantan are being logged and burned, cleared for palm oil plantations, at an increasing rate by a rapacious

---

[14] The different scientific classifications of forest, and the loser term 'jungle', and the divergence of species which occurred when the solitary Continent of Pangaea broke up 210 million years ago, are expertly described by Catherine Caufield in the chapter 'In the Beginning' in her book *In the Rainforest*.

oligarchy and planters, causing a haze fog which frequently enve-
lopes the islands of Indonesia, Malaysia and Singapore.[15]

Avid gardeners thinking of making a visit might care to note
that there are some 8,000 different flower species, 2,000 types of
trees and bushes and 200 different palms which are visited by 900
species of butterfly and 450 kinds of birds. Borneo hosts the largest
flower in the world, the metre wide rafflesia: it emits an odour best
not enlarged on for the gentle reader, except to recount that it is so
pungent it easily attracts from afar the necessary insect pollinators
for the short time it flowers every few years.

The capital town of Malaysian Borneo is Kuching, situated on a
turbulent stretch of the yellowish brown Sarawak River. It is something of a frontier town, but all the more friendly and enjoyable for
that – especially when one returns from a steamy, sweaty, sunless
visit to the rainforest – and the bolthole comes with a shower and
air-conditioning. The National Museum houses many interesting
ethnographic treasures, including a traditional old-style longhouse.
There is, apparently, a nice beach resort half an hour away by boat,
but the town is built near mangrove swamps which are home to
tetchy saltwater crocodiles, marshes and almost impenetrable
coastline jungle. Kuching is mainly a base for river trips into the
heart of the forest. There are many tourist-style longhouses in the
forest near to the town, but it is much more interesting to visit
those inhabited by indigenous people within the forest if possible.
The really professional travel agents will organise tours into the interior, along the Skrang, Baleh or Rajang rivers, which penetrate
deep into the forest, with visits to the local tribes arranged in such

---

[15] This postcard only considers the part ruled by Malaysia, which until recently was
protective of this precious relic of prehistoric times; so the wanton ecological sac-
rilege of the klepto-oligarchy next door need not intrude into our discourse. However, recently, over a million hectares of primary forest have been cleared for their
valuable timber and then planted with palm oil for biofuels. This creates huge
quantities of slurry and pollutes rivers and drinking water and kills fish. Now there
is the additional threat of ten dams being constructed by the construction company responsible for the Three Gorges dam on the Yangtze, which will displace
thousands of Dyak forest people. Again, traditional tribal people seem powerless
against the forces of crony capitalism.

a way as to respect and not undermine their traditional way of life. We were told that there was too much commerce due to logging on the Baleh and Rajang rivers so we chose the Skrang, which we joined upstream beyond a waterfall, after travelling a couple of hundred kilometres by road.

Our travel agent arranged for our little group to hire a professional forest guide, four or five long wooden canoes with outboard motors, and a couple of boatmen each. We were restricted by the tiny width of our canoes to taking only a small waterproof bag each, while two extra boats contained essentials – white wine, red wine, beer, elementary foodstuffs, coffee, concentrated milk, emergency medicines. The agency provided each of us with a couple of fresh sheets and a pillowslip; each of our longhouses had prepared rattan beds with mattress, pillow and mosquito net.

We subsequently spent an unforgettable time admiring the extraordinary scenery of this ancient Jurassic relic, trekked umpteen forest trails with specialist guides and instructors, slipping and sliding on the algae-covered rock and mud, arranged improvised picnics using natural utensils and bush-tucker collected on the way and visited the longhouses of the Dayaks and Iban. We bathed in secluded pools – downstream from where we collected water, while avoiding the attentions of such creepy-crawlies as mosquitoes, technicolour caterpillars, leeches and fire ants, centipedes, millipedes, if not megapedes. We were instructed in poison-dart-hunting and the use of bow and arrow by the *tuai ruarah*, or longhouse chief. I regret that I could not find out how exactly he, or his purveyor of fine hunting instruments, had manufactured a beautiful, smooth, two and a half metre long blowpipe, out of forest hardwood, with an interior core smooth and straight as a sniper's rifle. Apparently the wood is dried for months and a long steel rod slowly drilled through the shaft of wood for a hundred hours. Our marksman could hit the bull's-eye with a dart at twenty metres every time.[16]

---

[16] According to Eric Hansen, author of the fascinating record *Stranger in the Forests: On Foot across Borneo*, who once witnessed the iron age process, one trick

Our first accommodation was a good few hours upriver, past rocks and rapids, while dodging heavy logs and branch debris floating downriver. We watched the scene unfolding – the enveloping forest, lianas and foliage exuberantly draping the sunlit sides of the river, strange birds diving and swooping, skimming the surface, from one bank to the other. As awe-inspiring and unforgettable were the forest sounds, including the rude whoop, whoopings of the monkeys, especially the aggressive gibbons, although relatively quiet compared to the sunset chorus.

Our boats were not simple dugouts, though the same in length. Instead, they were made of three long, shaped planks of local hardwood carved with a *parang* (jungle knife), forming the two sides and a flat bottom, with a small trapezoidal stern to which the outboard motor was attached. They were thus much more manageable in rough water than simple though solid and heavier dugouts. We saw them being made and repaired by men of our longhouse every day. On arrival we hauled our boats far up the riverbank, securing them prow and stern; logical, since there were tropical downpours every night and the river could rise precipitately. Our refreshments were carefully placed in a sack tied with a long rope, the other end of which was tied to a tree, bottles were wrapped in leaves to prevent breakage, and gently lowered into a quiet pool in the river to serve as a cooler.

The longhouse, high up on the bank, was entered by mounting a deeply notched tree trunk – a relic of the old days, as mentioned above, when it could be quickly pulled inside in case some neighbouring tribesmen called without the appropriate RSVP. The barn-like interior housed twenty-one families and was divided lengthwise into a public and private area, with the private part partitioned for each family. During the daytime the women were busy in the public part weaving mats from palm branches, while one elderly artist tenderly carved the figure of a traditional local, fighting knife

---

was to start boring at the narrower of the dried hardwood lathe, shaping it round and then drawing certain vines through the bore to smoothen it to a mirror-like finish. I peered through our headman's specimen and it was dead straight and mirror-like for the full bore.

in one hand, severed heads in the other. Dinner was prepared by the Dayak ladies in their private rooms and served to us in the public part of the longhouse. It consisted of forest pig, chicken, rice and various local fruits and vegetables. Excellent and tasty fare, it was accompanied by French and Irish libations (the tropical-strength Guinness brewed at St James's Gate is popular in Malaysia and brought upstream by Chinese traders). Post-prandial toasts were offered with the local *tuak*, palm wine, and *arak*, distilled palm wine, then the ceremonies began. The ladies performed their dances, the local braves theirs, flaunting tattoos, in traditional costumes of course, accompanied by the resident orchestra of drums and reed instruments. As visitors we also had to sing or dance, or otherwise make fools of ourselves, to the great merriment of the children who gathered in a corner. We were too far from any radio transmitter so evening entertainment was just as it was in Ireland, *fadó, fadó,* what you made of it yourself.

Entertainment over, our little rattan beds were brought out and lined up, mosquito nets positioned over each. We dressed our 'beds', drew the nets, the storm lamps were quenched, and we lay back listening to the jungle chorus, before slipping into the embrace of Morpheus. I had not counted on the fact that Chinese salesmen regularly travel up the river, even this remote headwater, their canoes laden with modern knick-knacks to sell to the longhouses. Regularly, on the half hour, this outer world intruded: outside the chief's quarters was positioned a battery-powered, hi-fi clock, complete with loudspeaker, like a lethal combination of Big Ben and the Top Ten, which successively relayed another jewel of the canon of western musicology. Half hourly 'Little Ben' serenaded us with a quixotic medley, *The Blue Danube, Home on the Range, Colonel Bogey, There's No Place Like Home, Elizabethan Serenade, Qué Será Será, Swedish Rhapsody, Tulips from Amsterdam* ... I was half expecting to hear *Danny Boy* next when suddenly and prematurely, nature interrupted to treat us to a Rossini *crescendo* which was heralded by a blinding flash of lightning, followed by the earth-shattering *finale,* then by a tropical downpour which thundered on the palm leaf roof of our residence, and cascaded down the sides. But our house proved impermeable to the worst Borneo could throw at it; I finally dozed off thanking my lucky stars I was not dossing down *al fresco* in a tent or hammock, *a la* Redmond O'Hanlon who penetrated deep into the interior some years previously.

We witnessed the result of the downpour next morning, branches and leaves all over the place, and the river higher by a good three metres and almost twice as wide. The wisdom of securely tying up our canoes high on the bank became apparent. There could have been a real disaster had our guides not securely anchored our vital refreshments left to cool in what was previously a sidewater. Entire trees, logged tree trunks which had been torn loose and huge branches were floating down the churning torrent. Definitely not the day for river cruising.

We went instead for a trek through the forest, guides pointing out flora and fauna, creepies and crawlies. Even with binoculars it was difficult to spot our prey in the high canopy, even in the lattice of natural light from the grey skies which dappled the higher branches of the giants, some of which sprouted a good thirty metres high up the trunk. I was sorry I did not follow the advice of Mr O'Hanlon in his thoroughly engaging record, *Into the Heart of Borneo*, and bring some bird and plant field guides to study at leisure later. We were told which plants and jungle fruits were edible and which were to be avoided. Lunchtime came: we were a few hours from our base and thought it would consist of a drink from our water bottles and a biscuit or two. Not at all, our local guides carried rucksacks and knew how to whip up a decent meal in the middle of the forest, to rival the most accomplished Dublin 7 hostess. Pangas were wielded, bamboos felled, their interiors stuffed with improvised leaf-bags of hill rice; then followed meat brochettes, skewered on slivers of bamboo and cooked over an improvised fire. Bamboo was used not only as pots and pans, but smaller specimens were cut below a node (the segments along the stems), to make drinking cups – after all, there was Bordelaise in them there rucksacks. Large, shiny banana or pandanus leaves were chopped, the edges pleated and stapled with giant thorns, to serve as platters. Palm hearts were cut open, as well as hearts of bamboo, for our delectation. We sampled jungle fruits whose identity I have forgotten or had never heard of before. We held our noses and joined the guides in sampling *durians* – a wonderful taste, but one has to hold one's nose before biting (their scent has been described as similar to that of rotting flesh). This delicious repast despatched, washing up was easy: we just threw our crockery and cups to the ants, termites and leaf moulds to be ecologically recycled. Only the empty bottles and spoons remained to receive traditional treatment back at HQ.

This all appeared very simple, but we were being escorted by experts who have as innate a sense of direction in this twilight world as Bedu in the desert. A visitor should never, ever, venture more than a few paces from companions or try even a short stroll: the lack of sunlight and shadows, with almost perennial cloud cover, disorients non-forest dwellers and one will rapidly become completely lost.

The following day the level of the river had fallen so we could use the canoes to visit other tribal longhouses further up the river. Many of these had not been warned of our visit and had rattan baskets full of shrunken 'trophies' hanging from the rafters. The hosts kindly assured us they were not European heads, only Japanese, souvenirs of the War. I wondered what yarn they told the Japanese visitors. Still, they were extremely hospital people, especially as we came equipped with pencils, crayons, biros and sweets for the children. The one slightly disconcerting moment for me was when one elderly gentleman stared a little too intensely at my coiffure....

I had a little camera and film in a waterproof bag and took many shots of the local kids. Back in Europe I posted numerous copies of the prints to the head guide. Months later he wrote back to say he had revisited the longhouses and it caused a great outpouring of excitement as the kids crowded around to see if they featured. I often regretted I had not brought a Polaroid camera with me: there is no better device for breaking the ice with people in remote regions than taking their photos and watching them develop within a few moments. (But care must be taken to ask permission first: some people, especially in Africa, can get very agitated as they believe photos steal part of their spirit.)[17]

Staying in longhouses is an excellent way to enjoy a trip to Borneo though it does not involve the same degree of adventure and intimacy with nature as sleeping in a tent or hammock in the forest itself – and wakening each morning to find knapsack and clothing full of ants and beetles, with boots colonised by creatures resembling giant prawns with turned-up tails. The occasional visitor adds to the income of these kindly people, possibly encouraging them to preserve their culture and traditions, even if only to satisfy the visitors. Since the indigenous people know the forest intimately they also benefit by acting as guides and naturalists.

Yet they often pay a high price for living in the forest, which was brought home to us when staying in one longhouse. A father failed to return at sunset from tending his pepper plantation down river. A group of men went down with lamps to where his bushes grew. They came upon a large python, distended below the head. They opened it up with their parangs to find the unfortunate man's body inside. Since then whenever I use pepper I reflect on the price some poor folks must pay so we can indulge our appetites for spices.

On our way back to Kuching we stopped at a riverside village and visited the market. One saleslady had a large plastic barrel beside her sales stand. I peered inside, to see two pythons, each about two or three metres long and looking rather emaciated. I inquired of her, through the guide-interpreter, if they were intended as pets. I was looked at as if I were a right *amadán*. Her reply could be translated into Dublinese as, 'pythons as pets? Are ye out of yer mind? They're for making fresh soup, 5 Ringgits per kilo'.

On return to Kuching I enjoyed the air-conditioning in our hotel, especially the reduction in humidity from the 98 per cent of the previous couple of weeks, and spent longer than an American in the shower to rid myself of the grime of the forest. Curiously, it was

---

[17] Digital cameras have the advantage that one can let children check out their images immediately; the downside being that digital cameramen seldom bother to print out copies of their handicraft.

really only when I returned to the luxury of the modern hotel that I realised how hot and sticky things had been, constantly walking around in damp clothes. In the forest it seemed that one only hung up washed clothes to let gravity, not evaporation, reduce the water content. While lapping up the luxury, including newsagents and bookstores, I slowly felt a great void at abandoning the awesome majesty of primeval nature for the banality of westernised existence.

## Obergurgl – lofty eyrie midst Alpine peaks

There is one perfect antidote to lengthening autumnal shadows and looming winter doldrums: the pure exhilaration of gliding down a snowy mountainside on a pair of skis. Yet, this form of enjoyment can prove dangerous in more ways than the obvious; it's even more addictive than the siren game of golf once one gets hooked.[18] Unfortunately, the weather and location ensure that most of us can only participate for a few weeks a year. This leaves its devotees to indulge other pastimes, even golf, which at least offers the possibility of a pleasant, if interrupted, stroll outdoors during the warmer months. The glorious, winter-wonderland scenery, the bracingly-sharp air, the sapphire sky etched against the dazzling, silent, tapering white of the peaks, offer tranquillity to a frazzled soul. Then comes the main attraction, the unalloyed bliss of waltzing down a powder-snow glacier, sinuously alternating the weight and angle of one ski to the other, synchronously moving hips and shoulders, a biting wind whistling in one's ears, tears welling up in the eyes: it's not just sport, it's gymnastic lyricism – and therapeutic to boot. There is no better antidote to the melancholic languor of winter, *die grauen Stunden*, when, buffeted by wild westerlies,

> ... from whose unseen presence the leaves dead
> Are driven, like ghosts from an encounter fleeing,
> Yellow, and black, and pale, and hectic red,
> Pestilence-stricken multitudes: O thou,

---

[18] Some would argue that there is little comparison between the elation of carving arabesques on a pristine swathe of snow and what is essentially outdoor billiards played on lowland pasture, however imaginatively landscaped.

Who chariotest to their dark wintry bed
The wingéd seeds, where they lie cold and low,
Each like a corpse within its grave, until
Thine azure sister of the spring shall blow
Her clarion o'er the dreaming earth...

And what better spot to anticipate Shelley's 'azure sister' than the soaring beauty of a village which maintains its original charm and *gemuetlichkeit*, while restricting 'through' traffic. Better still, it is situated at the end of the road, way up the valley where the cool, obliterating snow is abundant and where the ski lifts are not constantly besieged by lengthy queues, and the sense of peace is palpable. One's pleasure is compounded when the village is so high it knows not autumnal leaves but the needles of the last coniferous sentinels of the vegetable kingdom.

Though highly therapeutic, sliding down the snowy slopes on a pair of planks is not entirely without risk. The celebrated political economist Kenneth Galbraith, author of *The Affluent Society* and *The Great Crash*, tells in his autobiography, *A Life in Our Times*, of his misadventure on the slopes. In 1955, just after his account of the 1929 Wall Street crash was published, he was called to testify at a US Senate Committee in case any similar crisis reared its head. He was circumspect in his testimony, suggesting some minor precautionary tightening of the rules. While he was testifying word leaked out and the stock market took a huge tumble. Billions were wiped of the value of shares. During subsequent days he was deluged by hate mail, 'denunciatory, defamatory, physically menacing or pious, the latter saying they were praying for [his] death or dismemberment'. To avoid the storm he took off to ski in Vermont where he promptly broke a leg. '[He] then learned he had done something for religion: the pious read the news and wrote to tell [him] that their prayers had been answered.'

## An Alpine Pearl

Obergurgl is a serene outpost in the Tirolean Alps at the very end of the Oetztal (Oetz valley), just 2,000 metres high, where the road peters out below the 3,700 metre levitating Wildspitz and slumbering glaciers. With its village twin of Hochgurgl at 2,100 metres it is one of the very highest permanently lived in villages in the Alps: no artificial skiing-factory this. As a UNESCO-designated model mountain village and Biosphere Park this Alpine pearl attempts to maintain its charm and quality by controlling rigorously the rate of expansion of its accommodation, avoiding mass tourism. The strategy is to promote a high level of service with a relatively low volume of visitors. The availability of accommodation ranging from five-star luxury hotels to impeccable B&B guesthouses built in the traditional Tirolean style allows it to cater for all classes: to paraphrase Thucydides, they discriminate not so much by social class as by ski class. The village manages to conserve a real skiing ambience rather than an artificial rendezvous for the *tres branchee*, long-fur-coat brigade. It is resolutely a ski-resort – not a tourist resort such as St Moritz or, God forbid, Davos. Obergurgl has no reason to feel embarrassed if the dominant garb is the anorak: like its equine equivalent, Cheltenham, where the horse is king, here it is the skiing, not the couture which is paramount.

The origin of the village name is lost somewhere in the recesses of time, presumably onomatopoeic from the gurgling of the mountain torrents as they descended from the melting glaciers. (As well as the annual cycle of melting and freezing the glaciers are now ablating as are most of the glaciers in the Alps due to global warming.) As a *Stamgast* of many years standing my only criticism is the recent introduction, even at that high altitude, of artificial snow-making hydrants. But that is as much an antidote to global warming as an attempt to ensure a longer season. I also believe that they should separate snowboarders from skiers – preferably by sending them over to the Rockies or, better still, to Kamchatka. The new technology ski lifts can effortlessly whisk large numbers of practitioners rapidly uphill. This eliminates the lengthy queuing of yesteryear when one could spend more time queuing than skiing, but the result is that at Carnival some ski *pistes* can resemble Henry Street on Christmas Eve. But that just shows the democratisation of the sport and a good democrat surely mustn't grumble. Well, just one further grumble: the immaculate blue skies of yore are increasingly scarred by the contrails of passing jets.

My first contact with Obergurgl was one unusually warm winter when there was little snow in the low-lying resorts round the Ehrwald/Zugspitzgletscher and one had to climb much higher to find adequate supplies of the fluffy white stuff. I first visited Vent in the Oetztal (Oetz valley). Though as high as Obergurgl, here the slopes are mostly south facing, so better suited for high mountain touring on combination skis than downhill skiing. I frequented the charming *Gasthof* of Heidi and Roman Scheiber for a few years, then reluctantly transferred my patronage to Obergurgl, where the runs are longer and mostly north-facing. I have seldom visited other resorts since. This is not due to a lack of initiative: one alternative was the Val di Fassa, in the Dolomites, which is excellent when there is plentiful snow, as the geology of the Dolomites lends itself to smoother slopes, but the South Tirol villages are not subject to the same planning restrictions that apply in Austria and are characterised more by traffic jams than traditional-style architecture.

At Obergurgl's highly acclaimed ski school I met, made friends with, and agreed to annually meet up with fellow ski aficionados such as Rudi, Anneke, Ria, Trevor, who, like me, frequent spotless and comfortable B&Bs, leaving us free to meet for dinner in one of the resort's many restaurants. Una and Hans, Agnes and David, Shane and Kate, on the other hand, stay at the elegant, traditional and centrally-located Edelweiss and Gurgl Hotel (first guests welcomed in 1898), with the main ski lifts located by their back door. Helena, Traudl and Mara, successive managers of the pristine Gasthof Kuraten (first guests 1849), strategically positioned one hundred metres from the main ski lift, kindly allow me to store my skis and encumbering boots in the *Keller* until the following season.

There is a plentiful supply of excellent restaurants in which to meet up with other friends staying on a B&B basis: a warm welcome and fine dining are provided by Rosi in the piquantly traditional, Tirolean-style, Gruener Stueben (1948), its carved timbers, redolent of a bygone era; from Doris in the Hexenkuechl; Helmut in his noctambulistic watering hole, the Josl Keller; and Rudi who organises

his weekly Tirolerabend at the exuberant 2,200 metre-high Neder-
hute. I pray that Petra and Roman Gruener never 'modernise' the
traditional Tirolean woodwork of their characteristically *gemuet-
liches Speisezimmer* – the local authorities should place a preservation order on this time capsule. Unfortunately Frau Hanna Scheiber
has vacated her traditional Sportzentrum where, for years, I collected my morning paper to return for a languid *Fruehstueck* at
Kuraten. Nowadays the stores which used to specialise in traditional Austrian and Italian quality mountain gear and *Strickwaren,*
have ceded to the ephemera of Fifth Avenue couture. Cili Riml's
eponymous sport store has kept me warm on the slopes for years.[19]

A chief attraction of Obergurgl is its north and west-facing
slopes: this means that the sun strikes the surface at a very oblique
angle, thus preserving the quality of the snow. So the skiing is not
just better, it's safer. My favourite run is along the Wurmkogl glacier in Hochgurgl. The very top stretch from 3,100 metres is a bit
steep for beginners but the snow is deep and soft if one tumbles.
The two lower stretches, which must run for five or six kilometres,
are wide and gently sloping, allowing the practice of nice *wedeln*,
wagging turns, so redolent of stylish Austrian skiing. The newer
Schermerspitz runs, leading down from about 3,000 metres, are
also magic in quality of snow and width of runs, and are little frequented. The Steinmannbahn, at the far end of the village, past the
Innsbruck University Alpine Research Centre, is less frequented
and has beautiful open runs along glaciers and open aprons of
slope. Those who feel energetic can plod on upwards on their skis
for half an hour from the top of the lift, along a silent, white piste,
to sample the hospitality of the Schoenwieshuette, nestling at 2,300
metres on a wide saddle between two high peaks – an intrinsic
element of the Hochalpine Skitour.

What a therapeutic effect the first morning's skiing has compared to recycled office air or strolling along a city sidewalk under a

---

[19] My sister Maureen's kids in Dublin were togged out each year on the advice of
Cili. Though she had never met either Daniel or Simone she invariably picked out
exactly the choice of gear they were delighted to wear.

sulphurous shroud. On a typical morning the gelid air is usually well below freezing in the village; being less dense at that elevation it is not penetratingly cold, more bracingly fresh. And what a joy it is to take the Hochgurgl lift *ungeheuer oben,* leaving the murmur of the village behind to enter a silent world, slipping the bonds from a more tawdry earth, to glide effortlessly past the last rime-feathered conifers, hoary sentinels of the vegetation kingdom, to be wafted over the wide, open snowfields and up towards the jagged crests, like the scales on some dinosaur's back, where dazzling white abruptly delineates the enzian blue skies. Just when you fear the flying chair of the Top Wurmkogl lift might launch you like Icarus over the crest towards the distant panorama of the Dolomites, its brooding Marmalada towering in distant haze, or like an old Roman criminal off the Tarpeian Rock, it briefly but gently descends to allow skis to touch the short landing strip just before the crest. You turn and point the skis towards the vast dazzling amphitheatre, the valley now far below, hovering anxiously for a moment before pirouetting and launching off into the powder snow of the high glacier. The instinctive reaction faced with such a vertiginous descent is to lean backwards on the skis, but this would invite a long inelegant tumble a few hundred feet through the fluffy white snow. Rather, overcome instinct, bend the knees, leaning forward on the skis but with upper body straight, start a series of controlled turns as the sharp inside edge of the bottom ski grips into the snow or icy surface. That's the trick with skiing; its mastery consists of learning the knack of steering, weight on the outer (downhill) ski while using flexed knees as personal shock absorbers. The other key challenge is to succeed in switching direction of shoulders and hips, and pressure from lower ski to the top, seamlessly changing direction, to *wedeln* (meaning to wag in German), a fluid movement which is the hallmark of the Austrian ski style. To execute a series of graceful turns, the wind whistling in one's ears, tears pouring from the eyes, while waltzing down the Wurmkogl is pure po-

etry in motion – especially when a benign tailwind encourages one
to chase some fleeting cloud-shadows.[20]

As an old ski bum I still tend to go on about certain rules for
safe enjoyable skiing: join a ski class with professional teacher, not
some big city *amadán* who has piste-bashed for a couple of years
and then scares the hell out of beginners by taking them on their
second day to runs they should only tackle with an expert teacher
in their third or fourth week; don't go off-piste skiing, especially on
one's own; if you don't know the runs don't explore on your own,
especially if it is approaching ski-lift closing time. Getting lost in
the late evening in a low cloud whiteout is scary: one loses all sense
of direction.[21] Despite many years' experience I still insist that the
ski shop adjust my safety binding to the lowest possible setting so
the skis will fall off in case of some abnormal shock, and not stay on
as levers to break my aging bones. Even with experienced teachers
one should not push to join a ski class in advance of one's abilities.
I once witnessed a young German lady who fell madly for the sport
and, in only her second year, joined our group of old codgers. But
she did not have the experience we had in case of difficulty, such as
a *Katzenjammer* (hangover); on a steep incline she fell and, instead
of rolling over, lay flat back on the ski ends to flash down the
mountain like a torpedo. She had to be helicoptered out and the
word was that she would never ski again, ever. A beginner, who
feels uneasy with the level of a class, if it is frightening and thus tir-
ing, should ask to be allocated to a less demanding group. After all,
it's a holiday, not a forced labour camp.

The Obergurgl Ski School (1922) is one of the most prestigious in
the Alps. Among the many teachers – and they all have their own
styles, methods of teaching and eye for imperfection – I can recall
the effortless elegance of Wendelin, and the demands of the gregari-

---

[20] In the older days of tight ski pants a major concern of the committed skier, especially during guest races, was that one's thigh muscles might embarrassingly
breach forth of pants – which would have made a disconcertingly embarrassingly
scene on arrival at the end station.

[21] If it ever happens the trick is to take off skis and tramp in what is probably the
correct direction.

ous, but energetic Adolf, especially on icy mornings, in queasy, sonambulistic torpor following elongated evenings spent in the timeless *gemuetlichkeit* of the Josl Keller, the ever-ascending columns of empty schnapps glasses and uncoiling cauliflowers of *Tabaksrauch* merging into a cumulus which clung to the ceiling. When chided by Adolf to put on a spurt in descending the Hohe Mut I silently reflected that in an earlier age he could have been in charge of personnel and productivity on a ship manned by galley slaves.

Obergurgl village was first inhabited in the thirteenth or fourteenth century. The paved road from the bottom of the Oetztal only reached the 1,400 metre-high Soelden village in 1904, and Obergurgl in 1932. It hangs, often precipitously, on either of the flanks of the Oetztal, winding its tortuous way through tunnels or under galleries constructed to allow avalanches to rumble overhead, until it finds its way past Soelden to Zwieselstein, where the road divides, one fork leading to Vent and the other to the Gurgls.[22]

### Oetzi the Iceman

The village celebrates two famous visitors. The French balloonist Auguste Piccard landed his pressurised capsule, the forerunner of modern aircraft, in the nearly hills in May 1931, having reached a new record altitude of 16,200 metres, putting the village on the international map. Earlier still a visitor called by the Similaun peak, parked bow and arrows under an overhanging rock for shelter during a snowstorm, and then seems to have died of exposure. In the exceptionally warm summer of 1991 a German couple was climbing nearby, accidentally departed from the correct track to the Similaun Hutte, and spotted an arm protruding from the ice. Though the person was already dead they raised the alarm, took a photo

---

[22] I once met a fellow visitor in Vent, whose job was to walk the German state railway tracks checking for faults in the line. Immediately after the war, when ski lifts were not yet operating, his daily holiday routine was to depart his Soelden lodgings in the morning, walk with skis on shoulder up to Untergurgl, continue past Hochgurgl at 2,100 metres to the Wurmkogl glacier, enjoy a packed lunch, then ski down to Untergurgl, even Soelden if conditions would allow, before enjoying a few well-deserved litres of *Abendessen*.

and awaited the arrival of a rescue helicopter from either the Italian or Austrian side of the border. The Austrians arrived first (the Italians are still due). The staff from the Similaun helped the rescue crew extract the body from the ice, presuming it was that of a mountaineer lost a few years earlier and whose body was never found. Normally bodies buried under the snow are slowly carried down the valley by the glacier to be eventually ejected from the melt-water often up to forty years later. As the rescuers hacked away at the ice they gradually realised from the apparel that they were dealing with a very old body. It was covered mainly in animal hides, with a curious peak-hatted cloak. Eventually the body was released and flown to the university hospital in Innsbruck where advanced scientific analyses were conducted. Carbon-14 dating concluded the body was over 5,000 years old. Later, looking at a photo they had taken, the couple noted a bow and arrows under an overhanging rock near the body's location. They had lain there undisturbed for 5,200 years! Had they been positioned further out they would have been carried away by glacial motion thousands of years ago. The arrowheads were made of bronze, thus allowing palaeontologists to date the beginning of the Bronze Age in Europe one thousand years earlier than scientists had believed up to then. Examining the animal-hide boots and leggings the scientists were able to identify the type of pollen picked up by the wearer (presumed to be a shepherd), and that of the deer from which the hides were made, and determined he had come up from the south. Many other extraordinary finds were made by a host of scientific investigators, which are described in the numerous books about this unique person, Oetzi, the Man from the Ice, as he is called, after the valley below the mountain where he was discovered. There was disagreement between the Italian and Austrian authorities as to which side of the border his body lay and, after more adventures, it was ultimately decided it was south of the border as it was drawn in 1918, a few metres into Italian territory. He now rests in a special museum in Bolzano, Italy.

## Ski Touring

From Obergurgl, or nearby Vent which triumphs at ski-touring, one can access the many *Huetten,* or mountain refuges, which serve winter skiers and summer climbers. These include the Ramolhaus at 3,005m, Hochwildehaus at 2,800 metres, Karlsruber at 2,400 metres and Schoenesweisehuette at 2,300 metres. It is probable they were originally designed as refuges for sheep and shepherds; the Martin Busch hut has markings indicating it was built in 1667. The refuges are provisioned by helicopter from Vent, which specialises in such vacations, from the month of March. During the *bergtouring* season one leaves a hut in the early morning with combination climbing/descent skis and *fellen* (strips of sealskin with hairs pointing backwards when climbing in deep snow, and attached temporarily underneath the skis) so as arrive at the next refuge by midday, when rising temperatures can trigger avalanches. To undertake such a trip is to commune with nature in a very special way: one leaves behind all the sounds of mankind's occupation of the earth to access a fairyland of snow, pristine peaks and deep blue sky – an increasingly unique experience in our times.

From about May to the end of September the Timmelsjoch mountain pass can be accessed from behind Hochgurgl. The road rises to some 2,509 metres to descend to the Italian province of South Tirol and the delightful town of Meran. In winter, travel to Meran from Obergurgl involves almost 200 kilometres via Innsbruck; in summer, over the Timmelsjoch, it is only 55 kilometres across the hair-raising, Himalayan-style switchbacks. As a bird flies it is only about ten kilometres. One may thus enjoy the pleasures of roaming in the high Alps one day, overnight in Obergurgl at very competitive summertime rates, and pop down to savour the special attractions of German-speaking Italy next day.

With increased global warming skiers are deserting lower-lying villages, where snow is either absent or too slushy, to experience the joy of the higher, more powdery article. It is to be feared that in future years this Alpine gem, through which traffic is prohibited, and which has largely rebuffed the commercial temptation of untrammelled expansion, may lose its timeless charm and resemble one of the more overrun present-day resorts.

Those responsible for regional employment-creation in both developed and less developed countries could well learn a useful lesson from Obergurgl as to the best means of developing local tourism skills and entrepreneurship, especially in the area of ecotourism. The Austrian system of encouraging locals to develop their own resorts, particularly by providing B&B accommodation in their own homes and expanding from this small base over time, rather than depending on homogenised multinational investment in massive facilities, with locals employed merely at the lowly manual level, should serve as an ideal to be emulated worldwide. The strategy of adapting a controlled rate of development while maintaining as much as possible of the domestic architecture and traditions marks the essential difference between developing a low value-added tourist slum which blights the landscape, and a destination with charm and ambience to the benefit both of visitors and locals.

In summer the village has a plethora of empty rooms with its Innsbruck University Alpine Research Centre and the excellent but little-exploited Piccard Hall in the town centre. The university conference centre researches the high mountain habitat for flora, fauna, humans, glaciology, climate change and high altitude sports medicine. It is a pity that the village does not organise an international ecotourism school, to their own benefit and the immeasurable benefit of those promoting the sustainable development of threatened ecosystems across the globe. An exemplary start has been made by three hotels, Mathiesen, Jenewein and Granat Schloessl, who organise summer schools in choral singing, instrumental music, dance and painting, in conjunction with a consortium of schools from Hamburg.

Still, what a loss for literature that on his crossing of the Alps someone did not direct Shelley higher up to the ultimate source of his celebrated, crystalline streams, to be enchanted by the white, feather-light carpets, pristine and tingling to the touch....

## Ethiopia – Faranji at Large

We can all come up with a convincing reason or excuse for visiting a certain destination; my enthusiasm for the ancient land of Prester John had been whetted by a recently-published account from the pen of the irrepressible and undauntable Dervla Murphy, with her tale of adventures with a mule in that exotic land. It merely aggravated my embarrassment each Monday morning when, as Roman tour guide, I pointed out to my new guests the strange obelisk (stele) located near the Circus Maximus, by the UN FAO building. This one, I explained, was different to all the other Roman obelisks, such as that in St Peter's Square or the Piazza Colonna, both of which had been 'liberated' from Egypt by the triumphant Romans. A fourth century, 24 metre tall granite stele, it was designed like a fourteen-story skyscraper with one small room on each floor, and was looted from Axum, Ethiopia, the legendary home of the Queen of Sheba, during the invasion of that sawdust Caesar, Benito Mussolini, in the 1930s.[23] Fearing I might be giving the false impression that Axum was a well-frequented watering hole, I determined to visit the mystery town to add to my credibility.

Ethiopia had long been a solitary, isolated Christian country[24] in the midst of other African religions, Muslim and animist. Gibbon hit the nail on the head when he wrote that the Ethiopians are 'encompassed on all sides by enemies of their religion and have slept for nearly a thousand years forgetful of the world by whom they were forgotten'. Though invaded many times during its long history it managed to repulse the invaders and preserve its old beliefs. The original language and unique script was *Ge'es*, from which the Amharic language has evolved over time – as Italian or French from Latin. Of course the rugged geography, high mountains, precipi-

---

[23] Admirably, a modern and more enlightened generation of Italians recently decided that it be returned to its Axum home after its lengthy exile, where it has eventually arrived.

[24] This is true since the fourth century, though with a tiny minority of Jews at Gondar and Muslims in Tigre. Muslim Eritrea is now independent.

tous gorges and ravines, arid desert and almost impenetrable savannah in the south, helped form natural barriers to invasion.

Though cyclically afflicted by famines and floods the country
boasts an extraordinarily beautiful landscape and architecture. This
includes the dreaded Danakil Desert, eons ago lying below the Red
Sea and now three times lower than Death Valley – and correspondingly warmer. Because it houses great reserves of old sea salt,
an invaluable resource with which mammalian life controls body
temperature, it is frequented by caravans of camels which brave the
excruciating heat to harvest blocks of salt for sale across north-
eastern Africa. In the 1960s a couple of friends explored the science
fiction landscape of old, its desiccated coral reefs and salt with a
dash of sulphur from volcanic eruptions, just making it out alive,
though one remained permanently debilitated after the expedition.

On the side of a road leading from Asmara (now capital of the
new Eritrea) in the direction of the coast at Massawa, a couple of
thousand metres lower, I noticed a parade of emaciated women
bent almost double, human beasts of burden, carrying huge bundles of dried branches to use as kindling for cooking. They had
carted them for miles – the male of the species being otherwise preoccupied with the more urgent task of discussing the meaning of
life, the finer points of ethics and the future of the universe, in the
local tea-houses. I asked to check out the weight of one of these
bundles and could hardly lift it; yet the impoverished lady porter
had to haul it many more miles towards her home. Some more affluent foragers had mules to carry their loads. I gave the good lady
a few pence to hire a mule, but she seemed to prefer walking and
retain the cash for some other purpose – hopefully to invest in
shoes. Most of her fellow porters were also barefoot. I began to realise that there are some parts of the globe where it is decidedly
preferable not to belong to the fairer gender.

The traditional directions offered to Ethiopia-bound travellers
were to turn left at Lake Chad and then right at Khartoum. Unfortunately I did not have the time, nor the courage and determination that Dervla Murphy and Thomas Pakenham devoted to their
travels to and around Ethiopia, so I initially took to the air. I had

saved all my annual leave so as to spend four weeks there. My first introduction was from the window seat of an Ethiopian B-707,[25] with about a half dozen passengers aboard, as was the custom of the day. The pilot entertained us with a running commentary as we flew up the Nile past various cataracts, the meeting of the White and Blue Nile at Khartoum, and over the Semien Mountains. The Semiens could be occasionally seen through the storm clouds which deluged rain onto the flat-topped mountains, washing away huge quantities of topsoil. It seemed as if an extraterrestrial giant had wielded a scythe cutting off the vertiginous peaks, so they appeared like gigantic stumps of felled trees, towering over the cavernous troughs. In fact the geological phenomenon happened in exactly the opposite way. It seems that millennia of rainfall have instead washed away the soil of the intervening valleys and ravines, some of which are a few thousand feet deep, so steep that the residents of these flat tops, known as *ambas*, never come down from their home territory, like some obdurate denizens of Trastevere in Rome who never crossed the Tiber in their lives. Some of these ambas are covered in exotic vegetation, including giant lobelias and rose trees. Rivers of deep brown-coloured water heavily suffused with nourishing soil flow from the tilled ambas converging into the Blue Nile, depleting the soil of Ethiopia but enriching the fortunate farmers lower down, though much of the fertile runoff is now deposited in Lake Nasser, behind the giant Aswan Dam. The exquisitely misnomered Blue Nile traverses the Highland plateau, contributing three-quarters of the total volume of the Nile when it converges with the White at Khartoum.

Thomas Pakenham tells the extraordinary story of the heirs-in-waiting to the throne of Ethiopia. Since the wily Emperors, not entirely unlike some flinty Irish farmers of old who resisted handing over the family farm to the eldest son, were scared that the successor to the throne might conspire to accelerate the process, all princes of the line were imprisoned on an almost-inaccessible

---

[25] At that time Ethiopian Airlines was considered one of the best managed airlines in the world.

mountainous pinnacle, a columnar thumb of rock, thousands of feet high, the access by steps and rope being closely guarded to prevent an unauthorised exit by one of the many inmates confined for years on the top.[26]

Addis Ababa of the 1960s showed all the signs of an insalubrious, newly-established African frontier town. It means 'New Flower' in the local dialect, which shows that, although they may not have a well developed trade descriptions act, they have a decided sense of irony. The Emperor had his palace here, many embassies were located in the better part of town, and the Organisation of African Unity had just set up their headquarters in the city. What motorised traffic there was mingled haphazardly with cattle, mules, donkeys, goats and camels. The majority of the populace was dirt poor and lived under tarpaulin or in corrugated-roofed dwellings, while a sprinkling of comparatively rich citizens lived in splendour – mostly friends close to or in the entourage of the Emperor. There is no need for me to describe the life of the Imperial court here: those who wish to gain an insight into the otherworldly ways of His Exalted Majesty, the Emperor Haile Selassie, should read the fascinating account of life and intrigue at that feudal court, *The Emperor: Downfall of an Autocrat*, by Ryszard Kapuscinski.

One problem with visiting such poor, if enchanting, countries is the need to harden oneself psychologically to eventually have to refuse the next pathetic beggar who importunes you just when the pile of small change in your pocket has run out. The poor, mobile, rag-covered beggars of Selassie's Addis were not the most unfortunate of his subjects; these were the many pathetic cripples, suffering from the most appalling disabilities including, I understand, leprosy. On my first day's reconnaissance of the town I had given away all my change, still secreting a small reserve of dollar bills, and had steeled

---

[26] Had they known the alternative practice in Turkey regarding succession to the throne they might have considered themselves comparatively lucky. Historically, when a Sultan inherited the throne his first act was to have his siblings garrotted, often, in the interests of certitude and a more reposing night's sleep, doing the job himself – which leaves one wondering if there was an old Turkish word for brotherly love.

myself to resist all further supplicants, when I was accosted by a leg-
less body in a cloth rag. This apparition was pulling him or herself
along the ground with a wooden peg in one hand. I just could not
ignore him or I would have been unable to swallow, never mind enjoy, a cool beer or three in the hotel bar that evening. I extracted the
lowest paper denomination, a five dollar bill, which was immediately
grabbed and hidden in the rags; the peg was then stabbed into the
ground and the figure shuffled away quickly, presumably for fear I
might change my mind. I then curtailed my stroll around the streets
of the city, especially the squalor of the impoverished Mercato area,
since the contrast between it and my hotel accommodation and the
constant importuning by the wretched of the earth was too distress-
ful during the early days. I mentioned my squeamishness to a fellow
imbiber in the bar that evening and he discouraged a repeat of the
gesture: not being used to such good fortune when panhandling in
Addis I risked giving the surprised recipient a fatal heart attack.

In contrast, His Most Gracious Highness, the Conquering Lion
of Judah, according to Kapuscinski, was accustomed to making a
display of his commiseration and generosity in the face of the
abysmal poverty of his loyal subjects. He would drive his Rolls
Royce over the pot-holed roads, accompanied by the Purse Bearer
to the Emperor's Treasurer, to a strategic location. The purser himself described the action:

> I also took care of another bag, a large one that was filled with
> small coins on the eve of national holidays: the Emperor's
> birthday, the anniversary of his coronation, and the anniversary
> of his return from exile. On such occasions our august ruler
> went to the most crowded and lively quarter of Addis Ababa,
> Mercato, where on a specially constructed platform, I would
> place the heavy, jingling bag from which His Benevolent Maj-
> esty would scoop the handfuls of coppers and that he threw
> into the crowd of beggars and other such greedy riff-raff. The
> rapacious mob would create such a hubbub, however, that this
> charitable action always had to end with a shower of police ba-
> tons against the heads of the frenzied, pushy rabble. Saddened,
> His Highness would have to walk away from the platform. Of-
> ten he was unable to empty even half the bag.

Being an Emperor, and sharing one's wealth, is obviously tougher than many realise!

If travel in the sixties was inconvenienced by the lack of infrastructure and means of transport at least there were no shoals of tourists in such places, and the occasional traveller was welcomed with openness which now seems improbable if not unbelievable. Also, in those days Emperors seemed to have much more class and were exceptionally hospitable to foreign visitors, if not to their own great unwashed. The gates of Haile Selassie's palace in Addis – like that of the Shah of Persia's in Tehran – were open to the overseas visitor. After all, as the Supreme Ruler why not impress the occasional foreigner with a view of your own imposing digs? It should also distract them from the surrounding misery. So yours truly availed of the offer and visited the Imperial reception rooms, gardens and private zoo, saw His pet lion and His leopard, although I must admit neither looked particularly imperial of mien. The old lion had a reasonable mane, but it could have benefited from the ministrations of His Master's coiffeur. In order to consolidate his image as the 'Lion of Judah', Haile took this pet (an Ethiopian male lion being a bit smaller than a savannah version, with a blacker mane) on a well-publicised stroll every morning, having first taken the sensible precaution of giving it a sufficient serving of victuals to ward off the pangs of hunger.[27] I passed a garage which harboured an old Rolls Royce and other rare limousines, whose grandeur intimidated me almost as much as the less favoured locals.

I have occasionally visited some *chico bello* restaurants in European cities to read that His Imperial Majesty, Emperor Haile Selassie had once dined there. Recalling the poverty I had witnessed I recoiled at his extravagance, as when I read reviews of exotic motors costing a fortune, of which only a handful had been build, with the inevitable addendum, Haile Selassie bought one of the first models. Years later, when I heard he had been overthrown in a coup and that

---

[27] I wondered if the Keeper of the Imperial Lion had arranged a severe manicure and dental job in case the old king of the jungle attempted to supplement breakfast with imperial fillet mignon. Otherwise the Keeper risked joining the ranks of the unemployed.

he departed his palace in the back of a VW Beetle, I did not register any great feeling of sadness: I regretted the fate of the people of that poor country, especially when conditions went from bad to worse under the brutal ideological regime of the Dergue.

Addis has little charm for the visitor, but it serves as a base for excursions. It had almost been abandoned for another location a hundred miles away at the beginning of the last century, as was the tradition of the Emperors when they had exhausted all the local resources, especially wood for building and cooking. Then an enterprising Frenchman introduced some Australian eucalyptus trees which took to the local soil like rhododendrons to Co. Kerry, and the relocation was put on permanent hold.

It was from Addis that the last of the great explorers, Wilfred Thesiger, whose father was the British Consul there, set out on his first expedition to find the as yet unknown source of the Awash River. When I first visited a short stretch of the same river it was still home to crocodiles and hippos.

I had wanted to join a small group in a jeep heading down the southern direction of the Great Rift Valley, along what is apparently a series of lakes and savannah of great beauty, by the Omo River, towards Lake Rudolf (Turkana). But transport was not immediately available or too costly to finance on my own, so I headed northwards to somewhat more frequented parts, along the Murphy trail in reverse. Years later, when in Kenya, I attempted to travel to Lake Rudolf and Turkana tribal territory; again it was only possible if there was a caravan of several jeeps for security, so I have yet to make the trip. Now it may be impossible as the Ethiopians are completing the gigantic Gibe III dam on the Omo River which will submerge hundreds of square kilometres of land and destroy the traditional way of life of some 500,000 people, among the poorest on the planet.[28]

---

[28] It is curious how some countries, so vociferous at demanding the developed world furnish them with aid, feel indifferent to the welfare of their own indigenous poor.

First stop outside Addis was at Bahr Dar which is located by Lake Tana, the source of the Blue Nile and the majestic Tissisat ('Water that Smokes' in the local language) Falls. The Nile is about as blue here as the Danube in Vienna, but the locals are honest enough to call it the Abbas River. My local guide took me along the rough trail to reach an observation point from which to see the Tissisat Falls which rival Victoria further south on the Zambezi. The 'watery smoke' spray promotes dense forest growth for about a mile around. The only other people present were another *feranji*, or foreigner, an American, and his local guide. We exchanged greetings. On hearing that I was Irish he enquired if I had ever met a certain Tom Barrington. 'Know Tom well, he's my big boss.' Apparently the American was teaching law at the Institute of Public Administration in Nairobi and Tom had just delivered a series of lectures there. 'That's the difference between Ireland and the US,' I told him, 'Ireland is a village, and if you don't know the particular person you will know someone who knows him or her.'

Next major stop for the visitor making his way north is the old imperial capital of Gondar, last destroyed by the Dervishes a couple of hundred years ago. The old palaces and castles are extraordinary in their African setting, a cross between medieval European castles and those of South Arabia. But what fascinated me most were the local Jews, know as *Falashas,* and the gorgeous little church of Debre Barhan Selassie with its majestic, traditionally-styled frescoes. I had just one roll of film during my entire trip, which I greatly regret, but I am glad that I had the good sense to steady my trusty little Agfa camera on a bench and keep the lens open for half a minute to record the beautiful faces of angels, with ancient Egyptian-style almond-shaped eyes, depicted on the ceiling. I have since heard a rumour that they deteriorated during the dictatorship of the Dergue, which would be a great pity since they represent an outstanding example of native African art.

The Falashas claim to be one of the lost tribes of Judah. I reminded the head man that we Irish have that reputation too. His reply was similar to that of an Irish playwright whose name I cannot recall: 'very unlikely, they couldn't have got all that lost!' Although the Ethiopian church follows the Eastern Orthodox rite they base their Christian teachings more on the Old Testament than the New, while the Falashas follow the Torah and believe they are the successors of Jews who followed the Queen of Sheba and her son Menelik back from the court of King Solomon in Jerusalem. Apparently Her Majesty, who travelled via the Yemen to Jerusalem, fell in love with Solomon's great wisdom and, reputedly, expressed her affection with the fullness of her heart. Among the souvenirs of Jerusalem this fullness evinced was a son, Menelik. He, in turn, visited his sage papa in Jerusalem later, reputedly returning with the Ark of the Covenant, which he is said to have deposited in the Church of St Mary of Zion in Axum.

The Falashas live in villages around Gondar, or at least they did, as in the 1980s the Israeli government decided they were legally Jews, and had a right to return to the Land of the Prophets. They were being moved to Israel a group at a time when the Dergue threatened to prevent any more leaving. A secret air transport shuttle, Operation King Solomon, was mounted by El Al through which most of the remainder was airlifted out.

A resourceful people, whenever travellers visited their villages they would erect little tables which they covered with black, baked earth souvenirs, mostly with Jewish motives, candelabras and the Star of David, even models of a crowned couple sharing a bed, presumably Her Majesty of Sheba and His Most Wise Majesty.

My next port of call was to have been Lalibela, but it was the rainy season and I was to travel in an Ethiopian Airlines Dakota DC3. These otherwise sturdy craft locate the third wheel in the tail, not the nose, so they can flip down on the cockpit nose if the two main forward wheels hit water on landing. The pilot flew over the field and declared it too dangerous to land on the flooded grass runway. It was bad enough to miss out on Lalibela with its magnificent rock-hewn churches,[29] but then the pilot overflew Axum for

---

[29] Apparently they dug their churches deep in to the rocky terrain so they would not be easily detected at a distance by invading Moslems, just as the old Irish monks built round towers to escape the Vikings.

the same reason, landing in Asmara. As I had come to Ethiopia especially to see Axum this was just too much. I insisted on being provided with land transport from Asmara. But, I was told, nobody travels from Asmara to Axum, the road is impossibly rough and infested with *shiftas* (armed highwaymen, often aggressive Somalis). My argument was that if they tell everybody that, nobody will travel and the shiftas will have given up hanging around waiting to rob travellers who never arrive, so are unlikely to be a threat to us. I was eventually provided with a jeep and made the arduous, but enchanting overland trip to Axum.

There's no doubt, if you really want to get to know a foreign country and establish rapport with the locals, however briefly, there is no alternative to overland travel. (The pinnacle of such travel must surely be that of Dervla Murphy who made the expedition on foot, or, more precisely, her two and Jock-the-mule's four. But Dervla is a far more stout-hearted and courageous voyager, physically and psychologically indestructible it seems; she hated roads, considering their use by a real traveller as cheating, so she crossed overland, over mountain and through ravine, instead. I tried to console my pusillanimous self with the excuse that there is one slight disadvantage to travelling by mule, *a la* Murphy: apart from the time constraints, it's like travelling on motorbike with a large helmet, what do you do with the accessory when you arrive? And if you have four extra hooves a-trailing how do you reply to a dinner RSVP from the local *ras*, 'mind awfully if I bring along my travelling companion?')

The road from Asmara was reasonably good at first, a souvenir of the nineteenth century occupation of Somaliland by the Italians with their great road-building tradition. Once we reached the boundary of the territory occupied by the Italians in the late 1930s, the road became a rutted dirt track, but the scenery – landscape and flora, together with the enigmatic silhouette of the distant Semien Mountains – was magnificent. We had a breakdown and had to pull into a small village for repairs. While waiting we visited a wee inn and sampled some of the local fare. The culinary highlights were uncomplicated: the menu consisted of two items, the staple Ethiopian diet of *wat* and *injera*. The latter is a form of mushy bread made from the local rye, or *teff*, while wat is like an Irish stew adapted to Ethiopian ingredients – and palates seemingly lined from birth with asbestos. Presumably to make up for a lack of refrigeration they season the wat and its mystery viands with copious quantities of curry. I scooped a portion from the opaque brown mix, which turned out to be a paw, complete with claws and residual fur. On reflection I figured, why not? In the elegant ski resort of Obergurgl, they serve *Schweinhaxen* (pigs' crubeens), so why not *Hyenahaxen* in the Semiens? In Hungary they serve goulash and in Italy minestrone: one wonders if the basic logic of such dishes is to use up the leftovers from the previous day's repast. The pot in which the wat was simmering seemed to have been topped up by a regular regime of addition/recycling. The refreshments were limited to two items, local beer, *talla*, and *tej*, the local 'looney soup', distilled from I know not what.[30]

My journey was interrupted by frequent stops, especially when we traversed villages. Obviously the message that travel should be avoided due to the presence of shiftas had sunk in, as most of the locals, especially the children, had seldom or never seen a *feranji*, which apparently implies not just a foreigner, but a pallid avatar from the next world.[31] The local kids peered at me from shambas and from behind bushes and ditches. I played along with this, to the evident satisfaction of the kids, who did not witness too many fun-fairs in their mountain fastnesses. I chased the kids, howling like a banshee, to the consternation of the very youngest and the great diversion and amusement of the older children. The bravest of the little boys were apparently those who could tolerate my

---

[30] I heard, but gratefully never witnessed, that in parts of the country it was then the custom to occasionally cut a portion of steak from a live cow, and sew back the skin over the wound. Had I succeeded in my original intention of travelling south from Addis down through Omoland to Lake Rudolf my diet would have consisted mainly of ox-milk porridge, ox blood and crushed berries.

[31] I recalled hearing of the fascination of nineteenth century Dubliners when, at some repulsive fun-fare, the 'Black Man from Borneo' was paraded for their amusement.

countenance the longest –about three seconds – the little ladies took one look, screamed and fled. One needs a thick skin when frequenting certain destinations!

Once in Axum I visited the Church of St Mary of Zion and, on offering a modest contribution, was regally escorted around the church and sacristy, where various ornaments, sacred vessels and ancient liturgical books, written on still-supple parchment in old Ge'ez, were presented to me to hold and inspect. The Chester Beatty Library would have them preserved behind double-glazed, bullet-proof glass. But I was obviously not invited into the side church where the Ark of the Covenant is said to be secreted, hidden from the eyes of the profane, the domain of the Orthodox priesthood alone.

Nearby were a number of stelae, or obelisks, similar to those I had known in Rome, including one massive one which had fallen and broken and which originally measured forty metres and weighed hundreds of tons. How they had been transported from the nearby granite-delivering hills is still a mystery. It is a fascinating experience to see these great engineering and artistic works of the ancient world *in situ*, akin to viewing the *maoi* of Easter Island for the first time.

I did not manage to visit the more eastern provinces where remains of early mankind's predecessors were discovered – the site where the Kenyan palaeontologist Richard Leakey, with his wife and team, discovered the three-million-year-old petite skeleton of early hominid 'Lucy', so-called because they were listening to the Beatles' tune as they were excavating.[32] Not too far away is Kaffa province, which gave rise to the names coffee and café, when the novelty beans were first introduced into Europe. Across the Red Sea top quality Arabica coffee also grows in the Yemen, the subject of another postcard. It was traditionally shipped out of Al Mokha, hence the alternative name *mocca* for coffee in Italy and France.

---

[32] The remains of 'Lucy' are apparently now on display at the National Museum in Addis.

## The Okavango Delta – Arid Desert, Lush Marshes

There are many highly desirable places across this wonderful world I have yet to visit, but there are some that I have already seen which are so memorable that I would choose a return visit to them instead. The Okavango Delta and the savage splendour of the Namib Desert, spread over the borders of Botswana and Namibia in Southern Africa, are high on my list for another and more extended visit. If East Africa is God's Garden this must be his secret hideaway. The area includes the delta flood-plain of the Okavango River as it spills into and disappears in a rich blaze of fauna and floral glory in a sublimely beautiful corner of the Kalahari Desert. Further north it is reinforced by the Chobe and Zambezi rivers. Just across the nearby mountains which form the frontier between the two countries lie the vast, parched wastes of the Namib Desert which stretch to meet the chill waters of the South Atlantic. Here, the prevailing winds and the iron oxide in the desert sands combine to create vast dunes which turn red as the iron oxidises in the billowing morning mists.

The landscapes of both territories are haunted by the ghosts of peoples past, the Bushmen of the Kalahari and the Herero, the latter ethnically cleansed after the German invasion of the early twentieth century, a harbinger of other outrages to come for less fortunate people during that brutal century's descent into savagery. The Bushmen of the Kalahari, now correctly called San peoples, are not strictly nomads but hunter-gatherers who hunted in extensive but delineated areas, while their good ladies gathered foodstuffs in perfect ecological harmony with nature – as they had done for tens of thousands of years. Now the diamond miners have largely taken over the Kalahari leaving little trace of this extraordinary people but their ancient rock carvings and paintings. Meanwhile they are forced to live lives of lassitude in soul-destroying shantytowns.

The Okavango is located in northwest Botswana and is not easy to access. There are no roads into the more exotic interior so one must fly in by small aircraft from nearby Maun airfield. In addition, the local authorities do not wish to encourage the overcrowding endemic in the more popular East African game parks and want to maintain exclusivity through high revenue and low volume. We stayed at Chief's Camp on Chief's Island, arriving in a small aircraft and were ferried to the camp by a jeep equipped with a snorkel – the better for fording rivers and lagoons. We made our way through vast herds of elephant amidst breath-taking scenery. Luckily they did not charge us, however, a few disturbed buffalo did take exception to our well-battered jeeps.

My accommodation at Chief's Camp was in one of only fifteen tents, mounted on raised wooden platforms to deter the local elephant from trampling on them – not conducive to a restful night. The large tents were equipped with mosquito nets and once you enter the tent at night you are under strict instructions not to venture forth, bathroom facilities being provided at one end of each ample pavilion. There is, apparently, a tacit agreement with the local wildlife that guests, once inside their tents, should not be rudely disturbed at night – such as by being eaten – on condition they did not venture out. I found it intriguing to lie in a nice comfortable bed, protected from the great outside by a mere sheet of cotton cloth and a mosquito net, especially as the local dominant male lion came past twice during the night growling threateningly. This was to inform and warn me that the local lionesses, who do the actual hunting, were his personal lady friends, any trifling with their affections and skin and hair would fly, not necessarily his. I was perfectly prepared to respect his domestic arrangements and dutifully, but with lingering trepidation, went back to sleep. Apparently as part of an ecological agreement the camp will be demolished fifteen years after construction, bathroom and other non-degradable equipment removed, and the wooden structures left to revert back to nature.

We spent the next few days exploring our corner of the delta. It consists of open water where there are river channels and lagoons, permanent swamp, floodplain grasslands and islands, each with its own flora and fauna. It was in keeping with the landscape that our jeep came equipped with a snorkel. There were gigantic herds of elephant, reminiscent of those in East Africa over a generation ago. Carnivores stalked the even more plentiful grazers, who are somewhat different from the East African variety. Instead of huge herds of gnus, and there were many of these, the most prominent of the deer-like genus are the *tsessebes*, smaller, skinnier, but speedier versions of hartebeest, which are considered the tastiest of haut cuisine by the local lionesses. We observed many predators on the hunt but the tsessebes were fleet of hoof – specially adapted to marshland – and would take off into the marshes and lagoons leaving the frustrated, hyperventilating, hydrophobic pursuers behind on shore.

There were many more herbivores, including waterbuck, red lechewe, sable antelope, which, because of the huge sweeping horns of the males should be called sabre antelope, as well as giant kudu, whose huge corkscrew horns could prove temptingly useful amidst the gigantic vats in the cellars of the Chateau Petrus. Lion, cheetah, hunting dogs, hyena were plentiful, especially the graceful if doleful-looking cheetah. There is a great wealth of wildlife also in the water-lily-flecked wetlands and lagoons, and on the unique islands which are formed from the remains of termite castles flooded in the rainy season (as comprehensively described by Chris McIntyre, in the highly informative Brandt guide to Botswana).

Having negotiated the exit from the delta to terra firma it is not too long a drive to Maun and from there to Windhoek, the capital of Namibia, just over the mountains. Or one can take a small commuter aircraft from Maun field. The departure lounge at Chief's Island airfield is my ideal: a small desk situated under a thorn tree and a covered bus shelter to protect passengers during the rainy season. There is no arrivals notice board, as at Entebbe of old, you just cock your ears.

## Namibia – Untamed wilderness

Windhoek, Windy Corner, presumably, is the old German colonial capital of South West Africa, and lies in the middle of Namibia. It has a certain old world charm, though some of its historic street names have given way to more progressive substitutes, such as Nelson Mandela Avenue and Fidel Castro Drive. Quixotically, there is a prominent equestrian statue of a First Reich cavalry officer in the centre square near the old Lutheran Cathedral, as surprising as a

statue of Oliver Cromwell in Drogheda. But Windhoek is more of a
base than a destination in its own right. Swakopmund on the coast
is far quainter with its old railway station so tastefully converted
into a hotel. For the nostalgic, sorry, *heimwehkrank*, this can be
found near the intersection of Von Molkte Strasse and the Kaiser
Wilhelm II Strasse.

The drive to the coast through the Namib-Naukluft Park is
hauntingly beautiful, the domain not just of exotic flora and fauna,
but of the enchanting, little meerkats so familiar to TV nature programme viewers. A defence mechanism they adopt is to play dead if
captured or picked up; this is to give the impression to certain birds
of prey that they are already carrion and not good for the digestion.
The Park is substantial, 4,976,000 hectares, compared to the 700
hectares of the Phoenix Park. It is home to desert gemsbok and
oryx, with their elegant, metre-long horns, while on the outer
fringes of this particularly arid desert, zebra with markings specific
to the region, giraffe and desert elephant flourish. The flora includes the extraordinary *Welwitchia* plant which grows for over a
thousand years and can survive without water for years; it resembles a shredded tyre. Other plants can lie dormant for years, yet
pour a few drops of water on them and within less than a minute
they will open up. Weaver birds weave gigantic nests in trees, like
upside down cones. This makes it difficult for smaller snakes to
visit for pickings.[33]

A few hundred kilometres from Swakopmund is the town of
Sesriem, the gateway to the Sossusvlei sand dunes, which can rise
to over three hundred metres. As already noted, they become
ochre-red in colour as the diaphanous early morning mists oxidise
their high iron content. They are best seen and climbed in the soft
early morning sunshine. To view these extraordinary red mountains from below, framed by one of the few camel thorn trees, is
one of the more memorable experiences of global travel – an ex-

---

[33] I approached one to inspect it more closely when our guide shouted a warning:
the tree's undergrowth is a favourite feeding spot for black mambas and king co-
bras which take up residence in the shade of the 'restaurant' overhead.

perience which would be even more enhanced were a cheeky mamba to rear up in greeting.

Further up the coast from Swakopmund, with its beautiful craft shops and ambience redolent of the fin de siècle, stretches the Skeleton Coast, so dreaded of mariners. To be shipwrecked here was to die a slow death from hunger and thirst, on the beach or attempting to cross the pitiless desert. Further inland, between Namib and the Kalahari, we visited some old rock paintings and sculptures in a cave which would have been used over thousands of years by the Bushmen. They apparently never killed a young animal which could reproduce, instead hunting only the very old, in effect, culling. Our guide told us a sad story of a wee bushman who was tracking game early one morning. He sighted an unusually large animal, crept up and dispatched it with poison arrows. The custom of the San was that, like the Bedu, game was shared with all other hunters. He spotted a large human emerging from a tent. Not realising he was witnessing the vanguard of the invading Prussian army heading for the Caprivi Strip, he kindly showed his dead quarry to the stranger, a cavalryman who did not appreciate sharing his recently deceased mount with an indigenous hunter, and who promptly shot him dead. Since then almost all his fellow tribesmen have been driven off their land, dispossessed and exterminated, while some who joined the South African army when it was in occupation were abandoned when it eventually left. Apparently the few San who remain suffer the fate which awaits all semi-nomadic hunter gatherers – dispatched unwillingly to a fixed encampment.[34]

Anyone considering a visit to this enchanting corner of the globe could do worse than see the film *The Gods Must be Crazy*, which was shot in the Kalahari, starring, inter alia, the endearing, inoffensive San.

---

[34] The official excuse is that this is in the interest of the San's development; nothing to do with the fact that their traditional hunting grounds are rich in diamonds. One can only hope that perhaps ecological tourism will offer some hope of employment, possibly through making and selling traditional craftwork, or acting as guides in the desert.